Christian Democratic Parties in Europe since the End of the Cold War

KADOC Studies on Religion, Culture and Society 1

Christian Democratic Parties in Europe since the End of the Cold War

Edited by
Steven Van Hecke & Emmanuel Gerard

Leuven University Press
2004

Published with the support of K.U.Leuven Commissie voor Publicaties

© 2004
Leuven University Press/Presses universitaires de Louvain/Universitaire Pers Leuven
Blijde-Inkomststraat 5, B-3000 Leuven (Belgium)

ISBN 90 5867 377 4
D/2004/1869/28
NUR 697

Table of Contents

Preface

The idea for this book arose in the context of an international workshop on "European Christian Democracy in the 1990s" (Leuven, 7-8 February 2003), organised by the Political Science Department and KADOC - Documentation- and Research Centre for Religion, Culture and Society - with the financial support of the Research Council of the K.U.Leuven.

Both the Political Science Department and KADOC have a long tradition in this field of study. We refer to the KADOC's 1995 colloquium and its ensuing publication: E. Lamberts (ed.), *Christian Democracy in the European Union (1945-1995)* (Leuven: Leuven University Press, 1997).

The aim of the workshop has been to update the academic research that has been carried out on European Christian Democracy, to exchange results among political scientists and historians, both junior and senior academics, and to study the European Christian Democratic parties in a comparative way by examining them according to a broad set of characteristics.

The success of this gathering of scholars convinced us to forge ahead with plans to publish the revised proceedings and to contact a number of additional scholars for further contributions. All the authors have conducted independent research and none has explicit political affiliations, except for Wouter Beke.

In preparing this volume, the editors incurred many debts from many individuals and institutions. We would like to express our gratitude to the Research Council of the K.U.Leuven, to the KADOC's chairman, Emiel Lamberts, and its director, Jan De Maeyer, to Luc Vints, publication coordinator at KADOC, and his team, to Hilde Lens, director at University Press Leuven, and her team.

Emmanuel Gerard

European Christian Democracy in the 1990s
Towards a Framework for Analysis

Emmanuel Gerard and Steven Van Hecke

"For the time being, it remains inexplicable why the fate of these [Christian Democratic] parties in Western Europe varies so much in the 1990s."[1]

The end of the Cold War challenged Christian Democratic parties in Europe in many different ways. One of the most striking events has been the collapse of Italian Christian Democracy as well as the loss of power in the Netherlands, Germany and Belgium. As Van Kersbergen rightly says, outcomes of this period have been very diverse and not yet fully examined. This volume updates scholarly research on European Christian Democracy since the end of the Cold War by studying the European Christian Democratic parties in terms of a broad set of characteristics. The result common to all the parties enables us to draw some conclusions about the particularities and generalities of European Christian Democracy in the 1990s. In this way, this volume contributes to the existing literature on European Christian Democracy by providing a comparative study on party politics in a period characterised by an acceleration in the European integration process, a changing pattern of political ideologies and the emergence of new political parties and issues.

This introductory chapter has a twofold objective. First, its aim is to shape the general framework of this volume. The topics are presented through an analysis of the literature, disciplines, theories and assumptions concerning Christian Democracy, while the various case studies and the general research questions of this volume are also examined. Second, by tackling these different issues, this chapter endeavours to give an impetus to the intellectual debate

---

1   K. Van Kersbergen, "Hopen op macht. De neergang van de Nederlandse christen-democratie in vergelijkend perspectief", in: *Jaarboek 1995. DNPP*, Groningen, 1996, 96: "Het blijft voorals-nog ondoorgrondelijk waarom het lot van deze [christen-democratische] partijen in West-Europa zo uiteen loopt in de jaren negentig." (authors' translation)

about doing research on contemporary Christian Democracy from a comparative and transnational perspective.

Assumptions

Christian Democracy is a topic that is as much under-researched as lacking in theoretical elaboration. As yet, no established body of scholarly know-ledge has accumulated on the subject. Moreover, that this phenomenon is even suitable for academic research is sometimes contested, due to the varieties of Christian Democracy in 'practice' (a problem not exclusive to Christian Democracy).[2] It is said that 'Christian Democracy' is nothing more than a generic term that merely brings together various kinds of political particularities. While research always implies a certain degree of generality, Christian Democracy seemingly cannot fulfil this condition. In many cases, this position is based on a tautology. Given that a relatively limited amount of research has been done, one could deduce that Christian Democratic practices have no common features (and that it must therefore necessarily be a temporary and spatially restricted phenomenon). The first of our basic assumptions takes the opposite stance: we consider Christian Democracy to be a distinct political type, despite its undeniable particularities. In addition, we regard these particularities as a challenge to our comparative approach.[3] Marked differences and similarities between European countries add colour to the common label of 'Christian Democracy'. The related problems of its nature and definition, which are an inevitable part of doing scholarly research on Christian Democracy, are dealt with in this volume by Alberti and Leonardi.

Furthermore, our point of departure is the simple fact of the existence of European Christian Democratic parties. This points to our second basic assumption: by 'Christian Democracy' we mean the parties in European countries that have historically called themselves 'Christian Democratic' and continue to do so.[4] Our third assumption follows from our view of Christian

---

2   D. Hanley, "Introduction. Christian Democracy as a Political Phenomenon", in: D. Hanley (ed.), *Christian Democracy in Europe. A Comparative Perspective*, London, 1994, 2: "(…) Christian Democracy is in many ways an elusive and shifting phenomenon (…)."

3   J. Gaffney, "Introduction", in: J. Gaffney (ed.), *Political Parties and the European Union*, London, 1996, 5.

4   We generally use the term 'Christian Democracy' in its post-Second World War meaning. For a historical review of the meaning of the term, see E. Gerard, "Christen-democratie in België tussen 1891 en 1945. De 'archeologie' van de Christelijke Volkspartij", in: *Trajecta*, 2 (1993) 154-175.

Democracy as a specific political phenomenon.[5] We therefore exclude European rightist and/or conservative parties that do not call themselves Christian Democratic.[6] Instead, our focus will be on the development of Christian Democracy in Austria, Belgium, Germany, France, Italy, Luxembourg, the Netherlands and Spain.[7] Scandinavian Christian Democracy covers one single chapter because the parties are rather small and can easily be compared. Christian Democracy in the United Kingdom is not included, as the country does not have a party (only a 'Movement for Christian Democracy') that calls itself 'Christian Democratic'.[8] In addition, one chapter is dedicated to the developments of the European Union (EU) given the impact of the European integration process on the status of Christian Democracy. In this way, our general framework is in effect the EU and its member states.[9]

Finally, our research focuses on the period since the end of the Cold War. This limitation arises from our third explicit assumption: we consider the period from the 1990s onwards to be politically distinct. Although all time delineations are somewhat arbitrary, we consider the events of the end of the 1980s and the early 1990s as marking the beginning of a new period. The fall of the Berlin Wall in the Autumn of 1989, German Unification in 1990, the agreement on the Maastricht Treaty and the break-up of the Soviet Union, as well as the war in Yugoslavia, all these events thoroughly transformed the political environment.[10] While old problems faded away, new issues started to dominate the political scene on both the national and international level. It is yet unclear how and when this (transition) period will finish, although it is

5   Both the 'Christian Democratic' label and Christian Democracy as a specific political type are highly problematic issues in the Italian case: see the chapter "From Dominance to Doom? Christian Democracy in Italy" in this volume.

6   As the title of this volume suggests, we also exclude Christian Democratic parties in Latin America, which we consider to be part of a different political environment.

7   As to the Dutch case, we do not cover the small 'Christian' (Protestant) parties. In the case of Spain, there is currently no Christian Democratic party except for the Catalonian *Unió Dem(ò)cratica de Catalunya* (UDC). However, because until recently there have been Christian Democratic parties in Spain (unlike, for instance, in Portugal), which though tiny have been absorbed into the *Partido Popular* (PP), because Christian Democrats can still be distinguished and because the PP plays a significant role in the European People's Party (EPP), we dedicate a separate chapter to the Spanish case.

8   For the same reason, neither Greece, Ireland nor Portugal is included.

9   This is the reason why there is no chapter on Christian Democracy in Switzerland. As a politically 'separate' case, it has no link with the rest of European Christian Democracy and therefore did not influence its particularities and generalities during the 1990s.

10   R. Ladrech, "Political Parties in the European Parliament", in: J. Gaffney (ed.), *Political Parties and the European Union*,. 301; K.R. Luther and F. Müller-Rommel, "Political Parties in a Changing Europe", in: K.R. Luther and F. Müller-Rommel (eds.), *Political Parties in the New Europe. Political and Analytical Challenges*, Oxford, 2002, 5.

sometimes said that it ended with the events of 11 September 2001. However, we think it is still too early to judge whether they are in fact another turning point in our history, whether its impact is at least comparable to that of the end of the Cold War.[11]

Literature

I t is customary when introducing a work on a familiar topic to justify the new contribution by referring to the inadequacies of the existing literature. In the case of Christian Democracy, however, one has to talk less in terms of adequacy than of non-existence. Considering the weight of this movement in the politics of contemporary Europe, it is astonishing how little academic attention it actually attracts."[12] Hanley's quote has almost become a commonplace but it is worth recalling. In comparison to Social Democracy, for instance, Christian Democracy has not inspired much research and/or many researchers, and there is certainly no 'organised' or continuous research tradition.[13] However, Hanley's statement should be qualified. There seems to have been a certain improvement in the literature on Christian Democracy with the publication over the last few years of a number of studies that have rapidly become 'classic'. Therefore, to speak (still) of 'non-existence' with regard to the literature on the subject is rather an exaggeration, though this does not mean that all the gaps in the existing literature have been filled.

Christian Democracy has primarily been studied from a national perspective, and there is therefore a relatively large body of literature in the languages of

---

11   For instance, Fukuyama disagrees with the thesis that the events of 11 September 2001 mark the beginning of a new era: F. Fukuyama, "Has History Started Again?", in: *Policy*, 2 (2002) 3. See also our concluding chapter "European Christian Democracy in the 1990s. Towards a Comparative Approach" in this volume.

12   D. Hanley, "Introduction. Christian Democracy as a Political Phenomenon", in: D. Hanley (ed.), *Christian Democracy in Europe. A Comparative Perspective*, 1. See also: K. Van Kersbergen, *Social Capitalism. A Study of Christian Democracy and the Welfare State*, London, 1995, IIX: "Christian Democracy has attracted surprisingly little scholarly attention. Whereas studies of social democracy could easily fill a small library, monographs on the Christian-inspired movements of Western Europe would probably scarcely fill a single bookshelf."; N. Huntington and T. Bale, "New Labour. New Christian Democracy", in: *Political Quarterly*, 1 (2002) 44: "(…) a surprising lack of academic analysis."

13   We leave aside the research being conducted on behalf of Christian Democratic political parties. As far as this area is concerned, the German *Konrad-Adenauer-Stiftung* generates the most research and is by far the biggest publisher.

the respective national parties.[14] With regard to comparative research on the history and the current situation of Christian Democracy, the harvest is much poorer.[15] As far as the historical perspective is concerned, Fogarty's study on the origins and development of Christian Democracy is well known.[16] Letamendia provides a more extensive but rather introductory work on the same topic.[17] Although Irving's focus is not primarily historical, he offers a detailed comparative view of the origins of Christian Democracy in Italy, Germany and France.[18] In his attempt to trace accurately the beginnings of Christian Democracy, Mayeur makes a distinction between Liberal and intransigent Catholics.[19] Contrary to previous opinions, Mayeur states that Christian Democracy originates in intransigent Catholicism.[20] Although Mayeur focuses largely on the French case, his thesis has sparked a debate about the very roots of Christian Democracy. Mayeur's position has been challenged by Kalyvas.[21] According to Kalyvas, to understand the origins of Christian Democracy one has to distinguish between the Conservatives and the Catholic movement. Out of their collaboration at the end of the 19th century emerged the confessional parties, later referred to as 'Christian Democratic'. In Kalyvas' analysis, the comparative approach prevails over the particularities of the national histories of Christian Democracy. Buchanan and Conway examine 'political Catholicism', of which Christian Democracy is an offshoot.[22] They compare the evolution of political Catholicism in France, Italy, Germany, Belgium and the Netherlands as well as Spain, Portugal, Ireland and Great

14   For instance, for the Belgian case we refer to W. Dewachter, E. Gerard, E. Lamberts et.al. *Tussen staat en maatschappij (1945-1995). Christen-Democratie in België,* Tielt, 1995; W. Dewachter, E. Gerard, E. Lamberts et al., *Un parti dans l'histoire (1945-1995). 50 ans d'action au Parti Social Chrétien,* Louvain-la-Neuve, 1996.

15   This is especially true when articles published in academic journals are not taken into account, as is the case in this introductory chapter.

16   M.P. Fogarty, *Christian Democracy in Western Europe (1820-1953),* London, 1957.

17   P. Letamendia, *La démocratie chrétienne,* Paris, 1977.

18   R.E.M. Irving, *The Christian Democratic Parties of Western Europe,* London, 1979, 1-28.

19   J.-M. Mayeur, "Catholicisme intransigeant, catholicisme social, démocratie chrétienne", in: *Annales,* 2 (1972) 483-499; J.-M. Mayeur, *Des partis catholiques à la démocratie chrétienne (XIXe-XXe siècles),* Paris, 1980.

20   J.-M. Mayeur, "Catholicisme intransigeant, catholicisme social, démocratie chrétienne", 490: "(…) la démocratie chrétienne des années 1890 et le catholicisme social du début du sciècle sont profondément liés au catholicisme intransigeant."

21   S.N. Kalyvas, *The Rise of Christian Democracy in Europe,* London, 1996.

22   T. Buchanan and M. Conway (eds.), *Political Catholicism in Europe (1918-1965),* Oxford, 1996.

Britain from the end of the First World War until 1965.[23] Gehler, Kaiser and Wohnout offer different country studies and contributions on Christian Democratic co-operation in the Interbellum and post-Second World War period (i.e. until the end of the 1960s).[24] The common denominator of the country studies is an assessment of the significance of Christian Democracy for 20th century politics, in Western, Central and Eastern Europe. Kselman and Buttigieg focus primarily on the intersection of religion and politics: European Christian Democracy is presented from a historical, thematic as well as comparative point of view by an examination, *inter alia*, of Christian Democratic parties in Germany, France and Italy.[25]

The comparison of contemporary Christian Democratic parties in different countries is a recent research objective. We recall the work by Irving who compares Italy, Germany, Belgium, the Netherlands and France, and also presents a thematic study on the relation between Christian Democratic theory and practice. Caciagli's appoach is rather patchy, covering Italy, Germany, Belgium, Catalonia and the EU.[26] Hanley deals with the ideological specificity of Christian Democracy, the status of Christian Democracy in the so-called peripheral regions, the international (i.e. European) dimension and the Christian Democratic parties in Belgium, the Netherlands, Italy, Austria and Germany.[27] Van Kersbergen examines the role of Christian Democracy in the creation and development of the welfare state, on the one hand, and the role of the welfare state in forging the distinctiveness of Christian Democracy on the other.[28] We take special notice of the KADOC study that combines the historical and contemporary perspectives. Lamberts offers historical, international and thematic contributions which explore Christian Democracy in Belgium, the Netherlands, France, Germany and Italy, taking into account the European dimension as well.[29] The evolution of Christian Democracy is

23   Also linked with the evolution of political Catholicism and Christian Democracy is the history of 'left Catholicism'. A historical and comparative study is offered by G.-R. Horn and E. Gerard (eds.), *Left Catholicism. Catholics and Society in Western Europe at the Point of Liberation (1943-1955)*, KADOC-Studies 25, Leuven, 2001.

24   M. Gehler, W. Kaiser and H. Wohnout (eds.), *Christdemokratie in Europa im 20. Jahrhundert/ Christian Democracy in 20th Century Europe/La démocratie chrétienne en Europe au XXe siècle*, Vienna, 2001.

25   T. Kselman and J.A. Buttigieg (eds.), *European Christian Democracy. Historical Legacies and Comparative Perspectives*, Notre Dame, 2003.

26   M. Caciagli (ed.), *Christian Democracy in Europe*, Barcelona, 1992.

27   D. Hanley (ed.), *Christian Democracy in Europe. A Comparative Perspective*.

28   K. Van Kersbergen, *Social Capitalism. A Study of Christian Democracy and the Welfare State*.

29   E. Lamberts (ed.), *Christian Democracy in the European Union (1945-1995)*, KADOC-Studies 21, Leuven, 1997.

analysed from the years after the Second World War to the beginning of the 1990s.

Apparently, there has been some renewal of interest especially in the internationalisation of Christian Democracy. In the case of most of the publications, this is due to the attention that has been paid both to the process of Europeanisation at the national level and to Christian Democracy's successes at the European level.[30] Pridham was the first to publish academic research on this matter.[31] Portelli and Jansen address different aspects of international Christian Democracy: its historical evolution, the status of Christian Democracy in Latin America and various thematic contributions on, for instance, political culture.[32] The final result is somewhat unbalanced because of the difference in the length and depth of the articles. Papini deals with Christian Democratic co-operation in Europe and Latin America.[33] In addition, a number of well-documented articles discuss the problems of contemporary Christian Democracy. Jansen provides us with an inside view of the European People's Party (EPP).[34] He examines its historical development and organisation rather than the supranationalisation of Christian Democracy as such. On the latter topic, a number of works have recently been published in various political science journals by scholars who, unlike those of the former generation, have no political affiliation with Christian Democracy.[35] In this volume, Van Hecke highlights the issue of Europeanisation as a key aspect of current and future challenges of (doing research on) Christian Democracy.

---

30   This tendency may stimulate research on other aspects of Christian Democracy. See for instance the publication of a series of monographs on Christian Democratic and Conservative parties by the *Konrad-Adenauer-Stiftung* and its relation with the Europeanisation of Christian Democracy: H.-J. Veen and L. Gruber, "Einführung", in: H.-J. Veen (ed.), *Christlich-demokratische und Konservative Parteien in Westeuropa 5*, Paderborn, 2000, 17: "Insofern tragen die Länderstudien zur Klärung der Kernfrage nach dem Vertiefungspotential der Parteienbünde und idealiter nach der Chance eines einzigen christlich-demokratischen und konservativen Parteienbundes in Europa bei."

31   G. Pridham and P. Pridham, "Transnational Parties in the European Community. The Party Groups in the European Parliament", in: S. Henig (ed.), *Political Parties in the European Community*, London, 1979; G. Pridham and P. Pridham, *Transnational Party Co-operation and European Integration. The Process Towards Direct Elections*, London, 1981; G. Pridham, "Christian Democrats, Conservatives and Transnational Party Co-operation in the European Community. Centre Forward or Centre Right?", in: Z. Layton-Henry, *Conservative Politics in Western Europe*, London, 1982, 318-346.

32   H. Portelli and T. Jansen, *La démocratie chrétienne, force internationale*, Paris, 1986.

33   R. Papini, *The Christian Democratic International*, London, 1997.

34   T. Jansen, *The European People's Party: Origins and Development*, Basingstoke, 1998.

35   See for instance the special issue entitled "The Europeanisation of Party Politics", in: *Party Politics*, 4 (2002), 387-503.

Disciplines and theories

Research on contemporary Christian Democracy, especially comparative research, is situated in the common ground of different disciplines. The research legacy of Christian Democracy focuses on the study of its history, while present developments are generally analysed within the framework of political science. With regard to the different countries in which Christian Democratic parties exist, the supranationalisation and/or Europeanisation of Christian Democracy, and the internal and external evolution of the Christian Democratic parties, the sub-disciplines of political science (comparative political science, international relations and political sociology, respectively) each play their role and stimulate cross-fertilisation. It is not our objective to prefer one (sub-)discipline over another; on the contrary, we have opted for a multidisciplinary panel and approach.

Although we consider Christian Democracy to be a distinct object of academic research, there is no widely established theory on Christian Democracy. Therefore, this volume is not based on any one single theoretical framework, unlike, for instance, Kalyvas' implicit rational choice application.[36] Our point of departure is fairly pragmatic and utilitarian: theories are relevant only if they contribute to a better analysis and understanding of contemporary Christian Democracy. Two chapters in this volume explicitly adhere to this criterion: Alberti and Leonardi develop a 'consociational' framework for explaining contemporary Christian Democracy as an alternative to the 'rationalist' and 'reflexivist' approach; Van Hecke reviews the concept of 'Europeanisation' and examines its impact on Christian Democratic parties. The various case studies of this volume are in varying degrees based on rather implicit theoretical approaches.

Case studies

Because the main focus of this volume is on political parties, the case studies will first of all focus on the traditional topics of research on party politics: electoral evolution, political ideology, party programmes and policies, internal organisation and ways of decision-making, party membership, party personnel (recruitment, gender, generation hand-over), positioning towards other parties and in the political system as a whole, etc. Secondly, attention will be paid to those items that are typical of (research on) Christian

36   S.N. Kalyvas, *The Rise of Christian Democracy in Europe*.

Democratic parties, such as the different party affiliations (women, youth, employees),[37] the electoral geography of the Christian Democratic vote (e.g. rural outnumbering urban voters), its positioning as a centre *versus* a centre-right party, its relation with civil society, etc. Finally, issues that have become important since the end of the Cold War will be included, such as the emergence of new political issues (globalisation, immigration, euthanasia, etc.), the rise of extreme-right parties, the so-called Liberal drift (with regard to the socio-economic and the cultural-ethical level),[38] the alleged tendency towards a bipolar political system, the 'Conservative challenge' with regard to ideology, the 'cartelisation' of party organisation,[39] etc. Overall, the case studies examine the ways in which Christian Democratic parties have changed as political parties in comparison to the period before the end of the Cold War.

Obviously, each case study also addresses the particularities of the party involved. As to the German case, Bösch addresses the transition from governing party to opposition party (at the federal level) of the *Christlich Demokratische Union Deutschlands* (CDU) and the Bavarian *Christlich-Soziale Union* (CSU), the consequences of this transition, its ensuing difficulties and opportunities, relations with the party's regional branches, the chancellorship's domination of the party organisation and programme, the leadership change and the financial resources and scandals. Fallend pays particular attention to the debate about the party programme, the electoral competition, the government coalition with the extreme-right and the policy changes of the Austrian *Österreichische Volkspartei* (ÖVP). Leonardi and Alberti explain the collapse of the *Democrazia Cristiana* (DC), discuss its development from a single party into a politically fragmented grouping and answer the question whether the phenomenon of 'Christian Democracy' still exists in Italy. Beke focuses on the widening divide in Belgium between the Flemish *Christelijke Volkspartij* (CVP) and the francophone *Parti Social Chrétien* (PSC), their change from government to opposition party and their new programmes and names. Lucardie discusses the sharp and sudden electoral ups and downs and the ideological renewal of the Dutch *Christen Demokratisch Appèl* (CDA). Poirier stresses the continuity in the central position of the *Chrëschtlech-Sozial Vollekspartei* (CSV) in Luxembourg politics and society.

37   D. Hanley, "Introduction. Christian Democracy as a Political Phenomenon", in: D. Hanley (ed.), *Christian Democracy in Europe. A Comparative Perspective*, 5.

38   *Ibid.*, 6: "(…) the liberal drift is seen as having helped enlarge parties' audiences beyond the initial core of believing or practising Christians, who are nowadays a commodity in declining supply."

39   R. Katz and P. Mair, "Changing Models of Party Organisation and Party Democracy. The Emergence of the Cartel Party", in: *Party Politics*, 1 (1995) 5-28.

The other case studies are particular by definition because, in comparison to the previous studies, they do not have a (single) party (in the classical meaning of the word) that calls itself 'Christian Democratic' as their primary subject. However, because of the reasons mentioned above, these case studies are necessary in order to make a complete analysis of Christian Democracy in Europe since the end of the Cold War. Massart adopts a historical approach in examining the current political weight of the French Christian Democrats and questions whether they still constitute a separate and autonomous political group (party). Madeley compares the different Christian (Democratic) parties in Scandinavia, their fortunes and misfortunes as well as their attitude(s) towards European integration, finally presenting them as an alternative to Continental Christian Democracy. Matuschek explains the failure of Spanish Christian Democracy and the electoral success of the *Partido Popular* (PP), assessing the role of the Christian Democrats therein and drawing lessons for other (Christian Democratic) parties. Finally, Van Hecke deals with Christian Democracy in the institutions of the EU, the changing nature of the EPP and its response to the widening and deepening of the EU.

Research questions

Beyond these case studies (but at the same time based on the analyses of them), this volume aims to offer some conclusions on the particular and general features of Christian Democratic parties since the end of the Cold War. We therefore present some questions that will be discussed in our concluding chapter "European Christian Democracy in the 1990s. Towards a Comparative Approach":

1. With regard to some Christian Democratic parties, is the electoral decline conjunctural or structural? Alternatively, have we seen only an accidental combination of circumstances related to the specific situation of those countries involved or are we witnessing the end of Christian Democracy in Europe?
2. How do we have to understand the simultaneous 'downs' for some Christian Democratic parties and 'ups' for others?
3. In which way has the European integration process challenged, not to say changed Christian Democratic parties? Has it brought any advantages or disadvantages to Christian Democratic party politics?
4. How have Christian Democratic parties responded to new issues such as the multicultural society, asylum seekers, illegal immigration, etc.?

5. What about the position of Christian Democratic parties on ethical problems such as euthanasia, gay marriage, etc.?
6. Did Christian Democratic parties move towards the right at the socio-economical and/or the cultural-ethical level, because of, respectively, the triumph of neoliberalism and the electoral success of the extreme-right?
7. To what degree and in which way have Christian Democratic parties opened their doors for non-Christian Democrats, i.e. Conservatives and Liberals? How is this *rapprochement* linked with the so-called end of ideology and the Social Democratic renewal in the second half of the 1990s?
8. Does a Christian Democratic 'core electorate' still exist? How should it be defined? How is it related to the electoral failures and successes of Christian Democratic parties?

Conclusion

The period since the end of the Cold War has turned out to be an unprecedented decade for European Christian Democracy. The 1990s fundamentally changed the face of Christian Democracy and in each country involved, the position of the Christian Democratic party was called into question. Even at the level of the EU, Christian Democracy found itself in a fundamentally altered situation. At the same time, it does not appear that this evolution has ended, let alone that the outcome has already been decided. Our list of research questions cannot hope to be exhaustive therefore, nor is it the aim of this volume to have the final word on Christian Democratic parties in Europe. However, we believe that, given the growing impact of the European integration process on these parties' politics and policies, it is only by comparative and transnational research that the development of European Christian Democracy can be fully understood.

The Consociational Construction of Christian Democracy

Paolo Alberti and Robert Leonardi

Despite its enduring influence and hegemony in many European political systems, most of the literature on Christian Democracy has difficulty in explaining what it is. Quite recently, however, a very significant improvement has been made, thanks largely to Kalyvas' *The Rise of Christian Democracy* and Van Kersbergen's *Social Capitalism. A Study of Christian Democracy and the Welfare State*.[1] Besides contributing to the understanding of this political phenomenon, these two works are particularly interesting as they also offer a remarkable sample of the two most typical alternative approaches underpinning the study of Christian Democracy, the rationalist and the reflexivist approaches. By adopting a third perspective that claims to seize the ground between these two classical approaches, the aim of this chapter is to bridge the gap between Kalyvas' and Van Kersbergen's theses by introducing a framework that might facilitate a better theoretical understanding of this political phenomenon's distinctiveness and formation process.

Introduction

Most of the existing literature on Christian Democracy usually tends to display either a 'rationalist' or 'reflexive' approach based on an individual ontology. In particular, rationalist accounts treat Christian Democracy as a unitary player, with a given set of preferences and interests and driven mainly by cost-benefit concerns. As a result, they tend to overlook the endogenous dynamics in the formation process of the Christian Democratic identity and its normative framework. Actually, rationalist scholars do not deny that ideas may influence Christian Democracy. However, these are generally assumed away and considered as mere independent variables rein-

---

1   S.N. Kalyvas, *The Rise of Christian Democracy in Europe*, Ithaca, 1996; K. Van Kersbergen, *Social Capitalism. A Study of Christian Democracy and the Welfare State*, London/New York, 1995.

forcing "actors' clarity about goals or ends-means relationships".[2] Hence, when it comes to actually defining Christian Democratic interests, these are often merely deduced from 'post hoc' functionalist explanations based on material capabilities and constraints.[3]

By contrast, reflexivist accounts reject the rational assumption according to which political players could be moved merely by the objective of interest maximisation. Generally their working hypothesis is that Christian Democracy is a distinctive political phenomenon with a consistent set of values intrinsically reflected in its political identity. Therefore, these works argue that a proper understanding of this phenomenon can only come from a recognition of the reflexive relation between initial normative values and political experience. However, this claim is usually not grounded in or combined with a theoretical account of the precise mechanisms underpinning the reflexive relationship between beliefs and political experience. Consequently, they often fail to notice that such a relation is not just univocal, but that there is rather a mutual and continuous interchange between these two levels. Indeed, although ideas definitely matter, they do not come out of a vacuum and, hence, their formation needs to be accounted for also.

In our opinion these two approaches are inadequate in highlighting and theoretically accounting for the actual DNA of Christian Democracy. Our perspective endorses the recent sociological turn in political science, according to which a more useful approach is offered by the emphasis on social interaction as a social phenomenon and on the consequent need to move from an individual to an inter-subjective ontology in which interdependence rather than anarchy is what actually characterises human behaviour[4]. In this context, interdependence requires the existence of effective 'institutions' that are in a position to create patterns of mutual understanding and shape behaviour.

---

2   J. Goldstein and R.O. Keohane, "Ideas and Foreign Policy. An Analytical Framework", in: J. Goldstein and R.O. Keohane (eds.), *Ideas and Foreign Policy. Beliefs, Institutions and Political Change*, New York, 1993, 3.

3   K. Thelen and S. Steinmo, "Historical Institutionalism in Comparative Politics", in: S. Steinmo, K. Thelen and F. Longstreth (eds.), *Structuring Politics. Historical Instiutionalism in Comparative Analysis*, Cambridge, 1992, 8.

4   B.G. Peters, *Institutional Theory in Political Science. The 'New Institutionalism'*, New York, 1999, 14; A. Wendt, "Collective Identity Formation and The International State", in: *The American Political Science Review*, 2 (1994) 384-385.

In contrast to the old institutionalism, however, neo-institutionalists define institutions in a broader sense, laying emphasis on their "relational character".[5] In their view institutions are seen as providing the rules of the game, establishing parameters for participant behaviour. Their key assumption is that "acting within an institutional framework involves commitments to values other than personal values, and has a pronounced normative element".[6] Hence, "as institutions provide moral or cognitive templates for interpretation and action", the players' behaviour is not fully strategic but is co-terminus with their worldviews.[7]

This perspective has been further developed by social constructivism, which claims "to seize the middle ground" between rationalist and reflexivist approaches.[8] Indeed, constructivists share some arguments with traditional reflexivisist works but also reveal the same rationalist concerns for theory building and empirical evidence. In Checkel's words, their quarrel with rational theories "is ontological, not epistemological".[9]

Social constructivism rests on the "notion of mutual constitutiveness of norms and agents".[10] Constructivists "believe that identities, interests and behaviour of political agents are socially constructed by collective meanings, interpretations and assumptions about the world" and, thereby, they underline the need to apprehend the embeddedness of the agent in its normative institutions.[11] However, according to constructivists, not just social facts are socially constructed, but also their 'significance' is the outcome of a process of social interaction and construction of meaning. Indeed, constructivism assumes

5   Hall quoted in: K. Thelen and S. Steinmo, "Historical Institutionalism in Comparative Politics", 6.
6   B.G. Peters, *Institutional Theory in Political Science*, 16.
7   Hall and Taylor quoted in: C. Jönsson and J. Tallberg, "Institutional Theory in International Relations", unpublished paper, 2001, 5.
8   E. Adler, "Seizing the Middle Ground. Constructivism in World Politics", in: *European Journal of International Relations*, 3 (1997) 327; A. Wendt, "Collective Identity Formation and The International State"; J.T. Checkel, "Social Construction and Integration", in: *Arena Working Paper*, 14 (1998); J.G. Ruggie, "What Makes the World Hang Together? Neo-Utilitarianism and the Social Constructivist Challenge", in: *International Organisation*, 4 (1998) 855-885; S. Guzzini, "A Reconstruction of Constructivism in International Relations", in: *European Journal of International Relations*, 2 (2000) 147-182.
9   J.T. Checkel, "Social Construction and Integration".
10   M. Brosig, "Three Roads to Europe or the Social Construction of European Affairs", in: *Politikon*, 5 (2002) 5.
11   E. Adler, "Seizing the Middle Ground", 324.

intersubjective "knowledge as constructed through process" as well as "the world 'out there' as constructed in itself".[12]

Moving from such a perspective, this chapter argues that Christian Democracy is an articulate phenomenon characterised by political moderation and originating from a 'consociational' pattern of interactions that have been more or less institutionalised in time and in space. Moreover, it holds that such a pattern theoretically accounts for the social construction of both Christian Democracy's organisational and ideational dimension. Quite interestingly such a perspective is also consistent with Christian Democrats' normative self-definition. Indeed, as Alcide De Gasperi, the founder of Italy's post Second World War Christian Democratic party, said, Christian Democracy "originates not just from a doctrine, i.e. a social and political philosophy, but also from a historical experience and that of this history of which we are both the object and the subject".[13] Likewise, according to Thomas Jansen, former secretary general of the European People's Party (EPP), "the Christian Democrat identity is not simply shaped by its philosophy. It also reflects the history of Christian Democracy".[14] In other words, as Michael Fogarty rightly stated, "en forgeant on devient forgeron".[15] Our hypothesis is, hence, twofold: (1) Christian Democracy is a distinctive political phenomenon resulting from a consociational development process of moderation and synthesis of the primordial vying pluralism within political Catholicism; (2) this consociational configuration has had an impact on the social construction of Christian Democracy's (collective) identity and ideology.

In consideration of this, we suggest applying to the study of Christian Democracy the analytical framework of consociational democracy first elaborated

---

12   A. Wiener, *Social Facts in World Politics. The Value-Added of Constructivism*, paper presented at the 42nd Annual Convention of the International Studies Association, Chicago, 20-25 February 2001, 13; H. Tsoukas, "False Dilemmas in Organisation Theory. Realism or Social Constructivism?", in: *Organisation*, 3 (2000) 534: "Insofar as we create structures through patterns of sustained interaction, from the micro-level of the small group right to the macro-level of global economic systems, we are confronted by real structures which we only partially and often indirectly and unintentionally have helped create. Such structures cause us to form beliefs about them. In turn, our descriptions of these structures (more precisely, how we describe them), are matters which depend on the language-based institutionalised meanings a community of actors have historically adopted. It is this process of (history-shaped) social construction, unfolding in time and space, that we, as organisational researchers, should seek to study."

13   De Gasperi quoted in: P. Alberti, *Il coraggio della moderazione. Dalla Dc al Ppi di Mino Martinazzoli*, Brescia, 2000, 284.

14   T. Jansen, "The Integration of the Conservatives into the European People's Party", in: D. Bell and C. Lord (eds.), *Transnational Parties in the European Union*, Aldershot, 1998, 105.

15   M.P. Fogarty, *Christian Democracy in Western Europe (1820-1953)*, London, 1957, 22.

by Lijphart. In our opinion, such a device enables us to highlight Christian Democracy's specific pattern of development and to set the basis for its comparative and theoretical understanding. Adopting a notion first put forward by Sartori in 1976, the assumption is that a political party is similar to a 'political system' (though smaller) and accordingly it can be analysed and interpreted in similar terms.[16]

The rationalist approach

The most recent and convincing advocate of a rationalist approach to the study of Christian Democracy is Kalyvas in *The Rise of Christian Democracy in Europe*. The author adopts a rational choice model and questions the Catholic Church's organic link to Christian Democracy as a confessional party. Kalyvas points out that if there were a complete overlap between the Church and Christian Democracy, there would be a fundamental contract between two institutions "represent(ing) the same constituency, lay Catholics". Indeed, he correctly argues that far from being a dependable instrument of the Church, **"confessional parties were formed in spite of and not, as is often assumed, because of the Church's intentions and actions. They emerged as an unplanned, unwanted, and ultimately detrimental by-product of the strategic choices the Church made under constraints. Nor did Conservative political elites intend that confessional parties be formed. In fact, both sets of actors who initiated the process that led to the formation of confessional parties had a compatible set of preferences that excluded the creation of these parties".[17]**

It is worth noting that Kalyvas' analysis is not particularly revolutionary or original in that the reluctance of Christian Democracy to project itself as a direct extension of the Church has been extensively recognised in most of

---

16   G. Sartori, *Parties and Party Systems. A Framework for Analysis*, Cambridge, 1976, 346-347:
      "Let us keep well in mind, therefore, that the outer moves of a party - the inter-party competi-
      tion - are also a function of its inner moves, that is, of intra-party competition. The question
      turns, then, on whether also the intra-party processes can be interpreted in Downsian terms.
      My conjecture is that this is very much the case. But this opens up a path of inquiry that
      cannot be pursed here." See also: B. Caillaud and J. Tirole, "Parties as Political Intermediaries", in:
      The Quarterly Journal of Economics, 4 (2002) 1454-1455.

17   S.N. Kalyvas, *The Rise of Christian Democracy in Europe*, 18.

the literature.[18] Besides, it is sufficient to recall the Vatican's trenchant position officially expressed in the 1901 papal encyclical *Graves de Communi Re* and in the 1902 *Instruction* written by the Congregation for Extraordinary Ecclesiastical Affairs. However, Kalyvas' undeniable merit is to advance the theoretical understanding of the Christian Democratic phenomenon by providing a convincing and methodologically accurate theory of its initial evolution. Regrettably, his theoretical effort covers only the primordial phase rather than the effective rise of Christian Democracy as a political phenomenon with its own distinctiveness. The weakness of his theoretical approach comes at the very beginning where Kalyvas declares his intention to "(…) avoid the debates on terminological issues such as the difference between 'social Catholicism', 'Christian Socialism', and Christian Democracy. Such debates quickly evolve into charting endless and almost imperceptible nuances. They also tend to be irrelevant with respect to party formation".[19] On the contrary, as Pridham underlines, the controversy within Christian Democratic movements reveals that it is "not merely a debate about terminology".[20] As a consequence, Kalyvas confuses the concept of 'Christian Democracy' with the broader category of 'political Catholicism', of which Christian Democracy is only one stream. Thus, conversely to his intention, he ends up accounting for the evolution of the genre rather than the species.

Indeed, Kalyvas correctly contests that "political Catholicism is the natural child of Catholicism per se", but in turn he unfortunately seems to assume that Christian Democracy is the 'natural' child of political Catholicism.[21] In fact, just as the pure presence of Catholicism per se does not necessarily account for the development of political Catholicism; neither does the mere development of political Catholicism automatically explain that of Christian Democracy,

---

18   M. Einaudi and F. Goguel, *Christian Democracy in Italy and France,* Notre Dame, 1952, 2; C. Brezzi, *I partiti democratici cristiani d'Europa*, Milano, 1979, 176; R.E.M. Irving, *The Christian Democratic Parties of Western Europe*, London, 1979, 28; J.-M. Mayeur, *Des partis catholiques à la démocratie chrétienne (XIXe-XXe siècles)*, Paris, 1980, 8; A. Giovagnoli, *La cultura democristiana tra Chiesa cattolica e identità italiana (1918-1948)*, Roma, 1991, 22; E. Gerard, "El catolicismo social en Bélgica", in: A.M. Pazos (ed.), *Un siglo de catolicismo social en Europa (1891-1991)*, Pamplona, 1993, 154-199; K. Van Kersbergen, *Social Capitalism*, 46; M. Conway, "Introduction", in: T. Buchanan and M. Conway (eds.), *Political Catholicism in Europe (1918-1965)*, Oxford, 1996, 2; J.-D. Durand, "La Mémoire de la Démocratie chrétienne en 1945. Antécédents, expérience et combats", in: E. Lamberts (ed.), *Christian Democracy in the European Union (1945-1995)*, Leuven, 1997, 18.

19   S.N. Kalyvas, *The Rise of Christian Democracy in Europe*, 1.

20   G. Pridham, "Christian Democrats, Conservatives and Transnational Party Cooperation in the European Community. Centre-Forward or Centre-Right?", in: Z. Layton-Henry (ed.), *Conservative Politics in Western Europe*, London, 1982, 338.

    21   S.N. Kalyvas, *The Rise of Christian Democracy in Europe*, 8.

which is only one of the possible outcomes. More precisely, it is undeniable that "a theory of Christian Democracy will have to account for the construction of a Catholic political identity"[22], but the construction of a Catholic political identity in itself does not explain the rise and peculiar nature of Christian Democracy, since that construction is preliminary to any other experience that develops from the womb of political Catholicism.

Indeed, Kalyvas dedicates 221 pages of his volume to developing a meticulous theory of the formation of Catholic political identity and only the final 42 pages to its further evolution towards Christian Democracy. In his conclusions, Kalyvas briefly hints at the further evolution of the Catholic movements, portraying them as the result of an "endogenous process" of secularisation "that took place during and right after their formation".[23] However, he does not further investigate this process but merely summarises its effects: "(…) in spite of Church pressure and internal dissent, they de-emphasised religion, declericalised party organisation, and displayed a surprising spirit of political moderation".[24] Regrettably, Kalyvas does not explain where such a "surprising spirit of political moderation" originates. Considering that such an outcome is precisely what defines Christian Democracy's distinctiveness, this explanation is obviously of primary importance.

Likewise, Kalyvas' last pages raise other very important questions about Christian Democratic parties: "As products of religious mobilisation they were socially heterogeneous. Hence they acquired a catch-all nature and a centrist orientation (often regarded by their adversaries as opportunism), cultivated the art of mediation, developed a moderate outlook, and avoided sweeping or radical programs and policies". Yet, it is still not clear how they did it; how such "socially heterogeneous" products then "acquired a centrist orientation", developed a moderate outlook" and "avoided radicalism". How can this process be accounted for? Kalyvas' conclusion does not solve this puzzle: "They relied on their confessional identity to keep their disparate social basis together, yet this identity clashed with their need to detach themselves from religion and the Church in order to survive autonomously and expand electorally. To solve this confessional dilemma, these parties moved in directions that shaped politics and society in important and unanticipated ways. They constructed an identity of their own, redefining its confessional nature in a way that did not discard Catholicism but secularised it, while embracing liberal democracy".[25]

22   *Ibid.*, 11.
23   *Ibid.*, 222.
24   *Ibid.*, 234.
25   *Ibid.*, 263-264.

Again, the question is: how did they manage it? Was that outcome the simple result of someone's imposition or of an articulated process? In the latter case, was its development an inertial one or did it require some determining conditions? Furthermore, was this the only possible outcome or could there have been some "variations over space" and "over time"?[26] If so, how can these differences be explained? What is their influence on the development of this political phenomenon? Unfortunately, Kalyvas' theory does not provide any interpretative tool or pattern for a further analysis of Christian Democracy, neither in its distinctiveness, nor in its elusiveness, nor in its cyclical or dynamical evolution both inside and outside the movement. Given its importance for the past and future of European politics, the dynamics of the Christian Democratic phenomenon still have to be adequately disentangled and explained.

The reflexivist approach

Quite the opposite to Kalyvas, *Van Kersbergen's Social Capitalism. A Study of Christian Democracy and the Welfare State* starts with a very clear and correct definition of what Christian Democracy is precisely. First of all, Van Kersbergen contests the propensity of the traditional literature to misread the distinctiveness of the Christian Democratic phenomenon. In summarising his review of that literature, he argues that what seems to emerge on Christian Democracy is that "it is a movement operating in the centre and it seems to have no basic theory on its own; rather it prefers to plagiarise elements of liberal, Conservative and socialist thought at will in order to blend these into a hotchpotch of ideology".[27] He correctly claims to the contrary that "Christian Democracy is neither a substitute for conservatism nor a duplicate of social democracy; it is a distinctive political actor".[28] Notably, Van Kersbergen rejects Christian Democracy's assimilation to conservatism: "It may be indeed the case that there are many similarities between conservatism and Christian Democracy (...). [However] those who refute distinctiveness by pointing to the resemblance between conservatism and Christian Democracy, still face the task of showing that no such analogy exists between Christian Democracy and other political ideologies, notably social democracy and liberalism".[29]

26   J.H. White, *Catholics in Western Democracies. A Study in Political Behaviour*, Dublin, 1981.
27   K. Van Kersbergen, "The Distinctiveness of Christian Democracy", in: D. Hanley (ed.), *Christian Democracy in Europe. A Comparative Perspective*, London, 1994, 33.
28   K. Van Kersbergen, *Social Capitalism*, 2.
29   K. Van Kersbergen, "The Distinctiveness of Christian Democracy", 32.

Equally, he also discards the tendency to attribute to Christian Democracy an imprecise physiognomy because of its pragmatic and inter-classist approach by indicating in the politics of accommodation a specific and distinctive feature of Christian Democracy: "Religious inspiration affects virtually every matter of policy. An articulate social theory of capitalism emphasises the vital role of social organisations and the subsidiary role of the state. A specific political ethic aims at reconciling conflicts and accomplishing social integration. Particularly relevant for social policy is the politics of mediation: the religiously inspired, ideologically condensed and politically practised conviction that conflicts of interests can and must be reconciled politically in order to restore the natural and organic harmony of society. The politics of mediation is a common characteristic of the Christian democratic movements of Western Europe. However, *the precise configuration of interest representation and accommodation within these movements has led to different outcomes in terms of social policy performance*."[30]

Unfortunately, this is also the very limit of his study. Indeed, Van Kersbergen simply postulates Christian Democracy's distinctiveness as the preliminary hypothesis of a scrupulous analysis of its ultimate effects on policy-making, but he does not seem to highlight sufficiently the theoretical background from which such a hypothesis develops. As emphasised in the above quotation, the research question of his study is how "the precise configuration of interest representation and accommodation within these movements has led to different outcomes in terms of social policy performance". Such a consideration seems overlooking the fact that a precise configuration of interest representation and accommodation within these movements and their dynamics and interactions affect the process of maturation and evolution of Christian Democracy itself even sooner than its social policies.

Indeed, by skipping to the ultimate effects, Van Kersbergen does not seem to pay enough attention to exploring the source of Christian Democracy's distinctiveness. In fact, the crucial question should not simply be 'What is Christian Democracy's distinctiveness?' or 'How can we depict it?', but more appropriately, 'Where does it comes from?' and 'How can it be explained and accounted for?'. If one reads carefully Van Kersbergen's illustration of the Christian Democratic phenomenon, it is clear that the author does not solve the puzzle. Indeed, his chief argument is that: "Christian Democracy is distinct from its competitors *by virtue* of its specific model of social and economic policy and *because* the religion accords the movement an unparalleled opportunity to adapt to changing circumstances".[31]

However, the first aspect (the policy model) is rather an 'effect' than a 'cause', while the second (religion) is essentially a 'means' (besides, is it the only one?). Therefore, this argument does not reveal how Christian Democracy's distinctive approach to politics (and consequent policy model) originates and develops or how such an 'unparalleled opportunity' is exploited. In a subsequent paragraph Van Kersbergen refers to Christian Democracy's formation process repeatedly by touching a variety of its features without grounding them in a theoretical framework that explains their reciprocal interaction: "The distinctiveness of Christian Democracy is corroborated by three elements. First, the possession of an elaborated body of (Catholic) social doctrine has historically distinguish-ed Christian Democracy from conservatism. Second, the typically centrist position of Christian Democratic parties in the political system in which they operate was not simply an effect of a pragmatic slackening of elementary principles in the course of political conflicts, but - on the contrary - *a consequence of the application* of a consistent political ethic, that resulted in a specific political project which aimed at social integration, (class) compromise, political mediation, accommodation and pluralism. Specifically, the argument is that 'Christian Democracy *voices, translates, codifies and restructures societal conflict within itself* in an attempt to arbitrate and accommodate societal discord. Class reconciliation and cooperation *lie at the heart* of what defines Christian Democracy as distinctive'. The 'essence' of Christian Democracy is, therefore, that *it always attempted to be the 'embodiment'* of the building of social and political consensus. Christian Democratic politics has been a politics of mediation, i.e. a religiously inspired, ideologically condensed and politically practised conviction that conflicts of social interests can and must be reconciled politically in order to restore the natural and organic harmony of society. Third, the religious inspiration of Christian Democracy has supplied the movement with an electoral catch-all identity of a specific type, because *religion had the capacity to canvass voters from a variety of social backgrounds precisely to the extent that the religion curbed the political weight of class*".[32]

Several times in this paragraph the author touches on the problem of Christian Democracy's formation process without ever fully coming to grips with it. For example, if "the typically centrist position of the Christian democratic

31   K. Van Kersbergen, "The Distinctiveness of Christian Democracy", 30; K. Van Kersbergen, *Social Capitalism*, 28 (own italics).
32   *Ibid.*, 28 (own italics).

parties is (...) a consequence of the application of a consistent political ethic", then, who and how did they apply it? Likewise, how exactly does "Christian Democracy voice, translate, codify and restructure societal conflict within itself"? Moreover, how does religion have "the capacity to canvass voters from a variety of social backgrounds precisely to the extent that the religion curbed the political weight of class"? Was that an automatic process or did it require someone's involvement and/or favourable condition? Actually, Van Kersbergen is right in pointing to Christian Democracy's politics of accommodation as being its very 'essence', but then he fails to clearly formulate its causal relationship to Christian Democracy's distinctiveness. Indeed, differently to what he points out, the distinctiveness of Christian Democracy is not corroborated by but it is precisely grounded in its continuous effort to amalgamate within the movement the societal conflict in order to embody the building of the social and political consensus.

The consociational explanation

At the end of the 1960s Lijphart started looking into how fragmented democracies can nonetheless develop political moderation. As we intend to demonstrate, his consociational model of democracy and Christian Democracy have a lot in common. To begin with, they emblematically share the same founding fathers and birth place. Interestingly, it is precisely those European Continental countries with Christian Democrats in power that have been also the pioneers of the consociational efforts characterising the politics of the European Union (EU).[33] Such a coincidence is further emphasised by the fact that both of these are typically absent in Anglo-American systems as well as, in our opinion, in Scandinavian countries.

More specifically, Christian Democracy and consociational democracy share the same elite origins within a pillarised framework, that is a pluralist context "fragmented into political subcultures".[34] Furthermore, the underlying 'spirit' or driving force behind these phenomena is also the same. As Lijphart precises, " the essential characteristic of consociational democracy is not so much any particular institutional arrangement as the deliberate joint effort by the elites to stabilise the system".[35] Indeed, this model hinges on "a self-conscious

33   D.N. Chryssochoou, *Theorising European Integration*, London, 2001.
34   A. Lijphart, "Consociational Democracy", in: *World Politics*, 2 (1969) 211
35   *Ibid.*, 213.

'union of the oppositions'"[36], a formula that sounds very similar to Christian Democracy's notion of stewardship and aims of "making strangers into friends".[37] As Fogarty argues, Christian Democrats "have a profound belief in the value of meetings of minds".[38] Moreover, according to Lijphart consociational democracy lays emphasis on the 'common good' and leans towards 'all inclusive coalitions'[39], conversely to the propensity of the Anglo-American systems (the so-called Westminster model) to rely on 'minimum winning coalitions' with a bare majority support.[40]

The key features of Lijphart's consociational framework are the role of political elites and of pillarised pluralism. According to his theory, the establishment or persistence of a consociational system is favoured by the presence of a number of conditions, at the level of the elites, of the rank-and-file, and of their inter-play. However, its success ultimately relies on four main factors that entail the political elites' coalescent effort.

As a quick review of a number of monographs on Christian Democracy immediately demonstrates, the development of this political phenomenon in Europe largely fits into the aforementioned framework. To different extents but unequivocally, the development of Christian Democratic parties is unanimously accounted for as a convergence at the elite level of a plurality of autonomous groups, each "combining distinct cultural identity with economic self-interest".[41] With regard to the Italian case, for example, Giovagnoli recalls that "the DC [*Democrazia Cristiana*] was founded in 1942 and 1943 through the convergence of different forces and groups from the Catholic world into a single political party".[42] Likewise, according to Koole, in the Netherlands, "the overwhelming presence of various societal organisations within the KVP [*Katholieke Volkspartij*, Catholic People's Party] was exactly what distinguished the KVP from other parties. Of course, other parties also had links with other societal organisations (...). But nowhere were these contacts represented as such in the party executive, the party council, and

---

36   *Ibid.*, 212
37   D. Hanley, "Introduction. Christian Democracy as a Political Phenomenon", in: D. Hanley (ed.), *Christian Democracy in Europe. A Comparative Perspective*, 8.
38   M.P. Fogarty, *Christian Democracy in Western Europe (1820-1953)*, 133.
39   Likewise, Christian Democrats in France, Germany, Italy and the Netherlands were coalition builders, even when they could have opted for a single party government: *Ibid.*, 92-93.
40   A. Lijphart, "Consociational Democracy", 215.
41   M. Donovan, "Democrazia Cristiana. Party of Government", in: D. Hanley (ed.), *Christian Democracy in Europe. A Comparative Perspective*, 76.
42   A. Giovagnoli, '*Il Partito Italiano. La Democrazia Cristiana dal 1942 al 1994*, Bari, 1996, 33.

The consociational framework

Factors conducive to consociational democracy:

1. Elites' ability to accommodate divergent interests and demands from the subculture
2. Elites' ability to transcend cleavages and join in a common effort with the elites of rival subcultures
3. Elites' commitment to the maintenance of the system and to the improvement of its cohesion and stability
4. Elites' understanding of the perils of political fragmentation

N.B.: These conditions are to be verified in the reverse order, since the latter are conducive to the former.

Favourable conditions to its establishment or persistence:

1st level: inter-subcultural relations at the elite level (relations among the elites of the subcultures):

1. Existence of external threats
2. Multiple balance of power among subcultures
3. Relatively low total load on the decision-making apparatus

2nd level: inter-subcultural relations at the mass level:

1. Existence of distinct lines of cleavage among encapsulated cultural units
2. Balance between transaction and integration (desirable to keep transactions among antagonistic subcultures to a minimum)

3rd level: elite-mass relations within the subcultures

1. Internal political cohesion of the subcultures (elites have to cooperate and compromise without losing the allegiance and support of their own rank and file)
2. Adequate articulation of the interests of the subcultures (elites provide a political articulation of the interests of their own subcultures)
3. Widespread approval of the principle of government by elite cartel

Source: A. Lijphart, "Consociational Democracy", in: *World Politics*, 2 (1969) 207-225.

had a reserved place on lists of candidates for the national elections".[43] In his summing-up Fogarty writes, "in the political field, the unity and effectiveness of Christian Democratic parties themselves is seen as based on a continuous exchange of views between the different classes and elements of which they are made up. Most of the parties object, as has been said, to allowing different groups or tendencies to organise fractions of their own. But they encourage the informal expression of opinions, and have usually formal machinery - joint or advisory committees - for keeping in touch with the other Christian Democratic or Christian Action movements".[44]

Indeed, contrary to the Communist and Social Democratic parties, which generally display a centralised and top-down development, Christian Democracy typically shows a pluralist and decentralised physiognomy that is usually the consequence of a bottom-up and confederal origin.[45] According to Becker, "as a result of their Catholic traditions, in particular, the Christian Democratic parties have remained anchored to a certain extent in society, outside their own organisation. This was expressed in an ideological and social view that transcended the more narrow political aims of the party, as well as in an intentional association with social or religious groups".[46] As a consequence, subcultures within Christian Democratic parties have been often tolerated to a greater extent, enjoying a remarkable degree of segmental autonomy and behaving as parties within the party itself.[47] In some cases, like in Austria, Switzerland and Belgium, the Christian Democratic parties were even founded jointly by different Christian associations (the farmers, the workers, and the employers) and for long maintained a system of indirect membership.[48] Often, this situation was additionally complicated by localism and regional claims. As Fogarty reminds us, "the Centre Party [*Zentrum*] and the CDU [*Christlich Demokratische Union Deutschlands*], like their colleagues in Belgium or Switzerland, have had throughout their history to accommodate

43   R.A. Koole, "The Societal Position of Christian Democracy in the Netherlands", in: E. Lamberts (ed.), *Christian Democracy in the European Union (1945-1995)*, 144.

44   M.P. Fogarty, *Christian Democracy in Western Europe (1820-1953)*, 133.

45   N.D. Cary, *The Path to Christian Democracy. German Catholics and the Party System from Windthorst to Adenauer*, Cambridge, 1996, 170; D. Broughton, "The CDU-CSU in Germany. Is There Any Alternative?", in D. Hanley (ed.), *Christian Democracy in Europe. A Comparative Perspective*, 111; C. Brezzi, *I partiti democratici cristiani d'Europa*, 125.

46   W. Becker, "The Emergence and Development of Christian Democratic Parties in Western Europe", in: E. Lamberts (ed.), *Christian Democracy in the European Union (1945-1995)*, 116.

47   R. Leonardi and D.A. Wertman, *Italian Christian Democracy. The Politics of Dominance*, Houndmills, 1989.

48   This was also the case of the three Dutch Christian Democratic parties, which in 1980 merged into one single party: R.A. Koole, "The Societal Position of Christian Democracy in the Netherlands", 143-145.

themselves not only to varying social class interests but also to the clash of regional interests".[49]

Nonetheless, these collateral linkages and variegated composition had a profound impact in enhancing Christian Democracy's crosscutting attraction and its search for moderation. However, as Fogarty noticed in 1952, "it has been a fairly general observation (in recent years) that, though coordination between the specialised Christian movements is often (not always) good at the top, it may be almost non-existent at the bottom. It would scarcely be claimed anywhere that the right balance between class organisation and collaboration has yet been found".[50] Likewise, more recently Kalyvas has underlined that "the unity has always been more effective at the top level than at the mass level", where such a convergence has never been sufficient to amalgamate these groups, constantly balancing between integration and autonomy. According to Conway, indeed, "within Christian Democratic ranks, there was a continual struggle for influence between professional and sectional lobbying groups".[51] In the Italian case, for example, "the extreme factionalism which marked the party led to a considerable decentralisation of power. The impact of the factions was such that in the case of a few, they were closer to elements in other parties than they were to some other factions in the DC".[52] Nonetheless, the Christian Democratic components eventually proved able to transcend their respective and mutual cleavages, join in a common effort with the elites of rival subcultures, and overcome the perils of political fragmentation for the fragile and new European democracies. A number of conducive factors and favourable conditions, both at the elite and elite-mass level, accounts for such an achievement.

At the elite level, indeed, the Christian Democrats were particularly aware of the fact that their political weakness and the 'maverick' divisions among them had been among the causes opening the path to the upsurge of nationalism in Europe.[53] Besides, the considerable and multiple balance of power among these subcultures (none of which could aim at 'converting' the others or openly prevail over them) combined with the existence of an increasing exter-

49   M.P. Fogarty, *Christian Democracy in Western Europe (1820-1953)*, 133.
50   *Ibid.*, 80.
51   M. Conway, "The Age of Christian Democracy. The Frontiers of Success and Failure", in: T. Kselman and J.A. Buttigieg (eds.), *European Christian Democracy. Historical Legacies and Comparative Perspectives*, Notre Dame, 2003, 54.
52   S. Koff and S. Koff, *Italy. From the First to the Second Republic*, London, 2000, 35.
53   N.D. Cary, *The Path to Christian Democracy*; De Gasperi quoted in: P. Alberti, *Il coraggio della moderazione*, 276.

nal threat (a radical Communist and Socialist bloc) proved particularly influential and effective in favouring a coalescent effort among Catholic leaders.

Yet, this development also required that Christian Democratic political elites be able to co-operate and compromise without losing the allegiance and support of their own rank-and-file. In other words, they had to have the power to take binding decisions for their own sub-subcultures whose internal political cohesion ultimately relied on the Christian Democratic leaders' ability to accommodate their divergent interests and demands. In effect, in contrast to the 'horizontal' pluralism within the party (mass level), at the elites-mass level these sub-cultures revealed a strong vertical cohesion and widespread acceptance of the principle of government by an elite cartel. As highlighted with regard to Italian Christian Democracy, "DC factions usually began as informal, face-to-face associations bringing together individuals with similar ideological orientations, experiences, or socio-economic and geographic backgrounds", which then evolve and "operate on the basis of commonly accepted hierarchical patterns of relationships in which the leaders are recognised as having the ability to make and enforce the decisions for the group".[54] With the passage of time, this consociational construct became more and more institutionalised. Such an evolution is consistent with Lijphart's analysis according to which the persistence of a consociational democracy is indeed further enhanced by the length of time it has been in operation.[55]

Another very interesting aspect of Lijphart's theory is that it can account not only for Christian Democratic distinctiveness, but also for its elusiveness or change. As Peters emphasises, institutional "change is rarely the rational, planned exercise found in strategic plans, but rather tends to be emergent and more organic".[56] Indeed, according to Lijphart, consociationalism is neither an inertial nor an ineluctable process. On the contrary, it is a dynamic one ultimately hinging on the actual combination of two key elements, namely societal pluralism and coalescent behaviour. Variations in one of these components may potentially provide an insight into the national nuances of this phenomenon. As Van Kersbergen correctly observes, "in general, Catholic politics was characterised by the attempt to integrate the entire Catholic population into a unitary movement. The extent to which this succeeded or failed accounts for considerable cross-national variation both in strength and complexion among the European Catholic parties".[57]

54   R. Leonardi and D.A. Wertman, *Italian Christian Democracy*, 17-18.
55   A. Lijphart, "Consociational Democracy", 216.
56   B.G. Peters, *Institutional Theory in Political Science*, 34.
57   K. Van Kersbergen, *Social Capitalism*, 3.

Typology of democratic regimes

		Internal Structure	
		Segmented pluralism	Homogeneous
Elite Behaviour	Coalescent	Consociational Democracy	Depoliticised Democracy
	Adversarial	Centrifugal Democracy	Centripetal Democracy

Source: A. Lijphart, *Democracy in Plural Societies. A Comparative Exploration*, New Haven, 1979, 106.

However, it is opportune to underline that these differences among Christian Democratic parties in Europe are in 'degree' and not in 'type'. Besides, such variations are more evident on a comparative level when part of a comparison of national cases. Indeed, as Lijphart outlines, "the degree of competitive behaviour by elites must also be seen as a continuum. Among the consociational democracies, some are more consociational than others".[58] For example, in Germany Christian Democracy unquestionably shows a more homogenous structure than in other European countries. This is partially a reflection of the respective features of the societies in these countries. As Lucardie observes, "German society has never been pillarised like its Belgian, Dutch or even Italian counterparts (...). Thus the CDU could (and would) not be part of a network of Christian organisations".[59]

However, it is also the outcome of a different historical evolution and of an internal composition that shows a lower level of support among the unionised working class and an over-representation of the upper-middle classes. In addition, this structural feature of the German Christian Democratic polity is also coupled with distinctive elite behaviour. Indeed, *vis-à-vis* its European counterparts, the initial set-up of the CDU was characterised by a more competitive effort, which led to a few centrifugal rifts and further enhanced the CDU's internal homogeneity. Even afterwards, the party leadership has typically displayed a less coalescent attitude towards the internal 'minority'. As a consequence of the German chancellorship system, such oppositions have been progressively marginalised and neutralised by the increasing influ-

58   A. Lijphart, "Consociational Democracy", 224.
59   P. Lucardie, "From Family Father to DJ. Christian Democratic Parties and Civil Society in Western Europe", in: E. Lamberts (ed.), *Christian Democracy in the European Union (1945-1995)*, 215.

ence and hegemony of the chancellor within the party. Hence, the combination of these two features could explain why, in contrast to other European Christian Democratic parties, the CDU typically displays a centripetal evolution and is less exposed to centrifugal drifts despite the presence of a less coalescent elite behaviour, but this may also account for the increasing depoliticisation due to the technocratic evolution of this party towards a cohesive 'machinery of the boss' in support of the chancellor. As in the German case, variations in the combination of these two elements emerge not only in 'space' but also in 'time'.

Indeed, as Fogarty observes, in each of these countries Christian Democracy does not show a linear but a cyclical evolution.[60] Far from being an irreversible achievement, in all these countries Christian Democratic leaders have revealed diverse consociational propensities: some intense, acting to traverse the Catholic borders and extend to the political system; some others so feeble as to undermine the persistence of the Christian Democratic project itself. In addition, these elements can also be concretely affected by a plurality of other factors and conditions. For example, a system of 'indirect membership' (individuals are members of an organisation which then joins the party) can make the creation of a consociational system more difficult, as the absence of an effective overarching loyalty (which in a consociational democracy is usually represented by common citizenship) may undermine the required balance between integration and autonomy. Equally, a similar situation can be determined by the presence of a unitary and independent labour movement instead of a separate confessional trade union representing the Christian workers.

Finally, "while consociational solutions may increase political cohesion", according to Lijphart the other side of the coin is that "they also have a definite tendency to lead to a certain degree of immobilism".[61] According to Fogarty, this tendency also affected Christian Democracy in Italy where "a continuous debate (…) between the centre or 'united front' section of Christian Democracy and the party's left and right wings" did not prevent "certain major social reforms" but also "led to a certain 'immobilism'".[62] In effect, one risk for Christian Democratic parties is also that of relying on a mechanical and self-referential perpetration of such a consociational system, preferring compromise to true synthesis and progressively losing contact with the vibrant plura-

---

60   M.P. Fogarty, *Christian Democracy in Western Europe (1820-1953)*, 149.
61   A. Lijphart, "Consociational Democracy", 225.
62   M.P. Fogarty, *Christian Democracy in Western Europe (1820-1953)*, 327.

lism of their societies. Indeed, particularly in Italy by means of a long-established and proficient system of mediation and political accommodation that had been institutionalised and improved throughout the years, the DC gradually transformed itself into a 'party-cartel' in a 'symbiotic' relationship with the state, which provided it with the means to ensure its own survival, despite its growing detachment from society, and a party capable of controlling its environment and defending itself from pressures for political change.[63] However, as Lijphart outlines, "consociational democracy presupposes not only a willingness on the part of the elites to cooperate but also a capability to solve the political problems of their countries".[64] And, indeed, the inability to forge political solutions is significantly also one of the causes of Christian Democracy's involution and consequent decline in France during the Fourth Republic and in Italy at the beginning of the 1990s, where a progressive deterioration of Christian Democratic consociational cohesion eventually opened the path to a ceaseless centrifugal whirlpool.

Conclusion

Moving from a criticism of the two main alternative approaches usually adopted by the literature on Christian Democracy, this chapter lays emphasis on the intersubjective nature of social phenomena. It argues that Christian Democracy is a distinctive political phenomenon characterised by political moderation. Such a distinctive identity derives from a process of social interaction based on consociational lines that has been shaping the Christian Democratic identity (i.e. party profile, organisation and policy) as well as normative self understanding (i.e. ideology). As Fogarty correctly observes, social construction is even more important for understanding Christian Democracy than Church teachings "because it belongs properly and exclusively to Christian Democracy".[65] Indeed, "the synthesis which Christian Democrats aim at creating is not arrived at only by abstract thought, or by any one movement on its own. A main factor is the interplay, with reference to concrete problems, of organisations and interest groups, each of which influences the rest".[66] The whole set of distinctive features that

---

63   R. Katz and P. Mair, "Changing Models of Party Organisation and Party Democracy. The Emergence of the Cartel Party", in: *Party Politics*, 1 (1995) 5-28. With regard to Italy, see our chapter "From Dominance to Doom? Christian Democracy in Italy" in this volume.

64   A. Lijphart, "Consociational Democracy", 218.

65   M.P. Fogarty, *Christian Democracy in Western Europe (1820-1953)*, 24.

66   *Ibid.*, xiv.

are usually said to characterise the Christian Democratic political perspective (moderate approach, centrist orientation, interclassism, subsidiarity, etc.) are all products of an incessant struggle between a plurality of interests, tendencies and experiences that Christian Democracy "voices, translates, codifies" and accommodates within itself.[67]

With regard to subsidiarity, for example, Fogarty correctly observes that "the principle of pluralism, 'vertical' even more than 'horizontal', is rooted very deeply indeed in Christian Democratic minds. For, apart from any merely intellectual acceptance, its value has been burnt into their consciousness by a generation of bitter experience (…). It would indeed be hard to name even one Christian Democratic movement that has not in the last three or four generations known what it was to be a minority, and often a seemingly permanent minority, to which even elementary justice was denied (…). To all this has been added opposition inside the Christian body itself. Christian Democracy has grown out of several generations of struggle and debate among Christians themselves".[68] Likewise, according to Jansen "in any given state or society, they [Christian Democrats] commit themselves to the development of a consensus that integrates the differing interests and concerns of all classes and groups. Constant endeavours to strike a balance and an agreement between divergent goals and, perhaps, conflicting principles, form a fundamental element in the Christian Democrat's approach to the resolution of political problems".[69] Such a balance has been described by the relevant literature as a ceaseless "battle between left and right", romantics versus realists, 'principled versus minimalists', radicals versus clericals. Still, with the passage of time, Christian Democracy has been shaping a "hard yet supple" doctrine, which "avoids the dangers of both 'massifications' and atomisation", "consistently oppose(s) (…) extreme federalist and separatist views" as well as "with equal force all tendencies towards centralisation".[70] Therefore, it has been correctly argued that "such parties can only be understood historically".[71] Indeed, as Jansen writes, "Christian Democracy cannot be understood as something abstract: there is no 'pure' form of it". Furthermore, "because the Christian Democrats in individual European countries have had different historical experiences, the Christian Democrat identity, too, has a varied content".[72]

67   K. Van Kersbergen, *Social Capitalism*, 28.
68   M.P. Fogarty, *Christian Democracy in Western Europe (1820-1953)*, 46-47.
69   T. Jansen, "The Integration of the Conservatives into the European People's Party", 104.
70   Biton quoted in: M.P. Fogarty, *Christian Democracy in Western Europe (1820-1953)*, 22, 42, 88.
71   D. Hanley, "Introduction. Christian Democracy as a Political Phenomenon", 3.
72   T. Jansen, "The Integration of the Conservatives into the European People's Party", 127, 105.

Finally, "since the programmes of Christian Democracy have been and are being shaped by experience, there is and can be no moment at which they attain their final form".[73] In conclusion, then, the framework here presented aims at being more than a mere heuristic model. Since social interaction is constitutive of distinctive social phenomena, both on an organisational and ideational level, this framework promises to enhance the theoretical understanding of Christian Democracy, and especially with regard to the distinctiveness and formation of the political phenomenon. Moreover, it could also provide a basis for a further comparative investigation into the nuances between the different Christian Democratic parties in Europe. However, what seems to be already emerging is that (1) at the end of the 1990s Christian Democracy's fortunes in Europe still relied heavily on its political elites' ability to preserve the vertical cohesion of their respective *standen* and their variegated pluralism, transcend the cleavages between them and join in a common and coalescent effort; (2) variations in degree and in the combination of these elements could account for these parties' respective differences and current evolution.[74] Undoubtedly, however, this framework may still needs some improvements, as a result of further testing and revision, but this is true for Christian Democracy as well as for consociational democracy. Indeed, a few authors, and particularly Boogards, have been arguing that Lijphart's model has a number of imperfections that would inevitably affects its applicability to Christian Democracy.[75] Nevertheless, what should be challenged it is not the analytical framework as such but rather our thesis, i.e. that Christian Democracy's distinctiveness intrinsically rests on a specific pattern of consociational interaction.

---

73 M.P. Fogarty, *Christian Democracy in Western Europe (1820-1953)*, 25.
74 See the different case studies in this volume.
75 M. Boogards, "The Favourable Factors for Consociational Democracy. A Review", in: *European Journal of Political Research*, 4 (1998) 475-496; M. Boogards, "The Uneasy Relationship between Empirical and Normative Types in Consociational Theory", in: *Journal of Theoretical Politics*, 4 (2000) 395-423.

Christian Democratic Parties and Europeanisation

Steven Van Hecke

In analysing Christian Democratic parties since the end of the Cold War, one cannot pass over the issue of what is called 'Europeanisation'. Although Europeanisation has become an umbrella term for all kinds of pressures, both implicit and explicit, coming from different directions and generating many changes, big and small, and although Europeanisation is not a totally new phenomenon, there is a growing awareness of the qualitative and quantitative impact of the European integration process on many, if not all, aspects of political life since the 1990s, the period in which the process of building a political Europe started.[1] Consequently, political parties have been linked to Europeanisation insofar as they have become increasingly involved in a (transnational) European environment. In this way, it has been one of the major influences on the politics and policies of Christian Democratic parties.

In this chapter I will examine the relationship between Europeanisation and Christian Democratic parties since the end of the Cold War. I will apply the concept of Europeanisation to party politics and develop it from three complementary perspectives: Europeanisation of political parties, Europeanisation by political parties and the mutual relationship between national and transnational parties. To a large extent, I rely on Ladrech's framework for the Europeanisation of political parties (my first perspective), further elaborating the issue of Europeanisation by political parties (my second perspective) and the specific nature of transnational parties and their relationship with national member parties (my third perspective).[2] Furthermore, I will present three cases in which different aspects of the impact of Europeanisation on Christian Democratic parties will be analysed: party labelling following the 1995 enlargement, the party leaders' meetings of the European People's Party (EPP) and the relationship between the EPP and the Spanish *Partido Popular* (PP).

1   C.M. Radaelli, "Whither Europeanisation? Concept Stretching and Substantive Change", in: *European Integration online Papers*, 4 (2000) 8, 2-6.
2   R. Ladrech, "Europeanisation and Political Parties. Towards a Framework for Analysis", in: R. Ladrech (ed.), *The Europeanisation of Party Politics*. Special Issue of *Party Politics*, 4 (2002) 389-403.

Questions regarding what factors make the 1990s a special period and in which cases parties may be called 'Christian Democratic' will not be dealt with here as they have already been discussed in "Towards a Framework for Analysis". The same applies to the European policy orientation of the various Christian Democratic parties and the evolution of the EPP and its party group in the European Parliament (EP).[3] However, I will pay considerable attention to Europeanisation as such, starting with some theoretical considerations and the current debate in the field of political science.

The issue of Europeanisation and political parties is generally presented in the literature as either lacking or warranting research. According to Gaffney, "the place and role of political parties in the European context is under-researched".[4] More recently, a similar conclusion was put forward by Luther and Müller-Rommel.[5] It is said that only limited research has been carried out on the impact of European integration on political parties and *vice versa*. Mair, on the other hand, has already acknowledged an expanding literature on the Europeanisation of party politics.[6] The question whether the glass is currently half-empty or half-full is, however, subordinate to the question whether research on Europeanisation and political parties is essential for understanding the changing nature of the latter. More precisely, is it right to assess the European integration process as one of the major challenges facing traditional research on party politics? Opponents to the connection between Europeanisation and party politics emphasise the role of non-partisan players and factors in the process of European integration or argue that the nation-state provides the optimal framework in which to analyse the role of (predominantly national) political parties.[7] Proponents emphasise the role of European integration as one of the main motors of the recent changes

3   See the different case studies in this volume and the concluding chapter "European Christian Democracy in the 1990s. Towards a Comparative Approach".
4   J. Gaffney, "Introduction. Political Parties and the European Union", in: J. Gaffney (ed.), *Political Parties and the European Union*, London/New York, 1996, 2.
5   K.R. Luther and F. Müller-Rommel, "Parties and Party Research in the New Europe", in: K.R. Luther and F. Müller-Rommel (eds.), *Political Parties in the New Europe. Political and Analytical Challenges*, Oxford, 2002, 343.
6   P. Mair, "The Limited Impact of Europe on National Party Systems", in: *West European Politics*, 4 (2000) 27.
7   I refer mainly to the intergovernmental approach to the European integration process and the 'classical' theories on party politics. See for instance S. Hix and C. Lord, *Political Parties in the European Union*, Basingstoke, 1997, 201-204; A. Ware, *Political Parties and Party Systems*, Oxford, 1999, 7-13; K.R. Luther and F. Müller-Rommel, "Political Parties in a Changing Europe", in: K.R. Luther and F. Müller-Rommel (eds.), *Political Parties in the New Europe. Political and Analytical Challenges*, Oxford, 2002, 3-7.

in Western European politics. Moreover, these changes constitute a fundamental challenge for political parties (and research on political parties).[8] I agree with the latter that the European Union (EU) constitutes a political environment *sui generis* in which (transnational) party interaction questions the traditional frameworks for analysing political parties. After all, the impact of European integration cannot be isolated from domestic party politics.[9] Therefore, assessing the impact of Europeanisation on political parties should be at the top of the research agenda.[10] This perspective is, however, fairly new as the EU is traditionally not analysed in terms of party politics.[11] Obviously, this "paradigm shift" requires a specific theoretical framework which can be applied to particular cases of the Europeanisation of political parties, Europeanisation by political parties and the relationship between national and transnational parties.[12]

The Europeanisation of political parties

Not surprisingly, there is hardly any consensus among political scientists about what Europeanisation exactly means. Different kinds of definitions cover various aspects of this broad phenomenon.[13] However, in almost none of these definitions are political parties the primary focus. Europeanisation is first of all defined as the impact of the European integration process on the politics and the policies of its member-states. Clearly, this reflects the fact that the effect of Europeanisation on political parties is a rather new research topic. In order to include the impact on political parties as well as the construction of a political Europe, Ladrech defines Europeanisation as "the *process* by which individuals and organisational actors and institu-

---

8   K.R. Luther and F. Müller-Rommel, "Political Parties in a Changing Europe", 7, 9-10.
9   S. Hix and K.H. Goetz, "Introduction. European Integration and National Political Systems", in: S. Hix and K.H. Goetz (eds.), *Europeanised Politics? European Integration and National Political Systems*. Special Issue of *West European Politics*, 4 (2000) 3. This position refers to the comparative approach as opposed to the intergovernmental or the neo-functional approach to the European integration process. See for instance: S. Hix and C. Lord, *Political Parties in the European Union*, 201-204 - who are clearly in favour of the comparative approach themselves -; K.M. Johansson, "Vers une théorie des fédérations européennes de partis", in: P. Delwit, E. Külachi and C. Van de Walle (eds.), *Les fédérations européennes de partis. Organisation et influence*, Brussels, 2001, 21-38; L. Bardi, "Parties and Party Systems in the European Union. National and Supranational Dimensions", in: K.R. Luther and F. Müller-Rommel (eds.), *Political Parties in the New Europe. Political and Analytical Challenges*, 293-294.
10   K.R. Luther and F. Müller-Rommel, "Political Parties in a Changing Europe", 10-16.
11   S. Hix and C. Lord, *Political Parties in the European Union*, 7.
12   K.R. Luther and F. Müller-Rommel, "Parties and Party Research in the New Europe", 344-346.
13   R. Ladrech, "Europeanisation and Political Parties", 391-393.

tions respond to the altered conditions generated by the development of the EU since the launch of the Single European Act".[14] The reference to the Single European Act is crucial because it marks the beginning of the direct involvement of political parties in the European integration process. Additionally, Hix and Goetz define Europeanisation as a two-way process, as both a source of change and an effect, neither of which can, in their view, exist without the other.[15]

If, however, the link between Europeanisation and political parties is made, "the theoretical focus shifts to such variables as the structure of society, the dimensions of ideological and party conflict, the institutional framework of the political system, the behaviour of political actors within the system, and the making of public policy".[16] Although there is relatively little literature on the Europeanisation of political parties, Ladrech distinguishes two camps, each covering some of the aforementioned variables[17]: first, the research on party groups in the EP and transnational party federations, and second, the considerable research on the European policy orientation of individual political parties.[18] What is lacking is a study of the connection between the two phenomena, on the change and adaptation of political parties, internally and externally, in response to the effects of European integration. It is worth recalling that this thesis only refers to political parties as such, because, as Mair argues, European integration has only a potential indirect impact and not a direct impact on national party systems.[19] If, however, one agrees that "the 'remaking' of European politics - and particularly the emergence of a supranational level of decision-making - constitutes a fundamental change in the operational context of political parties", then a particular theoretical model should be developed.[20]

---

14   *Ibid.*, 393 (Ladrech's italics). The launch of the Single European Act at the end of the 1980s is generally perceived as the starting point of the process of building a political Europe.

15   S. Hix and K.H. Goetz, "Introduction. European Integration and National Political Systems", 21.

16   S. Hix and C. Lord, *Political Parties in the European Union*, 203.

17   R. Ladrech, "Europeanisation and Political Parties", 390.

18   See our introduction and footnote 3.

19   P. Mair, "The Limited Impact of Europe on National Party Systems", 27-51. Notwithstanding the fact that the impact of Europeanisation on national party systems falls beyond the scope of this chapter, in my view this thesis should seriously be considered. See for instance the link between Christian Democratic parties and the electoral system of proportionality and my third case. See also my conclusion and footnote 53.

20   K.R. Luther and F. Müller-Rommel, "Political Parties in a Changing Europe", 5.

In order to grasp this "fundamental change", Ladrech proposes five areas of investigation for evidence of Europeanisation in parties and party activity: (1) programmatic change; (2) organisational change; (3) patterns of party competition; (4) party-government relations; and (5) relations beyond the national party system.[21] Obviously, plenty of overlaps exist between these different areas of the Europeanisation of political parties. Although Ladrech lists these five areas with regard to the Europeanisation of political parties only (my first perspective), I will also apply them in my cases of Europeanisation by political parties (my second perspective) and of the relation between national and transnational parties (my third perspective). Moreover, my cases will illustrate not only the overlap between these five different areas but also the interwovenness between the three perspectives. In this way, applying Ladrech's areas to my second and third perspective is warranted.

As to the Europeanisation of political parties, there are plenty of examples of individual parties (Christian Democratic or not) that have changed their politics or policies in one way or another. The 1995 enlargement of the EU to include Austria, Finland and Sweden offers one of the most explicit examples in the area of programmatic change. In each of these countries (and only these countries), although to varying degrees and within varying contexts, Christian Democratic parties changed their names to emphasise a growing identification with Continental Christian Democracy.[22] It should be noted that this process is not directly linked to the partisan Europeanisation by the EPP as the EPP does not exclusively call itself 'Christian Democratic' and neither does it consist merely of Christian Democratic parties.[23] In Austria, the 1995 party programme defined the *Österreichische Volkspartei* (ÖVP) as a 'Christian Democratic' party, reintroducing the confessional label of 'Christian' and at the same time underlining its social image. In Sweden the *Kristen Demokratisk Samling* (Christian Democratic Rally) changed its name in 1991 to *Kristdemokratiska Samhällspartiet* (Christian Democratic Social Party) and again in 1996 to *Kristdemokraterna* (Christian Democrats). In Finland a similar process took place: *Suomen Kristillinen* (Christian League) became *Kristillisdemokraatit* (Christian Democrats) in 2001. Since the Danish *Kristeligt Folkeparti* (Christian People's Party) changed in 2003 to *Kristendemokraterne* (Christian Democrats), all the Scandinavian Christian Democratic parties in the EU adopted the same

---

21   R. Ladrech, "Europeanisation and Political Parties", 396-400.
22   See the chapters "Rejuvenation of an Old Party? Christian Democracy in Austria" and "Life on the Northern Margin. Christian Democracy in Scandinavia" in this volume.
23   See "A Decade of Seized Opportunities. Christian Democracy in the European Union" in this volume.

name. In this way, one can speak of a process of 'Scandinavisation'.[24] Although simultaneity is not causality, the 'Christian Democratic' (re)labelling after the enlargement of 1995 reveals a striking paradox as the explicit references to Continental Christian Democracy were made in a period of electoral decline that has in some cases led to a reluctance to use the term 'Christian Democratic'.

Europeanisation by political parties

In his theoretical framework, Ladrech considers political parties as the objects of Europeanisation but makes no clear reference to the active role of political parties in the process of European integration. By contrast, I argue that political parties should be researched both as the object (dependent variable) and the subject (independent variable) of Europeanisation. As mentioned above, Europeanisation can be defined as a two-way process, both as a source of change and an effect.[25] Applied to party politics, this means that the relationship between Europeanisation and political parties is a "dialectical" process: the Europeanisation of political parties on the one hand and Europeanisation by political parties on the other.[26] In this way, political parties may be seen as players in the process of European integration. If the European level is presented as a higher level and the focus is on national political parties, Europeanisation then becomes both a top-down and a bottom-up process. To use Ladrech's framework again, it should be noted that he acknowledges Europeanisation as "a reflexive relationship" but uses the general term national actors only.[27] Even though it is difficult, most of the time, to trace which variable is dependent and which is independent, it is only through incorporating the active role of political parties that the process of the growing politicisation of the EU itself can be fully understood.[28]

Party leaders' meetings offer one of the clearest examples of Europeanisation by political parties - my second perspective - in the area of organisational change, although, as mentioned already, they are the result of a dialectical

24 Because of the limited scope of this paragraph, I simply assume that this change of labels covers a more profound change of party programmes (or that the change of label is the final result of this process).
25 S. Hix and K.H. Goetz, "Introduction. European Integration and National Political Systems", 21.
26 D. Hanley, "Christian Democracy and the Paradoxes of Europeanisation. Flexibility, Competition and Collusion", in: R. Ladrech (ed.), *The Europeanisation of Party Politics. Special Issue of Party Politics*, 4 (2002) 464-465.
27 R. Ladrech, "Europeanisation and Political Parties", 393.
28 J. Gaffney, "Introduction. Political Parties and the European Union", 3.

process. In these meetings, prime ministers, foreign ministers, members of the European Commission and national opposition leaders gather publicly on a partisan basis on the eve of the European Council meetings.[29] Moreover, "the EU's distinctive institutional environment made it sensible for the transnational party federations to concentrate on a task that has no parallel in national politics: that of coordinating the positions of party leaders prior to meetings of the EU's main agenda-setting body", the latter being an example of Europeanisation by political parties.[30] Attending these party leaders' summits provides informational advantages, (national) exit strategies and elite socialisation. Being involved in these kinds of "transnational partisan networks" creates a "closeness to fit" that is certainly an important element in trying to explain different trajectories of Europeanisation.[31]

Christian Democrats have been pioneers in establishing party leaders' meetings on a regular basis.[32] Their importance has been growing in accordance with the increasing politicisation of the European Council meetings and the role they have been playing in the decision-making process of the EU.[33] It is therefore no surprise that the impact of the Christian Democratic (EPP) leaders in the 1985 Intergovernmental Conference (IGC) that led to the Single European Act has been researched.[34] From the start of the IGC at the Milan European Council in June 1985 until the final Luxembourg Council in December 1985, Johansson shows the decisive impact of the various meetings of Christian Democratic party elites on agenda setting, timetable and content. The effectiveness of this strategy is, of course, dependent on the quality and

29   S. Hix and C. Lord, *Political Parties in the European Union*, 182-195; S. Van Hecke, "Het Europa van de opportunities. Analyse van de overlevingsstrategie van de christen-democraten in de Europese Unie", in: *Res Publica*, 4 (2003) 654-655, 668-669. Only the EPP, the Socialists and the Liberals organise such meetings on a regular basis. These meetings also include the chairmen of their respective party groups in the EP and, depending on the political affiliation, the president of the EP. See also "A Decade of Seized Opportunities. Christian Democracy in the European Union" in this volume.

30   S. Hix and C. Lord, *Political Parties in the European Union*, 20.

31   S. Hix and K.H. Goetz, "Introduction. European Integration and National Political Systems", 19; K.M. Johansson, "Party Elites in Multilevel Europe. The Christian Democrats and the Single European Act", in: R. Ladrech (ed.), *Special Issue on the Europeanisation of Party Politics. Party Politics*, 4 (2002) 426.

32   They date back to the 1970s, the period in which the EPP was founded and consisted of Christian Democratic parties only. In 1990, the meetings were given official status in the EPP's statutes. See also "A Decade of Seized Opportunities. Christian Democracy in the European Union" in this volume.

33   See also "A Decade of Seized Opportunities. Christian Democrats in the European Union" in this volume.

34   K.M. Johansson, "Party Elites in Multilevel Europe".

quantity of the Christian Democratic presence in the European Council.[35] Christian Democrats reached a comparable success during the 1990-1991 IGC that led to the Maastricht Treaty. From the Rome Summit in October 1990 until the Maastricht Summit in December 1991, Christian Democratic leaders were able to dominate the negotiation process and marginalise Margaret Thatcher, British Prime Minister, especially with regard to the criteria and the calendar of the Economic and Monetary Union (EMU).[36] The same happened with the introduction of the principle of subsidiarity, the co-decision procedure and the general framework of the new treaty. Given the massive impact of Maastricht and particularly of the EMU in the domestic and European arenas, it is not an exaggeration to claim that, in this respect, Christian Democratic party elites to a large extent shaped the politics and policies of the 1990s.[37] During the 1995-1996 and 2000 IGC, which led respectively to the Amsterdam and Nice Treaties, Christian Democrats failed to influence the outcome significantly as, first of all, they lacked the relative majority from which they had profited before.[38] With respect to the Convention on the Future of Europe (2002-2003) and the subsequent IGC (2003-), the provisional result is much more ambiguous. Many observers have witnessed the active contribution of Christian Democrats and other EPP members in the Convention and the efforts of the EPP Presidency to influence the outcome of the IGC. However, the success of the EPP party leaders' meetings can only be judged once the new treaty has been signed. Clearly, much will depend on the final position(s) of the various (Christian Democratic, Conservative and Liberal) EPP leaders in the IGC that currently, it is worth noting, includes twenty-five member state governments.

35   During the 1985 IGC, the Belgian, Dutch, German, Irish, and Luxembourg governments were headed by Christian Democrats (i.e. 5 out of 12) while Giulio Andreotti, the former and would-be Prime Minister, was Foreign Minister in the Italian government that presided over the European Council meetings.

36   S. Hix and C. Lord, *Political Parties in the European Union*, 170, 189. Hix and Lord also discuss the EPP's influence on the European Council of Edinburgh (December 1992), Brussels (December 1993) and Essen (December 1994): *Ibid.*, 190-194.

37   Once more, the outcome depended on the Christian Democratic 'quality and quantity' in the European Council. As far as the first is concerned, six out of twelve government leaders were linked to the EPP, including the President of the European Council. See also D. Hanley, "Le parti populaire européen au cœur du consensus décisionnel?", in: P. Delwit, E. Külachi and C. Van de Walle (eds.), *Les fédérations européennes de partis. Organisation et influence*, 190.

38   Only the Belgian, German and Luxembourg governments were lead by (traditional) Christian Democrats. Moreover, the position of Helmut Kohl, Federal Chancellor of Germany and one of the main architects of the Single European Act and the Maastricht Treaty, was weakened by the socialist majority in the Bundesrat (Higher Federal Chamber). The position of the Christian Democratic leaders was also weakened because they were more or less divided on the introduction of an employment title, something the socialists supported. K.M. Johansson, "Tracing the Employment Title in the Amsterdam Treaty. Uncovering Transnational Coalitions", in: *Journal of European Public Policy*, 1 (1999) 85-101.

National and transnational parties in a mutual relationship

In his framework, Ladrech focuses on political parties as part of the national political system. He therefore identifies national political parties as the primary subject of analysis and refers to transnational parties only insofar as relations beyond the national party system are concerned. I argue, however, that (1) both national and transnational parties should be considered; (2) Europeanisation of and by political parties often involves transnational parties as mediators; and (3) therefore the supranational level should be included in the analysis, alongside the nation-state level.[39]

My third perspective reflects the fact that the deepening of the European integration process has transformed party politics in the EU in a way that has increased the political weight of the transnational parties. In this development towards supranational parties, Article 191 of the Treaty on the European Union (TEU) offers a legal illustration of the (potential) importance and role of transnational parties at the European level.[40] At the same time, its introduction is the actual result of lobbying by the transnational party federations in the Council, the Commission, and the EP. However, potentiality is not reality, as has been shown by the long and difficult road to regulating the statutes and financing of European political parties.[41] For instance, the Nice amendment forbids transfers of EU funds to national member parties, as Ladrech rightly points out.[42] Moreover, direct access of national parties to EU decision-making is very unlikely in the near future. So far, national parties have only indirect influence through their partisan presence in the Council, the Commission and the EP. Therefore, the impact of transnational parties can only be analysed on a case-by-case basis.

---

39   K.R. Luther and F. Müller-Rommel, "Parties and Party Research in the New Europe", 346. Although beyond the scope of this chapter, this position implies a multi-level governance approach. See for instance L. Hooghe and G. Marks, *Multi-Level Governance and European Integration*, Lanham, 2001.

40   The introduction of the so-called party article dates from Maastricht. The Nice Treaty has added a second paragraph. Article 191 (ex-138A) TEU reads: "Political parties at European level are important as a factor for integration within the Union. They contribute to forming a European awareness and to expressing the political will of the citizens of the Union. The Council (…) shall lay down the regulations governing political parties at European level and in particular the rules regarding their funding." In its Draft Treaty establishing a Constitution for Europe, the European Convention classifies the party article, now article 45, under the principle of representative government (Title VI The Democratic Life of the Union), shortening it to "Political parties at the European level contribute to forming European awareness and to expressing the will of Union citizens."

41   L. Bardi, "Parties and Party Systems in the European Union", 296.

42   R. Ladrech, "Europeanisation and Political Parties", 395.

The relationship between the EPP and the PP offers such a case, especially in the areas of party programme (ideology) and elite personnel.[43] In the early 1990s, the PP relied heavily on the EPP programme to renew its policies and emphasise its break from its predecessor, the *Alianza Popular* (AP). Clearly, the PP took a more pro-integration stance on European issues and accommodated itself to the model of a social market economy.[44] During the 1989 EP election, for instance, the PP campaigned on the basis of the EPP manifesto. Later on, as the PP's position inside the EPP became stronger, the party started influencing the EPP's programme and voting behaviour in the EP. In the field of economic policy, the PP was rather successful, especially because other 'old' and 'new' member parties supported its neo-liberal stance (although the PP maintained its commitment to the essentials of the welfare state) and the EPP itself had shifted towards liberal economics. As to European integration (institutional reform, common foreign and security policies, etc.), the picture is much more ambiguous. On the one hand, the PP's position became less 'Christian Democratic' and increasingly inspired by national interests, something the opponents of the entry of the PP to the EPP had warned against.[45] In this way, the traditional pro-European stance of the EPP has been weakened. On the other hand, the PP did not manage to dominate the institutional agenda of the EPP. So far, the EPP has been faithful to its federal principles, although in the run-up to this ultimate goal, compromises with more intergovernmental approaches could not always be avoided.[46] Finally, the EPP and the PP have increasingly rejected the terms 'right' and 'conservative'. The latter was the first to downgrade its ideology by using 'modern', 'centre', 'reformist centre', etc.[47] The EPP soon followed by identifying itself as 'centrist', 'reformist' etc.[48] In the case of the PP, integration into the EPP has meant a softening of its ideology but not a re-ideologisation along Christian Democratic lines: traditional programmatic principles were abolished without being replaced by any new, clear-cut doctrine.

---

43 For an extended version of this case, see S. Van Hecke and P. Matuschek, *Europeanisation and Political Parties. The Case of the Spanish People's Party and the European People's Party*, unpublished paper, 2004.

44 P. Matuschek, "Aznars Ambitionen. Die spanische Volkspartei und ihr europäischer Führungsanspruch", in: *Blätter für deutsche und internationale Politik*, 1 (2002) 77-84.

45 *Ibid.*, 82. See for instance the Spanish position in the 2003- IGC.

46 The debate about the inclusion of a reference to the Christian heritage in the EU Constitution is one of the few examples in which traditional Christian Democrats and the PP share each other's point of view.

47 P. Matuschek, "Aznars Ambitionen", 81.

48 See for instance "A Union of Values" as agreed at the XIVth EPP Congress (Berlin, 13 January 2000): "(…)we as Christian Democrats, moderates, and centrists, members of the EPP…". On the web (<www.eppe.org>), the EPP presents itself as "a family of the political centre".

As far as elite personnel is concerned, a similar two-way process can be observed. In the domestic arena, from 1990 onwards, the PP has experienced a considerable increase in the representation of Christian Democratic politicians (most of them former members of small Christian Democratic parties), both within the higher ranks of the party organisation and in public office, although they have never constituted a coherent group or faction within the PP. In the European realm, several Christian Democrats were appointed to international posts. By the time the PP was at the centre of the EPP, senior officials of the PP had been appointed in the EPP and the EPP Group.[49] In this respect, the smooth relationship between José María Aznar, PP President and Spanish Prime Minister, and Wilfried Martens, President of the EPP, is both a cause and a consequence. Obviously, this form of "transnational partisan networking" leads to a fusion of interests and access to party representation in the Council, the Commission and the EP in which the appointment of elite personnel is only the first step. Failing however to provide any examples of the EPP's influence on the recruitment of the PP's senior officials, the issue of elite personnel shows the limits of Europeanisation by transnational parties.[50] However, this is not due to the weakness of the EPP as such, but is a simple consequence of the fact that "[t]he power to obtain political office in the EU ultimately rests with the sub-units of the EU parties: the domestic party organisations".[51] In this way, the mere status of the EU integration process limits the scope of Europeanisation of and by (trans)national parties.

[49]   Currently, one vice-president (EPP Group), one vice-president (EP), one committee chairman (EP), one committee vice-chairman (EP) and four coordinators (EPP Group) are PP MEPs. <www.epp-ed.org>. Alejandro Agag, personal advisor to Aznar, was EPP Secretary General from 1999 until 2002. His successor, Antonio López Istúriz, is another personal advisor to Aznar.

[50]   The only exception is Aznar's appointment as Vice-President of the EPP at the instigation of Martens in 1993, less than three weeks before the national elections, intended clearly to boost Aznar's chances.

[51]   S. Hix and C. Lord, *Political Parties in the European Union*, 208.

Conclusion

Europeanisation is indeed a very complex process. It is only through defining the concept and applying it to particular cases that this broad phenomenon can be understood and that its impact can be assessed.[52] Obviously, many cases have not been researched and plenty of questions remain unanswered, such as the impact of Europeanisation on the national party systems in which, among others, Christian Democratic parties operate, and on intra-party processes.[53] In other words, the analysis of the impact of Europeanisation on Christian Democratic parties has only begun. As for the parties themselves, Europeanisation is increasingly perceived as a 'challenge'. In this way, parties understand that one cannot oppose Europeanisation, let alone neglect or deny it. It is something that is simply there and probably will become even more important in the near future. Parties no longer operate exclusively on a domestic level but have to integrate the European dimension in their organisation, policies, personnel, etc. It goes without saying that the same applies to research on contemporary Christian Democratic parties: the hitherto dominant state-centred paradigm has to be replaced by a dual national-supranational approach.[54]

---

52   In his article on Christian Democracy and Europeanisation Hanley concludes: "Europeanisation reveals itself to be a matrix of powerful pressures not always pulling in the same direction. It is a complex process that proceeds at different speeds in different places (...). The interplay between national and supranational actors makes such an outcome anything but predictable." D. Hanley, "Christian Democracy and the Paradoxes of Europeanisation", 479.

53   See respectively S. Hix and K.H. Goetz, "Introduction. European Integration and National Political Systems", 15: "(...) the effect on domestic politics - notably political cleavages, voters, elections, parties, party competition, party systems and patterns of democratic legitimation - are only beginning to be researched."; P. Mair, "The Limited Impact of Europe on National Party Systems", 26: "As such, virtually no attention is paid to the question of how Europe may have provoked fissures within parties, or to the extent to which it may have encouraged the formation of internal party factions (...)."

54   K.R. Luther and F. Müller-Rommel, "Parties and Party Research in the New Europe", 346.

Two Crises, Two Consolidations?
Christian Democracy in Germany

Frank Bösch

The period between 1989 and 1991 - the end of the Cold War - marks a crucial point in European history. Many historians refer to this period as the end of a whole era, particularly Hobsbawn whose designation, "the short twentieth century" (1914-1991), has become a popular expression.[1] In many Western European countries the end of the Cold War marks the decline of Christian Democracy; in Germany, however, it ensured its continuity. The electoral results of the *Christlich Demokratische Union Deutschlands* (CDU) and the Bavarian *Christlich-Soziale Union* (CSU) remained quite stable and they did not lose their governmental power until 1998. The Western German CDU was united with the Eastern German CDU, but the programmes, statutes, leadership and organisation of the party were not significantly changed. The turn of the century seems to be the main turning-point in the history of the CDU/CSU. In 1998 they suffered an electoral decline and lost power. Helmut Kohl, Chairman for twenty-five years, resigned and many politicians of his generation stepped down as well. In 2000 the greatest scandal in the history of the CDU hastened this transformation. Since then, a new leadership has tried to reform the party's programmes, organisation and statutes.

In this chapter I argue that the CDU/CSU had to expect electoral and organisational problems similar to those of other Christian Democratic parties in Western Europe during the late 1980s, but German unification helped to hide them for another decade. During the 1990s, the CDU/CSU was discreetly changed, but was not reformed to cope with the new challenges of the 1990s. A new phase in its history started between 1998 and 2000. My chapter therefore highlights two crises and two consolidations: one at the end of the 1980s

---

1   E. Hobsbawn, *Age of Extremes. The Short Twentieth Century (1914-1991)*, London, 1994.
     For an early German contribution to this debate, see K. Tenfelde, "1914 bis 1990. Die Einheit
     der Epoche" in: *Aus Politik und Zeitgeschichte*, 40 (1991) 3-11.

and the other a decade later. Changes within the CDU/CSU will be analysed by examining different aspects: its electoral development, campaigns and voters, its policy, programmes and ideology, and its organisation, leadership and finances.[2]

Elections, campaigns and voters

At the end of the 1980s, the German Christian Democrats went through serious electoral crises. In 1989 they lost more than 8% in the European Parliament election. In the regional elections their results declined too. The CDU lost its governmental power in rural Protestant *Länder* (federal states) - such as the northern Schleswig-Holstein (1988) and Niedersachsen (1990) - and even in Catholic *Länder* like Saarland (1985) and Rheinland-Pfalz (1991), which had been governed by the CDU since the post-war period.[3] Since 1991 the Christian Democrats have been governing only two of the former West German states: Baden-Württemberg and Bavaria. The CDU/CSU became the main parties in the South, while the North and the West were dominated by the Social Democrats. The crises of 1989 were apparent not only in the electoral results: the party itself was in a miserable condition and completely indebted; Kohl's authority was weak and internal discussions revealed its disunity in public.

The year 1989 also marked the emergence of a new rival. For the first time in thirty years, an extreme right party, *die Republikaner* (the Republicans), succeeded in passing the 5% threshold and entered many regional parliaments. In the European election it also won almost exactly the votes (more than 7%) that the CDU lost. Many German Christian Democrats were afraid that this new competitor might become as successful as popular right-wing parties in other Western European countries.[4] The CDU/CSU lost voters from all kinds of social groups, but some in particular. As in other countries, above average numbers of young men switched to the Right and younger women

---

2   This chapter is based on a research project that analysed the development of the CDU since its foundation. The results are published in three volumes: F. Bösch, *Macht und Machtverlust. Die Geschichte der CDU*, Stuttgart/Munich, 2002; F. Bösch, *Die Adenauer-CDU. Gründung, Aufbau und Krise einer Erfolgspartei (1945-1969)*, Stuttgart/Munich, 2001; F. Bösch, *Das konservative Milieu. Vereinskultur und lokale Sammlungspolitik (1900-1960)*, Göttingen, 2002.

3   For an introduction to the regional development of the German states, see J. Hartmann (ed.), *Handbuch der deutschen Bundesländer*, Frankfurt, 1997.

4   See the excellent comparative study on the rise of the new right-wing parties in Western democracies: F. Decker, *Parteien unter Druck. Der neue Rechtspopulismus in den westlichen Demokratien*, Opladen, 2000.

with higher education preferred *die Grünen* (Green party). The CDU lost above average numbers of those voters who traditionally had a weaker affiliation with the party, namely the Protestants and the workers. Consequently, it could keep only its southern strongholds which still had a stronger Catholic and middle-class electorate.

Some reasons for this decline are obvious and can be found in other countries too. The end of the Cold War, the new growing secularisation and the change in traditional values threatened the CDU's anti-communist and Christian positions which had united its heterogeneous supporters. Conflicts with the peace movement led to differences with some churches, especially with the Protestant church. The high unemployment rate dissatisfied low-income voters. Bitter conflicts with the trade unions led to strikes and mobilised their members against the CDU/CSU.[5] Consequently, many academic researchers and observers expected that the *Sozialdemokratische Partei Deutschlands* (SPD) and the Green party would succeed in the forthcoming federal election in 1990.

Nevertheless, Kohl and the CDU/CSU won the election in 1990 with almost 44% of the vote -10 points more than the Social Democrats. This victory was a result of the sudden German unification, which solved many problems within the CDU. From an electoral point of view, the CDU was rescued by the new voters from Eastern Germany. Many researchers had expected that the East Germans would vote for the Social Democrats, because less than one third of the East Germans were members of the church, the well-off middle classes were weak and the Protestant regions belonged to traditional strongholds of the Social Democrats. In fact, workers in East Germany especially voted above the average for the CDU.[6] The generous promises of Kohl were much more attractive to them than the cautious scruples of his challenger Oskar Lafontaine. As the Nazi and Communist dictatorships had destroyed most of the traditional cleaveage structures and milieus, the new electorate voted rather as 'rational voters' for those parties that made the best promises and had the most popular candidates. Religion was the only traditional cleavage still visible in the East, but it was relevant only for a minority.

5   F. Neuhaus, *DGB und CDU. Analysen zum bilateralen Verhältnis von 1982 bis 1990*, Köln, 1996, 332.
6   Forschungsgruppe Wahlen. *Bundestagswahl 1990. Eine Analyse der ersten gesamtdeutschen Bundestagswahl am 2. Dezember 1990*, Mannheim, 1990; P. Schindler, *Datenhandbuch zur Geschichte des deutschen Bundestages*, Vol. 1, Berlin, 1999, 238.

Federal elections, 1987-2002 (per cent)

	CDU/CSU	SPD	FDP	*Grüne*	PDS	Turnout
1987	44.3	37.0	9.1	8.3		84.3
1990	43.8	33.5	11.0	5.1	2.4	77.8
1994	41.4	36.4	6.9	7.3	4.4	79.0
1998	35.1	40.9	6.2	6.7	5.1	82.2
2002	38.5	38.5	7.4	8.4	4.0	79.1

Less than one third of the East German voters were members of churches, but this minority still preferred the CDU well above the average. Even in the 2002 election, when the CDU received only 28% of the vote in the East, church members supported them well above the average (Catholics 52% and Protestants 40%). These religious core supporters are small in number but constitute a remarkable gain for the CDU.

CDU and SPD voters in East and West, 1990 and 2002 (per cent)

		CDU		SPD	
		West	East	West	East
Worker	1990	39	49.8	46.7	24.8
	2002	40	30	44	39
White-collar worker	1990	43	37	35.9	25.1
	2002	36	28	39	41
Official	1990	46.7	34.4	31.9	24.1
	2002	36	31	37	35
Self-employed	1990	56.9	50.3	17.9	16.2
	2002	47	47	21	17
In training	1990	32.1	18.1	33.5	23.1
	2002	30	18	39	43
Catholic	1990	56.3	65.8	26.6	11.5
	2002	52	52	31	30
Protestant	1990	39.6	53.4	39.7	20.1
	2002	36	40	44	37
No Religion	1990	25.7	33.3	45	28.7
	2002	26	22	35	38

The problems following the quick unification led to the emergence of the so-called post-socialist cleavage, which can be observed in other parts of Eastern Europe as well.[7] The post-communist *Partei des Demokratischen Sozialismus* (PDS) profited from pre-unification cultural networks, which were revived in the years after 1990. Since then, the PDS has almost regularly gained about 20% of the votes in Eastern Germany. These results fragment the Left and weaken the position of the Social Democrats.

The image of Kohl celebrated by the East German population at the end of the 1990s had some impact on West German voters. Kohl suddenly appeared as a statesman who had successfully negotiated between East and West. His official and private meetings with Mikhail Gorbachev and George Bush sr. were broadcast in the media and were seen as highly symbolic. This helped Kohl to regain his authority within his party. Economic and political problems seemed to be less important considering the national challenge of unification. At the same time, the extreme right party was somewhat marginalised due to these new national issues. Between 1990 and 1994 the CDU became the party of the Catholic and economically powerful South and of the poor atheistic East. Anti-communism and the trust in the economic competence of the Christian Democrats united those different kinds of strongholds. Furthermore, in the regional elections between 1990 and 1994 the CDU succeeded in four of the five new Eastern German *Länder*. Once more, the electoral decisions in the East were influenced by persons and issues and rarely by party identification.

There were many similarities between the federal election of 1994 and that of four years before. The SPD led the polls for a long time, but the CDU/CSU finally won the race. The Christian Democrats ran a very efficient campaign. A strict anti-communist campaign against the PDS mobilised the voters in the West. The CDU improved its use of the media and started to work with private TV-stations.[8] Kohl, who usually had problems in communicating on television, became a regular visitor on TV shows and the central guest in several. He even got his own show, called *Zur Sache Kanzler* (Get to the Point, Chancellor), which was shown on the SAT 1 channel owned by his friend and media tycoon, Leo Kirch.

---

7   H. Kitschelt, "Formation of Party Cleavages in Post-Communist Democracies", in: *Party Politics*, 4 (1995) 447-472; I. Jörs, "East Germany. Another Party Landscape", in: *German Politics*, 1 (2003) 135-158.

8   The dominance of the CDU in the media campaign is analysed in: O. Jarren and M. Bode, "Ereignis- und Medienmanagement politischer Parteien. Kommunikationsstrategien im Superwahljahr 1994", in: Bertelsmann-Stiftung (ed.), *Politik überzeugend vermitteln. Wahlkampfstrategien in Deutschland und in den USA*, Gütersloh, 1996, 87.

At the polls, the CDU lost a percentage of some social groups in the electorate. A close look at the 1994 results shows some similarities with the late
1980s. Voters in the northern cities, especially, and in those regions with a
traditional industry (Nordrhein-Westfalen, Saarland) turned away from the
CDU. Women under 35 switched over to the Green party and workers to the
Social Democrats. In Eastern Germany the CDU particularly lost the votes of
workers. However, the election was decided once more in Eastern and Southern Germany where the majority of the voters kept a distance from the Social
Democrats. Votes for the CDU/CSU increased especially in the South where
the excellent economic conditions were appreciated by the voters.

The voters of the CDU/CSU, 1983-2002 (per cent)

	1983	1987	1990	1994	1998	2002
Catholic	65	55	55	52	49	52
Protestant	40	32	39	39	32	37
Male	47.7	42.5	42	40.6	34.9	40
Female	49.2	45.1	44.8	42.2	35	37
Catholic worker	58	47	52			
Protestant worker	33	25	36			
Worker*				37	29	37
Catholic white-collar worker and official	67	58	55			
Protestant white-collar worker and official	47	35	34			
White-collar worker and official*				40	33	35
Catholic self-employed	76	71	72			
Protestant self-employed	45	45	52			
Self-employed*				52	44	47
Farmers	68	77	78	64	63	

* Not including their confession
Sources: *Datenhandbuch zur Geschichte des deutschen Bundestages (1953-1990)*, Berlin, 1999;
Forschungsgruppe Wahlen, *Bundestagswahl 1994/1998/2002*, Mannheim, 1994/1998/2002; *Infratest
dimap Wahltagsbefragung.*

The electoral decline of the CDU worsened in the second half of the 1990s. Setbacks in the country's unification led to protests by different social groups. For the first time the Catholic and the Protestant Churches protested against the social cuts of Kohl's government policies and demanded help for the huge number of unemployed. During the 1980s some priests had already protested against the policy of the CDU, but now the church's official leaders were raising their voices also. The trade unions kept quiet until 1996 when they organised one of their biggest demonstrations in the history of the Federal Republic and criticised the social policy of the government as too liberal. At the demonstration of the *Deutsche Gewerkschaftbund* (German Federation of Employees) in June 1996, for instance, 350,000 people demonstrated in Bonn against the "attack on our social system". At the same time, the employer organisations were criticising conditions in the German economy as not liberal enough.

The CDU declined in the polls and in regional elections particularly in East Germany. It became obvious that these new voters in the East had not developed a significant party identification with the Christian Democrats. In 1998, the CDU had its worst electoral result since 1949. The Christian Democrats were sent into opposition after having been in power for sixteen years in a coalition with the Liberal *Freie Demokratische Partei* (FDP). Many scholars have traced the radical decline back to Chancellor Kohl: voters decided for a personal change, not for the Social Democrats.[9] The new Chancellor Gerhard Schröder was much more popular than Kohl and voters believed that Schröder and the Social Democrats had more economic competence. The Social Democrats succeeded with an innovative media campaign which was closely mirrored on the campaigns of Tony Blair and Bill Clinton.[10] The traditional anti-communist campaign of the Christian Democrats against the 'red-green chaos' failed completely this time; eight years after unification, the fear of communism could not mobilise the electorate anymore. For the first time a huge number of voters (1,3 million) switched from the right to the left, from the CDU/CSU to the Social Democrats. The political shift of the Social Democrats towards the centre, suggested by their candidate Schröder, was based on this new volatility.

---

9   F.U. Pappi, "Die Abwahl Kohls. Hauptergebnis der Bundestagswahl 1998", in: *Zeitschrift für Politik*, 1 (1999) 1-29; M. Jung and D. Roth, "Wer zu spät geht, den bestraft der Wähler. Eine Analyse der Bundestagswahl 1998", in: *Aus Politik und Zeitgeschichte*, 52 (1998) 1-18.

10   H.-D. Klingemann and M. Kaase (eds.), *Wahlen und Wähler. Analysen aus Anlaß der Bundestagswahl* 1998, Wiesbaden, 2001.

Once more, the Christian Democrats lost voters from numerous social groups: 8% each of the workers, the self-employed, officials and white-collar workers. As mentioned above, these groups felt discontented with the government for different reasons, but with the same impact. The CDU/CSU lost in rural areas and in cities. They lost in all age groups, but especially among voters between 45 and 59 years who turned away from the CDU/CSU; this generation had been socialised by the leftist spirit of the 1970s and had not become conservative with age. In particular, women in this age group switched over (a loss of more than 12%) because they preferred more social security. On the regional level the biggest losses were in East Germany (minus 11%), where the poor economic situation and widespread unemployment led to a high rate of electoral volatility.

In the succeeding years the CDU could not really recover from this defeat, though its results have gone up and down in regional and national elections. For the first time since the 1980s, the CDU/CSU won several regional elections in the West in 1999 and were also successful in the European election in the same year. These results showed that 1998 had not been a 'critical' election that had led to durable new alliances between the Social Democrats and their voters. The political failures of the red-green coalition directly increased sympathy for the Christian Democrats. Even in 2000, the year of the donation scandal, the Christian Democrats gained some unexpected victories.

In the summer of 2002, the CDU/CSU seemed to have a real chance of winning the federal elections, having led the polls throughout the whole year almost. The Christian Democrats intensified their media campaign while the Social Democrats' campaign went rather badly. Nevertheless, the result was disappointing for the CDU/CSU. They made a small gain of 3% in the South, especially by the CSU in Bavaria. In the West and in the North the CDU stagnated at a low level. The CDU/CSU succeeded in winning back a bigger number of workers and unemployed, but failed to regain the huge group of retired people. Once more, the election was decided in East Germany, where during a tremendous flood Schröder was able to present himself as a generous chancellor, just as Kohl had done after unification. Once more, personality seemed to have had a decisive impact on the election result: the Christian Democratic candidate Edmund Stoiber was said to be less sympathetic although voters believed that he was more competent to solve the economic problems. Stoiber's media performance especially was worse than that of Schröder, as was evident in a live TV debate between the two candidates, the first ever in German history.

In comparison to other countries the German Christian Democrats are still rather strong. Since the election in 2002, the CDU/CSU has been leading the polls again - for many months by almost 50%. The East German voters might switch over again if the Social Democrats are not able to reduce unemployment. Whereas Christian Democratic parties in other European countries have lost supporters to right-wing parties, so far such new rivals have had only some regional success in Germany. The historical roots of political Catholicism still guarantee a loyal electorate; even in the election of 2002, 75% of regular churchgoing Catholics voted for the CDU/CSU. This group still constitutes 18% of the electorate.[11] Protestants do not show a significant preference for the CDU anymore and only in the East does the small Protestant community have a remarkably strong connection to the CDU. However, in future elections the German Christian Democrats might be confronted with three central problems: a decline in its female vote, which always stabilised the results of the CDU/CSU up to the late 1990s, a decline among the over-50 age group, and a decline in Northern Germany and parts of the West.

Programmes, ideology and political practice

German Christian Democracy consists of conservative, liberal and socialist elements and the CDU's basic programme explicitly recognises these three political traditions. Consequently, the CDU/CSU has had difficulty in developing concrete programmes. However, the success of the Christian Democrats does not rely on their vague platforms but on their politics. The social market economy, the anti-communist orientation and conservative family and educational values have remained the most important issues since the 1950s. The CDU succeeded as the party that had founded a democratic Germany. In the memory of the German voters it was the party that had initiated prosperity, stable prices, and a safe alliance with the West. Its strict anti-communism helped to integrate different political groups and in a divided country this was more effective than in other countries. Therefore, no programme was needed. An intensive programmatic debate was started only during the opposition period of the 1970s. After 1982, as a party in power, the CDU continued to pass several programmes, but they became more and more insignificant. Once more, it was governmental policy that shaped the political direction and public image of the CDU/CSU.[12]

11   J. Graf and V. Neu, "Analyse der Bundestagswahl vom 22. September 2002", in: *PolitikKompass*, 91 (2002).
12   F. Bösch, *Macht und Machtverlust*, 29-65.

In the late 1980s, the historic merits of the party were diminishing in the public memory and the CDU/CSU was facing several problems. Kohl's efforts to push European integration were successful, but not popular enough. The economic policy of the Christian Democratic government was successful - debts and inflation were reduced and the economy grew - but its efforts and its social cuts were not part of a long-term project. Many reforms - like tax and health care - seemed to fail, although they had been advertised throughout the years, and the unemployment rate remained particularly high.[13]

However, the CDU/CSU was lucky and succeeded in becoming the nation's founding party a second time. Since October 1989, it has promoted itself as the party of German reunification and created a new national myth. The CDU/CSU claimed that it was the only party that had always wanted unification and finally achieved it, although unification did not play a significant role in the Christian Democratic policy of the 1980s.[14] In this way, the CDU/CSU could appeal to patriotic emotions without becoming a nationalistic party. Once more, as in the Weimar Republic, Christian Democrats could accuse the leftist parties of a historical failure and blame them for their scepticism about German reunification. This strategy helped to integrate the voters of the right wing. Reunification led to a sudden economic improvement, though it later contributed to an economic crisis in the early 1990s when economic problems in Western Germany were attributed to problems in the East.

Since 1989, the programmes and the practice of the CDU/CSU have responded to the rise of right-wing parties. The Christian Democrats strictly forbade coalitions with extremist parties, even on the local level. The CDU/CSU banned public assemblies with the right-wing, calling them "extremists", and required the Office for the Protection of the Constitution to investigate them.[15] At the same time the CDU/CSU adopted the issues of those right-wing parties. It called for stricter laws against refugees and criminals, stressing the need for a reduction in immigration and a more rapid assimilation of foreigners. In public it appealed quite successfully to patriotic emotions: it used the colours of the German national flag for its posters, and although

13   G. Wewer (ed.), *Bilanz der Ära Kohl. Christlich-liberale Politik (1982-1998)*, Opladen, 1998; R. Zohlnhöfner, *Die Wirtschaftspolitik der Ära Kohl. Eine Analyse der Schlüsselentscheidungen in den Politikfelder Finanzen, Arbeit und Entstaatlichung (1982-1998)*, Opladen, 2001.

14   The unification policy of the 1980s is analysed in: K.-R. Korte, *Deutschlandpolitik in Helmut Kohls Kanzlerschaft. Regierungsstil und Entscheidungen (1982-1989)*, Stuttgart, 1998.

15   See the record of the 1989 party congress and the strategy paper of the party headquarters: *Die Republikaner - Analyse und politische Bewertung einer rechtsradikalen Partei*, 18 May 1989.

the Christian Democrats claimed to be the party of a united Europe, they used to sing the national anthem at public assemblies to show their patriotism.

The unification of the Western and Eastern German parties led also to some slight political changes in ideology. The East German Christian Democrats had a different point of view on many political issues. They preferred a stronger social policy and more public spending to counter unemployment. In institutional and ethical questions the East German Christian Democrats were more liberal, preferring plebiscites and a more liberal policy towards abortion and child-care. The programmes of the united CDU hardly considered these items.[16] However, the political practice of the Christian Democrats did consider these points after 1990. At least the East German Christian Democrats guaranteed plebiscites in the constitution of their East German States. The role of the state in economic matters was increased and public debts grew. New and higher taxes were raised to cover the costs of unification and health care, promises like a kindergarten place for every child were made and even the abortion law was liberalised after years of discussion. Consequently, unification led to a more liberal moral image of the Western CDU.

Kohl also tried to respond to charges that the CDU was not interested in programmes anymore and that it had lost its credibility as the founding party of the post-war German state. Right after the unification with the East German CDU, Kohl announced that a new basic programme would be developed, but the debate was fairly limited by comparison with the debate on the first basic programme of the 1970s. Kohl dominated the discussion and ensured that it was finished quickly.[17] In 1994, the basic programme *Freiheit in Verantwortung* (Freedom in Responsibility) was presented at the federal party meeting. The majority of media representatives criticised it as a boring document without any innovative ideas. However, it is an interesting source for analysing the party's ideas and ideology. At least three important points should be mentioned. First, the CDU still referred to God and Christianity, but at the same time, Kohl took care that the programme also included those

16   See for instance *Ja zu Deutschland – Ja zur Zukunft* (1990), *Dresdner Manifest* (1991) and the
       1994 basic programme.
17   For a critical analysis by a participant and political scientist, see I. Reichardt-Dreyer, *Macht und
       Demokratie in der CDU. Dargestellt am Prozess und Ergebnis der Meinungsbildung zum Grund-
       satzprogramm 1994*, Wiesbaden, 2000.

who did not belong to the Christian churches. In public, the CDU continued to avoid direct references to God. Second, the CDU changed its successful slogan "social economy" to "ecological and social economy". This ecological turn was justified in terms of the Christian mission to protect creation. In political practice the importance of ecological topics declined however after 1994. Third, it became obvious that the socio-economic chapters of the new programme were much more liberal than the old ones. The stress was no longer on social justice, equality or community but rather on "the free development of personality".

In the second half of the 1990s the policy of Kohl's government took a similar direction. A Protestant holiday (a day of prayer and repentance) was changed to a working day in order to pay for employers' taxes. The influence of economic groups was obviously more decisive than that of the Churches which protested against this decision. In 1996 and 1997, Kohl's government imposed strict social cuts on the German population. The age of retirement was raised and protection against dismissal reduced. Medical care became more expensive, and this especially became a symbol of the government's social cuts. Only families continued to receive tax reductions. Although the majority of the population agreed to structural reforms, these measures were not accepted because nobody witnessed any positive results. The unemployment rate increased even more and the economy stopped growing.

European integration remained one of the most important achievements of the Kohl government. Yet, in the late 1990s, although it was supporting the personal authority of the Chancellor, it was not improving the party's position. On the contrary, one could argue that European integration led to disadvantages for the CDU/CSU. Since the 1950s, the Christian Democrats had been celebrated as being the creator and guarantor of a stable German mark. In the late 1990s, exactly the same party decided to change the mark for the euro, a decision that was not at all popular.

The loss of governmental power in 1998 changed the party's ideology in many respects. Programmes now became more important than policy. As during its first period of opposition in the 1970s, the CDU planned to reform the party by means of an open debate. Angela Merkel , who succeeded Wolfgang Schäuble as party chairwoman in 1999 - Schäuble had to step down because of his involvement in the donation scandal - tried to put a new emphasis on ethical politics. The CDU still wanted to forbid homosexual marriages but supported more rights for gays and lesbians. Heterosexual marriage should be rewarded by tax reductions, but unmarried or divorced persons were explicitly accepted as families if they had children.[18] The CDU became more open-minded towards cultural changes. The biography of Chairwoman Merkel was an example of this development: a divorced woman without children and a Protestant from East Germany who was not a regular churchgoer.[19] However, the CDU/CSU still supports some specific Christian values. In 2002 the debate on embryonic research showed that they want to keep a specific Christian position on stem cell research and prenatal examinations, although the Liberal wing of the party demanded more rights for scientists and women.

After the defeat in 1998, the CDU/CSU's programmes promised a stronger social security system. Although the government was highly indebted, the party's platform of 2002 offered generous promises to all kinds of social groups. Taxes would be lowered and the regions in the Eastern states would receive more money. The cuts in health care would be scrapped and an extremely high children's allowance was promised.[20] The economic programme that Merkel presented in 2001 failed completely. Her new slogans, the "we-society" and the "new social economy" were dismissed and forgotten after one year. The economic profile was not represented through such programmes but through the political success of the Bavarian Prime Minister and candidate in the 2002 election, Stoiber. His economic policy cannot be called liberal. He privatised public property but spent the profits on regulating Bavarian industry and employment; furthermore, he organised the corporate integration of the trade unions in many ways. In general, since the loss of government in 1998, it is not Merkel's programme but the political practice of the regional parties that has become more important. The political practice of the CDU/CSU however shows significant differences in each region. The strongest man in the CDU, the Hessian Prime Minister Roland Koch, succeeded in his campaign against the reform of citizenship laws and a strict law and order policy. The new Prime Minister of the Saarland, Peter Müller, kept his distance from those issues and initiated more social reform oriented projects, like free kindergardens. The political future of the Christian Democrat party, then, does not depend on its programmes, but rather on the profile of its personnel who have been successful at the regional level and who will run in the next federal election.

18   Beschluss des Bundesparteiausschusses, *Lust auf Familie - Lust auf Verantwortung*, 13 December 1999.
19   J. Boyson, *Angela Merkel. Eine deutsch-deutsche Biographie*, Munich, 2001.
20   *Leistung und Sicherheit. Zeit für Taten. Regierungsprogramm CDU/CSU 2002-2006*, 6 May 2002.

The events of 11 September 2001 improved the chances of the Christian Democrats. In comparison to the Social Democrats, the CDU/CSU demonstrated a strict loyalty to George W. Bush. The emergence of a new Islamic enemy renewed the debate on common Christian values. In particular, the word *Leitkultur* (dominant culture), introduced by the parliamentary leader Friedrich Merz, initiated a major debate about the question as to whether the Christian culture should be favoured over other cultures in Germany. It also led to a debate on law and order politics that may strengthen the CDU/CSU's standing as a rather conservative party.

At the same time, the profile of the Christian Democrats has changed over the last decade. One might call this a 'liberal turn': in economic, social and religious respects the parties became more liberal. However, the distance from the FDP has not diminished, due to shifts in the programme of the FDP itself. Nevertheless, the CDU/CSU refers to values that are specific to Christian Democratic parties throughout Europe, and they still tend much more towards social and religious values than the FDP.

Members, organisation and leadership

The German Christian Democrats are a federally organised party.[21] The federal structure operates differently at different levels. One becomes a member of the regional party branches and those branches have different statutes and platforms. The regional groups are quite independent of the federal party; the existence of a completely separate party in the federal state of Bavaria, the CSU, is the most prominent example of the rather weak connection between the regional branches. In comparison to the Christian Democrats, the Social Democrats are quite a centralised party. The federal structure of the German Christian Democrats results from its different regional political traditions which were united after 1945. The unification of Catholic and Protestant traditions, which were strong in particular areas, led to a complex ideological and regional mixture. The programmes and the political practice still differ among the states. In regions with conservative attitudes like Bavaria, Hessian or Schleswig-Holstein, the CDU/CSU is a rather conservative party; in liberal regions like Baden-Württemberg it is a liberal one and in regions with a strong social Catholicism, like Nordrhein-Westfalen or the Saarland, it is a rather left party.

21   The federal structure is analysed in: J. Schmid, *Die CDU. Organisationsstrukturen, Politiken und Funktionsweisen einer Partei im Föderalismus,* Opladen, 1990.

The German Christian Democrats are represented by two parties: the CSU in Bavaria, which is more conservative, and the CDU in the rest of the country. Although the CSU is formally an independent party, it is closely connected to the CDU. Both never competed in the same area in any election and always shared a joint parliamentary group in the *Bundestag* (lower federal parliament). They also have some joint party organisations like the youth organisation *Junge Union*, the student organisation *Ring Christlich Demokratischer Studenten* or the Protestant *Evangelischer Arbeitskreis* (Evangelic Employees' Circle). Consequently, the CDU and CSU should not be treated as separate parties but as two branches of a common political group.

The organisational development of the CDU/CSU can be analysed from the ground up. Like most of the parties in Western Europe, the CDU/CSU has had organisational problems at the grassroots level since the 1980s. Its organisational efforts during its opposition period in the 1970s led to a growth of membership up until 1983. After that, not only the political interest of German voters declined but also the need for members due to the fact that the CDU/CSU was back in government. In 1989, the internal reports of the CDU highlighted the main problems of its membership: its members were too old, too academic and mostly male, with less than a quarter of its members female. German unification helped to stop the decline by integrating the strong membership of the CDU in East Germany, even though many of those members had a communist past. At the beginning, this unification of the Eastern and Western party organisations was highly controversial, but was accepted quickly as the Western Christian Democrats realised the advantages of the 'union'. Not only did they absorb new members but they also inherited a strong party organization in the East. This was a great advantage in comparison to the Social Democrats who had to start from zero in Eastern Germany.[22] The social profile of the East German membership also compensated for problems in the West: almost 40% of East German members were female, the percentage of workers was much higher, and they were younger than the members in the West.

---

22   K. Grabow, *Abschied von der Massenpartei. Die Entwicklung der Organisationsstruktur von SPD und CDU seit der deutschen Wiedervereinigung*, Wiesbaden, 2000, 295.

The membership of the CDU, 1968-2001

	Membership	Change per year (%)		Membership	Change per year (%)
1968	286,541	5.9	1985	718,590	-1.6
1969	303,532	8.4	1986	714,089	-0.6
1970	329,239	8.5	1987	705,821	-1.2
1971	355,745	8.0	1988	676,747	-4.3
1972	422,968	18.9	1989	658,411	-2.7
1973	457,393	8.1	1990	789,609	19.9
1974	530,500	16.0	1991	751,163	-4.9
1975	590,482	11.3	1992	713,846	-5.0
1976	652,010	10.4	1993	685,343	-4.0
1977	664,214	1.9	1994	671,497	-2.0
1978	675,286	1.7	1995	657,643	-2.1
1979	682,781	1.1	1996	645,786	-1.8
1980	693,320	1.5	1997	631,700	-2.2
1981	705,116	1.7	1998	626,342	-0.8
1982	718,889	2.0	1999	638,056	1.9
1983	734,555	2.2	2000	616,722	-3.3
1984	730,395	-0.6	2001	604,135	-2.0

Source: Zentrale Mitgliederkartei/Berichte der Geschäftsstelle

However, the CDU could not keep either these new members or the old ones in the West. Since the 1990s, the CDU has tried to react to this challenge. The rights of party members were strengthened and nowadays, members of several party districts are allowed to elect candidates directly or to vote in party referenda on important political subjects. The CDU has rarely used these innovations so far. On the other hand, the CDU has opened the party to non-members who were allowed to participate in local party meetings for a certain period.[23] As in other parties, it has also become more common to offer governmental ministries to non-members. In 1999, the decline in membership stopped. However, the donation scandal of 2000 signalled a further loss of members. The aging of the members continued: while in 1980 only 20% were over sixty years old, more than 44% had reached this age in 2002.[24]

23   S. Scarrow, *Parties and their Members. Organising for Victory in Britain and Germany*, Oxford, 1996, 199.
24   O. Niedermayer, "Parteimitgliedschaften im Jahr 2001", in: *Zeitschrift für Parlamentsfragen*, 33 (2002) 365.

Nevertheless, compared to other European parties, the German Christian Democrats still have a strong membership.[25] Furthermore, it is not declining as rapidly as that of the Social Democrats. The losses of the CSU especially remain quite low. Besides, it is questionable if a strong membership is really necessary for the electoral success of the CDU/CSU in future. The prosperity of the CDU/CSU has never relied on its members, most of whom are quite passive and do not know a lot about the programmes of their own party.[26] This passive behaviour may in fact have been helpful for the party: whereas members of the Social Democrats have often protested against the policy of their own party, the Christian Democratic members are easily satisfied.[27] Thus the CDU has appeared more compact than it actually ever was. This has been one of the major conditions for the party's success.

Powerful chairmen have compensated for the party's loose structure. Usually, they were federal chancellors or prime ministers in one of the states. In comparison to other countries, their long terms in office strengthened their positions. Chairmen Konrad Adenauer (1946-1966) and Kohl (1973-1998) held especially strong positions which led to a singular direction on central issues. Kohl's leadership relied on two different sources of power. On the one hand, he relied on a high number of loyal party secretaries in the local districts and kept in close contact with the grassroots representatives in order to protect his position in the states and in party meetings. Kohl also used the resources of his office. From 1982, decisions were made, not in the complicated and weak party committees but in the *Bundeskanzlei* (chancellor's office).[28] The distribution of posts was a common way of ensuring continuing loyalty. The prime ministers in the states also preferred to use their offices, the *Staatskanzleien*, rather than their party headquarters.[29] A close connection to the parliamentary group completed this system of control. In September 1989, some Christian Democrats, like the party secretary Heiner Geißler, demanded that the party undergo reforms. The debate included the question whether Kohl should resign as party chairman. Although his authority had significantly

---

25   P. Mair and I. van Biezen, "Party Membership in Twenty European Democracies (1980-2000)", in: *Party Politics*, 1 (2001) 18.

26   W.P. Bürklin et al., *Die Mitglieder der CDU*, Interne Studie Nr. 148 der Konrad-Adenauer-Stiftung, Sankt Augustin, 1996, 31.

27   P. Lösche and F. Walter, *Die SPD. Klassenpartei, Volkspartei, Quotenpartei. Zur Entwicklung der Sozialdemokratie von Weimar bis zur deutschen Vereinigung*, Darmstadt, 1992, 339-364.

28   The so-called Kohl System is described in: K. Dreher, *Helmut Kohl. Leben mit Macht*, Stuttgart, 1998; C. Clemens and W.E. Patterson (eds.), *The Kohl Chancellorship. Special Issue of German Politics*, 1 (1998).

29   H. Schneider, *Ministerpräsidenten. Profil eines politischen Amtes im deutschen Föderalismus*, Opladen, 2001, 282-306.

declined in that year, Kohl yet managed to disempower these rivals at the party convention and most of them lost their posts after the party meeting in Bremen in 1989.

Unification increased the centralisation of the organisation. Between 1990 and 1994, the CDU became a 'chancellor's party' as Kohl made all the major decisions on his own and his authority was rarely questioned. Party committees met less and less, and if they met Kohl dominated the meetings. The national party headquarters, with more than two hundred full-time employed members, helped to organise the party and prepare its campaigns but had no influence on political decisions. As the CDU lost power in several states, Kohl also lost potential opponents at the federal level. This also weakened the federal structure of the party. Only in the South of Germany, in Bavaria and Baden-Württemberg, did strong prime ministers maintain independent positions. By contrast, the Christian Democratic prime ministers in Eastern Germany were quite loyal to Kohl and adopted a similar style of party leadership in their own states. Wolfgang Biedenkopf (Saxony) or Bernhard Vogel (Thuringia) rarely paid attention to the party in the central office but organised the regional party branches from their offices.

Number of meetings of the CDU executive committees, 1990-2001 (absolute and per month)

Month/ Year	Präsidium (central executive committee)	Bundesvorstand (executive committee)
10/1990	16 (1.3)	14 (1.2)
12/1991	13 (0.9)	17 (1.2)
10/1992	9 (0.9)	5 (0.5)
09/1993	13 (1.2)	7 (0.6)
02/1994	5 (1.0)	4 (0.8)
10/1995	9 (0.5)	9 (0.5)
10/1996	14 (1.2)	11 (0.8)
10/1997	18 (1.8)	13 (1.3)
11/1998	26 (2.0)	20 (1.5)
04/1999	10 (1.7)	6 (1.0)
04/2000	29 (2.4)	20 (1.7)
12/2001	40 (2.0)	26 (1.3)

Source: Berichte der Bundesgeschäftsstelle

The power of the auxiliary organisations also changed. Unlike other Western Christian Democratic parties, the CDU/CSU could not rely on a close connection to a big Christian trade union. Instead, a group within the party organised the interests of the Christian employees. The *Christlich-Demokratische Arbeitnehmerschaft* (Christian Democratic employees' organisation) was quite influential from the the 1950s to the 1970s. During Kohl's government however it lost much of its power and one third of its members. Its leader in the late 1980s, Ulf Fink, criticised several decisions of Kohl's government as being too liberal and his influence within the party immediately decreased. In 1994, the new chairman, Rainer Eppelmann, was completely loyal to Kohl and consequently the employees' organisation lost its profile as an important social and left-wing organisation inside the party.[30] Instead, the influence and membership of the liberal *Mittelstandsvereinigung* (employers' association) increased.

Between 1995 and 1998, Kohl held on to his dominant position, but his leadership was often attacked by a group of young Christian Democrats in the Western states. They were called *die jungen Wilden* (the wild young men) in public, because most of them were in their mid-thirties. They demanded more democracy, more participation and more discussions. At least in the regional parties some organisational reforms took place. Kohl however rarely made concessions and became more and more resistant to his critical advisors. Many of his brilliant personal advisors and secretaries consequently retired from their jobs. In 1997, without consulting anybody in the party, Kohl simply announced to the media that he wanted to become chancellor for a sixth term. No one protested against his personal decision although many did not like it.

As the party was mainly centered on Kohl's leadership, the loss of government power in 1998 and his sudden retirement resulted in a power shift. The parliamentary group of the CDU/CSU in the *Bundestag* became more important, while at the same time the position of the party headquarters was strengthened. As a result, the party committees have been meeting much more regularly. However, because power was not centralised anymore, Merkel, who was now party chairwoman, had great difficulty in keeping the different wings and regions together as she lacked the authority of being chancellor. Finally, it was not the headquarters nor the party committees that took charge of the CDU but the prime ministers of the different *Länder*. They met

30   W. Schröder, "Das katholische Milieu auf dem Rückzug. Der Arbeitnehmerflügel der CDU nach der Ära Kohl", in: T. Dürr and R. Soldt (eds.), *Die CDU nach Kohl*, Frankfurt, 1998, 187.

regularly in the party central executive committee to co-ordinate their own strategies and those of the party.

Since 2000, the staff of the headquarters has become much smaller due to the fact that the CDU ran out of money after the donation scandal. It had to be reduced by more than 40% and this has added considerably to the decentralisation of the party. As a result, the large staff in the *Staatskanzleien* of the prime ministers and the parliamentary groups could expand their positions. Regional prime ministers like Roland Koch (Hessia), Peter Müller (Saarland), Erwin Teufel (Baden-Württemberg) and Edmund Stoiber (Bavaria) became the most powerful persons in the party. For this reason, it was not Merkel but Stoiber who stood for the chancellorship in the 2002 federal election.

Merkel often stated that the party should be reformed through open discussion. The atmosphere became more open for debates but, in fact, the 2002 election platform was written by a small group and rarely discussed in the party's committees. Merkel and Stoiber decided by themselves who would lead the 2002 campaign. Opinion polls about this question had great influence on this decision too, but not the party organisation itself. An open debate on their programmes or a free election of the candidates could have disturbed the internal balance of the party.

Since the end of the 1990s, the CDU has made great efforts to improve the participation of women within the party. In this respect, it responded to a new challenge: since 1996, one third of the CDU party leadership and candidates had to be female. This quota-system has proved to be quite successful. In 2000, there was not only a chairwoman leading the CDU but also a woman leading the youth organisation. For a Christian and conservative party this was a small revolution. The number of female members in the executive committees and among party secretaries in the regions also increased significantly. Compared to other conservative and Christian parties in Europe, there is a high percentage of women in the leadership of the CDU.[31] However, although this might help to stop the loss of female voters in the future, it did not stop the decline in the female share of the electorate in 2002. On top of that, the CDU, and especially the CSU, still have fewer women in leading positions than the German left-wing parties.

31   B. Höcker (ed.), *Handbuch politischer Partizipation von Frauen in Europa*, Opladen, 1998.

Women in the CDU, 1989 and 2001 (per cent)

Type of organisation	1989	2001
Präsidium (central executive committee)	15.3	28.6
Bundesvorstand (executive committee)	21.2	34.1
Bundestag (lower house of parliament)	7.7	18.4
Ausschußvorsitzende (chairwomen in parliamentary committees)	0	0
Landesvorsitzende (chairwomen of regional party organisations)	0	0
Landesgeschäftsführerinnen (party secretaries of regional organisations)	0	13.3
Kreisgeschäftsführerinnen (party secretaries of districts organisations)	17.2	27.5
Kreisvorsitzende (chairwomen of districts party organisations)	2.3	9.7
Ortsvorsitzende (chairwomen of local party organisations)		13.3
Members	2.8	25.2

Source: *Frauenberichte der CDU Deutschlands*

Financial resources and scandals

The CDU/CSU used to have the largest financial resources of all German parties. During the late 1980s, however, the financial problems of the CDU increased. It had spent too much money on its strong party administration. In the biggest party scandal in German history (the so-called *Flick-Skandal*), illegal charities were uncovered, resulting in a decline in charitable donations. The losses of members and elections further reduced the financial resources. In 1989, the CDU was completly in debt to the tune of 59 million euro. This was not only a catastrophe for the party machine and the forthcoming campaign but also for the party's image. German unification helped to solve these problems and averted bankruptcy. The unification with the former communist East German CDU brought new paying members, more public money and some (controversial) new financial means for the party.[32] The income of the CDU/CSU was still much higher than that of the Social Democrats; however, the CDU failed to reorganise its finances and continued to spend too much money on its vast administration.

The finances of the CDU, 1984 -1999*

Year	Revenue/Million DM			Donations (per cent)	Member- ship fees (per cent)	Direct public money (per cent)	Property/ Million DM	Debts/ Million DM
	CDU	CSU	SPD	CDU	CDU	CDU	CDU	CDU
1984	292.7	42.5	189.1	11.0	38.3	33.0	140.1	34.0
1985	176.6	39.5	193.7	12.6	46.0	31.3	139.9	40.1
1986	192.1	60.1	199.1	19.5	49.9	25.0	151.5	81.2
1987	193.0	48.2	214.0	16.0	45.3	31.0	148.3	92.8
1988	174.0	43.6	195.8	13.6	49.4	27.7	157.4	98.1
1989	198.2	57.1	241.2	21.6	42.3	25.0	146.2	115.4
1990	330.4	89.8	353.8	21.9	26.3	43.0	185.5	104.2
1991	212.8	51.7	339.6	18.1	43.8	24.8	175.8	84.0
1992	213.5	49.5	262.6	17.6	44.1	26.7	173.3	64.0
1993	225.8	56.0	280.7	19.5	42.4	27.2	201.8	57.5
1994	279.9	67.8	353.3	20.3	33.4	41.4	172.3	51.7
1995	218.3	52.8	285.1	16.5	45.3	33.7	169.1	37.1
1996	221.7	62.2	283.0	16.2	45.3	32.7	179.8	30.1
1997	218.2	56.0	280.9	15.5	46.1	33.6	202.7	24.5
1998	270.1	65.5	304.4	24.5	37.3	27.4	242.5	107.8
1999	258.9	63.7	306.0	25.2	40.7	29.6	226.1	127.4
2000	255.9	54.8	292.0	21.0	42.2	30.9	252.0	113.6
2001	265.2	67.6	312.8	19.4	43.5	31.6	259.2	145.8

* One German Mark/DM was equivalent to 0,51 Euro in December 2001.
Source:"Rechenschaftsberichte 1984-2001", in: Drucksachen des Deutschen Bundestages

Despite new regulations regarding financial transparency, illegal donations to the party were not stopped. As a result, in 2000, the CDU once again was accused of tax evasion and offences against the country's strict party financing laws. It was revealed that Kohl had used more than one million euro from hidden donations to strengthen his position within the party. His notorious Minister of the Interior, Manfred Kanther, was blamed for hiding more than ten million euro of illegal donations in Swiss banks. Corruption was suspected but was not proven in court despite strong evidence.[33] This time, the CDU reacted resolutely in securing its moral and financial basis. Those involved in the scandal had to resign immediately from their leading posts: Chairman Schäuble had to resign because he had not revealed illegal donations of 50,000 euro and Kohl, who refused to reveal the identity of the donors, lost his honourable chairmanship. A new kind of transparency was established and financial control was improved by means of new statutes. The high debts were reduced through staff layoffs and budget cuts. By taking clear measures with a direct impact, the Christian Democrats quickly regained the voters' trust. In the 2002 election campaign, the CDU still did not have as much money as the Social Democrats. Furthermore, the CDU could not spend any government money this time. However, the financial reforms built a moral basis for future. Moreover, the CDU was lucky in that in 2002 illegal funding of the SDP was also uncovered. This helped to re-establish a moral 'equality' between the parties.

Does money matter in the German party system? The history of the German elections suggests that there is a relation between the prosperity of the party and its electoral success. The crises of the CDU - whether in the late 1960s, the late 1980s or even in 1998 - have been accompanied by large debts. The rise of the Social Democrats in the 1960s and the late 1990s also corresponded with a positive financial situation.[34] The recent consolidation of the Christian Democratic financial resources, therefore, might be an indicator for future electoral success at the federal level.

---

33   H. Leyendecker et al., *Helmut Kohl. Die Macht und das Geld*, Göttingen, 2000, 189-244.
34   "Rechenschaftsberichte 1969-2001", in: *Drucksachen des Deutschen Bundestages*.

Conclusion

The German case may reveal some significant differences from other countries.[35] The end of the Cold War did not lead to a sudden decline of the German Christian Democrats, but rather helped to solve their various problems, at least for a while. At the end of the 1980s the CDU suffered a great crisis, which was significant for many Christian Democratic parties throughout Europe. It was losing voters and members and the organisation was divided; Kohl's reputation was low, his policy was considered obsolete and the party was in debt. The dismantling of the Berlin Wall and reunification produced new voters, members and financial sources. It bolstered Kohl's authority, helped to centralise the party organisation and led to new forms of political representation. Until the late 1990s, reunification hid many structural problems but did not solve them, and in 1998 the CDU suffered from many problems similar to those of the late 1980s. The donation scandal of 2000 prevented it from establishing itself as an opposition party. However, it led to an extensive reform of the CDU/CSU as a political organisation which has been conducted by close cooperation with Merkel. At the same time, its restoration as a powerful party can only be achieved by close cooperation with the different regional branches and prime ministers in office.

35   On the particularities of other Western Christian Democratic parties, see H.-J. Veen (ed.), *Christlich-demokratische und konservative Parteien*, Oplanden/Paderborn, 1983-2000; D. Hanley (ed.), *Christian Democracy in Europe. A Comparative Perspective*, London, 1994; E. Lamberts (ed.), *Christian Democracy in the European Union (1945-1995)*, Leuven 1997; other references in "European Christian Democracy in the 1990s. Towards a Framework for Analysis" and "European Christian Democracy in the 1990s. Towards a Comparative Approach" in this volume.

The Rejuvenation of an 'Old Party'? Christian Democracy in Austria

Franz Fallend

The 1990s was a period of steady electoral decline for Christian Democratic parties in Europe. The *Österreichische Volkspartei* (ÖVP) was not different in this respect, at least until the last general election. Indeed, in 2002 the ÖVP increased its share of the vote from 27 to 42% and became the strongest party in Austria for the first time since 1966. From the mid-1980s onwards, the ÖVP – like the *Sozialdemokratische Partei Österreichs* (SPÖ), its coalition partner of many years – lost votes to the right-wing, populist *Freiheitliche Partei Österreichs* (FPÖ), which claimed to be a reform-oriented 'movement' (as opposed to a traditional party) representing the interests of 'the man in the street', something the other, small opposition parties, *Grüne Alternative* (Green party) and *Liberales Forum* (Liberal party), refrained from doing. In contrast, the ÖVP and SPÖ were denounced as 'old parties', whose representatives allegedly formed an undemocratic *partitocrazia*, chiefly interested in their own privileges and incapable of reforms for the common good. In the 2002 elections, however, the ÖVP managed to reverse the trend. Not only did half of the former FPÖ supporters switch over to the ÖVP (a move that reduced the FPÖ to one third of its 1999 share), but the ÖVP also reconquered the (relative) majority of younger voters. While it had been the SPÖ between 1986 and 1995 and the FPÖ in 1999 that had attracted the most voters under 29 years of age, it was the ÖVP that succeeded in doing so in 2002 (33% of them voted for the ÖVP, 29% for the SPÖ and 14% for the FPÖ). In this respect, the ÖVP regained not only its previous strength, but was rejuvenated as well.[1]

---

[1]   However, the assertion of a rejuvenation within the ÖVP needs to be qualified. A look at the age structures of the party electorates reveals that the ÖVP and SPÖ are still 'old parties'. Only 15% of the ÖVP voters in 2002 were younger than 29 years old (the figures for the other parties, the SPÖ, FPÖ and Greens being respectively 15, 26 and 45%). See F. Plasser and P.A. Ulram, *Wahlverhalten in Bewegung. Analysen zur Nationalratswahl 2002*, Vienna, 2003, 219-221.

Only a few observers would have predicted such an overwhelming success a decade earlier. In the general elections of 1990 the ÖVP had suffered a disastrous defeat and its share of the vote plunged from 41 to 32%. In fact, at the beginning of the 1990s depression was the predominant feeling in the party leadership as well as among the rank and file of the ÖVP. In October 1991 the newly elected party chairman Erhard Busek, who hailed from the open-minded Vienna section of the party, identified six major problems his party had to solve in order to regain its position.[2] (1) The ÖVP was part of a government coalition from which only its partner, the SPÖ, profited, but not the ÖVP itself. (2) The ÖVP was not able to present its drive for reforms in a persuasive way. Instead, the coalition parties were perceived as constantly quarrelling. (3) Protest voting had become chic and both coalition parties suffered from it. (4) The party was confronted with issues (e.g. accession to the then European Community and immigration) for which it had no convincing answers that would address people's fears. (5) Almost every intra-party discussion, whether about personnel or specific issues, took place in public, with the media turning differences into conflicts and splits; this had the overall effect of damaging the party's image. (6) Within the party, the prevailing attitudes were of resignation to the existing situation and a conviction that they had a monopoly on wisdom.

Election results for the lower chamber of parliament, 1986–2002 (in per cent of the votes)*

	ÖVP	SPÖ	FPÖ	Grüne Alternative	Liberales Forum
1986	41.3	43.1	9.7	4.8	
1990	32.1	42.8	16.6	4.8	
1994	27.7	34.9	22.5	7.3	6.0
1995	28.3	38.1	21.9	4.8	5.5
1999	26.9	33.2	26.9	7.4	
2002	42.3	36.5	10.0	9.5	

*Only parties that won seats in the parliament are included.
Source: Homepage of the Federal Ministry of the Interior <www.bmi.gv.at>.

2   E. Busek, "Ziele der ÖVP-Regierungspolitik", in: *Österreichische Monatshefte*, 6 (1991) 19. The *Österreichische Monatshefte*, the major empirical source for this article, is the journal of the ÖVP published by the party's Political Academy.

At the beginning of the 1990s, the ÖVP lacked a clear mission and a coherent profile and as a consequence lost much of its electoral appeal. I will argue that the new popularity of the ÖVP, won in the elections of 2002, is the result of a deliberate move to sharpen the party's image, a move that, however, has not made the ÖVP more 'Christian Democratic'. For this purpose I will investigate the external challenges confronting the ÖVP in the 1990s, the electoral results and the party's strategic reactions in coping with the changing political environment. Furthermore, I will examine more closely the reactions of the ÖVP in five areas: party organisation, party programme, party competition, coalition building and, finally, three important policy areas: economic, social and immigration policy. To conclude, I will discuss the question whether the ÖVP has succeeded in solving the problems highlighted by former party chairman Busek and try to assess the Christian Democratic character of today's ÖVP.

External challenges

In the 1990s the ÖVP was confronted with three major external challenges. Two of them – global developments and changes in the national political culture – affected both the SPÖ and ÖVP, who joined in a 'grand coalition'. The third challenge – secularisation – is specific to the ÖVP, though it was not confined to the 1990s, but was a process that had been continuing since the 1960s.

Global developments

The breakdown of Communism after 1989 led to the end of the ideological East-West polarisation and to the triumph of (neo-)liberalism. With the collapse of 'the enemy on the left', Christian Democracy was pushed towards the right of the political spectrum, where it was confronted by the 'conservative challenge'. The forces of globalisation put the small Austrian economy under pressure and intensified the need to take part in the process of European integration, a predominantly liberal project, which accelerated in the 1990s (single market, EMU). Despite the reluctance of its coalition partner, the ÖVP succeeded in 1989 in submitting Austria's application for membership of the European Community. Finally, in 1995 Austria became a member of the European Union (EU). As a result of the opening up of the European borders, new problems, in particular intensified economic competition and the influx of (mostly economic) immigrants, had to be dealt with politically.

All these changes reduced the internal coherence of many Christian Democratic parties and deepened intra-party conflicts.[3]

Changes in national political culture

From the mid-1980s the ÖVP (like the other major party, the SPÖ) suffered from a substantial turnover in the Austrian party system. In 1986, both parties together could still attract 84% of the voters; by 1994 their share dropped to less than 63%. The de-alignment process that had gradually affected both parties from the end of the 1960s (first as a result of socio-economic changes, then as a result of political scandals and the ensuing highly emotional anti-party feelings) intensified from the mid-1980s. Opinion polls indicated that the number of voters periodically changing their party preferences increased from 26% in 1990 to 48% in 2000. Party membership decreased from 23% in 1986 to 15% in 2001. At the same time dissatisfaction with political parties and elites, though already very high in comparative terms, was on the increase. For instance, in 1996, 32% of the people agreed with the statement that "people like me have no influence on what the government does".[4]

The de-alignment process in the party system was aggravated by two factors: the 'grand coalition' type of government and the radical transformation of the FPÖ. In 1986 the SPÖ and ÖVP formed a coalition to carry out necessary but presumably unpopular reforms and budget-consolidation programmes. Soon both parties were perceived as 'two elephants sitting in a boat', neither of which could be held responsible by the voters, and with their persistent compromises, they lost their public profiles. In the same year Jörg Haider was elected party chairman of the FPÖ. He immediately started to transform the party, which had in the past been characterised by continuous internal conflicts between 'liberal' and 'national' forces, into a populist protest party, which exploited people's resentment of the 'old parties', privileged and corrupt elites, social-welfare cheaters, and foreigners.[5] Party competi-

---

3   This was also the analysis of Andreas Khol, long-term leader of the parliamentary party group of the ÖVP and one of its major theorists. See A. Khol, "Visionen statt Interessen. Perspektiven einer modernen Volkspartei zur Jahrtausendwende", in: *Österreichische Monatshefte*, 3-4 (1993) 24.

4   F. Plasser and P.A. Ulram, *Das österreichische Politikverständnis. Von der Konsens- zur Konfliktkultur?*, Vienna, 2002, 88, 105.

5   W.C. Müller, F. Plasser and P.A. Ulram, "Schwäche als Vorteil, Stärke als Nachteil. Die Reaktion der Parteien auf den Rückgang der Wählerbindungen in Österreich", in: P. Mair, W.C. Müller and F. Plasser (eds.), *Parteien auf komplexen Wählermärkten. Reaktionsstrategien politischer Parteien in Westeuropa*, Vienna, 1999, 209.

tion intensified and relations between the government and the opposition became more and more polarised.

Secularisation

The general secularisation of society in the 20th century has reduced the political relevance of the confessional issue and deprived Christian Democracy of one of its unique selling points. While 'religion' (besides 'class' and 'region') had been one of the key issues structuring the establishment of the Austrian party system at the end of the 19th century and in particular its development in the inter-war years, its relevance diminished significantly after 1945.[6] Although religious feelings in Austria in comparison to other European countries are still above the average, their intensity faded during the 1990s. While 75% of the predominantly Catholic Austrians described their religious feelings as 'very strong' or 'strong' in 1990, in 2000 only 67% did so.[7] Over the past 60 years, the ÖVP has become a catch-all party, a development initiated by the party leadership immediately after 1945. In 2001 only 33% of its sympathisers attended church services at least once a week (in 1955, 67% had still done so).[8] On the other hand, the ÖVP still is the most 'religious party' in the party system. In the general elections from 1990 until 1999, 59 or 60% of all regular churchgoing voters invariably voted for the ÖVP, in 2002 even 69% did so.[9] In a survey carried out in 1990, the ÖVP was regarded by 64% of the respondents as the only party whose policies represented Christian values.[10] To sum up, in the 1990s the ÖVP still had to come to terms with the dilemma of whether it should stick to its confessional roots or adapt to the requirements of a vote-maximisation strategy.

---

6   W.C. Müller, "Das Parteiensystem", in: H. Dachs et al. (eds.), *Handbuch des politischen Systems Österreichs. Die Zweite Republik*, Vienna, 1997, 228.

7   P.M. Zulehner, I. Hager and R. Polak, *Kehrt die Religion wieder? Religion im Leben der Menschen (1970-2000)*, Ostfildern, 2001, 27, 249.

8   F. Plasser and P.A. Ulram, *Das österreichische Politikverständnis*, 93. Considering that the ÖVP had won 2 million votes in the general elections of 1956 and only 1.2 million in 1999, the change is even more striking.

9   F. Plasser and P.A. Ulram, *Wahlverhalten in Bewegung*, 224. In 2002, 22% of regular churchgoers voted for the SPÖ, 3% for the FPÖ and 3% for the Greens.

10   F. Horner and P.M. Zulehner, "Kirchen und Politik", in: H. Dachs et al. (eds.), *Handbuch des politischen Systems Österreichs*, 495. The SPÖ and the FPÖ were mentioned by 8 and 2% respectively.

Characteristics of the electorate

A first indicator of how successfully the ÖVP managed to cope with the new political challenges of the 1990s is provided by the party's electoral performance. Until 2002 the ÖVP faced voter losses both at the national and at the regional levels. Only in the *Land* of Styria was the ÖVP able to reverse the trend. However, this happened only in 2000 and was above all due to the popularity of the incumbent provincial governor and to the fact that the ÖVP criticised some of the reforms of the new ÖVP-FPÖ coalition at the national level.

Traditionally, the ÖVP has been a catch-all party, gaining support from almost all groups in society. Nevertheless, during the 1990s it was heavily over-represented among farmers (who constitute only around 4% of the population) and to a lesser degree among self-employed and professional people. On the other hand, the voter share among young people (below 29) and blue-collar workers did not reach the level of the overall election results. Once more, the unusual nature of the 2002 election is evident in the fact that for the first time the ÖVP was able to attract a greater than average number of young people, white-collar workers and graduates of technical schools.[11]

Let us now take a closer look at the intra-party reforms and the strategic adaptations made by the ÖVP during the 1990s in reaction to external challenges, both international and national, and to stop electoral decline.

Party organisation and membership

The organisation of the ÖVP (like that of the SPÖ) has been traditionally that of a mass membership party. In the past, this was a source of strength. However, with the party competition in a very mobile electoral market, this type of organisation often proves to be a handicap in that it reduces the manoeuvring capabilities of parties and slows down their ability to adapt to new political circumstances.[12] Moreover, it is a peculiarity of Christian Democratic parties to strive to integrate and reconcile a plurality of societal groups with possibly opposing interests and, consequently, to be inter-

---

11   For an extensive report on the 2002 elections, see K.R. Luther, "The Self-Destruction of a Right-Wing Populist Party? The Austrian Parliamentary Election of 2002", in: *West European Politics*, 2 (2003) 136-152.

12   P. Mair, *Party System Change. Approaches and Interpretations*, Oxford, 1997.

Election results for the provincial parliaments, 1985–2001 (in per cent of the votes)*

Province	Year of election	ÖVP	SPÖ	FPÖ	Grüne Alternative	Liberales Forum
Burgenland	1987	41.5	47.3	7.3		
	1991	38.2	48.1	9.7		
	1996	36.0	44.5	14.6		
	2000	35.3	46.6	12.6	5.5	
Carinthia	1989	21.0	46.0	29.0		
	1994	23.8	37.4	33.3		
	1999	20.8	32.9	42.1		
Lower Austria	1988	47.6	37.4	9.4		
	1993	44.2	33.9	12.0		5.1
	1998	44.9	30.4	16.1	4.5	
Upper Austria	1985	52.1	38.0	5.0		
	1991	45.2	31.4	17.7		
	1997	42.7	27.0	20.6	5.8	
Salzburg	1989	44.0	31.2	16.4	6.2	
	1994	38.6	27.0	19.5	7.3	
	1999	38.8	32.3	19.6	5.4	
Styria	1986	51.7	37.6	4.6	3.3	
	1991	44.2	34.9	15.4		
	1996	36.2	35.9	17.1	4.3	3.8
	2000	47.3	32.2	12.4	5.6	
Tyrol	1989	48.7	22.8	15.6	8.3	
	1994	47.3	19.9	16.2	10.7	
	1999	47.2	21.8	19.7	8.0	
Vorarlberg	1989	51.0	21.3	16.1	5.2	
	1994	49.9	16.3	18.4	7.7	
	1999	45.8	13.0	27.4	6.0	
Vienna	1987	28.4	55.0	9.7		
	1991	18.1	47.8	22.5	9.1	
	1997	15.3	39.2	27.9	8.0	8.0
	2001	16.4	46.9	20.4	12.5	

* Only parties that won seats in the respective parliaments are included.
Source: H. Dachs et al. (eds.), *Handbuch des politischen Systems Österreichs*, 388-392; Homepages of the Provincial Governments.

Social and demographic composition of ÖVP voters, 1986–2002
(in per cent of the total number of the respective social and demographic groups)

		1986	1990	1994	1995	1999	2002
Gender	Male	38	29	25	26	26	44
	Female	43	33	30	29	27	40
Age	Below 29	33	24	19	18	17	33
	30–44	37	32	26	25	23	35
	45–59	48	34	30	33	32	38
	Over 60	44	34	33	34	33	48
Occupation	Farmer	93	85	73	72	87	95
	Self-employed and profession	60	51	40	39	41	58
	Civil servant	33	30	23	20	30	41
	White-collar worker	36	27	25	28	23	37
	Blue-collar worker	27	19	15	13	12	34
	Pensioner	41	32	31	32	30	46
	In education	38	29	18	22	18	20
Education	Obligatory school	42	33	28	27	28	38
	Professional school	38	27	24	25	23	42
	School leaving, examination or university degree	46	38	32	32	30	44

Source: Exit polls quoted in F. Plasser and P.A. Ulram, *Wahlverhalten in Bewegung*, 216.

nally divided into factions or wings.[13] The ÖVP, too, claims to be a people's party, in which the interests of the major groups of society are represented and balanced for the common good.[14]

In the ÖVP these interests are quasi-institutionalised in six *Teilorganisationen* (constituent organisations), the most important being the three *Bünde* (leagues): the *Bauernbund* (Farmers' League), the *Wirtschaftsbund* (Business League) and the *Arbeiter- und Angestelltenbund* (Workers' and Employees' League). Other organisations (for women, youth and pensioners) were given the same formal status in the 1970s, but contrary to the leagues, they lack

13   K. van Kersbergen, "The Distinctiveness of Christian Democracy", in: D. Hanley (ed.), *Christian Democracy in Europe. A Comparative Perspective*, London, 1994, 36.
14   For the 1995 party programme, see <www.oevp.at/download/000298.pdf> (17/03/2004).

real power. The power of the leagues, which finds expression in their right to nominate an equal share of candidates for state functions (e.g. seats in parliament), is based on their dominance in the various corporatist interest organisations: the Farmers' League dominates the Chamber of Agriculture and the Business League dominates the Chamber of Business. By contrast, the Workers' and Employees' League, which accounts for about 50% of all party members, is in a minority position *vis-à-vis* the Social Democratic trade unionists in the Trade Union Congress and the Chamber of Labour. Although party members (since 1980) first become members of the party and only then of the leagues, the members are *de facto* still primarily recruited and organised by the leagues, making the ÖVP a party of indirect party membership.[15] The electoral defeat of 1990 provided the party leadership with a chance to enhance its position *vis-à-vis* the leagues. The defeat was seen as the result of the predominance of the leagues, especially the Farmers' and the Business Leagues, in intra-party decision-making. In a reform of the party statutes in 1991 more autonomy was granted to the party leadership. Subsequently, the influence of the Business League was reduced so that its representatives for some time considered separating from the party.[16]

At the same time, however, the *Land* (regional) party organisations, the second major intra-party player besides the leagues, tried to gain more autonomy *vis-à-vis* the national party organisation. During the 1970s and 1980s the ÖVP had been stronger in most of the regions than at the national level. After a series of electoral defeats from the late 1980s on, the regional parties tried to keep a distance from the national party. They stressed their own identity in electoral campaigns (e.g. by using the name 'Tyrolean People's Party' instead of 'Austrian People's Party' or by eliminating the party's name altogether from election posters). Moreover, they criticised the national party or ÖVP members of the national government if it served their electoral purposes, or they made clear that they preferred representatives of the national party not to appear in the regions during the campaigns.[17] In a few regional party organisations even a split from the party and the formation of independent organisations was a serious option during the 1990s.[18]

15   W.C. Müller and B. Steininger, "Christian Democracy in Austria. The Austrian People's Party", in: D. Hanley (ed.), *Christian Democracy in Europe. A Comparative Perspective*, London, 1994, 87.
16   W.C. Müller, F. Plasser and P.A. Ulram, "Schwäche als Vorteil, Stärke als Nachteil", 221.
17   *Ibid.*, 222.
18   W.C. Müller, "Die Österreichische Volkspartei", in: H. Dachs et al. (eds.), *Handbuch des politischen Systems Österreichs*, 275.

The high degree of internal factionalism did not make the ÖVP very attractive to potential new members or voters. In the 1990s, therefore, the party leadership tried time and again to mobilise party activists and members. First, several intra-party ballots were organised but they had the negative effect of worsening splits within the party.[19] Second, following a reform of the electoral system in 1992 (which left the system of proportional representation intact but introduced smaller regional constituencies in order to boost the personality element in the election process), primaries were held before the general elections of 1994 in order to find the 'best' candidates. However, the party machine was not particularly enthusiastic about the primaries and some regional party organisations responsible for carrying out the primaries even refused to accept the results.[20] For that reason, the party did not repeat the experiment.

As a consequence of the party's failure to reform its structure and contrary to its claim, as expressed in its name, to be a people's party, ÖVP members in the 1990s continued to deviate significantly from the general social structures. While the gender structure of the voters corresponded roughly to that of the overall population, male domination of the party membership even increased from the 1980s to the 1990s. The traditional core group of farmers was more than twice as strong in the party's membership than among ÖVP voters (while the other core group, self-employed and professional people, showed a consistent ratio). By contrast, the representation of blue-collar workers among the members was half that among the voters. With regard to both voters and members, the ÖVP 'aged' from the mid-1980s: the share of young people was below the national average and even shrank further, while the share of old people was above average and continued to rise.

19   W.C. Müller, F. Plasser and P.A. Ulram, "Schwäche als Vorteil, Stärke als Nachteil", 217.
20   L. Leitner and C. Mertens, "Die Vorwahlen der Österreichischen Volkspartei zur Nationalratswahl 1994. Analyse und Reformvorschläge", in: *Österreichisches Jahrbuch für Politik 1994*, 1995, 199-218.

Social and demographic composition of ÖVP voters and members, 1985 and 1993
(in per cent of the total number of voters and members)

		Voters		Members	
		1985	1993	1985	1993
Gender	Male	45	45	57	69
	Female	55	55	43	31
Age	Under 29	24	20	21	18
	30–44	27	27	29	30
	45–59	23	23	29	20
	Over 60	25	30	23	32
Occupation	Farmer	10	9	17	20
	Self-employed and profession	6	6	8	5
	White-collar worker	23	24	27	22
	Blue-collar worker	17	17	9	7
	Housewive	16	13	16	17
	Pensioner and unemployed	30	31	24	28
Education	Obligatory school	37	33	40	30
	Professional school	47	48	43	56
	College	12	14	15	11
	University	4	5	3	3

Source: W.C. Müller and P.A. Ulram, "The Social and Demographic Structure of Austrian Parties (1945–93)", in: *Party Politics*, 1(1995) 149 and 155.

Party programme

Wheras the ÖVP party organisation and membership did not change significantly during the 1990s, the party revised its programme. Since 1945 the ÖVP's concept of itself has been that of a *bürgerliche Sammlungspartei* (non-socialist catch-all party) integrating different ideological tendencies: Catholic social doctrine, conservatism and liberalism. Catholic social doctrine, based on the principles of subsidiarity, personalism and solidarity, has been the most important element in the party's programme, determining its conception of human nature and its approach to social justice (social interests should not be subordinated to the dictates of the economy). The party's upholding of property rights, its respect for legitimate authorities and its repudiation of extremist views may be called conservative. Liberalism has constituted its ideas about the constitution and human rights, the conviction that the state should be restrained and, especially in practical politics, the party's economic positions. In the 1980s, in line with the international trend, the ÖVP adopted a neo-liberal economic programme. At the end of the decade, when ecological concerns came to dominate the political agenda, the party developed the vision of an 'eco-social market economy', in which environmental protection was to be achieved by market incentives rather than by state regulation.[21]

The need for changing the party programme, which was adopted in 1972, became even more pressing at the beginning of the 1990s, thanks to radical changes in the political environment. At the same time, the intra-party discussion about the new programme was intended to have an integrating effect and smooth the conflicts between the traditional Christian democratic wing (centered on Andreas Khol, chairman of the parliamentary group, and Alois Mock, former party chairman, both members of the Workers' and Employees' League) and representatives of a more progressive 'politics of the centre' wing.[22] Despite (or because of) the ongoing secularisation trend, the 'traditionalists' pressed for a more distinctive, ideologically oriented programme to counter the enormous electoral losses of the past years.

21   R. Kriechbaumer, *Parteiprogramme im Widerstreit der Interessen. Die Programmdiskussionen und die Programme von ÖVP und SPÖ (1945–1986)*, Vienna, 1990, 505, 515; W.C. Müller and B. Steininger, "Christian Democracy in Austria", 87, 95; C.M. Auer and W. Marschitz, "Die Diskussion zum neuen Grundsatzprogramm der Volkspartei 1995", in: *Österreichisches Jahrbuch für Politik 1995*, 1996, 176.
22   A similar confrontation had been observed during the discussion of the 1972 programme. See R. Kriechbaumer, *Parteiprogramme im Widerstreit der Interessen*, 493.

Eventually, the new programme defined the ÖVP as a 'Christian Democratic party', based on the Christian commitment to the dignity of the human being, personal responsibility and a rejection of ideological extremism. In 1945 the Austrian Christian Democrats had dropped the label 'Christian' from their party denomination. Its predecessor party of the inter-war years had been called the *Christlich-Soziale Partei* (Christian Social Party). In the 1972 programme the label 'Christian Democratic' had been subordinated to the party's definition of itself as the 'party of the progressive centre' (reflecting an *aggiornamento* to the 'leftist' spirit of that period).[23] At the same time, however, the notion of a 'social integration party', which was perceived as a contradictory concept, was not removed in 1995, leaving the matter of the principal orientation of the party open for discussion.

The 1995 ÖVP programme picked up elements of the communitarianism debate in the United States of America, which had developed as an answer to the growing trends of societal fragmentation and individualism. The programme stressed the value of different kinds of communities (family, churches, associations, etc.) and the responsibility of the individual towards them (as well as towards the natural environment). It stated that the integration of people into communities should provide for belonging and security. The list of major values was revised: new values (e.g. security, sustainability, responsibility and tolerance) were added while the value of equality was dropped in favour of a recurring emphasis on the differences between individuals in disposition and capabilities (e.g. 'equality' was restricted to equality before the law).[24] The value of tolerance was defined as respect for different convictions and different cultural, religious, ethnic and social forms of life, though with the qualification that this did not imply that all positions had the same 'value'. Due to the influence of Khol, tolerance for different sexual orientations was not explicitly mentioned in the relevant paragraph. At the same time, the family issue was the most controversial issue during the programme discussions. Conflicts were not resolved. As a result, a commitment to family (and marriage) appears alongside allusions to new forms of life. Abortion in the first three months of pregnancy (its legalisation in 1974 resulted in a basic conflict between the SPÖ government on the one hand and the ÖVP opposi-

---

23   *Ibid.*, 494.
24   The press officer of Caritas, the charity organisation of the Catholic Church, criticised the excessive notion of 'effort' throughout the programme that, according to him, lacked any Christian basis. See W. Bergmann, "Christliche Spurensicherung", in: *Österreichische Monatshefte*, 1-2 (1995) 24.

tion and the Catholic Church on the other) was still rejected, though the prosecution of women seeking abortions was not supported any longer.[25]

The communitarian line was further developed by Khol, who published several books on the matter.[26] He warned of the emergence of a therapeutic police state unless an active *Bürgergesellschaft* (citizens' society) based on the principle of solidarity could be realised. The idea of a *Bürgergesellschaft* was also incorporated into the papers of the ÖVP's 'future congress' in 2001. Critics pointed to the fact that many of the associations Khol and the ÖVP envisaged as the backbone of a new model of society were in crisis due to recruitment problems, ageing, etc. Besides, it was argued that Khol's proposals (e.g. the installation of citizens' offices and academies for associations, the awarding of badges of honour by the state and a solidarity service controlled by the state) would not lead to the development of a society of self-responsible political subjects but only to networks of social services under state control.[27] So far, however, the debate about the *Bürgergesellschaft* has been limited to academic and intellectual circles.

Party competition

The ÖVP aimed at developing a more distinctive party profile not only in the orientation of its programme but also with regard to party competition. Until the end of the 1980s the political leaders of the ÖVP had not reacted to the profound de-alignment processes that had started to affect both major parties. Only in 1990, when the ÖVP lost almost a fourth of its voters, did the party leadership wake up. The old pattern in which the losses of one of the major parties resulted in gains for the other (typical for a two-party system) obviously no longer held true as both major parties lost voters, above all in favour of the 'new' populist FPÖ.[28]

In spite of their electoral losses, public estimation of the socio-economic competencies of the SPÖ and ÖVP remained relatively high, the SPÖ clearly performing better than the ÖVP. On the other hand, with regard to 'new'

25   C.M. Auer and W. Marschitz, "Die Diskussion zum neuen Grundsatzprogramm der Volkspartei 1995", 186 and190.
26   A. Khol, *Mein politisches Credo*, Vienna, 1998; A. Khol, *Durchbruch zur Bürgergesellschaft*, Vienna, 1999.
27   W. Marschitz, "Bürgergesellschaft. 10 Thesen zur aktuellen Debatte", in: *Österreichische Monatshefte*, 3 (1998) 9-12.
28   W.C. Müller, F. Plasser and P.A. Ulram, "Schwäche als Vorteil, Stärke als Nachteil", 213.

issues on the authoritarian-libertarian dimension (to use Kitschelt's terms), both parties were overtaken by the FPÖ (the issue of fighting criminality excepted).[29] It is worth noting that it was the ÖVP above all that performed poorly. In three out of four issues it was surpassed by the SPÖ and in none of the six issues (which people considered to be the most urgent issues facing politicians) was the ÖVP judged to be the most competent party.

Party competencies, 1990-1996 (per cent) *

	Secure jobs	Secure pensions	Prevent waste	Fight corruption / privileges	Fight criminality	Get a grip on the 'foreigners' question'
ÖVP	20	20	10	12	18	13
SPÖ	47	49	11	8	31	21
FPÖ	5	4	25	31	14	28

*The six items listed in the table represent the ones endowed in opinion polls with highest priority in the period of 1990-1996 (with changing ranks). The percentages give the averages of 9 opinion polls carried out in this period.
Source: W.C. Müller, F. Plasser and P.A. Ulram, "Schwäche als Vorteil, Stärke als Nachteil", 229.

The electoral defeats both at the national and regional levels between 1987 and 1994 and the poor ratings increased the turmoil within the ÖVP. The so-called steel helmet faction wanted to stress traditional, conservative Catholic positions in cultural and ethical questions, while the 'moderate-liberal faction' pleaded for a more open and clear market-oriented positioning of the party and for greater respect for the plurality of lifestyles. The ÖVP wavered between a concentration on the core groups of the party (Catholics, rural dwellers, farmers, self-employed and professional people) and a catch-all strategy. As a consequence, it sent out rather diffuse signals to the voters. Around the mid-1990s the party finally abandoned its catch-all strategy in its election campaigns and gave priority to its core groups.[30]

In 1995 the newly elected party chairman, Wolfgang Schüssel, who had long been secretary-general of the *Wirtshaftsbund*, proclaimed that it was time for a change. *Verändern, um zu bewahren* (Change in order to preserve) was his

29   H. Kitschelt and A. McGann, *The Radical Right in Western Europe. A Comparative Analysis*, Ann Arbor, 1995, 13.
30   W.C. Müller, F. Plasser and P.A. Ulram, "Schwäche als Vorteil, Stärke als Nachteil", 225.

motto. He attributed the rise of the FPÖ since 1986 (when Haider took over the party chairmanship) to the postponement of vital reforms (privatising and deregulating the economy, improving the efficiency of the civil service, fighting the abuse of social benefits, etc.), which the SPÖ as a leading government party had been blocking. The fact that the ÖVP had decided in 1987 to enter a coalition with the SPÖ (as a junior partner) was primarily motivated by reasons of state, and not by a high degree of political consensus with the SPÖ. According to Schüssel, the only defense against the radical attacks of the populist FPÖ on the political establishment was a "credible, autonomous, non-socialist alternative". Schüssel literally said that "he (she) who votes for Schüssel, votes for less socialism. He (she) who votes for Schüssel weakens Haider's radicalism".[31] The ÖVP tried to free itself from the bonds of the coalition and moved to the right of the political spectrum, and this was reflected in the general public's perception of the party.[32]

The strategic dilemma of the ÖVP was that it addressed the same anti-socialist, liberal-conservative voter segment as the FPÖ.[33] In order to stress its uniqueness *vis-à-vis* the FPÖ (as well as *vis-à-vis* the SPÖ and Greens), the ÖVP emphasised its non-extremism, drawing clear lines between itself and the parties on the left and right. Yet, while accentuating its neo-liberal economic positions, it claimed at the same time to be the exclusive occupant of the political centre. For instance, in its campaign for the general elections of 1999, the Social Democrats and Greens were both denounced as leftist parties with anachronistic, semi-Marxist ideas and radical elements, concentrating on marginal issues and groups, while the ÖVP allegedly stood "in the middle of life".[34] On the other hand the ÖVP attempted to counteract efforts by the FPÖ to attract conservative voters and began to adopt more and more conservative Catholic positions on socio-cultural questions.[35] Yet, the ÖVP was careful not to appear too conservative. When the FPÖ agreed on its new party programme in October 1997, which contained a clear commitment to

---

31   W. Schüssel, "Es ist Zeit für einen Wechsel", in: *Österreichische Monatshefte*, 7 (1995) 7.
32   While 31% of the respondents said that the ÖVP occupied a 'right' position in 1993, 37% did so in 2000. See A. Pelinka, F. Plasser and W. Meixner, "Von der Konsens- zur Konfliktdemokratie? Österreich nach dem Regierungs- und Koalitionswechsel", in: A. Pelinka, F. Plasser and W. Meixner (eds.), *Die Zukunft der österreichischen Demokratie. Trends, Prognosen und Szenarien*, Vienna, 2000, 450.
33   A. Khol, "Die FPÖ im Spannungsfeld von Ausgrenzung, Selbstausgrenzung, Verfassungsbogen und Regierungsfähigkeit", in: *Österreichisches Jahrbuch* für Politik 1995, 1996, 205.
34   C.M. Auer, "Entscheidung 99. Politik in einem Wahljahr", in: *Österreichische Monatshefte*, 1 (1999) 6.
35   W.C. Müller, "Die Österreichische Volkspartei", 281.

"a Christianity that defends its values" (against Islamic fundamentalism, sects, aggressive capitalism and consumerism)[36], the ÖVP condemned the FPÖ for its conservative Christian fundamentalism and accused it of leading a *Kulturkampf* (cultural war), against the open society and the liberal constitutional state.[37] Still, liberal party members of the ÖVP were anxious about the variety of opinion within the party and in 1996 founded a 'platform for open politics'. In 2000 a 'Christian Democracy Initiative' was established for a similar purpose, which promised to represent young urban opinion leaders and speak out for the weak in society and for liberalism.[38]

Coalition building

The finding that the ÖVP and FPÖ were supported by the same voter segment raises the question why they had not formed a coalition before 2000. As had already been the case between 1947 and 1966, from 1987 onwards Austria was governed by a 'grand coalition' between the SPÖ and the ÖVP, with the difference that now the ÖVP was in the junior position.[39] A grand coalition was deemed by the leadership of both parties to be an appropriate type of government for a situation where big reforms (e.g. privatisation of nationalised industries, reforms of the public sector and of the social welfare system) - in general seen as 'hard', unpopular and costing votes - topped the political agenda. Only a government with broad parliamentary support and close links with the major interest groups (the so-called social partners) was seen as strong enough to carry through the necessary reforms. Yet, the two parties had underestimated the degree to which the opposition, in particular the FPÖ under its new, charismatic party leader Haider, would profit from such government decisions.[40]

Both coalition parties lost votes and the FPÖ correspondingly gained. At the same time no alternative composition of governing parties seemed possible. After its transformation from a party at the political centre (with its partici-

---

36   This alienated traditional anti-clerical FPÖ party members, particularly within the Viennese party organisation.
37   O. Karas, "Kulturkampf und kein Damaskus-Erlebnis", in: *Österreichische Monatshefte*, 4-5 (1997) 5.
38   T. Köhler and C. Mertens, "Neue Wege zur 'neuen Mitte'", in: Österreichische Monatshefte, 3 (2000) 11-4.
39   Between 1966 and 1987 the national governments were drawn from the ÖVP (1966-70), the SPÖ (1970-83) and the SPÖ and the FPÖ (1983-87).
40   W.C. Müller, F. Plasser and P.A. Ulram, "Schwäche als Vorteil, Stärke als Nachteil", 227.

pation in a 'small coalition' with the SPÖ from 1983-1987 as a highlight) to a right-wing, populist party radically opposed to the established political class and its consensual style of politics, the FPÖ disqualified itself as a serious coalition partner, at least for the SPÖ, Greens and Liberals.[41] Somewhat paradoxically then, the FPÖ, the party that brought more competition into the party system also succeeded in stabilising the 'grand coalition'. However, the judgement that it was unfit to govern applied only at the federal level. At the regional level the FPÖ had been integrated into government functions for many years. The main reason for this is that in the provinces, in seven originally but just five since 1998, governments are formed according to the *Proporzprinzip* (principle of proportional representation), which guarantees each party a constitutional right to be represented in government in proportion to its strength in the elections. By 1998 the FPÖ was participating in all seven *Proporz* governments as a result of its electoral successes in the provinces since the mid-1980s.[42]

At the beginning of the 1990s, the ÖVP still refused to consider forming a coalition with the FPÖ at the national level. Busek, party chairman from 1991 to 1995, condemned the friend-foe politics of the FPÖ, which were characterised by continuous mobilisation and polarisation with the ultimate goal of either victory or doom.[43] As the influential leader of the parliamentary group of the ÖVP, Khol declared in 1996 that the FPÖ under Haider was beyond the *Verfassungsbogen* (constitutional arch) and therefore declared it *nicht regierungsfähig* (unfit to govern).[44] He listed four criteria the FPÖ had to meet in order to qualify as part of the *Verfassungsbogen* : (1) a renunciation of its strategy of 'cultural revolution' (amounting to the establishment of a 'Third Republic'); (2) an affirmation of social partnership (the Austrian form of corporatist intermediation between organisations of employers, employees and the

---

41   A. Schedler, "Zur (nichtlinearen) Entwicklung des Parteienwettbewerbs (1945 bis 1994)", in: *Österreichische Zeitschrift für Politikwissenschaft*, 1 (1995) 31; W.C. Müller, "Austria. Tight Coalitions and Stable Government", in: W.C. Müller and K. Strøm (eds.), *Coalition Governments in Western Europe*, Oxford, 2000, 94.

42   The common experience of ÖVP and FPÖ representatives in the provincial governments may therefore have eased the establishment of the two parties' coalition at the national level in 2000.

43   E. Busek, "Politik als Auftrag zur Gestaltung der Zukunft", in: *Österreichische Monatshefte*, 1-2 (1993) 16.

44   Although sounding legal, the *Verfassungsbogen* is a political concept that originally referred to the exclusion of the Italian communists from government participation, known as *arco costituzionale*.

state in the fields of economic and social policy); (3) unconditional support for the EU; (4) an unambiguous condemnation of Nazism.[45]

Besides the radical nature of the FPÖ, two other factors seem to have restrained the ÖVP. First, a coalition between the ÖVP and FPÖ would have ignored the importance of the corporate arena (social partnership). The SPÖ still controlled the trade unions whereas the FPÖ was (and is) clearly under-represented. Second, opinion polls revealed consistently that the vast major-ity of the voters preferred a continuation of the grand coalition between the SPÖ and the ÖVP. For instance, in 1995, 63% of the respondents supported the latter whereas only 19% favoured a 'small coalition' between the ÖVP and the FPÖ.[46] As a consequence, in his campaign for the general elections of 1994 party chairman Busek proclaimed that the ÖVP would form a coalition with the SPÖ "without any ifs or buts". The result, however, was disappointing. From then on the ÖVP started to play the card of the FPÖ option more overtly than in previous coalition negotiations with the SPÖ.[47]

Because of the ÖVP's pivotal position in the party system between 1986 and 2002, its members were not unanimously negative in their evaluation of the FPÖ's fitness to govern. The SPÖ severely restricted its strategic options in coalition negotiations by categorically renouncing any coalition with the FPÖ. However, no alternative coalition with the Greens and/or the Liberals ever reached the necessary parliamentary majority. Moreover, differences in important policy fields (e.g. welfare state reform, immigration or environmen-tal policy) would have made such coalition-building difficult. As a result, the SPÖ was bound to the ÖVP as its only possible coalition partner. The ÖVP, on the other hand, which has drawn the median voter on the socio-economic left-right divide (the major cleavage within the Austrian party system) in every election since 1983, numerically would have been able to form a major-ity coalition with the FPÖ ever since 1986.[48] Moreover, the major policy differ-ences between the SPÖ and the ÖVP did not seem to favour an SPÖ-ÖVP

---

45 A. Khol, "Die FPÖ im Spannungsfeld von Ausgrenzung, Selbstausgrenzung, Verfassungsbogen und Regierungsfähigkeit".

46 31% preferred a coalition of SPÖ, ÖVP and Liberals, 28% a coalition of SPÖ, Greens and Liber-als and 14% a coalition of SPÖ and FPÖ. See F. Plasser and P.A. Ulram, "Konstellationen und Szenarien des Parteienwettbewerbs in Österreich", in: W.C. Müller, F. Plasser and P.A. Ulram (eds.), *Wählerverhalten und Parteienwettbewerb. Analysen zur Nationalratswahl 1994*, Vienna, 1995, 513.

47 W.C. Müller, F. Plasser and P.A. Ulram, "Schwäche als Vorteil, Stärke als Nachteil", 239.

48 With the exception of a short period between 1993 and 1994 when five FPÖ rebels had founded the Liberal party and thereby weakened the parliamentary group of the FPÖ.

coalition in the first place. A survey of the deputies in the national parliament in 1997 and 1998 showed that in socio-economic and socio-cultural matters the ÖVP was closer to the FPÖ than to the SPÖ.[49] Therefore, in the campaigns of 1995 and 1999 the ÖVP identified the SPÖ as its main political opponent and warned of the terrible consequences of a 'turn to the left'. Opinion polls indicating that a majority of the people did not want a 'red-green' coalition were used as ammunition.[50] This, in turn, enabled the SPÖ, Greens and Liberals to make an impending 'black-blue' coalition one of their (negative) campaign issues.

The judgement of the FPÖ as unfit to govern at the federal level ended in February 2000 when the SPÖ-ÖVP coalition , which had governed Austria since 1987, was replaced by an ÖVP-FPÖ coalition.[51] Khol, once again, had played a decisive role in paving the way. Shortly before the election he declared that the FPÖ had moved back into the *Verfassungsbogen,* without offering any precise arguments. As coalition negotiations between the SPÖ and ÖVP failed, President Thomas Klestil - who had been put forward as presidential candidate by the ÖVP, but would have preferred a continuation of the SPÖ-ÖVP coalition - saw no alternative but to swear in the new government and nominate Schüssel as the first ÖVP chancellor for 30 years.[52] The ÖVP became the leading party, although it had suffered its worst election result since 1945 and it had gained 415 votes less than the FPÖ. The ÖVP put forward several arguments to justify its decision to form a coalition with the FPÖ. First, it was alleged that the SPÖ had refused to commit itself to necessary reforms but was only interested in maintaining its own power. Second, although he had signed the coalition agreement, Haider did not become a cabinet member. Third, a preamble with clear statements on Nazism and EU membership was incorporated in the coalition agreement, which was used by the ÖVP as proof that its new coalition partner was on the way to becoming a 'responsible government party'. Fourth, the ÖVP argued that government participation would prevent the FPÖ from becoming the leading party in the next elections.[53]

49   W.C. Müller and M. Jenny, "Abgeordnete, Parteien und Koalitionspolitik. Individuelle Präferenzen und politisches Handeln im Nationalrat", in: *Österreichische Zeitschrift für Politikwissenschaft*, 2 (2000) 144.

50   W. Schüssel, "Es ist Zeit für einen Wechsel", 7; C.M. Auer, "Entscheidung 99", 6.

51   F. Fallend, "Austria", in: *Political Data Yearbook 2000. Special Issue of European Journal of Political Research*, 3-4 (2000) 323–37; F. Fallend, "Austria", in: *Political Data Yearbook 2001. Special Issue of European Journal of Political Research*, 3-4 (2001) 238–53.

52   In the 1990s, both chancellors, Franz Vranitzky (1987-1997) and Victor Klima (1997-2000), were from the SPÖ.

53   C.M. Auer, "Die große Aufregung", in: *Österreichische Monatshefte*, 1 (2000) 11-13.

After a while, the initial excitement, both national and international, concerning the FPÖ's participation in government faded away. The so-called sanctions that the governments of the other EU member states (EU-14) had imposed on the new Austrian government right after its inauguration proved to be counterproductive as they had stirred up national feelings in the country and intensified the bonds between the two governing parties. The new government also won EU-wide respect as it managed to consolidate the federal budget (provisionally) by the end of 2001 (albeit at the cost of pushing the tax burden to record levels of 45.5% of the GDP). The plan of the ÖVP-FPÖ coalition was to impress the people by carrying through tough, but allegedly necessary measures in a decisive manner. For this reason, the governing parties agreed to reduce the political influence of the social partnership, which was depicted as an anachronistic institution blocking reforms. The goal was also, of course, to hit an important power base of the SPÖ. The plan of the ÖVP to 'tame' its coalition partner was successfully implemented, at least in the eyes of the party itself. It was convinced that the often populist positions of the FPÖ (e.g. towards the EU) had 'cooled down'. The ÖVP, on the other hand, was able to continue on its course without having to reposition itself with regard to its political programme (except in relation to its immigration policy).[54]

The rather bright prospects for making a new start in Austrian politics faded significantly after the break-up of the ÖVP-FPÖ coalition in September 2002. The key reason for this was that the government's performance did not pay off equally for both coalition parties in electoral terms. Provincial elections and opinion polls showed that the ÖVP gained in support whereas the FPÖ lost as the budgetary measures contradicted the party's electoral promise to represent the interests of 'the man in the street'. A rebellion by FPÖ delegates to the national party congress, backed by former party chairman Haider who opposed the government's decision to postpone a tax reduction for low-income people from 2003 to 2004, finally led to the resignation of party Chairwoman and Vice-Chancellor Susanne Riess-Passer, Finance Minister Karl-Heinz Grasser (the most popular cabinet member) and the chairman of the parliamentary group. In spite of the intra-party turmoil in the FPÖ that had caused the collapse of the coalition and in spite of the fact that the ÖVP 'cannibalised' the FPÖ in the subsequent elections (more than half of the former FPÖ voters, over 600,000 in absolute terms, switched over to the ÖVP), the 'black-blue' coalition was renewed in February 2003. Schüssel who had clearly won

54   T. Köhler, "Partei der politischen Mitte", in: *Österreichische Monatshefte*, 1 (2001) 7, 10.

99

the snap elections became chancellor for the second time. The ÖVP, now four times as strong as the FPÖ, obviously saw in the (drastically weakened) FPÖ a coalition partner that guaranteed the highest spoils of office and the best chance to implement most of its own policy positions.[55] However, its subsequent, constant criticisms of common government decisions (e.g. concerning pension reform, tax reform or the full privatisation of *Voest Alpine*, a still partly nationalised steel company) show that the FPÖ so far has not managed to change into a 'responsible' government party. The problem, still unresolved, is that "such a transformation would require the FPÖ to abandon precisely the strategy responsible for its electoral breakthrough".[56]

Policy continuities and changes

An evaluation of ÖVP policies in the 1990s must first of all take into account the fact that a modern party which has to act in an increasingly mobile electoral market and takes part in a coalition government is restricted in its room for manoeuvre and simply cannot implement Christian (Democratic) values in a pure form. Josef Pühringer, Chairman of the powerful regional party organisation and Governor of Upper Austria, stressed this in the so-called 'dialogue for Austria', a series of talks held in 1998 between representatives of the Catholic Church and the parliamentary parties. He declared that he respected the Church's emphasis on its 'option for the poor'. Nonetheless, he warned that ethics should be based not only on wishful thinking but on the feasibility of policies as well. The ÖVP, he explained, has to look for majorities in the population and has to do what is necessary, even if unpopular.[57] The head of the Political Division of the ÖVP, Clemens Martin Auer, concurred with his party colleague in stating that "the competence of several hundred socially engaged initiatives at the basis of the Christian churches is impressive, but not always particularly high".[58] The gap between Christian values and ÖVP policy positions is particularly apparent in three major policy fields – economic, social and immigration policy.

---

55   K.R. Luther, "The Self-Destruction of a Right-Wing Populist Party?", 148.

56   W.C. Müller, "Evil or the 'Engine of Democracy'? Populism and Party Competition in Austria", in: Y. Mény and Y. Surel (eds.), *Democracies and the Populist Challenge*, Basingstoke, 2002, 174.

57   J. Pühringer, "Als Christ Politik machen. Der Beitrag der Kirche zu einer menschlichen Gesellschaft", in: M. Wilhelm and P. Wuthe (eds.), *Parteien und Katholische Kirche im Gespräch. Fünf Studientage der Österreichischen Bischofskonferenz mit FPÖ, Liberales Forum, SPÖ, ÖVP, Die Grünen*, Graz, 1999, 156.

58   C.M. Auer, "Gerechtigkeit braucht soziale Veränderung", in: *Österreichische Monatshefte*, 1 (2002) 35.

With regard to economic policy, the ÖVP was able to introduce its major demand for a neo-liberal re-orientation (towards privatisation, deregulation, tax reduction and budget consolidation), although it was only a junior partner in the 'grand coalition' with the SPÖ from 1987 until 2000.[59] The principle of an 'eco-social market economy', as laid down in the new party programme of 1995, did not play a significant role in practical politics during the 1990s. Instead, pragmatic political interests and classic economic topics dominated the political agenda, first in the context of Austria's rapprochement with the EU and afterwards as a consequence of the increasing necessity for budget consolidation and cutbacks in social benefits.[60] The responsibility for these drastic measures was attributed to the SPÖ's 'debts policy' of the past. Moreover, the ÖVP argued that only a balanced budget could guarantee the functioning of the welfare state in the long run. Leading representatives of the party emphasised the principle of *Leistung* (effort), which was given a prominent place in the 1995 party programme. *Leistung* was seen as a precondition for social security and stability. Excessive re-distribution, they argued, weakens the competitiveness of the economy and menaces the welfare state.[61] 'Real' poverty in modern society has, it was believed, "something to do with a breakdown in the lives of individuals and little or nothing with societal or economic structures".[62]

As to social policy, the ÖVP has always rejected reproaches that its programmes are characterised by *Soziale Kälte* (social coldness).[63] Yet, the neo-liberal elements of government policy from time to time prompted criticisms from the Catholic Church or affiliated social organisations. During the aforementioned 'dialogue for Austria', Franz Küberl, Chairman of *Caritas*, a humanitarian organisation of the Catholic Church, defended the Church's negative attitude towards current tendencies in capitalism. He asked whether the ÖVP was not in danger of changing from a 'people's party' into a 'party for the economy' and criticised the ÖVP's appeal to voters in the 'political centre'

---

59   W.C. Müller and B. Steininger, "Christian Democracy in Austria", 97; F. Fallend, "Austria", in: *Political Data Yearbook 1997*. Special Issue of *European Journal of Political Research*, 3-4 (1997) 316. Nonetheless, one has to acknowledge that the breakthrough towards privatisation was much more a matter of government declarations than of practice and that structural budget problems could not be solved despite several consolidation programmes.

60   W.C. Müller, "Die Österreichische Volkspartei", 281.

61   See for instance E. Busek, "Ziele der ÖVP-Regierungspolitik", 21; J. Pühringer, "Als Christ Politik machen", 160; M. Bartenstein, "Leistung muss sich lohnen", in: *Österreichische Monatshefte*, 5 (2001) 4-7; W. Schüssel, "Lupenrein solidarisch", in: *Österreichische Monatshefte*, 6 (2001) 4-7.

62   C.M. Auer, "Am Leben vorbei", in: *Österreichische Monatshefte*, 4 (2001) 33.

63   See for instance W. Schüssel, "Lupenrein solidarisch".

and its consequent lack of care for people at the margins of society, in particular the unemployed. A policy that aims at reducing social benefits in order to widen the gap in salaries and to increase people's motivation to look for jobs is, argued Küberl, cynical. He also rejected the model of *Bürgergesellschaft* as relying on romantic considerations. He feared that this model would serve as an argument for the state to delegate the solution of social problems to small units, charity organisations and families.[64]

In fact, social policy is a contested matter within the ÖVP and has often split the leagues. The *Wirtschaftsbund* is usually reluctant on issues concerning the maintenance or even expansion of the (high standards of the) Austrian welfare state. The *Arbeiter- und Angestelltenbund*, on the other hand, shares with the SPÖ a desire to expand the welfare state. It differs from the Social Democrats, however, not only in its special concern for its primary clientele (civil servants and white-collar employees), but also in asking that the distributed financial benefits be devoted to those truly in need (in accordance with the Catholic social doctrine of subsidiarity) and that particular support be given to families with children.[65] As for the ÖVP, family policy was used to demonstrate the continuing 'social' character of its policies. The benefits for families and the duration of paid maternity leave for mothers were increased several times (also as a means of fighting poverty).[66] In this way, the ÖVP tried to reconcile its neo-liberal economic policy with its Christian social roots.

As far as immigration policy is concerned, the FPÖ managed to influence government policies and party programmes indirectly even if it did not actively participate in national government from 1987 until 2000. In the field of immigration especially, the SPÖ and the ÖVP integrated the FPÖ's proposals, for instance in a package of laws enacted in 1992.[67] As to the ÖVP, the new party programme of 1995 stressed the 'right of Austrians to their own home' and stated that the number of foreigners should not exceed the capacity of the national labour, school and housing markets to absorb them. At the same time, the ÖVP wanted to maintain Austria's commitment to being an asylum country and stated that refugees should be guaranteed fair and humane treatment. Foreigners living legally in Austria for a long time should be actively

---

64   F. Küberl, "Dialogbedarf und gemeinsame Aufgaben von Kirche und ÖVP", in: M. Wilhelm and P. Wuthe (eds.), *Parteien und Katholische Kirche im Gespräch*, 143 and 148.

65   W.C. Müller and B. Steininger, "Christian Democracy in Austria", 95.

66   J. Pühringer, "Als Christ Politik machen", 165; W. Schüssel, "Lupenrein solidarisch".

67   W.C. Müller, F. Plasser and P.A. Ulram, "Schwäche als Vorteil, Stärke als Nachteil", 230.

integrated, provided that they were ready to learn the German language and respect Austrian laws and customs. The *Caritas* press officer criticised the chapter on foreigners as totally unrespectable, given the "daily inhumane practice" of asylum procedures and the "notorious" breaches of immigration laws.[68]

However, in 1997 and 1998 the SPÖ and ÖVP government further lowered the quotas for immigrants and reserved them for so-called 'key workers' and for family reunification (against the warnings of economists who predicted a shortage of workers). The claims of asylum seekers were to be checked in a short preliminary procedure at the frontier, with only 48 hours allowed for an appeal. The Liberals, Greens, *Caritas*, prominent lawyers and the UNHCR criticised these new regulations. The UNHCR and Amnesty International disapproved of the unclear criteria for defining so-called safe third countries to which asylum seekers could be immediately deported, the low approval rate for Kosovo-Albanians and the short procedure allowed for 'obviously not-justified' claims. The Constitutional Court approved the latter criticism by repealing the two-day appeal period. An ordinance of the SPÖ Interior Minister declared all neighbours of Austria to be safe third countries, with the consequence that only refugees coming by plane had the chance of being allowed apply for asylum.[69] According to *Caritas*' Chairman, Küberl, Austria had lost its status as a safe asylum country. He condemned the fact that the legal security of refugees and foreigners had deteriorated radically and wondered whether those who had agreed to the new laws (including, of course, ÖVP deputies) were not occasionally ashamed.[70] The 'Christian Democracy Initiative' departed from the restrictive ÖVP course and demanded that municipal buildings in Vienna be opened to foreigners and that they be given passive voting rights in works councils and in the Chamber of Labour.[71] Admittedly, immigration policy was the central issue where the ÖVP had to give in to the FPÖ's demands, especially after the government change in 2000. For instance, a proposal by the new ÖVP Interior Minister to remove the family reunification provision from the annual immigration quota was turned down by the FPÖ.[72]

---

68   W. Bergmann, "Christliche Spurensicherung", 25.
69   F. Fallend, "Austria", in: *Political Data Yearbook 1998*. Special Issue of *European Journal of Political Research*, 3-4 (1998) 351; F. Fallend, "Austria", in: *Political Data Yearbook 1999*. Special Issue of *European Journal of Political Research*, 3-4 (1999) 334.
70   F. Küberl, "Dialogbedarf und gemeinsame Aufgaben von Kirche und ÖVP", 147.
71   T. Köhler and C. Mertens, "Neue Wege zur 'neuen Mitte'", 14.
72   T. Köhler, "Partei der politischen Mitte", 8; R. Heinisch, "Success in Opposition - Failure in Government. Explaining the Performance of Right-Wing Populist Parties in Public Office", in: *West European Politics*, 3 (2003) 106.

Conclusion

During the 1990s, the Austrian Christian Democratic party clearly moved to the right of the political spectrum. The catch-all character of the party's profile was identified as the major reason for a series of electoral defeats from the end of the 1980s. The loss of 'the enemy on the left' following the breakdown of Communism, its long grand coalition as junior partner with the Social Democrats, together with the necessity for constant compromises, intensified attacks by the opposition parties and in particular the 'new' populist FPÖ. Continuous splits between the major intra-party players (the leagues) led to disorientation and conflicts within the party and created an unattractive public image.

The ÖVP reacted by stressing its liberal-conservative traditions: liberal in economic terms, conservative in cultural terms. The neo-liberal philosophy was proclaimed as a necessary strategy to maintain the competitiveness of the national economy and to secure the welfare state. Reproaches of *Soziale Kalte* were rejected with hints about the long-term rewards of budget consolidation and the expansion of benefits for families. Caught between the SPÖ and the *Grüne Alternative* (two parties with allegedly 'socialist', anachronistically state-centred economic policies) on the left and the FPÖ (a party with supporters in the same liberal-conservative voter segment but with polarising and destructive intentions) on the right, the ÖVP presented itself as the only party of the 'political centre'. It tried to hide the fact that in economic as well as in cultural terms it had clearly moved to the right (or it sensed correctly that the 'political centre' in Austria at that time was in fact liberal-conservative).

Considering itself to be a more responsible and reliable party than the FPÖ and to be able to 'tame' it, the ÖVP risked entering another coalition government. The official reason for the centre-right coalition in 2000 was that the SPÖ was not prepared to take responsibility for the necessary hard decisions. However, it turned out that the FPÖ was not prepared to do so either. Instead of proving itself to be fit to govern, it instead revealed self-destructive impulses. As a result, around half of the former FPÖ supporters voted for the ÖVP in the general elections of 2002 and the ÖVP became four times as strong. Whether the ÖVP party leadership foresaw this development or whether it was even the underlying but ultimate motive for forming the ÖVP-FPÖ coalition, it was nevertheless a masterpiece of political strategy. Whether the ÖVP has increased its electoral appeal on a permanent basis, however, remains to be seen.

From Dominance to Doom?
Christian Democracy in Italy

Robert Leonardi and Paolo Albert

At the beginning of the 1990s, Italy witnessed a thorough transformation of its party system. Within two years, between 1992 and 1994, almost all the old parties collapsed and were replaced by or had to change into new parties. Such a change, commonly dubbed the passage from the 'First' to the 'Second Republic', did not save the *Partito della Democrazia Cristiana* (DC), which for almost fifty years had been the main pillar of the Italian political system. Unable to avoid the increasing disarticulation of its traditional constituency, the party eventually entered a downward spiral whose causes and effects have yet to be adequately explained.

Using the framework laid out in 'The Consociational Construction of Christian Democracy', this chapter will first try to explain the involution of the DC, secondly analyse the end of the single party period, then discuss the era of "endless transition" after the collapse of the DC[1], and finally see what, if anything, has remained of Italian Christian Democracy and its distinctive features within the two new political coalitions and the parties that claim to receive their inspiration from the DC.

Explaining the collapse of Italian Christian Democracy

The crisis of Christian Democracy in Italy during the 1990s raises at least two fundamental questions, concerning the cause and effect of such an implosion: (1) Why did the DC collapse and split into so many competing factions? What were the causes of the implosion?; (2) To what extent is it possible to assert that Christian Democracy still exists in Italy? More precisely, does it still make sense to talk about a Christian Democratic presence in Italy?

---

1   G. De Rosa, *La transizione infinita. Diario politico 1990-1996*, Bari, 1997.

Unfortunately, most of the literature on Italian politics during the 1990s does not tackle these issues. Indeed, apart from a very few specifically Italian works on this subject, little attention is given to the Christian Democratic crisis. In most cases, it is mentioned only in passing while in others what is presented is a mere recounting of events. On the whole, however, the usual explanations can be summarised as referring either to external or internal factors, i.e. outside or within the 'Catholic world'. Among the former, most authors point to some structural changes in the national or international situation. Most of these explanations generally refer to the extensive judicial investigations on political corruption that took place in Italy from 1992 onwards, i.e. the so-called *Mani pulite* (Clean Hands) enquiry[2]; to the referendum campaign for new electoral rules and the subsequent adoption of a prevalent majoritarian system; or to some major structural changes coming from outside, e.g. the fall of the Soviet-Union or the Maastricht constraints on public spending.

Among the studies examining the evolution of the 'Catholic world', an often-cited structural change is the increasing secularisation of Italian society. Partially related to this, another change noted is the progressive shift away from a unitary approach to Catholic political mobilisation, to the extent that at times, during the 1990s, it was doubtful whether the Christian Democrats were, in fact, the preferred party of the Church.[3] In a similar vein, it was increasingly less and less evident that practicing Catholics continued to vote only for the Christian Democrats. In fact, they were increasingly voting for competing political parties.

A final explanation for the demise of the DC focuses on 'last minute' internal failures. Quite surprisingly, this explanation often tends to largely overlook the evident corrosion already affecting the party prior to 1992, which had already begun to lose votes in a number of European, national and local elections throughout the 1980s. For these authors, some of whom are active political leaders, the leadership responded inadequately to the political crisis of 1992, the danger signs of electoral alienation among voters in the North and

2   Partially from this perspective, the usual argument that is all the rage among the supporters and leadership of *Forza Italia* (FI) is that the demise of the DC was the result of a plot by Communist judges against the political establishment. See P. McCarthy, *The Crisis of the Italian State. From the Origins of the Cold War to the Fall of Berlusconi*, Palgrave, 1995, 170-180. However, in contrast to the FI's leader Silvio Berlusconi (the beneficiary of the plot, if there was one), the Christian Democrats have always been reluctant to support this explanation.
3   M. Donovan, "Italy. A Dramatic Case of Secularisation?", in: D. Broughton and H.-M. ten Napel (eds.), *Religion and Mass Electoral Behaviour in Europe*, London, 2000.

the desire to introduce new electoral rules. According to Sandro Fontana, for example, who was among the founders of the *Centro Cristiano Democratico* (CCD), the end of the DC was a "deliberate suicide" brought about by a selfish leadership in search of a "mislaid victory".[4] For Marco Follini, current leader of the *Unione dei Democratici Cristiani e di Centro* (UDCi), it derived instead from the party's attempt to save its identity while forgetting its political and social mission. Likewise, Giovagnoli blames the last DC leadership for accepting the idea that, with the end of Communism, the party had accomplished its historical mission. Such an idea, on the contrary, is maintained by Sorge and, partially, by Scoppola, who nonetheless criticises the Italian Christian Democrats for failing to adapt to the end of proportionalism and the introduction of majority voting.[5] According to Scoppola, social and liberal Catholics should have split instead of insisting on a joint centrist position, thereby further exacerbating the radicalisation of the political debate.[6] Yet, as Donovan observes, "poll evidence, however, indicated that the party was likely to lose whichever way it went, left or right".[7]

Quite likely most, if not all, of the aforementioned factors, may have played a role in the demise of the Italian DC. Nevertheless, what these explanations generally lack is a theoretical base explaining the causal link between Christian Democracy and these factors. For example, the end of Communism did not bring about the collapse of all the anti-communist parties in Western Europe. Hence, why and how had the Communist menace influenced the development of Christian Democracy in Italy? Likewise, the explanations tied to the impact of secularisation, the *Mani pulite* enquiry into party bribes or the electoral reforms: how did these serve to undermine Christian Democracy among the voters? It is quite obvious that a party's fortunes are heavily dependent on the possibility of allocating financial resources and delivering benefits to supporters and that these opportunities can be severely constrained by a sharp drop in government spending. However, such a situation does not usually force a governmental party to collapse (especially when a party is as well established as the DC) but, at most, leads to its being replaced by the opposition. Otherwise, we would have a change in party systems every time a financial crisis occurs. Why then was the DC so sensitive to and dependent on the presence of all of these factors?

4   S. Fontana, *Il destino politico dei cattolici*, Milano, 1995, 3, 117.
5   B. Sorge, *I Cattolici e l'Italia che verrà*, Casale Monferrato, 1994, 202.
6   P. Scoppola, *La Repubblica dei Partiti. Evoluzione e crisi di un sistema politico (1945-1996)*, Bologna, 1997, 493.
7   M. Donovan, *Church and State in Italy. Beyond Christian Democracy*, ECPR Joint Sessions, Copenhagen, 2000, unpublished paper, 11.

Moreover, without a well-defined theoretical base, these explanations do not help us to understand what happened later on and to assess what has survived of the Christian Democratic legacy in Italian politics today. Are *Forza Italia* (FI) and the whole range of parties generated by the collapse of the DC - *Partito Popolare Italiano* (PPI), CCD, *Cristiani Democratici Uniti* (CDUi), *Cristiano Sociali* (Social Christians), *Unione dei Democratici per la Repubblica* (UDR), *Unione dei Democratici per l'Europe* (UDEUR), *Rinnovamento Italiano* (RI), *Democratici* (Democrats), *Margherita* (Daisy), UDCi, etc. - equally Christian Democratic parties? On which basis (and to what extent) can we still assume that there is a Christian Democratic presence in Italy? Clearly enough the answer depends on what we mean by Christian Democracy.

From a methodological point of view, that kind of question does not concern the Christian Democrats alone. Indeed, it would equally emerge if one wanted to analyse to what extent, for instance, the Chinese Communist Party is still a communist party or whether New Labour is still a socialist force. Or, more generally, when is a revolutionary movement still revolutionary? A well-defined theoretical framework is even more important in undertaking a comparative study of Christian Democracy in Italy during the 1990s if for no other reason than the lack of a 'physical' continuity in the party over time. Although historically the official heir of the DC is the PPI, politically a number of parties are now claiming that legacy. Clearly enough, our analysis cannot merely rely on their own ideological claims nor the labels of these parties, whose meanings differ from country to country. For example, the Swiss *Union Démocratique du Centre* (Democratic Union of the Centre) is an unlikely centrist party and unquestionably not at all akin to the Italian UDCi. Likewise, the Bavarian *Christlich Sozialen* (CSU) are certainly not politically equivalent to the Italian *Cristiano Sociali*. Nor could our analysis rely on their own claims to be identical.

The problem is also not solved by trying to decide which political party has attracted the better part of the former Christian Democratic political elite or electorate because the data point in different directions. If we merely look at political elites perhaps, the centre-left still has more former DC 'surnames' than the centre right. On the other hand, most of the former DC voters have dispersed to the centre-right. None of these criteria is sufficient per se to document the persistence of a Christian Democratic political tradition. Indeed, it is almost certain, for example, that many Italian citizens who earlier supported the fascist regime later voted for the democratic parties that emerged after the Second World War. This obviously did not make any of those parties fascist or even post-fascist forces. Indeed, beside the extent of a certain political mobilisation, what matters is what is politically on offer and not just how the electorate orients its preference. In other words, it is one thing to record that the disappearance of the DC prompted its electorate to vote for other parties; it is something else to argue *sic et simpliciter* that these therefore can be considered to be Christian Democratic parties. In conclusion, our understanding of what the Italian case shows particularly well is that the analysis of Christian Democracy must begin from a clear definition of that political phenomenon based on a theoretical framework capable of accounting for the Christian Democrats' distinctiveness, establishment and persistence.

From the end of the single party ...

In "The Consociational Construction of Christian Democracy" we have argued that Christian Democracy is a political phenomenon characterised by political moderation and originating from a consociational formation process. We also maintained that this is not a linear but a dynamic and continuous process whose proper understanding is fundamental to the analysis of the development and, now, the demise of Christian Democracy. Up till the end of the 1980s, regardless of their electoral results and political decisions, the DC leadership could still keep control of the party and the electorate.[8] Indeed, despite the increasing involution of the party's consociational structure, the DC cartel still had access to the resources and basic requirements necessary for its survival and massive presence.[9]

However, in 1980 the party decided to throw itself into a long-term alliance with the *Partito Socialista Italiana* (PSI) rather than keeping its options open and playing off one opposition party with another. With limited alternatives from the outside and unable to redefine its internal relationships with the

---

8   G. Pasquino, "Shaping a Better Republic? The Italian Case in Comparative Perspective", in: *Estudios/Working Papers*, Juan March Institute, 1994, 39: "To be more precise, for a long time, it would have been clearly wrong to speak of Italian civil society as if it were a more or less numerous and lively set of social, economic, professional, cultural groups organisationally autonomous and willing to confront the political class. On the contrary, most of what could be defined as civil society had been promoted and shaped by the Italian political parties, by a network of subcultural socio-political organisations, and it was and remained, at least until the eighties, largely dependent on their respective parties".

9   R. Leonardi, "Political Party Linkages in Italy. The Nature of the Christian Democratic Party Organisation", in: K. Lawson (ed.), *Political Parties and Linkage. A Comparative Perspective*, New Haven, 1980, 243-265.

other parties in the five-party coalition, the DC was engaged with its government allies in a very expensive and mutually self-destructive struggle for maintaining the status quo and power-sharing. The hope was that the electoral losses of the Christian Democrats would be made up by the electoral gains of the PSI, but the latter never achieved its self-proclaimed goal of going over 15% of the vote and becoming the leading party of the Left. However, the personal returns to the shrinking group of party elites in terms of financial and political pay-offs made it impossible to see the warnings welling up from civil society. The first signs of a grassroots revolt in the North, demanding more local control of policy and a more transparent relationship between leaders and led, went unheeded. The calling of early elections in 1987 provided clear evidence of this state of affairs. The early dissolution of parliament was determined by the in-fighting between the DC and the PSI over the so-called *patto della staffetta*.[10] In effect, the mounting disaffection from political elites did not immediately translate into an open split because there was still no alternative. During the last party congress, in February 1989, Ciriaco De Mita was forced to resign as party chairman but he thwarted any possible alternative candidate from his own faction. He preferred to search for an agreement and share power with his opponents.[11] Such a decision was bitterly criticised by a large part of his own faction, but still without severely compromising the principle of allegiance and the internal cohesion of the party's subculture.

By the end of 1989, however, that situation had already changed. Using Hirschman's well-known, two-steps model, a number of new conditions made the disaffection with the DC pass from 'voice' to 'exit'. First of all, in November 1989 the fall of the Berlin Wall marked the end of the communist threat. At the mass level, Italian Catholics no longer felt the need to remain politically loyal to the DC. An example of this came in 1991, in relation to Italy's participation in the Second Gulf War. For the first time, a large part of the Catholic hierarchy and groupings openly manifested their disapproval of the party's stance. The party elites no longer provided an adequate political articulation of the interests (and consciences) of their own subcultures.

At the beginning of the 1990s a number of factors arose that definitely aggravated elite-mass relations within the party and disrupted the internal political cohesion at the base of its traditional consociational approach.

10   At the beginning of the mandate, DC and PSI agreed to alternate in the control of the PMs office, but at mid-term, Prime Minister Bettino Craxi did not accept leaving his position to the DC leader, Ciriaco De Mita.
11   De Mita was replaced by Arnaldo Forlani as party leader but was rewarded with the chairmanship of the party's National Council.

Among other factors, the corruption investigations, the financial crisis, and the elites' immobilism gradually detached believers, clients and activists from the party. In particular, from 1992 the judicial investigations broke the tie linking elites and masses on two levels, the moral (i.e. delegitimation) and the physical (removing from the scene numerous political leaders who had to spend time defending themselves in court rather than running the party). However, for various months this "radical discontinuity"[12] advancing from the outside contrasted sharply with the reaction of the DC leaders who strenuously defended their power positions and blocked any change.[13]

Suddenly, the involution of the consociational construct of Italian Christian Democracy could no longer be ignored. At the elite level, the DC leaders were still engaged in a coalescent effort that however did not originate in their understanding of the perils of political fragmentation but merely in their commitment to give continuity to agreements with coalition partners. Indeed, after the fall of the Berlin Wall, the better part of the DC elite assumed that the only consequence would be the crisis of the *Partito Comunista Italiana* (PCI). Only a few - above all the former President of the Republic, Francesco Cossiga - realised that the effects of that crisis would inevitably affect the entire Italian party system and the DC in particular. Yet, the risk of political fragmentation was still completely disregarded, particularly given the vague programmes of the main alternative forces.[14] Besides, up until 1994 the Church continued to give official backing to the unity of Catholics in politics. Consequently, the electoral disaffection with the DC was essentially interpreted as an episodic matter of the temporary departure of voters (*'voti in libera uscita'* or 'votes on a holiday') who would eventually return to the party.

Likewise, the advance of the *Lega Nord* (Northern League) and the secessionist menace were perceived differently in the North than in the rest of the country. Obviously, the northern DC leaders were more aware of the perils of

---

12 A. Giovagnoli, *Il Partito Italiano. La Democrazia Cristiana dal 1942 al 1994*, Bari, 1996, 271; L. Morlino, "Crisis of Parties and Change of Party System in Italy", in: *Estudios/Working Papers*, 1996. From 1992 to 1998, the enquiry *Mani pulite* conducted by the Court of Milan concerned 5000 people. During the 1992-1994 legislature 11% of the MPs received at least a warning that a formal investigation was underway, which in those dramatic years inevitably meant exclusion from the political scene.

13 P. Alberti, *Il coraggio della moderazione. Dalla Dc al Ppi di Mino Martinazzoli*, Brescia, 2000, 80.

14 Three days after the fall of the Berlin Wall, the PCI leader Achille Occhetto urged his party to transform itself into something different (emblematically called *La Cosa di Sinistra*, i.e. The Left Thing) and open themselves to other progressive traditions. That evolution provoked a split on the left and the formation of a new party, *Rifondazione Comunista* (Communist Refoundation), which was not compensated by new forces entering from the right.

political fragmentation than their counterparts in other regions where the party did not need to cope with such a threat.[15] This misunderstanding was also reflected at the national level given the gradual but persistent loss of leaders from the North and the growing influence of Southern political elites. By the spring of 1992, the only external threat worrying the DC leaders was that arising from the judicial enquiries. In effect, that menace had the effect of inducing the party elites (and their allies) into an even closer relationship. However, this did not lead to any improvement but only reinforced the impression of an immobile system clinging to its defensive line (whose main armour was Parliament's prerogative to authorise or forbid the investigation and prosecution of its members). Eventually, the DC leaders could not avoid the overwhelming crisis, especially when the new President of the Republic, Oscar Luigi Scalfaro, a Northern DC leader, blocked the appointment to the government led by Guiliano Amato of any leader being investigated for corruption. Gradually, the consociational cohesion begun to deteriorate at the elite level, too.

Three factors, among others (and besides the misjudgement of the perils of political fragmentation), can account for the DC's consociational failure at the elite level.

First, the political elites' multiple balance of power and their inability to transcend their cleavages proved ineffective. Up till the very end, the balance of power among DC factions was systematically reduced to an exhausting mutual veto among the DC leaders. An exemplary case of this was in May 1992, during the election for the President of the Republic, when each faction could block the election of the leader of the other factions but was not capable of imposing its own candidate.[16]

Second, the political elites were unable to formulate effective and lasting solutions to pressing political problems. Indeed, the success of consociational

15   The *Lega Nord*'s first astonishing breakthrough was at the local election in Autumn 1991, when in a number of cities the movement obtained more votes than the DC. By contrast, at the national level, up until the general election of 1992, the *Lega Nord* could only account for one senator elected in 1987, i.e. its leader Umberto Bossi.

16   After many days and unsuccessful ballots, these games were finally and tragically ended by the bomb blast that killed Giovanni Falcone, the judge in charge of the anti-Mafia investigations. The Parliament met quickly and chose Scalfaro as president, an outsider who a few days before had been elected speaker of the Chamber of Deputies. The death of Falcone and, soon after, of Paolo Borsellino, the other anti-Mafia judge from Palermo, helped to fuel a strong public reaction against the establishment in Sicily and reinforced Catholic dissident movements such as *La Rete* (The Network).

democracy requires not only a willingness on the part of elites to co-operate but also an ability to solve political problems. In other words, a deideological and coalescent approach is not by itself sufficient to stabilise power; it is also essential to be programmatically effective and able to perform in responding to the country's needs. However, during the 1980s and early 1990s the government coalition led by the DC openly limited itself to *tirare a campare* (trying to survive), inexorably convinced that *"il potere logora chi non ce l'ha"* (power weakens those who do not have it). Year after year, political immobilism considerably increased the load on the decision-making apparatus and the need for reforms could no longer be ignored.[17] Lacking effective change the system inevitably stalled until, at the beginning of the 1990s, it collapsed. The DC leaders' immobilism dissatisfied not only the rank-and-file but also the party elites.

One of the best examples of a dissatisfied party elite was Leoluca Orlando who, following disagreement with the national leadership, abandoned the DC in 1991 and founded a new movement, *La Rete* (The Network). Likewise, after the general elections in 1992, when the party fell under 30% for the first time in its history, forty DC backbenchers set up the *Gruppo dei 40*, and called for the resignation of Party Secretary Arnaldo Forlani together with an extensive change in the party's national nomenclature.[18] Gradually, the outcome was a sort of de-pillarisation within Christian Democratic supporters not as the result of an augmented cultural homogeneity but rather of the subcultures' vertical disarticulation at the elite-mass level.

Third, the political elites were unable to accommodate divergent interests and demands from the party's subcultures as a result of the need to engage in debt reduction. As observed by Bufacchi and Burgess, "because of the nature of particracy, (…) the relationship between the electorate and the DC is dependent on the latter's success in resource allocation".[19] However, at

17   In 1991, the last government led by Giulio Andreotti was precisely, though ineffectively, formed to promote a comprehensive institutional reform. Another significant indicator of the emergency of that situation was the extensive adoption of urgent decrees by the governments during the next legislature that lasted from 1992 and 1994: 9.8 per month against the 3.5 per month in the previous legislature from 1987 until 1992: M. Fedele, Democrazia referendaria, Roma, 1994, 130.

18   In the period between April and October 1992, almost all of the main DC factions underwent a split between the faction leaders and a large part of their cadres and rank-and-file. On the Left, De Mita was opposed by Mino Martinazzoli, Guido Bodrato, Mario Clemente Mastella, and Pierluigi Castagnetti; in the rightist *Forze Nuove*, Franco Marini and Fontana went their separate ways; and in the *Grande Centro*, Antonio Gava was abandoned by Sergio Scotti: P. Alberti, Il coraggio della moderazione, 83-85.

19   V. Bufacchi and S. Burgess, *Italy since 1989. Events and Interpretations*, Basingstoke, 2001, 47.

the beginning of the 1990s, two external factors combined to upset the relationship between party and electorate and the former's chances of success. Thanks to the combined effects of the international financial crisis and of the constraints set by the Maastricht Treaty, the Italian government was obliged to tackle and curb the massive debt that had accumulated over the 1980s. As Fedele correctly concludes, "the very nature of the Italian case is that having wanted to give something to everybody, at the end the system gave little and, anyway, more than it was realistically possible to give. A vicious circle developed which eventually led to the crisis of the Christian Democratic party-State".[20] The new government nominated after the 1992 election - first led by Amato and subsequently by Carlo Azeglio Ciampi - had to undertake a number of exceptional measures to cut government spending and privatise firms in the public sector in an attempt to bring down the deficit and prepare the country for entry into the Economic and Monetary Union (EMU).[21] Such a financial emergency enhanced the government's decision-making powers and autonomy *vis-à-vis* the parties, but it reduced the party elites' ability to accommodate the interests and demands of their clientele.

Additionally, a number of cross-party activities developed, not at the elite but at the mass level. In this context the referendum campaign for electoral reforms led by Mario Segni, a DC backbencher and son of a former President of the Italian Republic, must be mentioned. Although belonging to the more conservative and rightist side of the DC, his proposals were soon backed by a large section of the ranks from Social Catholicism and the Left. For example, the support of part of the Catholic trade union was decisive at the organisational level and in collecting signatures for the referendum petition. The *Patto* (Covenant) established by the referendum supporters not only exceeded the traditional borders of their original parties and subcultures, but it also constituted an overt challenge to the power of the Italian *partitocrazia*. Their slogan was "people instead of parties".[22] First and foremost, this movement - significantly named *Popolari per le riforme* (People for Reform) - represented a further challenge to the DC. Segni eventually left the party in March 1993

---

20 M. Fedele, *Democrazia referendaria*, 32.
21 Ciampi is the actual President of the Italian Republic. Significantly, he had been the first Italian PM who had not been a party leader nor even an MP. He had been Governor of the Bank of Italy before.
22 F. Bianchi, "Vecchie e nuove forme di comunicazione politica. Le competizioni elettorali del 1992 e del 1996 a Firenze", in: *Quaderni dell'osservatorio elettorale/Semestrale della Regione Toscana*, 1998, 11.

following new allegations of Mafia connections against some prominent party leaders.[23]

Much of the literature seems to consider the introduction of a predominantly majoritarian electoral system in August 1993 as the main factor in setting off the DC crisis.[24] Certainly, the proportional system was instrumental to the DC in projecting its consociational nature on to the entire political system.[25] However, even more than electoral reform, it was the introduction in 1991 of the single preference vote that extensively affected allegiances within the different subcultures; for the first time, members from the same faction were brought into direct competition, thereby undermining factional cooperation.[26] As Bianchi correctly points out, the single preference vote "constituted a potential weapon of disintegration for the inner cohesion of organised groups by preventing the creation of an electoral cartel and tying one's candidacy to the prestige of a political leader".[27] Besides, as a further consequence, the electoral innovation enhanced the process of personalisation in politics, an aspect that according to Bianchi "goes back to the well known distinction between different types of democracy: the majoritarian democracies which would push to personalisation on the one hand and consociational democracy which instead would make it almost impossible, on the other".[28] Indeed, the single preference vote (by writing down the candidate's surname) boosted the candidates' struggle for visibility, enhancing their autonomy and eventually the chance of subverting with an unexpected electoral result the existing internal hierarchy of a faction and its inner cohesion.

In spite of the mounting signs of dissatisfaction, the DC factional leaders proved unwilling to undertake any sort of change up till the very end.[29] Finally, however, the situation worsened such that they had to accept the

---

23   M. Donovan, *Church and State in Italy*, 10; M. Follini, *C'era una volta la DC*, Bologna, 1994, 41.

24   S. Fontana, *Il destino politico dei cattolici*; P. Scoppola, *La Repubblica dei Partiti*.

25   See our chapter "The Consociational Construction of Christian Democracy" in this volume.

26   G. Pasquino, "Shaping a Better Republic?", 9: The new law "reduced the number of preferences a voter could cast from three or four, depending on the size of the constituency, to one. Moreover, in order to reduce the possibility of fraud, this preference vote had to be expressed by writing on the ballot the name of the preferred candidate and not any longer only his/her list number".

27   F. Bianchi, "Vecchie e nuove forme di comunicazione politica", 64.

28   Ibid., 64.

29   Between April and October 1992, Forlani stepped down twice as party Chairman, but the first time the other factional leaders eventually convinced him to return; the second time he withdrew his resignation after a few days.

leadership of Mino Martinazzoli.[30] The peculiar profile of the new chairman was expected to be the answer to all of the DC's problems. First of all, he was a lawyer with a reputation as an honest and respected politician who in the past had often criticised the factional deterioration of his party and of Italian politics. Moreover, he was a DC leader (from the Left of the party) but not a factional one, whose rectitude and experience appealed to both Catholics and non-Catholics. Finally, he was a Northern leader, especially aware of the perils of political fragmentation to the party in his region and, what is more, the winning candidate at the general election in April 1992 against the *Lega Nord's* representative in a contested electoral district in Brescia.

However, when Martinazzoli was elected party secretary the consociational configuration of Italian Christian Democracy had already been severely compromised. The 'full powers' which the DC accredited to the new leader (he was not voted, but simply elected 'by acclamation' or, as he ironically commented, "by desperation") were the most evident epitome of the failure of the party's multiple balance of power and consociational process.[31] During the first months, he tried to restore the old party and put new life into it. The new leader's action was based on two fundamental pillars: continuing with the virtues and breaking with the vices of Italian Christian Democracy. In particular, he tackled the factional involution of the party-cartel in an attempt to open up a direct link with the *standen* traditionally closer to the DC. As Donovan notes, the party "sought to purge its delegitimised membership and to bolster it with Catholic activists".[32] Hence, Martinazzoli cancelled the existing membership, called for a new and more transparent enrolment of members and endorsed an extensive renewal of the party candidates and representatives. Moreover, a "second important aspect of the projected reform was a proposed regionalisation of the party's organisation".[33] Finally, he firmly impelled his reluctant MPs to support the government's autonomy and efforts to deal with the financial crisis. However, whilst these initiatives further affected the remaining resources and electoral potential of

30 At the local elections of 27 September 1992, the DC suffered a further decline.
In Mantova, for example, one of the main Northern cities, the party lost 13% and maintained only 14% of its voters.

31 In this respect, it appears totally groundless to argue that Martinazzoli was at the mercy of powerful factional leaders and could not find support for his reform: J.L. Newell, *Parties and Democracy in Italy*, Brookfield, 2000, 29, 64.

32 M. Donovan, *Church and State in Italy*, 10. Besides, DC had just suffered from a substantial loss of membership (nearly 720,000 members between 1990 and 1991).

33 L. Bardi and L. Morlino, "Italy. Tracing the Roots of the Great Transformation", in: R.S. Katz and P. Mair (eds.), *How Parties Organize. Change and Adaptation in Party Organisations in Western Democracies*, London, 1994, 254.

the party-cartel, they proved to be insufficient in rehabilitating the DC, which still continued to be blamed for and associated with the ongoing crisis of the Italian political system. Additionally, since the end of 1992, a number of its top national and local leaders (including Forlani, the seven times Prime Minister Giulio Andreotti and the former chairman of the DC parliamentary group Antonio Gava) had been charged with crime, ranging from corruption to links with the Mafia and political murder.

Persuaded that the historical phase of the DC was over, Martinazzoli decided at the beginning of the 1993 to continue the Catholic political tradition through a new instrument.[34] Therefore, he proposed to create the 'second' PPI, a new party open to co-operation with other centre-leaning forces and anchored to a vision of political moderation.[35] "When we talk about a moderate vocation we do not think of a place to occupy or of avoiding a choice. Rather, once again evoking Don Luigi Sturzo, we reaffirm our natural inclination that makes us hostile to every form of radicalism, to every pretension to dictate separate identities instead of living in the fire of the moral, cultural, social and civil life. In this context the centre does not allude to political neutrality but to a strong and authentic synthesis that is dynamic and not static, that conquers but does not possess".[36] Indeed, the resurrection of the old name was not meant to be a negation of the political experience of the DC, but rather an attempt to mark the reinstatement of a political party as conceived by Sturzo: a 'light' organisation (as the first PPI and, originally, the DC were) in contrast to the party-cartel that eventually defeated the consociational synthesis of Italian social pluralism.[37]

Up until December 1993, "Martinazzoli managed to organise in support of his project a large internal majority, ranging from the left to a section of the moderate leaders and of the old notabili".[38] However, despite his attempt to attract a large range of perspectives and subcultures into the new format, he could not avoid the ongoing diaspora of individuals no longer tied to the

---

34 According to Follini, the PPI presented itself as the party of "good-willed Christian Democracy": M. Follini, C'era una volta la DC, 63.

35 The 'first' PPI was founded in 1919 by the priest Don Luigi Sturzo.

36 Martinazzoli quoted in: P. Alberti, Il coraggio della moderazione, 266-267.

37 As Parisella emphasises, "De Gasperi's conception of the role of the party was precisely that of channelling into a project to govern society the electoral consensus gathered from a number of associations and social, professional and religious groupings": A. Parisella, "La base sociale della Democrazia cristiana. Elettorato, iscritti e organizzazione", in E. Lamberts (ed.), Christian Democracy in the European Union (1945-1995), Leuven, 1997, 191; P. Alberti, Il coraggio della moderazione, 31.

38 M. Follini, C'era una volta la DC, 57.

traditional leaders of their respective subcultures. Indeed, the societal fabric Martinazzoli faced and had to deal with had in the meantime gone through profound changes. Above and beyond its typical horizontal fragmentation, it had also become looser and with less vertical integration within its constituent subcultures. Moreover, at that point the supply-side of the political equation was changing. Orphaned by their traditional leaders, a large number of voters at the mass level became attracted by new outsiders entering the political arena, above all, the businessman and media tycoon Silvio Berlusconi and his party *Forza Italia* (FI), which had been founded in 1993. At the end of 1993, Martinazzoli rejected Berlusconi's proposal to join an assorted anti-Left coalition together with the post-fascist party *Movimento Sociale Italiano* (MSI) and the secessionist *Lega Nord*. In contrast with the party's decision to compete in the election on the basis of a centrist coalition, a few DC back-benchers started to contact Berlusconi and, on 18 January 1994, the same day the DC transformed itself into the PPI, they founded the CCD claiming a common inheritance with the party of founding father Alcide de Gasperi.

Martinazzoli's insistence on positioning his party at the centre had been criticised and defined in fact as the result of a "non-choice".[39] According to this view, Martinazzoli did not want to choose any unnatural alliance uniquely to preserve the identity of the new party. However, the very limit of this perspective is that of distinguishing between Christian Democracy's identity and its role as a "moderate party" essentially identified in the activity of government itself.[40] On the contrary, Martinazzoli's obstinate safeguarding of the PPI's centrist vocation was based on the consideration that in these circumstances, with an escalating level of political radicalisation, standing on one side or the other would have affected both the new party's nature and chance to accomplish its political role. Besides, the PPI was politically isolated in the emerging political system, and the only one still supporting it, from the outside, was the European People's Party (EPP). Therefore, in March 1994 the PPI contested the election together with Segni's *Patto* in an attempt to oppose the radical polarisation of the Italian political system with a centrist and moderate alternative.[41] Basically, Martinazzoli's strategy was grounded in the expectation of an electoral stalemate which would have neutralised the radical polarisation of the system and impelled it to abandon the extreme wings, bringing 'the

39   *Ibid.*, 100-101; P. Scoppola, *La Repubblica dei Partiti*, 506.
40   M. Follini, *C'era una volta la DC*, 99; A. Giovagnoli, *Il Partito Italiano*, 272.
41   The CCD's founders, instead, did not present their own list but joined the FI's in order to avoid the risk of not achieving the 4% threshold. Thanks to the new electoral system and pre-electoral agreements with FI, they and the PPI won the same number of seats.

ball back to the centre' for a consociational 'grand coalition'.[42] However, as Dono-van notes, the aim of creating a Catholic centrist party holding the balance of power between Left and Right and enabling the PPI to become a quasi-permanent party of government, had failed.[43]

... to the "endless transition" (1994-2001)

At the general elections of March 1994, Berlusconi's rightist pole gained 43% of the votes, the Left pole 31%, and the Centre coalition obtained only 15.8%. This result could, nonetheless, have been sufficient for Martinazzoli's goal, since in one of the two Chambers (the Senate) the rightist alliance did not achieve the absolute majority necessary to elect a new government. However, instead of strengthening the centre positioning of the PPI, that result soon after the election reopened at the elite level the traditional dialectic between the 'intransigents' and the 'collaborationists'. Disappointed by an outcome that he had incessantly tried to overcome during his leadership, Martinazzoli accepted responsibility for the electoral result and unexpectedly resigned. After less than two months, Berlusconi persuaded four centrist senators not to oppose his new government, thereby getting the necessary votes to create a new majority.[44]

Berlusconi's first administration lasted only seven months as the *Lega Nord* withdrew its support and, together with the PPI and a majority of the Left, endorsed a new transitional government led by Lamberto Dini, former Deputy Governor of the Bank of Italy and at the time Treasury Minister in Berlusconi's cabinet. In spite of this outcome (the so-called *ribaltone*), a few weeks later the PPI leadership once again quarrelled over the party's ultimate strategy and suddenly the party split into two: one side (which kept the name PPI) backing Romano Prodi's attempt to promote a new centre-left *Ulivo* (Olive Tree) coalition, the other (which kept the party symbol) aiming to join the *Polo della Libertà* (Freedom Pole). The latter called itself the CDUi and was led by Rocco Buttiglione who had replaced Martinazzoli as party chairman.

---

42 To a certain extent, this result was effectively achieved. In January 1995, the post-fascist MSI's decision to change into a new conservative party, *Alleanza Nazionale* (AN), provoked a split on the right of a few nostalgic supporters. Likewise, the Left coalition split between maximalist and moderate, who began to search for co-operation with the PPI. As a result of these developments, at the general election in 1996 the two main protagonists were significantly a centre-left (*Ulivo*) and a centre-right coalition (*Polo della Libertà*).

43 M. Donovan, *Church and State in Italy*, 11.

44 Among the four was Luigi Grillo who was nominated deputy secretary in Berlusconi's Cabinet. Likewise, Berlusconi's centrist opponent in the Rome constituency became Minister for Family Affairs: P. Alberti, *Il coraggio della moderazione*, 162, 255.

Electoral results of 'Christian Democratic' parties, 1992-2001 (per cent)

	General Elections April 1992	General Elections March 1994	General Elections April 1996	European Elections June 1999	General Elections May 2001	North 2001	South 2001
DC	29.7						
PPI		11.1	6.8	4.3			
Patto Segni		4.7	4.4	10.3*			
Democratici			7.7				
RI			4.3	1.1			
Margherita					14.5	15.1	13.3
UDEUR				1.6			
DE					2.4	1.4	3.6
CDU			5.8	2.1	3.2	2.3	3.9
CCD			**	2.6			

* In coalition with AN
** The CCD candidates joined the list of Forza Italia
Source: Parlamento Italiano/Camera dei Deputati (proportional ballots only)

As Donovan correctly notes by quoting two analyses published in the major Italian newspaper: "To a significant extent the split was between the traditional DC of left and right that emphasised the autonomy of the political sphere, and the newcomers - epitomised by [Rocco] Buttiglione - whose political culture was widely seen as clerico-conservative and hence extraneous to that of the traditional DC (Petrarca, *Corriere della Sera*, 3 August 1994). Clerico-conservatism was widely seen as resurgent in 1994 and it was feared that it could easily take on Catholic fundamentalist or integralist, anti-pluralist tones.(...) Grassroots support, however, mushroomed throughout the country and opinion polls indicated two-thirds of the PPI's electorate supported Prodi's candidacy (Mannheimer, *Corriere della Sera*, 13 March 1995)." The PPI split took place amidst intense disputes over the application of rules that led to two party secretaries (Buttiglione and Gerardo Bianco) being elected and the factions resorting to the courts to resolve their financial situation. The result was that the patrimony (including debts) of the DC was divided, the central property in Rome's Piazza del Gesù, for example, being split between the two groups. From that moment onwards, Italian Christian Democracy entered an endless downward spiral.[45]

45   M. Donovan, *Church and State in Italy*, 12.

The Italian Christian Democracy's diaspora

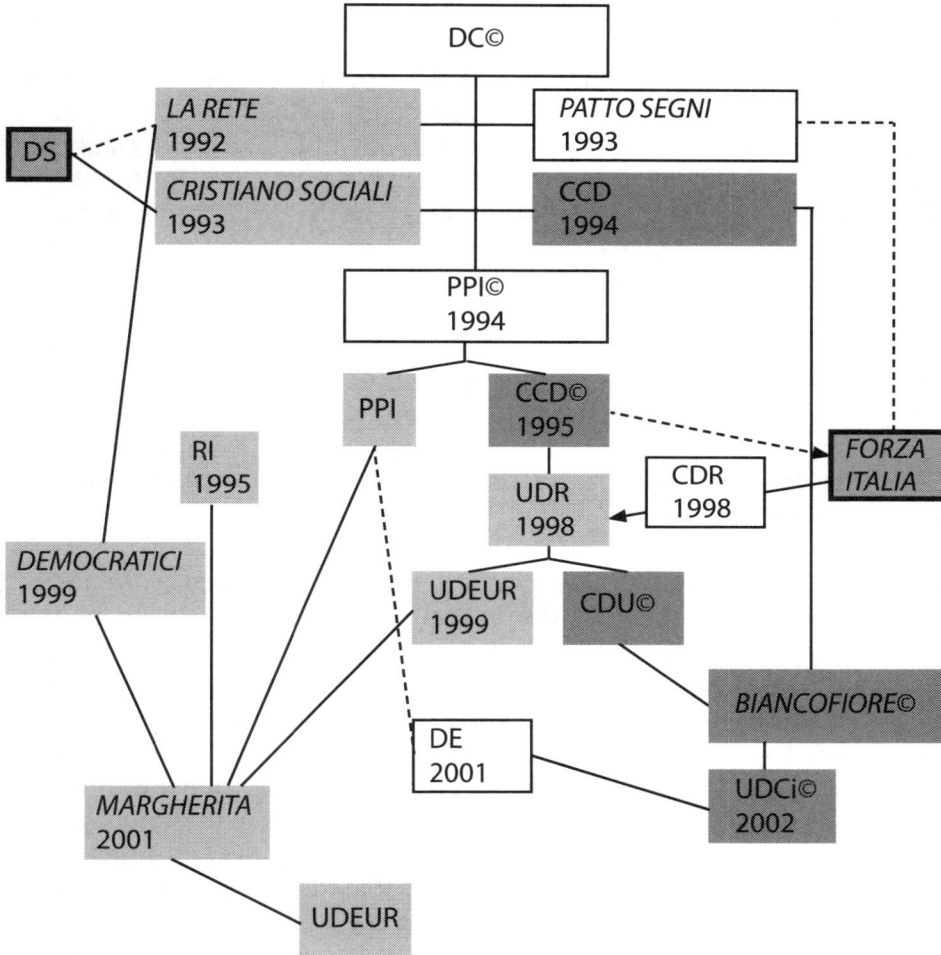

DC©

LA RETE
1992

PATTO SEGNI
1993

DS

CRISTIANO SOCIALI
1993

CCD
1994

PPI©
1994

PPI

CCD©
1995

RI
1995

UDR
1998

CDR
1998

FORZA
ITALIA

DEMOCRATICI
1999

UDEUR
1999

CDU©

MARGHERITA
2001

DE
2001

BIANCOFIORE©

UDEUR

UDCi©
2002

Party swings ───────
Individual swings ·············
© = DC's emblem

In 1996, the reorganisation of the Catholic parties led one party into the centre-left coalition (PPI) and two (CDUi and CCD) into the Berlusconi camp. In addition, the centre-left was also joined by the small but long established *Südtoriler Volkspartei* (SVP) founded in 1945 by the Christian Democrats of the local German-speaking minority. That year at the national election the overall Catholic vote reached 21.3% and remained steady up until the 2001 parliamentary elections, when these parties along with other small forces gathered around the centre-left *Margherita* and the centre-right *Biancofiore* (the 'White Flower', after the title of the DC's old anthem), now the UDCi. The leadership of the centre-left coalition by Prodi, a former Christian Democratic minister, gave the advantage to the PPI, which became twice as strong as the Christian Democrats in the centre-right bloc. The advantage of the PPI bloc was further reinforced during the 2001 parliamentary elections in which Berlusconi's coalition of parties won, though the CCD-CDUi attracted only 3.2% of the vote by comparison with the 14.5% achieved by the *Margherita*. However, a new party on the centre-right, *Democrazia Europea* (DE), led by the former Catholic trade union leader Sergio D'Antoni, gave the Catholics allied with Berlusconi another 2.4%.

As far as electoral geography is concerned, both centre-left and centre-right Catholic parties are fairly evenly distributed. However, the *Margherita* tends to be marginally stronger in the North *vis-à-vis* its right-wing rivals.[46] This feature seems particularly significant as it is reminiscent of the difference between the DC's initial establishment, when it was much stronger in the North of the country, and its later development from the 1960s onwards when the party's electoral strength (and its clientelistic organisation) in the South become increasingly dominant. More generally, however, the bulk of the voters for both the PPI and the CCD/CDUi still comes from the Catholic constituency. In 1999 als Berlusconi's FI party has joined the EPP in the European Parliament, but a number of surveys indicate that FI is not the party privileged by Italian Catholics. Segatti, Bellucci and Maraffi show that as many Catholics vote for the FI as for the leftist *Democratici di Sinistra* (DS) and its predecessor, the *Partito Democratico della Sinistra* (PDSi).[47] The successor of the post-fascist MSI, *Alleanza Nazionale* (AN), also attracts a relatively high percentage of the Catholic voters.

---

46 See <http://rost.dti.supsi.ch/~forti/lente/Confronto_Proporzionale.htm> (22/03/2004).
47 P. Segatti, P. Bellucci and M. Maraffi, "Stable Voters in an Unstable Party Environment. Continuity and Change in Italian Electoral Behaviour", in: *Estudios/Working Papers*, Juan March Institute, 1999; Diamanti quoted in M. Donovan, *Church and State in Italy*, 26.

Share of practising Catholics* among political parties' voters (per cent)

	Parties Eurisko (1994)	Università Cattolica (1994)	Avvenire-Cra (1996)
AN	19	23.6	19
FI	32	31.1	22
CCD-CDU	62	49.1	63
Lega Nord	21	24.1	12
PPI	70	63.4	66
Verdi (Greens)	23		
PDSi	14	14.3	19
Rifondazione Comunista		9.5	12

* Catholics going to Church at least once a week
Source: D. Dosa, "Il futuro dei cattolici italiani in politica", in: *Impegno Cristiano*, 1998, 39.

Vote distribution of practising Catholics in 1996

Party	Percentage
AN	8
FI	12
PPI and CCD-CDU	23
Lega Nord	3
PDSi	11
Rifondazione Comunista	3
Others	5
None	29
Total	100

Source: D. Dosa, "Il futuro dei cattolici italiani in politica", in: *Impegno Cristiano*, 1998, 39.

On the whole, the electoral bulk of Christian Democracy has nowadays dispersed towards both coalitions. Although tempting, it would be misleading to reduce what happened to a clear-cut split between the leftist and rightist DC factions. Indeed, the implosion of the DC has in fact to be understood as the result of a much deeper cleavage that determined a cross-cutting disarticulation at both the elite and mass level with a larger part of the former poisitioning in the centre-left and the better part of the latter moving instead towards the centre-right. More in detail, the centre-right coalition, the *Casa della Libertà* (Freedom House, that succeeded the *Polo della Libertà* in 2001) seems to have attracted most of the young and depoliticised voters, largely those most disappointed with politics (74% of those voting for the centre-right in 2001 declared they had little or no trust in politics, against 48% of the centre-left electorate), notably in the northeastern regions, in the South and on the Islands (Sicily and Sardinia).[48] On the contrary, the *Ulivo*'s electorate seems older and more politicised than that of the *Casa della Libertà*. At the last general election, 60.1% of the centre-left electorate had already decided their vote before the electoral campaign, while for the centre-right this percentage drops to 40.1%. In 2001 *Ulivo*'s political priority was the improvement of the health system. For the *Casa della Libertà* it was the reform of the judicial system. Although Italians are on the whole enthusiastic about the European Union (EU), the centre-left electorate is slightly more pro-European than the centre-right one: 46.4% against 37% think the EU should have more powers. Moreover, in the *Ulivo* support for the role of the family and collective organisations is above the national average, while the *Casa della Libertà* displays a remarkable confidence in entrepreneurs.

According to a study focusing on the northeast of Italy, men, graduates, professionals and entrepreneurs are more favourable to the centre-right whereas in the centre-left there is more support among women and retired people with a low level of education.[49] This result is partially reversed by another national survey that challenges the assumption that the coalition led by Berlusconi is essentially a political force representing the well-off.[50] What all these surveys agree on is that a large part of the centre-right vote comes from a more marginal and peripheral electorate, typically disaggregated and

48 Data from Fondazione Censis, "Le Motivazioni dell'Alternanza" in: *Censis/Note e Commenti*, 6 (2001).
49 I. Diamanti and F. Bordignon, "Verso il declino dell'identità regionale? Indagine sul comportamento degli elettori in Veneto il 13 maggio 2001", in: *Quaderni Fondazione Nord Est*, Collana Sondaggi, 3 (2001) 5.
50 ITANES, *Perchè ha vinto il centro-destra*, Bologna, 2001.

depoliticised and that it is therefore "difficult to recognise in the vote of the *Casa della Libertà* the social milieu of the DC"[51], which was typically involved in and connected with the pervasive Catholic social network. The profile of the centre-right electorate is surprisingly not mirrored at the elite level. As Mattina has observed with regard to the legislature of 1994-1996, while "almost 11% of MPs belonging to the PPI were members of Catholic organisations", 23% of candidates of the FI were entrepreneurs and 19% were managers, tradesmen or people from the private sector; 7% of the candidates of the *Lega Nord* were also entrepreneurs and 36% belonged to the other three sectors".[52]

Finally, the *Casa della Libertà* reveals a catch-all ability and an ideological flexibility that are more pronounced than its counterpart on the centre-left. For instance, in 2001 six out of the eight parties within the centre-right coalition were voted for by 12% that defined themselves as "leftist voters".[53] By contrast, only two out of six parties in the *Ulivo* have been preferred by self-confessed "rightist voters". Moreover, while in 1996 the centrist electorate was equally divided between centre-left and centre-right (33%), during the last national election the balance clearly switched in favour of the *Casa della Libertà* (41.7% versus 22.8%). Within the two coalitions, the FI and the *Margherita* are the two forces that are in the best position to capture the votes in between the two poles and to find support among voters who make up their minds at the last minute (21.7% of their respective total share of the vote). The actual difference among them seems to lie in the motivations of their respective voters: in the *Margherita* the ideological component is predominant while in the FI the programme and the leader are key factors. In spite of the predominant ideological component the *Margherita* is equally trying to transform itself into a modern opinion party whose evident aim is to become the direct competitor of the FI (which it has also partially emulated in its organisational profile). On the contrary, in laying more emphasis on its traditional identity, the UDCi is still perceived as a mainly centrist force with a low catch-all profile. Although the UDCi is an established member of the *Casa della Libertà*, surveys show that in 2001 only 0.4% of the rightist electorate voted for it *vis-à-vis* the 31.8% captured by the FI.

---

51   I. Diamanti and F. Bordignon, "Verso il declino dell'identità regionale?", 5.
52   Mattina quoted in L. Morlino, "Crisis of Parties and Change of Party System in Italy", 23.
53   As this was clearly a vote of disaffection with the *Ulivo* governments' performance, the challenge for the *Casa della Libertà* in 2006 will be to secure these votes until the end of their five-year period in office.

Is there still such a thing as 'Christian Democracy' in Italy?

What analogy can be possibly drawn between Christian Democracy and the coalitions that emerged after its involution? As explained in "The Consociational Construction of Christian Democracy", we regard Christian Democracy as a 'thick' people's experience intrinsically originating from a distinctive pattern of social interaction, whose establishment and persistence are aided by a few favourable factors and conditions and which ultimately requires the combination of two fundamental elements that are at the basis of its consociational process directed towards political moderation: a pillarised form of pluralism and the coalescent behaviour of its elites. For almost fifty years, the DC had always been characterised by a very high degree of internal fragmentation. Indeed, as happened in other countries, Christian Democracy developed in Italy from a consociational effort to overcome political fragmentation within political Catholicism. During the concluding phase a new level of fragmentation was achieved with regard to the party's internal pluralism. Eventually, such a new configuration thwarted the consociational approach that had been the bedrock of political Catholicism's ability to recompose its historical fragmentation.

The other factor affecting the consociational making of the DC was the increasing vertical disarticulation of the elites-mass relations within the party. Such a corrosion severely influenced the results of Martinazzoli's leadership, which still marked the last attempt to keep the ensemble of social and liberal Catholicism in a single party and to reactivate Italian Christian Democracy's consociational process directed towards political moderation. As Bardi and Morlino correctly observed, "Martinazzoli's project was simply the latest attempt by a DC Secretary to 're-establish', 'revitalise' or 'reorganise' the party. And while earlier attempts to improve the party's machinery during the 1970s and the 1980s had proved disappointing, they nevertheless confirmed, at least for the DC, that organisational inadequacy pre-dated the crisis of the 1990s by at least two decades".[54] Eventually, however, his effort was not sufficient to prevent the mounting polarisation that affected the Italian political debate after 1993 and 1994. As Donovan correctly observes, "post-war Italy has seen the pluralisation of Catholic identity (...). More recently, since 1993 and especially in and since 1996, it has seen a process of electoral bipo-

54   L. Bardi and L. Morlino, "Italy", 255.

larisation".[55] Indeed, whilst the inner pluralism has remained substantially unchanged, political Catholicism in Italy has internally intensified the basic clash between left and right, which Christian Democracy precisely aimed to overcome. From the mid-1990s onwards, Italian Christian Democratic political elites have increasingly switched from a coalescent to an adversarial behaviour, whose result within Italian political Catholicism has been a centrifugal involution of this experience and, ultimately, the departure from Christian Democracy's distinctive pattern of consociational development.[56] This point is also made by Morlino, according to whom in today's Italy "there is no longer a centre occupied by one party because of the crisis and the fragmentation of Christian Democracy".[57]

At present, neither of the two opposing coalitions can legitimately or entirely claim to be the successor of the Christian Democracy's experience. In each component there are some signs of that legacy but there is still not enough to re-establish the consociational process capable of achieving political moderation. The comparison of these two antagonistic political forces allows us to suggest a few concluding remarks. Apparently, the memory and historical assessment of the Christian Democratic experience is less controversial in the *Ulivo* than in the *Casa della Libertà,* which also includes two political forces, the AN and *Lega Nord*, previously excluded by and fiercely opposed to the political system that hinged on the DC. In general terms, the *Casa della Libertà* has a more neo-liberal approach than the former Christian Democrats, notably in the UDCi, who try to balance on the left by emphasising social solidarity, respect for state institutions and procedures, Italian unity and support for European integration. In contrast, the *Ulivo* has a platform that in principle seems more in line with Christian Democracy's traditional aim for a political synthesis between liberty and solidarity but whose implementation has to be constantly negotiated with the maximalist Left. Finally, the *Casa della Libertà* has so far demonstrated a more successful horizontal cohesion at the elite level but is still weak in connecting the elites to the mass base. Conversely, the *Ulivo* reveals a stronger vertical cohesion at the elite-mass level (within its constitutive sub-cultures) but still fails to achieve a horizontal cohesion at the elite level and consequently it appears more 'pillarised' than its counterpart.

---

55   M. Donovan, "Italy", 153.
56   See the figure in our chapter "The Consociational Construction of Christian Democracy" in this volume.
57   L. Morlino, "Crisis of Parties and Change of Party System in Italy", 29.

Indeed, in 1995 the *Ulivo* was founded as an assorted coalition of different sub-cultures (Catholic, lay, socialist, liberal, green, etc.), whose distinctive strength was expected to derive precisely from its political pluralism. Initially, its elitist nature seemed to replicate Christian Democracy's consociational pattern of development, although cutting across the borders of a single party and of Italian political Catholicism. Following the 1994 electoral defeat and the rightward drift of the country, the Centre and Left political elites proved successful in transcending cleavages and joining in a common effort to overcome their previous political fragmentation. At the beginning, the effort to combine different political traditions was more effective at the elite than at the mass level. Afterwards, however, that situation was almost reversed. While the rank-and-file have gradually integrated, the political elites have increasingly switched from a coalescent to a hostile (or at least a competitive) stance, opening the path to intense centrifugal drives.[58] Indeed, at the elite level all three conditions identified by Lijphart as favourable to the establishment and persistence of a consociational arrangement progressively changed.

First, the *Ulivo*'s electoral success in 1996 had the effect of neutralising or at least temporarily removing the external threat hitherto represented by the risk of a new electoral defeat by the Right. Second, the internal balance of power became increasingly undermined by the PPI-DS dualism[59] and, furthermore, by the external veto exercised by *Rifondazione Comunista* (Communist Refoundation), whose external support was vital for the government majority in parliament. Finally, the increasing burden on the decision-making apparatus gradually intensified the burden on the governing coalition, notably in connection with a number of very delicate issues, such as the international emergency in Kosovo, institutional reforms and, above all, the reduction of the annual deficit as a prelude to joining the EMU. As a result of all these, the apogee of the centre-left coalition's crisis was reached at the end of the 1998, when Prodi, the *Ulivo*'s main promoter and leader, lost a vote of confidence and had to resign as Prime Minister. The resignation of Prodi and his replacement by the DS leader Massimo D'Alema (alleged to be one of Prodi's main

---

58   See for this paragraph our chapter "The Consociational Construction of Christian Democracy" in this volume.

59   As Lijphart outlines, a dual balance of power instead of a multiple one makes consociation more precarious and unstable. "When political parties in a fragmented society are the organised manifestations of political subcultures, a multiparty system is more conducive to consociational democracy and therefore to stability than a two-party system". Indeed, "in a society with two evenly matched subcultures, the leaders of both may hope to achieve their aims by domination rather than cooperation, if they expect to win a majority at the polls": A. Lijphart, "Consociational Democracy", in: *World Politics*, 2 (1969) 217-218.

opponents, together with Cossiga and the new PPI leader Franco Marini) further exacerbated the reciprocal distrust between the centre-left leaders and eventually led a few MEPs close to Prodi (mostly from the PPI) to establish a new party, *I Democratici* (The Democrats) with a view to running in the 1999 European election. Paradoxically, on one side the new party was founded for overcoming these divisions within the coalition by boosting the creation of a single centre-left on the model of the Democrats of the United States of America, on the other it made its debut on the political stage (and inside the centre-left coalition) under the motto 'competion is competion'.

In contrast with this involution within *Ulivo*, at the elite level the centre-right leadership has until recently demonstrated a higher degree of horizontal cohesion. Their ability to transcend cleavages and to join in a common effort is the result of a combination of factors. Among others, the external threat represented by the Left may have had some influence. Moreover, contrary to their opponents, the centre-right elites undeniably demonstrated a major understanding of the perils of political fragmentation and an awareness of their respective parties' limited political fortunes outside of the *Casa della Libertà*.[60] Ultimately, however, such cohesion is still to a large extent the result of Berlusconi's hegemonic position in the coalition. Without him the coalition would not exist. Thanks to his personal charisma and extensive access to the mass media, Berlusconi has successfully exploited the crisis of the representativeness of the traditional parties and established a direct (though ethereal) relationship with the unorganised mass of individuals who in the 1980s voted for the *pentapartito*.[61] From this point of view, his leadership appears as an example of a "Caesaristic breakthrough", which is a continuing risk for fragmented societies as a consequence of their political immobilism and consociational failure.[62]

In spite of such a horizontal cohesion at the elite level, the *Casa della Libertà* has not yet succeeded in establishing pervasive elite-mass relationships with the main *standen* in Italian society. As Morlino outlines, when the FI was

---

60 Because of the majoritarian system, this is particularly clear for the rightist AN, but also for the FI and the *Lega Nord*, which in 1996 experienced the harsh consequences of its political detachment, the former ending in opposition and the latter obtaining fewer parliamentary seats than its share of votes. Likewise, the CCD is firmly tied to the *Casa della Libertà* since its original split from the DC was precisely motivated by the decision to join the centre-right coalition.

61 That is the 'five-party coalition' that had for long run the Italian Republic. Indeed, FI's manifest aim is to collect the legacy of that coalition rather than uniquely that of the DC. See, for example, Berlusconi's speech at the FI's 1st National Congress in Assago at 18 April 1998.

62 Almond quoted in: A. Lijphart, "Consociational Democracy", 208.

founded "the key organisational role was performed by the staff of *Publitalia*, a company, which is part of *Fininvest* (the conglomerate owned by Berlusconi) and which is a leading firm in advertising at a national level".[63] This failure to penetrate the Italian societal network is also confirmed by the profile of FI's candidates, most of whom have been selected for their professional background rather than for their connections and identification with a specific political subculture. Hence, the very problem for the centre-right is still its failure to provide an adequate political articulation for its electorate. In contrast to the fragmented and pillarised pluralism characterising the *Ulivo*, the *Casa della Libertà* is substantially more homogeneous because it still appears as an indistinct and blurry mass of unorganised individuals rather than as an articulation of cohesive units internally integrated at the elite level. As the combined result of its internal structure, political elite behaviour, and the characteristics at the elite and mass level, the *Casa della Libertà* resembles more the model of a depoliticised democracy rather than of a consociational one.[64] Such a conclusion finds empirical confirmation in a number of recent surveys that have stressed the "depoliticisation" of the centre-right electorate, precisely depicted as the fundamental consequence of an extensive distrust of others and the absence of social links.[65]

Furthermore, the internal configuration of the centre-right seems more consistent with the model of political participation typical of traditional liberalism and conservatism, from which Christian Democracy differs precisely in its distinctive emphasis on the role of intermediate bodies and social groupings. In consideration of this, Jansen's remarks on the affinities between Christian Democratic and Conservative parties do not seem appropriate. According to the former EPP Secretary General, these movements are substantially related given the similarity in their respective electorates.[66] Actually, such an assessment is based only on the socio-economic identity of these parties' respective voters. However, what one should consider is not the individual profile of its voters but rather the political articulation of the parties. In contrast with traditional conservative parties, Christian Democracy is a people's movement developing from a composite social interaction whose 'thickness' or 'density' is a key factor. In the end, therefore, the crucial differ-

63   L. Morlino, "Crisis of Parties and Change of Party System in Italy", 20-21.
64   See the figure in our chapter "The Consociational Construction of Christian Democracy" in this volume.
65   ITANES, *Perchè ha vinto il centro-destra*.
66   T. Jansen, *The European People's Party. Origins and Developments*, Basingstoke, 1998, 124; T. Jansen, "The Integration of the Conservatives into the European People's Party", in: D.S. Bell and C. Lord (eds.), *Transnational Parties in the European Union*, Aldershot, 1998, 103, 115.

ence between Christian Democracy and conservatism is precisely this diverse 'thickness', that is the amount of social capital that underlies the development of the Christian Democratic experience.

In conclusion, with the end of the single party, the former Italian Christian Democrats (elite and rank-and-file) are nowadays spread throughout the political spectrum. Recently, however, a few aggregative initiatives (*Margherita* and UDCi) are taking place on both sides. These might lead to two alternative models of interpreting and continuing the DC legacy. One is more in line with the traditional Catholic setting, while the other is more 'original' and innovative. The success of the first will mainly depend on its ability to articulate sensitive elite-mass relationships within Italian society. In this regard, a significant improvement can be seen in the UDCi's progressive attempt to establish a privileged relation with the Church and some of the most important Catholic organisations. On the other side, the reinstatement of a consociational process directed towards political moderation will ultimately rely on the centre-left political elites' ability to transcend their cleavages and join again in a common effort. Significantly, after the defeat in 2001, the *Ulivo*'s internal political agenda has for long been dominated by the controversial debate on the adoption of majority rules to overcome the political immobilism that has created a system of mutual vetoes. In addition, the centre-left's search for cohesion has been recently boosted by Prodi's proposal to contest the 2004 European elections on the basis of a single coalition list, whose positioning in the European Parliament is still unclear and open to dispute. However, it seems rather unlikely that the MEPs of the *Margherita*, now divided between the EPP-ED and the Liberal Group, will continue to join the EPP. For both sides the challenge is to construct a new post-cartel political force, combining the political interplay and organisational benefits of the cartel while at the same time returning to grassroots social forces. Otherwise they risk recreating another version of the clientelistic party-cartel of the 1980s (UDCi) or a progressive derailment from the Christian Democratic tradition (*Margherita*).

Living Apart Together
Christian Democracy
in Belgium

Wouter Beke

This chapter is entitled 'Living apart together', because two autonomous Christian Democratic parties exist within one and the same political system. The *Christelijke Volkspartij/Parti Social Chrétien* (CVP/PSC) was founded in 1945 as a single party, but was split into two autonomous wings in 1968. In the 1970s, the Liberal and the Socialist parties were also split up. In this way, it is fair to say that only regional parties still exist in Belgium. So when talking about Christian Democracy in Belgium, a distinction should be made between the Flemish and French-speaking Christian Democrats.[1] Moreover, in this chapter I will argue that the fact that Belgian Christian Democratic parties operate in a regional context has ideological, strategic and organisational consequences.

The period since the end of the Cold War can be divided into two distinct parts. Up until 1999, the Christian Democrats were the leading political branch. They provided the prime minister and determined the political agenda. This changed in 1999 when they found themselves in opposition for the first time in 40 years. Until then they had been preoccupied with running the country, whereas after 1999 they were mostly occupied with themselves. The electoral evolution, the parties' policies and programmes, the ideological changes and the relations with civil society will therefore be analysed in the

---

[1] Actually the situation is even more complex as there is also a Christian Democratic party, although relatively small, in the German-speaking part of Belgium called the *Christlich Soziale Partei* (CSP), and as both the CVP (Flanders) and the PSC (Wallonia) also compete in Brussels. In this chapter however I will mainly discuss and compare the CVP in Flanders and the PSC in Wallonia.

context of these two periods as well as in relation to the existence of two Christian Democratic parties in Belgium.[2]

Electoral evolution

The political landscape in Belgium is divided between parties as well as regions. Besides Christian Democrats, there are also Socialist, Liberal, Green, regionalist and extreme right parties. Apart from the nationalists and the Flemish extreme right, all parties are split up into distinct Flemish and Wallonian parties. As parties can oppose each other on a partisan basis and/ or a regional basis, the result is a broad asymmetrical federal political landscape and a complex system of decision-making processes.

In various countries, the Socialist parties are the main challengers of the Christian Democrats, and for a long time, this was the case in Belgium as well. After the Second World War, Christian Democrats and Socialists were on an equal footing for a long time, and the Liberals were traditionally the smaller party. Because the largest political party also provided the prime minister, this was most of the time a (Flemish) Christian Democrat.

This situation changed in the 1980s. While the Socialists were stagnating or even slightly declining, the Christian Democrats were experiencing a continuous decline. From 1988 until 1999, the Christian Democrats formed a coalition with the Socialists. The Liberals consistently targeted the right wing of the Christian Democratic party that gave them limited but almost systematic growth. Therefore, the Christian Democrats' main challengers were the Liberals rather than the Socialists. Liberal parties usually play a minor role, but during the 1990s in Belgium, the Liberals grew to become the country's major political power instead of the Christian Democrats. This is why the Liberals now occupy a unique position in Belgium. While the Liberals were competing with the Christian Democrats' right wing, the Green party was competing

2   The analysis is to a great extent based on the annual articles "Overzicht van het Belgisch politiek gebeuren" by M. Deweerdt published in the political yearbook of *Res Publica*, (1991) 3-4, 286-344; (1992) 3-4, 292-338; (1993) 3-4, 233-268; (1994) 3-4, 281-312; (1995) 3-4, 501-525; (1996) 3-4, 468-531; (1997) 4, 311-375; (1998) 3-4, 162-238; (1999) 2-3, 166-246; (2000) 3-4, 215-315 and (2001) 2-3, 155-252. For the period since 1999 I mainly rely on: W. Beke, "Tussen Van Acker en Verhofstadt. Enkele kanttekeningen bij verschillen en gelijkenissen voor een CVP in oppositie", in: *De Gids op Maatschappelijk Gebied*, 8 (2000) 34-52; S. Van Hecke, "De oppositie van de christen-democraten in België", in: *Christen-democratische Verkenningen*, 2 (2002) 20-35; S. Van Hecke, "Oppositie, vernieuwing, oppositie. Kroniek van enkele gelijkenissen en verschillen tussen CVP en PSC", in: *Nieuw Tijdschrift voor Politiek*, 1 (2001-2002) 37-59.

with its progressive wing, and more specifically, it was trying to establish linkages with the *Algemeen Christelijk Werknemersverbond/Mouvement Ouvrier Chrétien* (Christian Labour Movement) that has traditionally had close and exclusive ties with the Christian Democrats. In Wallonia, this seems to have worked better than in Flanders, not least because the Wallonian Christian Labour Movement has always been more distanced from the PSC than their Flemish counterparts from the CVP.

Generally, the Christian Democrats occupy a different position in Flanders than in Wallonia. In Flanders the CVP was the largest political party until 1999. Since then, the *Vlaamse Liberalen en Democraten* (VLD)[3] took over the political leadership, and in 2003, the *Socialistische Partij Anders* (SPA-SPIRIT)[4] also overtook the Christian Democrats. Despite losing just one seat, compared to 1999, they were now relegated to third place due to the increasing popularity of the Socialists and Liberals. What is remarkable in Flanders is not only the systematic growth of the Liberals, but also the rise of the *Vlaams Blok* (Flemish Block). The opposite was true for the Flemish regionalist *Volksunie* (VU).[5] Similar to the *Vlaams Blok*, the Green *Anders Gaan Leven* (AGALEV) gained with every election. In 2003 however, after a four-year participation in the federal government, they suffered their worst result ever and lost their representation in the Federal Parliament.

In Wallonia, the *Parti Socialiste* (PS) has always been the largest party. In 1981, the PSC lost its second place to the *Parti Libéral Réformateur* (PRL), and in 1999 it even had to relinquish its third place to the *Ecologistes Confédérés pour l'Organisation des Luttes Originales* (ECOLO). In the 2003 elections, the Wallonian Christian Democrats became the third largest party once again. However, this was not due to their own electoral success but rather to the decline of ECOLO, whose position nevertheless remained stronger than that of their Flemish counterparts.
In comparison to Flanders, the extreme right *Front National* (National Front) is less strong and therefore in no way poses a threat to the established parties. The regionalist *Front Démocratique des Francophones* (FDF), which was especially strong in Brussels, entered into an alliance with the PRL after the 1991 elections. The PRL-FDF alliance was refounded in 2002 as the *Mouvement Réformateur*

---

3 In 1992 the Flemish Liberal *Partij voor Vrijheid en Vooruitgang* (Party for Freedom and Prosperity) changed its name to VLD.

4 In 2000 the *Socialistische Partij* (Socialist Party) added the word '*Anders*' (different) to its name. In 2003 they formed an electoral cartel with the left-liberal wing of the former Flemish nationalist party called *Sociaal, Progressief, Internationaal, Regionalistisch, Integraal-democratisch en Toekomstgericht* (SPIRIT).

5 The VU split up in 2001. One party group became SPIRIT, another one that called itself the *Nieuw-Vlaamse Alliantie* (NVA) stayed an independent party until 2004, while several individual politicians joined the VLD.

(MR) which also took in some Christian Democrats who had left the PSC some time before.

Federal election results in the Chamber of Deputies, 1991-2003

Political Group	1991	1995*	1999	2003
Christian Democrats	26.9%	27.3%	21.4%	19.3%
	57	41	32	29
CVP/CD&V	18.4%	19.3%	14.7%	14.0%
	39	29	22	21
PSC/CDH	8.5%	8.0%	6.7%	5.3%
	18	12	10	8
Socialists	29.7%	27.3%	22.0%	32.0%
	63	41	33	48
PS	16.5%	14.0%	12.7%	16.7%
	35	21	9	25
SP/SPA-SPIRIT	13.2%	13.3%	9.3%	15.3%
	28	20	14	23
Liberals	21.7%	26.0%	27.3%	32.7%
	46	39	41	49
PVV/VLD	12.3%	14.0%	15.3%	16.7%
	26	21	23	25
PRL/MR	9.4%	12.0%	12.0%	16.0%
	20	18	18	24
Greens	8.0%	7.3%	13.3%	2.7%
	17	11	20	4
AGALEV	3.3%	3.3%	6.0%	0.0%
	7	5	9	0
ECOLO	4.7%	4.0%	7.3%	2.7%
	10	6	11	4
Vlaams Blok	5.7%	7.3%	10.0%	12.0%
	12	11	15	18
VU/NVA	4.7%	3.3%	5.3%	0.7%
	10	5	8	1
Others	3.3%	0.9%	0.5%	0.5%
	7**	2FN	1FN	1FN

* As result of constitutional reform of 1993, the number of seats in the Federal Chamber of Representatives has been diminished since 1995 from 212 to 150.
** The Walloon FDF obtains three seats, a Flemish libertarian protest party also three seats and the *Front National* one seat.

With regard to the geographical distribution of election results, the Christian Democrats are still particularly strong in the more rural regions but weak in the more urban areas. For example, in the 2003 election, the Christian Democrats achieved barely 10% of the vote in the cities of Brussels, Antwerp and Charleroi. In medium-sized towns located in more rural areas such as Bruges, they still gained 25 and 30%, but in the other towns such as Ghent and Liège, they scored less than the national average. The same patterns emerged in the provincial distribution. In the rural provinces, the Christian Democrats remain fairly strong, whereas in more urbanised provinces they score below average.

Federal election results of the Christian Democrats in urban areas, 1991-2003 (per cent)

Constituency	Province	1991	1995	1999	2003
Brussels PSC		11.3	10.4	8.3	8.7
Brussels CVP		5.2	4.2	3.1	2.2
Antwerpen	Antwerpen	14.3	13.7	12.4	10.6
Brugge	West-Vlaanderen	28.8	29.3	24.5	23.2
Gent	Oost-Vlaanderen	19.3	20.7	17.0	13.0
Leuven	Vlaams-Brabant	22.8	22.9	18.7	18.1
Charleroi	Henegouwen	16.2	22.1	12.2	9.5
Luik	Luik	17.3	17.9	15.4	13.2
Kortrijk	West-Vlaanderen	33.1	33.9	35.1	30.3
Aalst	Oost-Vlaanderen	21.0	22.5	18.3	17.1
Oostende	West-Vlaanderen	18.1	15.8	13.5	13.3
Namen	Namen	25.0	21.7	19.1	17.9
Hasselt	Limburg	24.3	25.6	17.7	16.7
Mechelen	Antwerpen	19.2	20.7	15.9	16.1
Bergen	Henegouwen	21.6	17.4	10.4	10.1
Roeselare	West-Vlaanderen	28.5	30.2	30.1	27.6
Turnhout	Antwerpen	32.2	31.1	25.6	23.7
Vilvoorde	Vlaams-Brabant	20.2	19.7	16.7	14.8
Genk	Limburg	33.5	33.2	26.2	23.8
Sint-Niklaas	Oost-Vlaanderen	25.5	26.0	18.6	16.9
Doornik	Henegouwen	25.9	23.0	17.0	13.4
La Louvière	Henegouwen	13.1	12.0	8.3	8.7
Verviers	Luik	34.7	32.9	15.2	18.1
Moeskroen	Henegouwen	39.0	33.4	31.8	23.4
Aarlen	Luxemburg	30.0	28.6	25.4	30.0

At the 1989 European elections, the Belgian Christian Democratic parties obtained 7 out 24 seats, i.e. one seat in three. The CVP achieved 34% in Flanders and the PSC 21% in Wallonia. This was the last true electoral success for the Christian Democrats in Belgium. Since 1989, the Belgian voters have been to the polling stations four times to vote for a new parliament at the national/federal and the regional levels.[6]

In the autumn of 1991 Belgian voters were called to the polls for early national elections. The results were so remarkable that the date of the election, 24 November and the term *Zwarte Zondag* (Black Sunday) became common expressions. All of the established government parties, whether in government or in opposition, lost votes. The CVP lost 4 seats and the PSC lost 1 seat out of 212. The big winner in Flanders was the *Vlaams Blok* while in Wallonia ECOLO triumphed. The dramatic result was in general considered to be the consequence of a number of scandals, fights and several other incidents within the outgoing coalition of Christian Democrats, Socialists and the VU. It also marked the end of the career in Belgian politics of Wilfried Martens who had personified the CVP during the 1980s.

By contrast, the 1995 federal and regional elections did not cause such a great upset. The Flemish governmental parties (Christian Democrats and Socialists) made a slight recovery from the loss they suffered four years earlier while the Wallonian Christian Democrats and Socialists experienced a marginal decline. The VLD and the PRL won 1.7 and 3.6% respectively. However, the Liberals suffered a moral defeat, as the VLD did not manage to become the country's largest political party (and failed to break up the ruling coalition). The *Vlaams Blok* gained another 1.7%. Since the ruling coalition was not penalised and still had a majority in the national and the regional assemblies, the Christian Democrats and the Socialists continued to rule the country.

The governmental parties, especially the CVP, were confident about the federal and regional elections of 1999 (thanks to the succesful entry of Belgium into EMU). However, due to the dioxin crisis that broke out a couple of days before the election date, Belgium experienced another political earthquake. The CVP now lost 7 seats and the PSC 2 (out of 150). Both AGALEV and ECOLO were very successful ('a Green Sunday') while the *Vlaams Blok* became the

---

6   Since 1995 regional parliaments have directly elected deputies. However, it was only with the federal elections in 2003 and the regional elections in 2004 that the two have been split in time.

third largest party in Flanders. More important, the CVP was overtaken by the VLD as the country's largest political party. Therefore the right to form a federal government now was in the hands of the Liberals. In a minimum amount of time, Guy Verhofstadt, VLD President, put together a cabinet of Liberals, Socialists and Greens.[7]

After four years in opposition, the *Christen-Democratisch en Vlaams* (CD&V) as the Flemish Christian Democrats were now called, was unable to stop its electoral decline. They lost another 1.4% (one seat out of 150) at the federal elections of 2003. The *Centre Démocrate Humaniste* (CDH) as the French-speaking Christian Democrats were now called, even lost two seats. The Liberals and Socialists strengthened their positions whereas the Greens suffered the worst electoral result since they had first entered the Federal Parliament. Consequently, Guy Verhofstadt continued to be Prime Minister of a cabinet of Liberals and Socialists. The Christian Democrats prepared themselves for another legislature in opposition.

Policy versus programme

The Maastricht Treaty and in particular its budgetary requirements dominated the political debate in many Western European countries during the 1990s. Maastricht established a number of criteria that the member states of the European Union (EU) would have to meet in order to enter into the Economic and Monetary Union (EMU). This was also the case in Belgium. Between 1992 and 1999, Jean-Luc Dehaene headed two consecutive cabinets of Christian Democrats and Socialists. His prime target was to have Belgium enter the EMU. With a 6.7% budget deficit in 1991 and a debt rate that had risen to 130%, the need for serious cost savings was obvious. Apart from Maastricht, state reform was also high on the political agenda in the first half of the 1990s. After 1999, however, party programmes and not government policies were at the centre of the political debate within the Christian Democratic parties in Belgium.

7   It would later become known that the Wallonian Socialists and Liberals had already sealed a
     coalition agreement in the summer of 1997.

The Flemish Christian Democrats

In September 1992, an agreement was reached between the Christian-Democrats, Socialists and Greens concerning the state reforms that would transform Belgium into a fully-fledged federal state. The major institutional reforms were the introduction of directly elected regional parliaments, reform of the federal parliament and the transfer of a large number of policy competences and financial means to the regions. The agreement temporarily cooled down tensions between the Flemish and the Wallonian parties so the federal government could fully concentrate on the pending economic and budgetary problems.

The agreement on state reform enabled Prime Minister Dehaene to reinforce his position within the CVP since the party had only reluctantly approved his coalition with the Socialists. After the European Council of Corfu in June 1994 where he narrowly failed to become President of the European Commission because of a British veto, he really became the undisputed leader of the CVP. This increased the party's self-confidence so the trauma of the 1991 defeat could be forgotten. Consequently, the CVP put Dehaene at the centre of its electoral campaign and presented itself as a genuine government party that offered stability and security. At the 1995 federal and regional elections, the CVP's share of the vote increased slightly. This marked the start of the second Dehaene-led government of Christian Democrats and Socialists.

In the aftermath of the 1991 defeat, the new party president Johan Van Hecke initiated a renewal of the CVP that entailed a new manifesto of fundamental principles, the direct election of the president, the principle of open local executives (every member who had signed a declaration of commitment could become a member of the local executive) and the renunciation of the influence of social organisations, the so-called *standen* (professional interest groups). However, after some time the momentum of change was lost because of the positive governmental record. The image of a genuine government party, personified by Dehaene, eclipsed party renewal. Following the successful 1995 elections, the plans for renewal were shelved. In addition, they were hampered by a number of other factors: the Agusta and Dassault bribery affair in 1995 (which affected the Flemish and the Wallonian Socialist coalition parties), the unexpected resignation of Van Hecke in June 1996 (for private reasons) and the Dutroux pedophilia scandal that erupted in

1996.[8] The Dutroux scandal caused a state of shock in the entire country. In the so-called *Witte Mars/Marche Blanche* (White March) 300,000 people protested in Brussels and voiced their indignation. Prime Minister Dehaene was at pains to keep the tensions under control. The fact that the public voiced emotional indignation rather than making material demands made it very hard for the government to strike the right chord. Stefaan De Clerck, the Flemish Christian Democrat and Minister of Justice at the time of the Dutroux scandal, partially succeeded in dissipating the mistrust in the judiciary system. However, when Dutroux managed to escape (though only for a couple of hours) in April 1998, De Clerck resigned as Minister of Justice. Paradoxically, his resignation made him even more popular as was later shown by his personal success in the 1999 federal elections.

The fact that government policy, especially with regard to the EMU, prevailed over the party programme, was clearly shown during the party congress of June 1998. Two important decisions were taken: the abolition of the fiscal discrimination of married couples by 2002 and the establishment of a legal framework for *werknemersparticipatie* (employees' shareholding). Abolishing the fiscal discrimination would cost 1.5 to 2 billion EUR, money that was not available if Belgium wanted to comply with the standards imposed by the Maastricht Treaty. Consequently, Prime Minister Dehaene and Herman Van Rompuy, former CVP President and Minister of the Budget, slammed on the brakes and tempered the ambitions of the congress. They agreed that the fiscal discrimination should be abolished, but also insisted that Belgium should first strive to enter the EMU at all costs. The confrontation between the 'administrators' (policy) and the 'innovators' (programme) was finally won by the former, although the party congress was originally intended to flesh out the party's plans for renewal.

8   The investigation into the murder of a former Wallonian Socialist Party President and Minister led to the Agusta and Dassault scandal. At the end of the 1980s a number of Socialist Ministers had accepted bribes for distributing contracts for the Belgian army. In the Dutroux scandal, a number of people were arrested for the kidnapping of at least six girls and the murder of at least four girls. In the particularly tense atmosphere generated by this affair, a Wallonian Socialist Minister was falsely accused of paedophilia. A parliamentary enquiry committee was set up to investigate the failure of 'the Belgian system'. The escape of Dutroux finally triggered an overall reform of the police and judicial system which was supported by the Christian Democrats, the Socialists, the Liberals and the VU. This prevented the Dutroux scandal from becoming an electoral issue in 1999.

After Belgium had entered the EMU on 1 January 1999, the CVP became very self-confident and even believed they could win the forthcoming elections of June 1999. However, the so-called dioxin crisis caused consternation.[9] The CVP campaign that had been premised on a positive economic climate and the reliable leadership of Dehaene now fell to pieces. Eventually Dehaene withdrew from the campaign and tried to get the crisis under control but an electoral defeat could not be avoided. Dehaene immediately assumed all responsibility and withdrew as the figurehead of the Flemish Christian Democrats. The party president, Marc Van Peel, also resigned. Soon after the elections coalition governments were formed at the federal and the regional levels, which excluded Christian Democrats.[10] The former Minister of Justice De Clerck was elected to be the new party president. Immediately after the local elections of October 2000 - the CVP lost 4% overall but still largely remained the biggest party with an average of almost 27% - De Clerck finally started work on the promised renewal. In September 2001 he organised a congress in his home town of Courtrai that changed the name (CVP became CD&V), the organisation (from one based on the informal decision-making processes of a leading government party into a new structure for an opposi-tion party) and the programme of the Flemish Christian Democrats.[11] Three policy proposals caused an upheaval within the party: gay marriage, the right of non-EU immigrants to vote in local elections and confederalism. Against the wishes of the party executive, the congress approved gay marriage and confederalism. The right of non-EU-immigrants to vote in local elections was rejected, as voting rights continued to be linked to Belgian nationality.

Many Christian Democrats or affiliated groups joined the debate about the renewal of the CVP and its future strategy and policy choices. The former president Van Hecke especially wanted the party to make radical decisions. He advocated a left-of-centre course. By the end of 2000, he had already formed a pressure group within the CVP called *Christen-Democratische*

---

9   Two weeks before the elections, the VLD announced that chickens had been contaminated with dioxin on a number of farms. The media painted a picture of mounds of poisoned food and suggested that the government had tried to cover up the whole affair. Although two ministers resigned, the outgoing government lacked the time and the serene political atmos-phere to deal with the sudden crisis. Solutions could not be provided before the elections.

10   The regional government of Brussels was the only exception. Support from the Flemish Christian Democrats was needed in order to ban the *Vlaams Blok* from executive power.

11   The most important change was the establishment of a *Directiecomité* (Executive Board) that included the party president, the leaders of the parliamentary party groups, the secretary general and the director of internal affairs. This body replaced the informal structure of Federal prime minister, Federal deputy prime minister, Flemish regional prime minister and party president that had led the CVP until 1999.

Vernieuwing (Christian Democratic Renewal). However, for many Christian Democrats he did not stimulate but undermined the delicate transition process. Barely a month after the 2001 congress, Van Hecke and a number of other Christian Democrats announced that they wanted the Liberals and Christian Democrats to merge into one wide-ranging people's party. President De Clerck forced Van Hecke to leave the party. Van Hecke immediately founded a new party, *Nieuwe Christen-Democratie* (New Christian Democracy), which explicitly intended to merge with the VLD. This finally happened in 2002.

It remained difficult however for the reconstituted CD&V to change into an opposition party. The Christian Democrats were unable to capitalise on the economic recession and the regular disagreements within the governments of Liberals, Socialists and Greens. Even the introduction of a new socio-economic programme, adopted at the 2002 party congress in Antwerp, could not alter this situation and was hardly referred to during the 2003 campaign. The party's profile was rather ambiguous as it was concentrated on both Dehaene's and De Clerck's records, representing respectively the old CVP policy and the new CD&V programme. Consequently, the Christian Democrats lost the 2003 federal elections, although only slightly (but not sufficiently to change the downward trend). De Clerck stepped down as party president and was replaced by Yves Leterme who was then leader of the party group in the Chamber of Deputies and had got a relatively good electoral result.

The French-speaking Christian Democrats

In contrast to the CVP, the early 1990s were relatively calm for the PSC. Their defeat in 1991 was not a major one and the leadership of president Gérard Deprez was not really questioned. The PSC lived in the shadow of the CVP, and despite being only the third largest party, they remained assured of governmental participation thanks to their close connection with the CVP. Deprez, who became the party's president as early as 1982, was re-elected in 1991 (being the only candidate). The continuation of his presidency reconfirmed the party's stability.[12] From 1994 onwards, however, this came to an end.

---

12   See about the PSC's presidency S. Fiers, *Partijvoorzitters in België of 'le parti, c'est moi'*, Leuven, 1998.

In 1994 Deprez was re-elected as president with only 51.1% of the vote, a result that clearly illustrated the fact that he was no longer the party's undisputed leader. At the 1995 congress celebrating the 50th anniversary of the PSC's foundation, Deprez surprisingly announced that he wanted to make an early exit as president of the PSC. He nominated Political Secretary Joëlle Milquet as his successor. It was the start of great discord within the PSC. Charles-Ferdinand Nothomb, former party president, minister and chairman of the Chamber of Deputies, also put himself forward as a candidate with the support of a number of senior party officials. The party members now had the choice - at least, that is how they perceived it - between a process of renewal under Milquet's guidance or a return to the good old days with Nothomb. Nothomb was finally elected, beating Milquet by 23 votes out of a total 30,941. Deprez in particular was disappointed by Nothomb's election and soon came to play a leading role in the party's internal opposition. At the same time, Nothomb failed to reunite the party. For instance, by ostentatiously moving Milquet aside inside the party and by vetoing her as chairwoman of the party group in the Senate, Nothomb did not resolve the internal crisis of the PSC but rather created more chaos and discontent.

Nothomb started secret but informal talks with the PRL, directed towards the establishment of a broad right-of-centre confederation between Liberals and Christian Democrats. As these conversations were leaked to the press, the PSC's left wing heavily criticised the idea of an alliance and managed to quash any further efforts. This put Nothomb's leadership in jeopardy as the idea of an alliance with the PRL had never been formally discussed within the party. An emergency conclave of some twenty senior party officials discussed the whole issue, decided not to join the PRL but re-affirmed Nothomb as party president. Nothomb's opponent, Deprez strongly supported the idea of a confederation between the PRL and the PSC and publicly announced that he too had been talking with the PRL for some time (but without Nothomb's knowledge). According as Deprez went ahead with the Liberals, he gradually lost support, for instance from Milquet, and was finally removed from the party.

However, this outcome did not reinforce Nothomb's position. At another party'conclave in early 1998, he announced his early resignation. A consensus was then reached to put forward Philippe Maystadt, then Deputy Prime Minister and Minister of Finance, as his successor. Maystadt, who preferred to remain in government, eventually agreed under pressure from Prime Minister Dehaene. The collapse of Dehaene's sister party, which the polls had warned about, would have been a major setback for the CVP. Maystadt assumed the party's presidency until the next elections while Milquet was promised the presidency after that. In the meantime, Milquet became Vice President so the Maystadt-Milquet team campaigned for the 1999 elections. This leadership change could not completely compensate for Deprez' departure. In the summer of 1998, he obtained the support of two other members of the Chamber of Deputies, and in the autumn of 1998, he officially founded the *Mouvement des Citoyens pour le Changement* (MCC). Finally the new movement joined the PRL (and the FDF that already formed an alliance with the PRL).

After the 1999 elections, which saw the Wallonian Christian Democrats lose another two seats in the Chamber of Deputies and become smaller than ECOLO, the PSC ended up on the opposition benches. Maystadt handed over his presidency to Milquet. In contrast to the period between 1982 and 1996, which was characterised by a very stable leadership, by 1999, the PSC had now seen four presidents in four years. After the local elections of October 2000, Milquet started a process of party renewal. A new party manifesto was to be drawn up and the party was to be given a new organisational structure and a new party name. This new party manifesto called *Charte de l'humanisme démocratique* (Charter of Democratic Humanism) was adopted in June 2001 at the party congress in Liège. By virtue of its central theme, Democratic Humanism, Milquet wanted to establish a 'fourth way' beyond the classic conflict between left and right and as an alternative to the Liberals' individualism, the Socialists' collectivism and the Greens' ecologic fundamentalism. Every reference to Christianity was carefully avoided and the concept of personalism was removed from the original memorandum. The PSC wanted to liberate itself from its historical ballast and intended to do so in an ideological sense as well.

The Liège congress reinforced the party's internal cohesion, despite the criticism of (and scepticism about) abandoning the idea of a party established for and run by Christians. In May 2002 however, Milquet managed to convince the other party senior officials to change the party's name into CDH. Some people regarded this as a subtle marketing ploy, because despite the absence of a Christian reference in the name, there was still the letter 'C'. Opponents founded a new party called *Chrétiens Démocrates Francophones* (Francophone Democratic Christians). According to them, it was not the Christian references that had led to the electoral defeats, but rather the lack of those references and the resulting vague political line. They explicitly wanted to position itself as a right-of-centre party and distanced itself from the left-of-centre course taken by Milquet. Cooperation with the PRL was very likely but an electoral alliance such as that of Deprez' party was rejected.

By choosing a left-of-centre position, Milquet was convinced she could win back most of the voters the party had lost to ECOLO. This position caused some disagreement. On the one hand, Deprez' contribution in building a powerful alternative to the etatist PS met with little sympathy; on the other hand, her argument that thereby the dominance of the PS in Wallonia could be broken was shared by several national representatives. Many others feared that Milquet was driving her party towards a coalition with the Socialists and the Greens rather than trying to cooperate with the Liberals in furthering Wallonia's economic revival. Because of the dissidence many predicted the end of Christian Democracy in Wallonia. The 2003 federal elections did not confirm this thesis, despite the loss of two seats in the Chamber of Deputies. Milquet personally received a relatively high score while the CDH 'survived' and thanks to the collapse of ECOLO became the third largest party again. After the elections Milquet was reconfirmed as party president of the CDH.

Similarities and differences

A number of remarkable similarities but also differences can be noted between the Flemish and French-speaking Christian Democrats. A first similarity is the fact that the Christian Democrats' electoral strength has always been based on defending Christian ideas and interests and that the CVP and the PSC have profiled themselves as reliable government parties. This has distracted the voters' attention away from the actual party programme, especially in the case of the CVP. With every election, the CVP staked everything on cashing in on the so-called prime minister's bonus. In the 1990s, the party could effectively be reduced to the character and image of Dehaene. This was less the case in Wallonia, even though the PSC also banked on its image of reliability in government with people such as Maystadt. When this image was completely destroyed as a consequence of the 1999 dioxin crisis, both parties had to pay the price to the degree that they were associated with government policies (which means that the CVP paid a higher price than the PSC).

A second similarity can be found in the fact that two former CVP and PSC presidents both established their own (personal) Christian Democratic movements, which finally became part of the Liberal parties. Coincidentally or not, both were members of the European Parliament and referred to the European People's Party (EPP) as the prime example of a reallocation of Christian Democrats, Liberals and Conservatives in one powerful political party. Nevertheless, there is also an important difference. Deprez wanted a rightist alliance with the Liberals in order to counter the Socialists' dominace in Wallonia whereas Van Hecke favoured a leftist course, although he ended up with the Liberals as well.

A third similarity is the fact that after the 1999 elections, both parties had new presidents who started a parallel (but not coordinated) process of party renewal. Both had to deal with much internal (and external) opposition, including the dissidence of former presidents, and faced many attacks on their leadership. Both however managed to change their parties' names, organisation and programmes. Neither succeeded in winning the 2003 elections although both secured the Christian Democrats' position in the Belgian political landscape. Whereas Milquet continued to be president, De Clerck resigned and was replaced by Leterme.

The first difference between the evolution of the CVP and the PSC is a result of the asymmetrical political landscape in Belgium and the relative weight of the *familles politique* therein. The immediate competitor of the Flemish Christian Democrats has been the VLD whereas the French-speaking Christian Democrats have mostly been challenged by ECOLO. During the 1990s, the CVP lost most voters - mainly from its right wing - to the Liberals. The PSC lost most of its voters - from its left wing - to the Greens. These respective situations have influenced the political strategy of the CVP and the PSC and emphasised the divergence between the two Christian Democratic parties.

A second significant difference is the fact that the CVP chose to keep the reference to Christianity in its new party name whereas the linkages with traditional Christian organisations, particularly the Christian Labour Movement, have gradually been loosened. The PSC dropped the term 'Christian' but made many efforts, especially since Milquet became president, to (re)established close(r) ties with (religiously inspired) civil society.

A third point of difference has been the extent to which both parties have developed 'regionalism' in their political programmes. Traditionally, the CVP was more regionalist than the PSC which had always to a certain degree defended Belgian interests. These different attitudes strengthened after 1999. Both parties were now in opposition so there was no longer any need to mitigate their policy preferences with regard to each other or other coalition parties. This evolution was clearly illustrated by the parties' positions during the fifth state reform process, the so-called *Lambermont/Saint-Polycarpe* Agreements of 2000-2001.[13] Whereas the PSC was in favour of this new agreement not because it further weakened the federal institutions and competences but because it was very beneficial for French-speaking education, the CVP opposed it because it did not adequately strengthen Flemish institutions and competences and because the French-speaking Community gained most (financial) advantages in the short and the long run.

Ideological changes

With regard to political ideology, one can also list some remarkable similarities and differences between the Flemish and the French-speaking Christian Democrats. First of all, Flanders and Wallonia have a different political environment and therefore different political dynamics. Flemish political parties have to deal with the *Vlaams Blok* which makes it difficult to discuss problems like migration, security, etc. because nobody wants to be accused of being aligned with the extreme right. In Wallonia, the left-right polarisation is growing. The Liberals have taken over the role of the Christian Democrats as the non-Socialist centre party, while the Socialists and the Greens cooperate with (a part of) the Christian Labour Movement in a left-wing block, explicity inviting the progressive Christian Democrats to join them in this effort. In this way, the rightist wing is pulled toward the Liberals whereas the leftists are drawn to an alliance with the Socialists and the Greens.

The Christian Democratic party, which since the Second World War has presented itself a 'people's party', seeks to promote mutual consultation between employers and employees in socio-economic matters. As an alternative to Socialist collectivism and Liberal individualism, the CVP/PSC stood for a 'third way': the path of a guided market economy, providing profitability for businesses in exchange for social redistribution. From 1999 onwards, the

---

13   The term *Lambermont* was used in the Flemish press and refers to the prime minister's residence in Brussels where negotiations took place; the term *Saint-Polycarpe* was used in the francophone press and refers to the date of the final agreement (similar to the Saint Michael Agreements a decade before). The fifth state reform enlarged the competences and the fiscal autonomy of the three Regions (Flanders, Wallonia and Brussels), consolidated the budget of the French-speaking Community and changed the institutions of the Brussels' Region and the statute of the German-speaking Community.

government, which did not include Christian Democrats, implicitly applied these principles so it was extremely difficult for the Christian Democrats to attack the government's policy. Ideologically speaking, they had very few arguments against the reconciliation of a free market economy (Liberalism) with a system of social redistribution (Socialism).

However, Christian Democrats still tried to distinguish themselves from Liberals and Socialists in the way they attributed more importance to the role of civil society, particularly in the areas of education and social service. Whereas the government considered them to be an integral part of the state, Christian Democrats emphasised the autonomy of the (mostly Catholic) schools, hospitals, etc. This was a hazardous undertaking for the Christian Democrats. In criticising the lack of respect for the autonomy of civil society, they sometimes relapsed into their old habits of solely defending Catholic interests. Even though the Christian Democrats proclaimed the intrinsic value of civil society, they still found it hard to present themselves as the party both for the Catholic and non-Catholic civil society organisations.[14]

In the area of ethics the Christian Democrats also kept a distance from the government. Whereas the Christian Democrats had great reservations about giving individuals complete self-determination, the Socialists and Liberals agreed on the legalisation of (a number of cases of) euthanasia in 2002 and gay marriage in 2003. In general, every Christian tenet was relegated to the realm of private life and stripped of its communal dimension. Ideologically speaking, the Christian Democrats' position was close to communitarianism and drew them away from libertarian Liberalism.[15] Christian Democrats tried to put off criticism that they were old-fashioned, conservative and resistant to societal developments by submitting their own proposals or even supporting regulations in the final legislative stage after their amendments had been turned down (with regard to the gay marriage as far as CD&V is concerned).

14   While in opposition, the Christian Democrats rediscovered the values of civil society, making implicit or sometimes explicit references to the concept of 'Social Capitalism' as it became known in the 1990s and most notably represented by Putnam: R. Putnam, R. Leonardi and R. Raffaella, *Making Democracy Work. Civic Traditions in Modern Italy*, Princeton, 1993; R. Putnam, *Bowling Alone. The Collapse and Revival of American Community*, New York, 2000.
15   With regard to Tönnies' distinction between *Gemeinschaft* (community) and *Gesellschaft* (society), Dierickx considers Christian Democracy to be a *Gemeinschaft* ideology whereas Socialism and Liberalism are *Gesellschaft* ideologies: G. Dierickx, "Het middenveld en de politieke ideologieën", in: *De Gids op Maatschappelijk Gebied*, 6 (2001) 26-36; G. Geudens, "Communitarisme in het Vlaamse politieke bedrijf", in: *Christen-Democratische Verkenningen*, 10 (2002) 14-19.

Despite repeated refusals, Flemish Christian Democrats have been urged to redirect their position towards conservatism in order to regain rightist voters from the *Vlaams Blok*, especially since the VLD presented themselves as the new centre party.[16] However, there are a variety of reasons, both ideologically and strategically, why the CVP/CD&V has refrained from labelling itself as 'Conservative'. First, Christian Democrats have rejected the left-right and the progressive-conservative oppositions because its ideology (personalism) is said to be constituted beyond these distinctions. Second, if the CVP/CD&V were to opt for a conservative stance in socio-economic affairs (in favour of the employers), it would lose its wide support among employees and within the Christian Labour Movement in particular. Moreover, the essence of the CVP - a 'people's party' in its name - has always been to appeal to all social classes. Third, exit polls have revealed that the CVP only came fourth as a provider of votes for the *Vlaams Blok* (after the SPA, the VU and the VLD). Analyses of voting behaviour also showed that Catholics - the core electorate of the CVP - vote less for the *Vlaams Blok* than non-Catholics. Also in terms of ideological orientation, the average Christian Democratic supporter had a different profile compared to that of the average *Vlaams Blok* supporter. For instance, CVP voters are less in favour of the hard repression of criminals and are less politically alienated than *Vlaams Blok* voters.[17] If the Christian Democrats were to change their programme in order to attract *Vlaams Blok* voters, they fear they would lose their traditional electorate at the same time.

In Wallonia too, the PSC/CDH's position as a centre party and 'pivotal player' between Liberals and Socialists has been discussed since Deprez' movement joined the PRL-FDF and the latter claimed to be a centre party. During the 1990s, the PSC/CDH lost an important part of its left wing electorate to ECOLO, a process strongly influenced by the openness of the Christian Labour Movement towards the Greens and *vice versa*. However, Milquet's ambition to win back voters from ECOLO with a post-materialistic programme is still far from being realised. At the 2003 federal elections, ECOLO lost the votes it had previously won from the Christian Democrats to the Socialists instead of the newly CDH. As both the Liberals and the Socialists won votes, the trend towards a bipolar political landscape in Wallonia was strengthened.

---

16   W. Beke, "Over CD&V en het rechts electoraal gat", in: *De Gids op Maatschappelijk Gebied*, 9 (2001) 61-64.

17   K. Deschouwer, "De smeltende ijsschots. Religie, kerkpraktijk en stemgedrag", in: M. Swyngedouw and J. Billiet, *De kiezer heeft zijn redenen. 13 juni 1999 en de politieke opvattingen van de Vlamingen*, Leuven, 2002.

Party organisations and civil society

External depillarisation

The tradition of Sunday mass-going in Belgium has become an almost marginal phenomenon. Loyalty towards the socio-political segments of Belgian Catholicism has drastically decreased as well. A 1996 survey showed that only 36% of the members of the *Christelijke Mutualiteit/Mutualité chrétienne* (Christian healthcare insurance organisation) and 46% of the members of the *Algemeen Christelijk Vakverbond/Confédération des syndicats chrétiens* (Christian trade union) voted for the CVP. When they were asked about their political sympathies, both Greens and Socialists appeared to be attractive alternatives to the CVP.[18]

At first sight, these facts seem quite remarkable, given the fact that both the Christian trade union and the Christian health care insurance organisation (which belong to the Christian Labour Movement) saw their membership grow enormously during the last decades. Currently, the Christian trade union has more than 1,600,000 members while the Christian healthcare insurance organisation has as many as 4,500,000. When compared with the number of CVP/PSC members, the difference really becomes apparent. Today, the Belgian Christian Democrats barely have 110,000 members. This means that the CVP/PSC have lost half of their members and voters since the early 1980s. However, the rate of organisation - the ratio between the number of members and the number of voters - has remained constant at about 10%. Whereas the CVP seems to have dropped to its sociological minimum, the organisations of the Christian Labour Movement seem to have reached their sociological maximum. Insofar as the 'corporative' channel has been disconnected from the 'electoral' channel (CVP/CD&V) within the Christian pillar in Flemish society, one can speak of 'external depillarisation'.[19] Comparing the CVP with the Christian trade union, the first obtained 20% of the votes in Flanders in 1999 while the latter was able to attract 57% during the so-called social elections (of trade union representatives in private firms) in 2000.

18   J. Billiet, *De kiezers van de CVP in de jaren negentig*, Leuven, ISPO-Bulletin, 2002.
19   Depillarisation refers to the undoing of social and religious segregation or 'pillarisation', a phenomenon that has characterised Austrian, Belgian and Dutch society and politics. See for instance: A. Lijphart, "Segmented Pluralism. Ideological Cleavages and Political Cohesion in the Smaller European Democracies", in: *Comparative Politics*, 2 (1971) 141-175.

Membership of Christian Democratic parties and Christian socio-economic organisations, 1990-2000

	Farmers	Health care	Employees	SME's	CVP/ CD&V	PSC/ CDH
1990	100.0	100.0	100.0		100.0	100.0
1991	98.6	100.9	102.2		100.0	99.5
1992	96.5	101.4	105.7	100.0	96.0	105.9
1993	93.5	101.1	108.1	102.5	94.7	103.1
1994	92.4	101.6	110.3	103.9	92.2	103.7
1995	92.7	101.8	110.6	105.3	82.5	97.9
1996	91.3	102.1	111.7	107.2	88.2	96.9
1997	90.0	102.2	112.4	111.2	80.3	90.2
1998	89.6	102.7	112.9	113.8	80.6	82.9
1999	88.6	102.9	114.8	114.4	80.4	80.0
2000	87.3	102.9	116.4	115.0	78.6	67.3
Meanly annual growth	-1.3	+0.3	+1.6	+1.9	-2.1	-3.3

Internal depillarisation

The debate about the relationship between Christian civil society, especially the socio-economic interest groups, and the CVP is as old as the CVP itself (as the party was officially founded in 1945 as *standenloos*, i.e. without formal linkages to its *standen*). Unlike the situation in Wallonia, Christian civil society in Flanders and especially the Christian Labour Movement had developed close formal and informal ties with the CVP and therefore had great influence on the government's policies. During the 1990s this issue became more prominent than it had been before. Once Van Hecke had become CVP president in 1993, he wanted to change the CVP into an 'open' civil society party, which meant that the power of the traditional Christian socio-economic organisations in intra-party affairs would be downsized. This stance was heavily criticised by the Christian Labour Movement. A number of its organisations even proclaimed a complete and immediate severing of ties with the CVP and cooperation with other parties (Socialists and Greens) instead. Despite this rhetoric, the Christian Labour Movement continued to regard the CVP as its privileged political party (and supported 'its' personnel within the CVP).

Many observers expected that the Christian civil society would distance itself from the CVP once it had become an opposition party. A number of incidents seemed to confirm this expectation. A leadership change within the Christian Labour Movement eased the contacts with Socialists and Greens. Officials of the Christian Labour Movement joined the cabinets of Green ministers or stood for election for AGALEV (breaking the CVP's monopoly in this respect). The Christian Labour Movement ciriticised the CD&V's new socio-economic progamme before it was discussed at the 2002 congress in Antwerp, even though it had had the opportunity to amend it and managed to do so.[20] The Christian Labour Movement also criticised the plan to establish an alliance for the 2003 federal elections between the CD&V and the *Nieuw Vlaamse Alliantie* (NVA), one of the successors of the regionalist VU. The Christian Labour Movement feared a shift to the right because the NVA was perceived to defend the interests of employers and SME's and because the VU had always attacked the *standen* system of the CVP. CD&V however continued its negotiations with the NVA but the electoral alliance was rejected by the NVA.[21]

Despite these various incidents, a total rift between the Christian Labour Movement and the CD&V did not take place. The Christian Labour Movement still regards the CD&V as the only party with which it has 'structural' cooperation (by contrast with the mere 'case by case' cooperation with the Socialists and the Greens). For instance, after the 2003 elections, they acknowledged 57% of the CD&V representatives in the Chamber of Deputies as politicians with whom they maintained a privileged relationship. In political committees, they meet these politicians on a regular basis to review the political situation and to inform them about their contacts with the various governments' cabinets.

20   S. De Smedt, "Sociaal-economisch congres CD&V. Het roer omgooien en de boot in evenwicht houden", in: *De Gids op Maatschappelijk Gebied*, 8 (2002) 35-45.
21   However, early 2004, CD&V and NVA decided to form an electoral alliance for the 2004 European and regional elections.

Representation of Christian socio-economic organisations in the CVP/CD&V*,
1991-2003 (per cent of the total number of seats of the party group)

	Employees	Farmers	SME's	*Standenloos*
1991	45	16	21	11
1995	49	14	22	11
1999	55	17	19	9
2003	57	10	19	14

* Party Group in the Chamber of Deputies
Source: 1991 and 1995 figures: J. Smits, "De organisatie en werking van de CVP-PSC", in:
W. Dewachter (ed.), *Tussen staat en maatschappij. De christen-democratie in België tussen 1945 en 1995*, Tielt, 1995, 161; 1999 and 2003 figures: CD&V Party Group in the Chamber of Deputies.

Apart from the Christian Labour Movement, there are also organisations for SME's and for farmers who traditionally have had a close relationship with the Flemish Christian Democrats. As far as the first is concerned, the *Nationaal Christelijk Middenstandsverbond* (National Christian Organisation for the Self-Employed) officially changed its name in 2000 to the *Unie van Zelfstandige Ondernemers* (Union of Self-Employed Entrepreneurs) . The organisation wanted to be open to all (Catholic and non-Catholic) self-employed entrepreneurs in Flanders and Brussels and independently (from the Flemish Christian Democrats) bring together the interests of the self-employed, the SME's and the legal professions. In contrast to the Christian Labour Movement, it had already been loosening its ties with the CVP for some time. In some constituencies, there was still a strong link to the party whereas this link was completely absent in others. Although it emphasises its autonomy *vis-à-vis* party politics, after the 2003 elections, it acknowledged 19% of the CD&V members in the Chamber of Deputies as 'its' candidates. In fact, it continues to maintain a 'structural' relationship (through its political committees) with CD&V only.

The *Boerenbond* (Farmers' Union) did not make any statements about the party's new attitude towards socio-economic interest groups. However, when the CVP ratified a plan to implement the European nitrates directive, the Farmers' Union no longer considered the Christian Democratic Minister of Agriculture to be a privileged discussion partner and announced it would limit its relationship with the CVP to the minimum. Because of the decreasing number of farmers in Flanders, close relations with them have become less important for the Christian Democrats. In this way, the Farmers' Union established closer contacts with the VLD once the Christian Democrats were excluded from executive power. However, their privileged relationship with the Christian Democrats never came into question Since the 2003 elections, the Farmer's Union's privileged representatives still account for 10% of the CD&V members in the Chamber of Deputies.

So while there is a certain trend towards 'internal depillarisation', there are still close contacts between the Christian Democrats and the main socio-economic groups. After the 1999 elections, only 9% of the CVP members in the Chamber of Deputies were labelled as 'independent' (i.e only 5 deputies in absolute numbers). Political committees in which Christian Democratic representatives regularly meet with the leadership of the socio-economic organisations continue to exist, although the party's influence has decreased significantly. From the other parties' point of view, the 'structural' cooperation has continued but from the Christian Democrats' point of view, it has become more 'individualised'.[22] For instance, during his prime ministership, Dehaene personally initiated and organised consultations with the socio-economic organisations on an informal basis. However, this trend towards 'personalised' cooperation is vulnerable as its effectiveness depends on the careers of individual politicians. When Dehaene withdrew from Belgian politics in 1999, the socio-economic organisations suddenly lost their direct contact person for federal government policies.

Cartelisation?

The gradual weakening of the relationship between the Flemish Christian Democrats and their affiliated socio-economic organisations can be interpreted as an indication of the trend towards the cartelisation of party politics.[23] By 'cartelisation' is meant the transition of a mass party towards a 'cartel party'. This transition can be characterised by, *inter alia*, the party's changing attitude towards civil society. On an electoral level as well as with regard to programmes, finances and personnel recruitment, a 'cartel party' is more autonomous *vis-à-vis* civil society in comparison with a mass party. Is this the case for the Flemish Christian Democrats?

---

22   For instance, the so-called *Agendacommissie* (agenda committee), the party's 'sanhedrin' where the leaders of the Christian Democratic socio-economic organisations met with the leadership of the Christian Democrats and that existed since the 1950s, has barely convened since the early 1990s.

23   R. Katz and P. Mair, "Changing Models of Party Organisation and Party Democracy. The Emergence of the Cartel Party", in: *Party Politics*, 1 (1995) 5-28.

Since the 1990s, the CVP/CD&V has tried to make clear that they are steering a new political course with regard to healthcare, education and socio-economic issues. In these areas particularly, Catholic organisations run Catholic hospitals and healthcare institutions, Catholic schools, Catholic trade unions, etc. The Christian Democrats no longer want to be considered merely as lobbyists for these Catholic institutions. They want to be perceived as defenders of the freedom of initiative and of all forms of civil society, Catholic and non-Catholic, as the emphasis no longer lies on the Christian element. In addition, these Catholic organisations now present themselves primarily as organisations that deliver reliable services of high quality. This image of quality and reliability was also a very important reason to vote for the CVP in the 1990s. In this way, parallel to its affiliated organisations and the services they provide, Christian Democratic politics has become "a job rather than a vocation".[24]

'Cartel parties' are also characterised by direct communication between the party and the voters, rather than by indirect communication through the party members. This trend is however not unique to the Christian Democrats as all the Flemish parties present themselves directly to the electorate through the mass media (especially television), nationwide mailings and electronic information. This is also the case with the party's finances. Following a number of scandals involving corruption and bribery, direct financing of political parties by the state has been introduced in Belgium. This has eliminated the parties' financial dependency on private firms and civil society. As for the Flemish Christian Democrats, financial support of affiliated organisations has become something of the past.

However, in a number of domains, the Flemish Christian Democrats have not evolved towards a 'cartel party' but become more of a 'mass party'. For instance, the position of the individual party members has been strengthened in the new statutes of the CD&V. Party members have a right to vote at party congresses and directly elect the party president. Although this is not an exclusive characteristic of the Christian Democrats, these new regulations further weaken the position of the Christian socio-economic groups because they were traditionally the most important mediator between the members and the party's central office (for instance in terms of recruitment). These new regulations also try to address the problem that an opposition party does not have a large number of cabinet members who are paid to campaign in the run-up to elections. As an opposition party without ministers who can personalise the party's policies, the CD&V has instead put more emphasis on

24   *Ibid.*, 23.

its programme. This is another element that does not belong among the characteristics of a 'cartel party'.

Conclusion

The prediction that the Christian Democrats would cease to exist once they were driven from power has not come true. Nevertheless, there is the pressing question of how they will position themselves in the future. Several attitudes towards this question persist. According to Deprez, there is no longer any hope of (French-speaking) Christian Democracy forming the backbone of Belgian politics. A number of senior Flemish Christian Democrats are in favour of a right-of-centre position in order to counter the ever growing *Vlaams Blok*. Others question the positioning of the CVP/CD&V and the PSC/CDH as centre parties since many European countries seem to be evolving towards a bipolar political system consisting of one major centre-right block and one major centre-left block. Officially though, the parties still favour the political centre, as evidenced by their new name and programmes.

After the electoral defeat of 1991, the CVP tried to renew itself, but this was hampered by the fact that they were the leading party in a coalition government based on compromises with other parties. For renewal to happen, attention had to be focused on the political programme and ideology. However, the programme, which was geared towards government participation, tried to avoid renewal as much as possible because this could have led to difficulties with the coalition partners. At the same time the party tried to convince its voters with the record of its policies, embodied by its prime ministers and ministers, and not merely with its programme. The PSC was less traumatised after 1991 so the call for renewal was less vociferous. Everything remained stable until 1996 when an enduring leadership crisis severely harmed the party's position. The PSC now had to fight for its own survival, whereas the CVP tried to remain the biggest party in Flanders.

In 1999, both the CVP and the PSC ended up in the opposition. Nothing could stand in the way of renewal now, but it soon became apparent that being in opposition and renewal were not necessarily compatible either. Its organisations were not prepared, the possibilities of creating new figureheads were limited, and it had lost the reputation for reliability and quality in public policy that had been one of its most important attractions for potential voters. After the local elections of 2000, the CVP and the PSC each finally started a process of change with regard to organisation, name, programme, personnel and strategy. Despite the different political landscapes in which they both had to operate and their growing mutual indifference, the processes they adopted showed a remarkable parallelism. In this way, the relationship between the Flemish and the French-speaking Christian Democrats can be characterised as 'living apart together'.

Since secularisation and de-pillarisation were said to have been among the main causes of the electoral decline, both the CD&V and the CDH tried to attract new (non-Catholic) voters. The French-speaking Christian Democrats removed the Christian reference in the party's name and drew up a new programme based on secularised 'Democratic Humanism'. The Flemish Christian Democrats have consciously chosen not to do so. They still refer to Christianity and Christian values in particular. At the same time, personalism has been replaced by communitarianism. However, both parties claim to be a party of values offering an alternative to the growing individualism and libertarianism in Belgian politics and society. Moreover, they are convinced that this strategy will be succesful as society is said to be evolving towards an increased sensitivity to common values, individual obligations and social responsibilities. A recent survey has confirmed a 'revival', albeit slight, of ethical sensitivity with regard to citizens' duties, family life, etc.[25] The fact that only a small share of the electorate chose the political programme as the main reason to vote for the Christian Democrats remains a weakness. The crucial question therefore is whether political programmes will have a greater impact in future elections and will bring back success to Belgian Christian Democracy.

---

25   M. Elchardus, J.M. Chaumont and S. Lauwers, "Morele onzekerheid en nieuwe degelijkheid", in: K. Dobbelaere, M. Elchardus, J. Kerkhofs, L. Voyé and B. Bawin-Legros (eds.), *Verloren zekerheid. De Belgen en hun waarden, overtuigingen en houdingen*, Tielt, 2000, 153-192.

Paradise Lost, Paradise Regained?
Christian Democracy in the Netherlands

Paul Lucardie

In 1989, the *Christen Democratisch Appèl* CDA (Dutch Christian Democratic Appeal Party) was the most powerful party in the Netherlands. In the parliamentary elections of that year, it had won 54 seats (out of 150), five more than its main rival, the *Partij van de Arbeid* (PvdA). With more than 120,000 members, the CDA was also by far the largest party in the country as far as membership was concerned; the PvdA had barely 97,000 members, the right-wing Liberal *Volkspartij voor Vrijheid en Democratie* (VVD) less than 70,000. Moreover, the Christian Democrats occupied a pivotal position in the party system, as the two other major parties had excluded each other as possible coalition partners since 1952. From its foundation as a party in 1980, the CDA had always provided the Prime Minister. From 1982 to 1989 its political leader Ruud Lubbers had led a government with the VVD, but when the latter broke up the coalition, he formed a coalition with the PvdA - which was only too happy to leave the opposition benches. Hence, it was almost paradise on earth for the Christian Democrats.

At the end of the 1990s, however, paradise was lost. The Christian Democrats lost 25 of their 54 seats in parliament, 40,000 of their 120,000 members, their pivotal position in the system and their popular leader. Worse, in 2001 the party was torn by a conflict between the party president and the parliamentary leader that ended in the resignation of both, leaving the party without leadership seven months before the parliamentary elections. Some observers started ringing the death-knell of Dutch Christian Democracy. Yet in May 2002 the party rose from its deathbed and won 43 seats in the elections, leaving its main rivals, the PvdA and the VVD far behind (with 22 and 23 seats respectively). Its new leader, Jan Peter Balkenende, became prime minister. Had the CDA regained paradise? It looked like it. In the elections of January 2003 it consolidated its electoral gains as well as its pivotal position.

In this chapter I will analyse the decline and recovery of the CDA from different angles: electoral ups and downs, ideological development, party organisation and party membership, and the interaction with the political environment. First of all, I would like to highlight what makes the Dutch Christian Democratic party different from its sister parties in other European countries. The CDA originated in three confessional parties: the *Anti-Revolutionaire Partij* (Anti-Revolutionary Party), which shared its leadership with the *Gereformeerde Kerken* (Calvinist Reformed Church); the *Christelijk Historische Unie* (Christian Historical Union), even more conservative in some respects, which was informally linked to the moderate orthodox centre of the *Nederlands Hervormde Kerk* (Dutch Reformed Church); and the *Katholieke Volkspartij* (Catholic People's Party), which was, of course, Catholic. These three parties held an absolute majority of seats in parliament from 1918 until 1967, whilst preferring to govern in a coalition with either the Liberals or Social Democrats. It was only in the 1970s that the three parties decided to merge into one party, the CDA. The merger was formalised in 1980.[1]

Electoral ups and downs

During the 1980s the Christian Democrats consolidated their share of seats in parliament: 48 in 1981, 45 in 1982 but 54 in 1986 and again in 1989. Thus at first sight the party appeared invulnerable to the processes of secularisation and de-pillarisation, which had begun in the 1960s and gathered speed in the 1980s. Surveys have shown that by 1991 more than half of the adult population declared no affiliation with any church. Moreover, church attendance had declined even among people who remained members of a church. Whereas almost one fifth of the population went to church every Sunday in 1980, only one tenth did so in 1991.[2] At the same time, the influence of the churches and of Catholic and Calvinist organisations in society had gradually declined since the 1960s - a process that is usually described as

1   P. Lucardie and H.-M. ten Napel, "Between Confessionalism and Liberal Conservatism. The Christian Democratic Parties of Belgium and the Netherlands", in: D. Hanley (ed.), *Christian Democracy in Europe. A Comparative Perspective*, London, 1994, 51-70; R.S. Zwart, *"Gods wil in Nederland". Christelijke ideologieën en de vorming van het CDA (1880-1980)*, Kampen, 1996; J.A. Bornewasser, *Katholieke Volkspartij (1945-1980), Deel II, Heroriëntatie en integratie (1963-1980)*, Nijmegen, 2000, 19-24. For the history of the foundation, see also H.-M. ten Napel, *"Een eigen weg". De totstandkoming van het CDA (1952-1980)*, Kampen, 1992.

2   B. Pijnenburg, "De 'C' van CDA: Een analyse van het christen-democratisch electoraat", in: K. van Kersbergen, P. Lucardie and H.-M. ten Napel (eds.), *Geloven in macht. De christendemocratie in Nederland*, Amsterdam, 1993, 117-140.

ontzuiling (depillarisation). As a consequence, the core electorate of the CDA, people attached to confessional organisations in every section of society, shrank slowly but steadily.[3]

General election results, 1981-2003

	1981	1982	1986	1989	1994	1998	2002	2003
CDA								
%	30.8	29.4	34.6	35.3	22.2	18.4	27.9	28.6
seats	48	45	54	54	34	29	43	44
Left parties*								
%	34.5	36.9	36.6	36	28.8	39.8	28	38.7
seats	53	56	55	55	44	61	42	59
Liberal parties**								
%	28.4	27.4	23.5	22.5	35.5	33.7	20.5	22
seats	43	42	36	34	55	52	31	34
Protestant parties								
%	4	4.2	3.6	4.1	4.8	5.1	4.3	3.7
seats	6	6	5	6	7	8	6	5
Other parties***								
%	2.3	2.1	1.7	2.1	8.7	3	19.3	7
seats	0	1	0	1	10	0	28	8

Total number of seats: 150
*PvdA, SP, GL or its predecessors
**D66 and VVD
***Seats of extreme right parties in 1982, 1989 and 1994 and of LN and LPF in 2002 and 2003

3   H. van der Kolk, "Het afnemende belang van godsdienst en sociale klasse", in: J. Thomassen, K. Aarts and H. van der Kolk (eds.), *Politieke veranderingen in Nederland (1971-1998)*, The Hague, 2000, 121-138.

Yet in the 1980s the decline of the core electorate was hidden from view, as it were, or compensated for, by the prime minister bonus and the popularity of Christian Democratic leaders and policies. The governments led by the pragmatic and conciliatory Catholic Lubbers weathered several crises in this period. First, they had to comply with the NATO decision on the modernisation of nuclear armaments, specifically the deployment of cruise missiles, which sparked off the largest mass demonstrations ever held in the history of the Netherlands. Second, in order to deal with rising unemployment and public deficits in the 1980s and early 1990s, they imposed cutbacks in the salaries of civil servants and in social security, which inspired almost equally intense protests. The mass protests, usually initiated by leftwing organisations, may have triggered a backlash that in the end benefited Lubbers and his party. Thus the CDA could mobilise the support not only of its core electorate, but also of the so-called cultural Christians who stayed away from church but cherished similar values; and even from voters who had left the church altogether but approved of Lubbers' policies and leadership. In 1986 and 1989, 16 or 17% of CDA voters did not belong to any church; most of them (12%) were former members, while 4 or 5% had been raised in a completely secular environment.[4] Of course, a majority of Christian Democratic voters were still members of a church: a little more than 50% were Catholic, about 30% Protestant (Dutch Reformed or Christian Reformed). At the same time, a majority of Catholic and Christian Reformed church members still lent their support to the CDA, while those of the Dutch Reformed denomination remained split between different parties, as they always had been. The declining number of churchgoing Christians in the Netherlands did not threaten the electoral position of the CDA - at least not yet.[5]

In 1989 the party had campaigned with the slogan *Laat Lubbers zijn karwei afmaken* (Let Lubbers Finish His Job) and again won 54 seats. The 'job' included reducing the public debt, reforming social security and promoting job creation. Apparently in 1993 Lubbers' job was done, as he retired and the party executive nominated a new leader, Elco Brinkman, at the time chairman of the parliamentary group. Though Lubbers had previously expressed a preference for Brinkman as his successor, he soon began to harbour doubts. Brinkman was a Protestant with neo-liberal ideas and a decisive managerial style, and was much less conciliatory than Lubbers. Shortly before the elec-

4 A. Need, "Moet het CDA verder als niet-christelijke partij?", in: *Christen-Democratische Verkenningen*, 7/8 (1998) 263-269.
5 R.N. Eisinga, *Data per datum. Profijt van regelmatig herhaalde surveys toegelicht aan de hand van electorale compositie, convergentie en cycli*, Nijmegen, 1998, 11-15.

tions in 1994, the Prime Minister announced he would not vote for Brinkman, who headed the party list, but for Ernst Hirsch Ballin, number three on the list. Brinkman himself declared later that the party leaders had insisted on an exclusively Christian party, whilst he had wanted to open the party to newcomers.[6] Whatever the exact reasons, the party was perceived as divided, and its new leader scored low on trustworthiness, competence and sympathy, especially among secular voters without strong ties to the CDA.[7] Moreover, the party was held responsible for drastic cuts in social security, especially industrial disability insurance, while future cuts were announced, possibly in old age pensions.[8] The combination of these factors - an unpopular leader, weak positions on important issues, depillarisation and secularisation - led to the most dramatic defeat in Dutch electoral history: the number of CDA seats decreased from 54 to 34.[9] The Christian Democrats managed to retain only their core electorate of older, less-educated, churchgoing Christians. Even in its regional strongholds in the Catholic South and the Calvinist East, the CDA lost almost 40% of its electorate. Younger, better-educated and more secular supporters switched in large numbers to the two liberal parties. The conservative and somewhat populist VVD won over 13% and the radical or leftwing-liberal *Democraten 66* (D66) 9% of all former CDA voters. Some older voters preferred the new senior citizens' parties, which attracted 3% of all former CDA voters.[10]

In spite of this electoral defeat, the CDA might have retained its pivotal position in the party system and in the government, if it had closed ranks behind

6   *Trouw*, 26 April 2000; M. Metze, *De stranding. Het CDA van hoogtepunt naar catastrofe*, Nijmegen, 1995; B. Steinmetz, *Ruud Lubbers. Peetvader van het poldermodel*, Amsterdam, 2000, 201-213.

7   H. Anker, "Kiezers, politici en partijkeuze", in: J.J.M. van Holsteyn and B. Niemöller (eds.), *De Nederlandse kiezer 1994*, Leiden, 1995, 205-222.

8   These social cuts - more exactly, freezing the general old-age pensions - were proposed in the draft election manifest but cancelled under pressure from senior citizen organisations. However, in the perception of many voters this did not improve the party's trustworthiness. See M.Metze, *De stranding. Het CDA van hoogtepunt naar catastrofe*, 207-210, 216-220; G. Irwin, "Tussen de verkiezingen", in: J.J.M. van Holsteyn and B. Niemöller (eds.), *De Nederlandse kiezer 1994*, 10-13.

9   According to Andeweg, the alienation of secular voters (who had voted for Lubbers and his policies in 1986 and 1989) explained 7% of the loss whereas depillarisation and secularisation explained 4% and 2% respectively: R. Andeweg, "Afscheid van de verzuiling", in: J.M. van Holsteyn and B. Niemöller (eds.), *De Nederlandse kiezer 1994*, 122-123.

10 CBS, *Statistiek der verkiezingen. 1994*, Voorburg/Heerlen, 1994, 15. In 1989 the CDA attracted more than 40% of the vote in the provinces of Limburg, Northern Brabant and Overijssel, whereas it retained less than 30% in 1994. In the more secular northern provinces of Northern Holland, Groningen and Drenthe its share dropped from about 25% to less than 20%. CBS, *Nationaal kiezersonderzoek 1989-1994*, Voorburg/Heerlen, 1995, 15.

its leader and pursued a clever strategy of divide and rule, as it had done in the past. However, its traditional coalition partners, the PvdA and the VVD, which had been arch-enemies in the 1960s and 1970s, had already started informal talks before the elections. The ideological distance between them had lessened, mainly because the PvdA had shifted towards the centre and dropped most of its socialist ideas. Moreover, traditional class conflicts had lost much of their political vigour and significance. As a result, Christian Democracy may have lost its historic function as mediator between Capital and Labour, as Van Kersbergen has argued.[11]

So it may be due to structural as well as conjectural factors that in 1994 the CDA lost not only almost half of its seats in parliament but also all of its seats in the government. The Christian Democrats had to lead the opposition against the so-called purple coalition of PvdA, VVD and D66.[12] This was a new experience as the Christian Democrats or their predecessors had been in government since 1918. Opposition proved difficult, especially against the socio-economic policy of the purple coalition, which did not differ significantly from what the Christian Democrats had always advocated: moderate cutbacks, deficit reduction and modest job-creation programmes.
An economic boom contributed to the government's popularity. Only in the area of socio-cultural policies and ethical issues did the CDA have the political means of fighting the secular coalition: the observance of Sunday closing as opposed to the liberalisation of shopping hours; the prosecution as opposed to tolerance of drug use and the prohibition instead of (partial) legalisation of euthanasia.

The opposition proved insufficient. In the 1998 elections the CDA suffered another defeat, losing five seats and its position as the second-largest party in parliament (which the VVD took over, winning 38 seats). The party again lost younger and urban voters - mainly to the PvdA and VVD - in spite of its serious attempt to renew and rejuvenate its list of candidates. Even in (former) strongholds like Overijssel, Limburg and Northern Brabant, only one in four voters expressed support for the CDA. Support remained fairly high among old-age pensioners (36%), farmers and small businessmen (24%) and

11   K. van Kersbergen, "Hopen op macht. De neergang van de Nederlandse christen-democratie in vergelijkend perspectief", in: *Jaarboek 1995 DNPP*, Groningen, 1996, 92-112;
K. Van Kersbergen, "Contemporary Christian Democracy and the Demise of the Politics of Mediation", in: H. Kitschelt et al. (eds.), *Continuity and Change in Contemporary Capitalism*, Cambridge, 1999, 346-370.
12   The government was called 'purple' because of the combination of red (socialism) and blue (liberalism).

housewives (21%), but sank to 15% or less among blue- and white-collar workers, managers and civil servants, students and the unemployed.[13] Its core electorate of churchgoing voters had shrunk further between 1994 and 1998.[14] Moreover, the Christian Democrats lacked issues they could clearly 'own' and that were considered important by the voters. The elections had been dominated by the leaders of the PvdA and VVD. Curiously, both leaders fought each other fiercely, especially in the area of social policies and immigration, despite their clear preference for another purple coalition without the Christian Democrats.

Frequent changes of leadership - three in four years - proved to be another handicap for the CDA in an election campaign that was highly personalised in the media.[15] Brinkman had already resigned as parliamentary leader in 1994; his successor Enneus Heerma - wary of the growing criticism from within his own party - stepped down in 1997 and was replaced by Jaap de Hoop Scheffer. The latter was a Catholic diplomat, more easygoing than his Protestant predecessors, but not yet well-known among the voters in 1998.[16] In 2001 he also resigned as party leader, after a clash with the party president over the list of candidates for the next parliamentary elections. He was succeeded by Balkenende, a Protestant professor of Christian Social Thought at the Free University of Amsterdam who had been elected to parliament only in 1998 but had worked before that as a policy consultant in the party's research institute.

This change of leadership happened only eight months before the elections of May 2002. With a relatively unknown leader, the Christian Democrats did not really look forward to these elections, even though elections for the provincial parliaments and the European Parliament in 1999 had shown an upward trend for the party. Economic prosperity seemed to favour the purple coalition. At the same time, the latter did not seem to have proper control over issues like crime, insecurity and immigration. Yet even here the CDA's

---

13   CBS, *Statistiek der verkiezingen. 1998*, Voorburg/Heerlen, 1999, 16;
      <www.statline.cbs.nl/statweb> (10 July 2003).
14   H. van der Kolk, "Het afnemend belang van godsdienst en sociale klasse", in: J. Thomassen,
      K. Aarts and H. van der Kolk (eds.), *Politieke veranderingen in Nederland (1971-1998)*, 131.
15   J. de Vries and J.W. Wiggers, "Je kunt een plantje niet aan zijn blaadjes de grond uittrekken.
      Een blik op de CDA-campagne", in: P. Kramer, T. van der Maas and L. Ornstein (eds.), *Stemmen in
      stromenland. De verkiezingen van 1998 nader bekeken*, The Hague, 1998, 29-37.
16   De Hoop Scheffer was Minister for Foreign Affairs in the first and second governments led by
      Balkenende until he became NATO Secretary General in January 2004.

opposition looked pale in comparison with the fiery attacks on the government by a new opposition party founded by Pim Fortuyn.

Fortuyn had been a sociology professor and a member of the PvdA, but left this party in 1989 and acquired a reputation as an independent critic of the purple coalition. He had entered politics in 2001 to head the list of *Leefbaar Nederland (*LN), a moderate populist party. In February 2002 he was forced to step down because of his statements about Islam ("a backward religion") and his call for a repeal of the first article of the constitution (that forbids discrimination) in order to enhance freedom of speech. Hence he decided to present his own list of candidates, the *Lijst Pim Fortuyn* (LPF) at the elections in May 2002. He was assassinated nine days before the election, yet his list won 17% of the vote and 26 seats.[17]

Unlike other party leaders, Balkenende had avoided personal criticism of the charismatic and flamboyant Fortuyn and agreed with much of Fortuyn's critics of the purple coalition and the so-called multicultural society. However, he rejected Fortuyn's drastic solutions (e.g. closing the Dutch borders) and argued for more moderate reforms instead. His campaign was nearly flawless. Even so, the party leadership and its senior officials were pleasantly surprised by the results of the 2002 general elections. With 28% of the popular vote and 43 seats the Christian Democrats had again become the largest party in the *tweede Kamer* (second chamber of the national parliament). Surveys and exit polls suggested they had regained not only their former supporters but also had attracted quite a few secular voters who were dissatisfied with the purple coalition but distrusted the new populist party of Fortuyn.

As a consequence, Balkenende formed a coalition government with the VVD and the LPF. It collapsed within three months, mainly due to internal squabbles within the LPF, which lacked not only a coherent ideology and a formal party organisation, but also - following Fortuyn's assassination on 6 May 2002 - a political leader. At the snap elections held in January 2003, the LPF lost more than two thirds of its electorate, whereas the CDA did even better than in 2002: 44 seats and 29% of the vote. The Christian Democrats had focused

---

17   F. Obbema and P. van Praag, "Moord op Fortuyn versterkte trends onder kiezers", in: *De Volks-krant,* 16 May 2002. According to exit polls, 13% of all secular voters and 29% of Muslims and Hindus voted CDA in 2002. See also J.J.M. van Holsteyn and G.A. Irwin, "Never a Dull Moment. Pim Fortuyn and the Dutch Parliamentary Election of 2002", in: *West European Politics*, 2 (2003) 48-49; D. van Eijk, "Kiezers vooral ontevreden met het politieke aanbod", in: *NRC Handelsblad*, 16 May 2002.

their campaign on their leader with the slogan *Betrokken, Betrouwbaar, Balkenende* (Committed, Reliable, Balkenende). Balkenende may have benefited from the prime minister bonus and won over quite a few former Fortuyn voters (14% of them).[18] Yet though relatively young, Balkenende attracted mainly the elderly: exit polls indicated that more than half of his voters were 50 years or older.[19]

Provincial elections, held in March 2003, confirmed the upward trend of the Christian Democrats. With 28% of the vote they remained the largest party in the country. As a result, the CDA won three more seats in the *Eerste Kamer* (first chamber of the national parliament), which is indirectly elected by the members of the provincial parliaments. Thus the coalition forged by Balkenende in May 2003, consisting of CDA, VVD and D66, enjoyed a solid majority in both houses of parliament. Despite this majority, the government led by the Christian Democrats faces difficult times: economic conditions have been deteriorating, feelings of insecurity and discontent remain widespread and their most faithful voters continue to age and die.

Ideological renewal or rapprochement with Conservatism?

The ideology of the Christian Democratic party in the Netherlands resembles that of its two Belgian sister parties - not very surprising, given the close contacts between them. Yet there are differences, owing to the impact of the Calvinist parties. Following intensive debates in the 1970s between (and within) the three merging parties, it was decided that the party programme would not be based on the Bible directly, as many Calvinists would have preferred, but only indirectly. The political conviction or ideology of the CDA was considered to be "the answer to the appeal made by the Bible".[20] In the programme adopted in 1980 and renewed in 1993, four main principles were elaborated: public justice, differentiated responsibility, solidarity and stewardship.[21]

---

18   P. van Praag, "The Winners and Losers in a Turbulent Political Year", in: *Acta Politica*, 1 (2003) 20.
19   According to exit polls of Interview/NSS. See also D. van Eijk, "De jeugd heeft de toekomst, het CDA de ouderen", in: *NRC Handelsblad*, 23 January 2003.
20   See the original Dutch version: "In antwoord op de oproep van de Bijbel krijgt de politieke overtuiging van het CDA gestalte" in: CDA, *Program van Uitgangspunten*, The Hague, 1993, 17. For the debate, see H.-M. ten Napel, "Een eigen weg", 303-305, 344-353.
21   CDA, *Program van Uitgangspunten*, The Hague, 1980.

Public justice represents the application of the biblical conception of justice to politics. All political action, and especially all government action should satisfy this criterion. However, the exact meaning of the notion should be defined depending on the circumstances of time and place.[22] Thus Christian Democrats may favour an interventionist social welfare state at one point in time (for example in the 1960s and 1970s) but prefer a more passive (liberal) state at other times (in the 1980s). This pragmatic or relativist conception distinguishes them from Liberals or Socialists.

Yet there are limits to this relativism: Christian Democrats will never accept a minimal or a collectivist state. The state should always respect the autonomy and responsibility of other sections of society - called *kringen* (circles) in the tradition of Dutch Calvinist thought - like the family, science and education or economic production. This principle, referred to as 'sovereignty in one's own circle' by Dutch Calvinists, was redefined in the 1970s as *gespreide verant-woordelijkheid* (differentiated responsibility). It resembles the Catholic principle of subsidiarity, but lacks the hierarchical implications of the latter.[23] The principle of differentiated responsibility implies respect for institutions that mediate between citizens and the state. Dutch Christian Democrats share this respect with Conservatives, but differ from the latter in their emphasis on a more or less equal distribution of responsibilities. Even so, they share the Conservative aversion to democracy in a radical or direct sense, for example when it comes to referendums.[24]

Christian Democrats, as well as Conservatives, usually conceive of society as an organic unity. They prefer society to be a *Gemeinschaft* (community) rather than a mere *Gesellschaft* (society), although they do not go as far as nationalists or ecologists.[25] Thus the principle of solidarity implies more than social security for the needy. It also implies a 'social-personalist' view of the individual: in order to develop herself (or himself), a person needs social relationships, relatives, neighbours and friends. Social personalism reconciles or

---

22 Wetenschappelijk Instituut voor het CDA, *Publieke gerechtigheid. Een christen-democratische visie op de rol van de overheid*, Houten, 1990, 116.

23 *Ibid.*, 133-135.

24 The CDA has consistently voted against any proposal to introduce a referendum in the Netherlands, even if some of its members disagreed. See A.P.M. Lucardie, "Vox populi of vox diaboli? Het debat over het referendum in de Nederlandse politieke partijen", in: *Jaarboek 1996 DNPP*, Groningen, 1997, 109-128. In 1999 a constitutional amendment in favour of a referendum became stranded in the first chamber because of opposition from the CDA, Protestant parties and one VVD dissident.

25 G. Dierickx, "Christian Democracy and Its Ideological Rivals", in: D. Hanley (ed.), *Christian Democracy in Europe. A Comparative Perspective*, London, 1994, 15-30.

transcends both collectivism and individualism. During the 1980s the CDA tended to emphasise the dangers of collectivism and to favour privatisation and competitiveness, but in the 1990s it began to worry more about individualism and to oppose economic liberalism. Actually, it adopted the term 'social personalism' in its party programme only in 1993 - about one decade after the Belgian Christian Democrats, although the latter have also been inspired by the CDA as far as political ideology is concerned.[26]

Personalism also has a religious dimension: a person is not a self-sufficient entity, she (or he) depends not only on social relationships but also on God. Human beings are God's stewards on earth. Thus, they may reap the fruits of the earth but should refrain from destroying or polluting God's creation. Some Christian Democrats interpret this principle of *rentmeesterschap* (stewardship) in a radical ecological, even ecocentric sense, but as a party the CDA has always refused to choose between economic growth and protection of the environment.[27]

The Christian Democrats have not substantially changed their ideology since 1980, only shifted from a critical to a more conservative perspective. In 1980 they were particularly concerned about the concentration of power in (multinational) corporations and called for the production of *maatschappelijk zinvolle producten (*socially meaningful products).[28] This critical attitude towards capitalism had practically disappeared by 1993, no doubt mainly as a result of a change in the *Zeitgeist*, particularly with the collapse of communism and the rising tide of neo-liberalism.[29] Other issues appeared on the Christian Democratic agenda. In its new party programme, the CDA paid more attention to environmental problems and ethical questions in science and health care (genetic manipulation, euthanasia), the public debt and European integration. The heavy electoral defeat in 1994 inspired renewed reflection on policy. In 1995, a committee headed by the former Catholic party leader (and finance minister) Frans Andriessen and assisted by Balkenende,

26   *Ibid.*, 22; CDA, *Program van Uitgangspunten*, 1993, 8. See also J. Alberts and K. Berkhout, "De nieuwe antithese van het CDA. Jaap de Hoop Scheffer verdedigt nu de publieke sector", in: *NRC Handelsblad*, 10 September 1999.

27   Compared to other parties, the CDA seems less 'green' than the GL, PvdA, D66 and the small Protestant parties but more than the VVD. See P. Lucardie, "Greening and Ungreening the Netherlands", in: M. Jacobs (ed.), *Greening the Millennium? The New Politics of the Environment*, Oxford, 1997, 183-191.

28   CDA, *Program van Uitgangspunten*, 1980, 8.

29   The collapse of the Soviet system was mentioned in the introduction to the new party programme as a reason for renewing the programme: CDA, *Program van Uitgangspunten*, 1993, 7.

the party's policy consultant and later Prime Minister, wrote a report with the significant title *Nieuwe wegen, vaste waarden* (New Ways, Old Values). It did not revise the party programme as such, but added a slant that one might classify as 'socially conservative' (as distinguished from neo-liberal conservatism): it was critical of liberalism - which had become increasingly dominant in this decade - and of excessive tolerance in the Netherlands, for example with respect to drugs.[30] Apart from drugs, more emphasis was also placed on issues such as security and the protection of life as well as on reducing the public debt and introducing social policies to protect the family and the poorer sections of society.

The trend towards social conservatism continued after 1995.[31] The election manifesto of 2002 also reflected this trend.[32] It called for 10,000 more policemen (thus outbidding all other parties), less tolerant drugs policies, a more restrictive refugee and immigration policy, less government intervention and more room for *maatschappelijk verantwoord ondernemen* (socially responsible entrepreneurship). Though the party leadership had firmly rejected the conservative label in the past, it was less adamant now. Prominent members (especially Catholics) like the former Prime Minister Dries Van Agt argued that "the time has come for conservatism" and joined the Edmund Burke Foundation, a think-tank founded in 2000 to spread the conservative gospel in the Netherlands.[33] In 2003 Alphons Dölle, member of the first chamber and professor of constitutional law, suggested that the tag 'social-conservative' be adopted as the CDA's sub-title in order to appeal to secular voters.[34] Others, however (especially Protestants) continued to reject Conservatism and emphasised the differences with Christian Democracy.[35] Balkenende, who was elected party leader in 2001, avoided these terms, yet his *gemeenschapsdenken* (communitarianism) does not seem to differ much from social

30   CDA, *Nieuwe wegen, vaste waarden*, The Hague, 1995, 7.
31   A. de Jong and B.J. Spruyt, "Een politieman tussen de oren. CDA-leider De Hoop Scheffer mist bij paars ethisch-moreel kader", in: *Reformatorisch Dagblad*, 26 August 2000; CDA, *Samenle-ven doe je niet alleen*, The Hague, 1998.
32   CDA, *Betrokken samenleving, betrouwbare overheid*, The Hague, 2002.
33   A.A.M. van Agt, "Hoogste tijd voor conservatisme", in: *Christen Democratische Verkenningen*, 5 (2002) 12-22.
34   A. Dölle, "CDA behoeft ondertitel 'sociaal conservatief'", in: *Christen Democratische Verkenningen*, 2 (2003) 76.
35   A.M. Oostlander, "Conservatieven vreemde eend in de EVP-bijt", in: *Christen Democratische Verkenningen*, 5 (2002) 33-38; K. Klop, "Fatsoen als vijfde kernbegrip?", in: Christen Democratische Verkenningen, 5 (2002) 27-32; A. Klink, "Conservatieven houden christen-democraten spiegel voor", in: *Christen Democratische Verkenningen*, 5 (2002) 23-26; F. Fennema, "Het CDA is geen conservatieve partij", in: *De Volkskrant*, 5 June 2002.

conservatism. Both communitarianism and social conservatism defend civil society, the 'organic' fabric of voluntary associations and traditional communities, against pressure from the market (pushed by the Liberals) and from the state (promoted by the Socialists). In a book published during the 2002 election campaign, Balkenende refers explicitly to communitarianism restoring the balance between (exaggerated) individual liberty and responsibility and emphasising common values rather than cultural diversity.[36] He rejects both the Liberal notion of a (morally neutral) minimal state and the Socialist notion of a redistributive state; above all, the state ought to maintain the legal and moral order and exercise authority. Not surprisingly, the Edmund Burke Foundation recognised Balkenende as a Conservative, even if he did not meet all its criteria - for one thing, he seemed to underestimate the need for an internal moral order, traditional virtues and self-restraint.[37]

However, whereas Conservatives lack explicit ideological principles, apart from a diachronic 'historicist' interpretation of the present and a belief in the extra-human origins of the social order, Christian Democrats refer to explicit principles - public justice, personalism, stewardship, solidarity, responsibility.[38] As a consequence, Christian Democrats can be more critical of established institutions than Conservatives - at least in theory. In practice, the fluidity and abstract nature of their principles may open the door for (some) historicist and conservative ideas. Thus one may conclude that even if the CDA has not yet turned into a (social) conservative party, it seems to be moving somewhat reluctantly in that direction.[39]

36   J.P. Balkenende, *Anders en beter. Een pleidooi voor een andere aanpak in de politiek vanuit een christen-democratische visie op de samenleving, overheid en politiek*, Soesterberg, 2002.
37   B.J. Spruyt, "Balkenende maakt debat over waarden onnodig ingewikkeld", in: *NRC Handelsblad*, 14 November 2002; M. van Houten, "De C van Conservatief", in: *Trouw*, 24 July 2003.
38   M. Freeden, *Ideologies and Political Theory*, Oxford, 1998, 332-336.
39   P. Lucardie, "De ideologie van het CDA. Een conservatief democratisch appèl?", in: K. van Kersbergen, P. Lucardie and H.-M. ten Napel (eds.), *Geloven in macht. De christen-democratie in Nederland*, Amsterdam, 1993, 39-58; P. Lucardie and H.-M. ten Napel, "Between Confessionalism and Liberal Conservatism", 67-68.

Party organisation and party membership: renewal, but no rejuvenation

While its electorate shrank rapidly in the 1990s, party membership declined slowly: from 142,000 in 1980 to 124,000 in 1990, 95,000 in 1995 and 80,000 in 2000. In 2001 it sank to 78,000, but in the election year 2002 it went up again to reach 79,000 by 2003. As the PvdA and VVD lost members at a similar rate, the CDA has remained the largest party in terms of membership. Its member/voter ratio remained (slightly over) 5%, until it fell in 2002 to 3%, paradoxically owing to the sudden electoral upsurge. Most of its funding (almost 75 % in 2000) came from membership fees, only a small part from state subsidies (16%) and donations (8%).[40] Rank-and-file members are active not only during the election campaign but also in between elections. Yet, to be involved in Christian Democratic party politics, membership is not a 'social obligation' any longer. Hence the CDA describes itself rightly as a people's party. It is not as large and tightly-knit as an ideologically integrated mass party, but not as small and elitist as a cadre party either.[41]

The party has maintained the traditional structure of local and provincial branches. At the local level, it is the largest and probably the most active party. The *afdelingen* (local branches) select their delegates to the *partijcongres* (party congress); the provincial branches send their delegates to the *partijraad* (party council). The party council elects the *partijbestuur* (party executive) and votes on the election programme, but can be overruled in certain cases by the party congress. Candidates for parliament are selected by the local branches and their preferences are collected at the national level,

40   M. van Rij, "Financiering partijen vereist controle", in: *De Volkskrant,* 9 October 2000; K.G. de Vries, *Notitie Herijking Wet subsidiëring politieke partijen,* The Hague, 2002, 8-10; R.A. Koole, "Ledenpartijen of staatspartijen? Financiën van Nederlandse politieke partijen in vergelijkend en historisch perspectief", in: *Jaarboek 1996 DNPP,* Groningen, 1997, 156-182.
41   The term 'people's party' seems more adequate than 'catch-all party', which refers to a specific strategy (catching as many voters as possible) rather than to a type of party organisation. See P. Lucardie, "From Family Father to DJ. Christian Democratic Parties and Civil Society in Western Europe" in: E. Lamberts (ed.), *Christian Democracy in the European Union (1945-1995),* Leuven, 1997, 210-221; R. Koole, "The Societal Position of Christian Democracy in the Netherlands", in: E. Lamberts (ed.), *Christian Democracy in the European Union (1945-1995),* 137-153.

though the 'advice' of the party executive is rarely ignored.[42] The central office employed about 30 people in 2002, the parliamentary party more than 70.[43]

The CDA has probably more affiliated organisations than any other Dutch party. Like most other Dutch parties it has a youth organisation (*Christen Democratisch Jongeren Appèl*), a research institute (*Wetenschappelijk Instituut voor het CDA*), a centre for political education and training (*Steenkamp Instituut*) and an association of local and provincial politicians (*Bestuurdersvereniging*).[44] Unlike most other parties it also has a women's organisation (*Vrouwenberaad*) as well as a Senior Citizens' Platform (*Ouderenplatform*). International solidarity has been promoted by the Eduardo Frei Foundation, which was established in 1990, while Christian Democratic immigrants have set up an Intercultural Council (*Intercultureel Beraad*).[45]

Party membership is open to anyone who accepts the party programme. In 1992 a Hindu joined the parliamentary party group, though not all party members approved. In 2003, two Muslims and one Hindu were elected. Even so, surveys suggest that the overwhelming majority of CDA members belong to one of the three major Christian denominations: in 1999, 45% were Catholic, 32% Christian Reformed and 20% Dutch Reformed; only 4% professed another religion or none at all. More than half of all members (54%) attended church every week, a quarter did so at least once a month and 20% seldom or never. In 1986 these figures were only slightly different as far as the denominations were concerned: 51% Catholic, 32% Christian Reformed, 15% Dutch Reformed, 2% no religion or "other". Yet church attendance was more frequent in the 1980s: more than three quarters (78%) went at least once a week. Compared with other parties, the CDA had more older and less-educated members. In 1999 more than two thirds (68%) of the members were 55 years or older (43% were 65 or over) and just over a third had completed higher education (university or college). In 1986 these numbers were somewhat lower. If this trend continues, the CDA will become a senior citizens' party in the (not very distant) future. As in other parties, not even one third of the

42   R. Hillebrand, *De antichambre van het parlement. Kandidaatstelling in Nederlandse politieke partijen*, Leiden, 1992, 32-56.
43   <www.cda.nl> (4 December 2003).
44   P. Lucardie and G. Voerman, "Party Foundations in The Netherlands", in: K.-H. Nassmacher (ed.), *Foundations for Democracy. Approaches to Comparative Political Finance*, Baden-Baden, 2000, 321-339.
45   C. van Beveren and I. Moerman, "Organisatorische vernieuwingen in het Christen-Democratisch Appèl", in: I. Hartman (ed.), *Sporen van vernieuwing. Een inventarisatie van recente organisatorische veranderingen in acht politieke partijen*, Amsterdam, 1996, 6-20.

members devoted at least an hour a month to the party, while more than two thirds were not active at all. On a left to right scale, most members placed themselves close to the centre, though slightly more often right-of-centre than left-of-centre (48 and 44% respectively; 6% placed themselves further to the right, only 2% further to the left). In 1986 a larger majority preferred the right half of the spectrum (69%).[46]

After the electoral shock of 1994, the CDA not only discussed ideology and strategy, but also tried to renew its organisation. Until 1999, however, this was a rather slow process. In 1995 younger members set up an informal network, 'Confrontation with the Future', which tried to stimulate a renewal.[47] In 1998, the parliamentary party - now reduced in size to 29 - included 14 newcomers. Marnix van Rij, elected party president in 1999, tried to speed up the process of renewal. He founded a 'Centre for Politics, Religion and Spirituality' in order to attract (more) Muslims, Hindus, perhaps even New Age people. He also promoted more involvement by members and even sympathising non-members in the decision-making processes. In a 'Competition of Ideas', members contributed about 20,000 propositions, one hundred of which were included in the final version of the 2002 election manifesto.[48] Although Van Rij resigned in 2001 following a conflict with the parliamentary leader de Hoop Scheffer, his ideas seemed to have caught on. His successor was elected by rank-and-file members in a postal vote in October 2002, after the party council had nominated two candidates in June. The party constitution had allowed this since 1996, but it had not been done before.[49] The constitution was again revised in 2003 in order to allow all members to vote at party assemblies. This had been proposed by a committee on 'Party Development' and approved by the party council in 2001. The party council and the party congress were merged into one members' assembly (*ledenvergadering*). This 'one-person-one-vote' system had been practiced by D66 since its foundation in 1966 and by the leftist green party *GroenLinks* (GL) since 2001, but not by any larger party in the Netherlands.[50]

---

46 J.J.M. van Holsteyn and R.A. Koole, "Generaties christen-democraten. Enkele bevindingen van een onderzoek onder CDA-leden", in: *Christen Democratische Verkenningen*, 2 (2000) 10-21; M.L. Zielonka-Goei and R. Hillebrand, "De achterban van parlementariërs: kiezers en partij-leden", in: *Jaarboek 1987 DNPP*, Groningen, 1988, 116-137.

47 R. Moerland and H. Staal, "Een stille revolutie. De vernieuwing van het CDA in de acht paarse jaren", in: *NRC Handelsblad*, 1 June 2002.

48 A. Krijger, "Nieuw ontwerp-verkiezingsprogramma krijgt vorm", in: *CDAKrant*, 3 (2001) 9.

49 CDA, *Statuten en huishoudelijk reglement*, The Hague, 1997, 20, 71-72.

50 In 200 GL was constituted from different small parties, inter alia the *Evangelische Volkspartij* (Evangelical People's Party).

The Christian Democrats in the Dutch party system: a provisionally pivotal position

The recent discussion on whether the CDA should be described as a conservative party is not a purely academic affair, but bears on its position in the party system now and in the future.

As mentioned above, Christian Democrats and their confessional predecessors used to hold a pivotal position in the system, occupying the centre between the Left - PvdA, D66, *Socialistische Partij* (SP), GL and its predecessors - and the Right - mainly the VVD. This socio-economic cleavage, which was dominant in Dutch politics (at least from about 1918), intersected with the secular-confessional cleavage, where the CDA almost monopolised moral and religious issues. Admittedly, on this religious level it had to compete with three Protestant parties: the *Staatkundig Gereformeerde Partij* (Political Reformed Party), the *Gereformeerd Politiek Verbond* (Reformed Political Association) and the *Reformatorische Politieke Federatie* (Reformed Political Federation). Yet these were quite small and appealed only to specific denominations. When the GPV and RPF merged in 2000 into the *ChristenUnie* (Christian Union), they lost some of their traditional voters.

The Christian Democrats maintained strong ties with large Christian organisations, like the *Christelijk Nationaal Vakverbond* (Christian Trade Union), associations of farmers, small businessmen, employers, teachers and broadcasting associations, specifically the *Katholieke Radio Omroep* (Catholic Broadcasting Association) and the *Nederlandse Christelijke Radio Vereniging* (Christian Reformed Broadcasting Association). Admittedly, the ties had become more informal and casual than in the heyday of *verzuiling* (pillarisation), but they were still significant - and mutually beneficial.[51] The organisations supported the CDA and in turn enjoyed access to the corridors of power, as the CDA was practically indispensable for any coalition government.

However, when the Christian Democrats lost power in 1994, the ties with the pressure groups and organised interests weakened. The Christian trade unions, employers, farmers and teachers did not want to alienate the purple

51   J. Woldendorp, "Christen-democratie en neo-corporatisme in Nederland. Het CDA en het maatschappelijk middenveld", in: K. van Kersbergen, P. Lucardie and H.-M. ten Napel (eds.), *Geloven in mach*, 141-161; R. Koole, "The Societal Position of Christian Democracy in the Netherlands", 137-153.

government and established regular contacts with the PvdA and (to a lesser extent) the VVD.[52] Moreover, Christian farmers' leagues, employers' and small businessmen's organisations were merging with their secular counterparts, while the Catholic and (to a much lesser extent) the Protestant broadcasting associations cherished their independence from the churches as well as the parties. Whereas in the 1980s still more than half of the members of the Christian Trade Union and of the Christian Reformed Broadcasting Association had voted CDA, in 1994 this dropped to about a third.[53] The leaders of these organisations were usually still members of the CDA, but they no longer wished or managed to 'deliver the vote' of their rank-and-file members. Though the CDA continued to invite the Christian organisations for informal talks and formal conferences, it realised that relations had changed and had become more casual and non-committal.[54] Together with the decline in class conflict and the end of the Cold War, weaker ties with the social 'partners' have reduced the importance of Christian Democrats as a mediators in socio-economic conflicts. Van Kersbergen argues this may be the main reason for the decline of Dutch Christian Democracy as well as Christian Democracy in Western Europe.[55]

Obviously, another important factor is secularisation, which has affected the Christian organisations as well as the Christian Democratic electorate. By the end of the 20th century Christians (all denominations taken together) had become a minority in Dutch society. The religious cleavage did not disappear, however, but was confined more and more to ethical questions - abortion, euthanasia and gay marriage. Moreover, a new cleavage seems to have emerged in the Netherlands, based on social and cultural values or lifestyles: between on the one hand 'progressive' cosmopolitans calling for an open, multicultural society; and on the other hand 'conservative' communitarians favouring a culturally homogeneous (national) community that should assim-

---

52   E. Vrijsen, "Bij een ander te biecht. Confessionele organisaties laten het CDA vallen als een bak-steen", in: *Elsevier*, 28 May 1994; K. Versteegh, *De honden blaffen. Waarom het CDA geen oppositie kan voeren*, Amsterdam, 1999, 81-86, 245-260.

53   J. Kuit, "Kritische noten van middenvelders", in: *Christen Democratische Verkenningen*, 7/8 (1994) 280-288.

54   K. Versteegh, "Andere banden met middenveld. Secretaris C. Bremmer over de verankering van de partij", in: *NRC Handelsblad*, 26 May 1995; M. Meijer, "Waardevolle gesprekken tussen CDA en maatschappelijke organisaties", in: *CD/Actueel*, 5 (1996) 8-9.

55   K. van Kersbergen and A. Krouwel, "De strategische opties van de christen-democratie", in: *Socialisme & Democratie*, 4 (2002) 14-22. See also the references in footnote 11.

ilate immigrants - if it cannot keep them out altogether.[56] The latter position was articulated eloquently by Fortuyn in 2002. After his untimely death, the movement he had mobilised began to disintegrate rapidly. Some of his followers voted for the CDA in 2003. Though the Christian Democratic leadership did not appreciate Fortuyn's populism and aggressive style, it shared some of his values - and so did its voters.[57] Analysis of its 2002 election manifesto suggests the CDA occupied a position between LPF and VVD as far as this dimension is concerned.

The two dimensions of the Dutch party system, 2002*

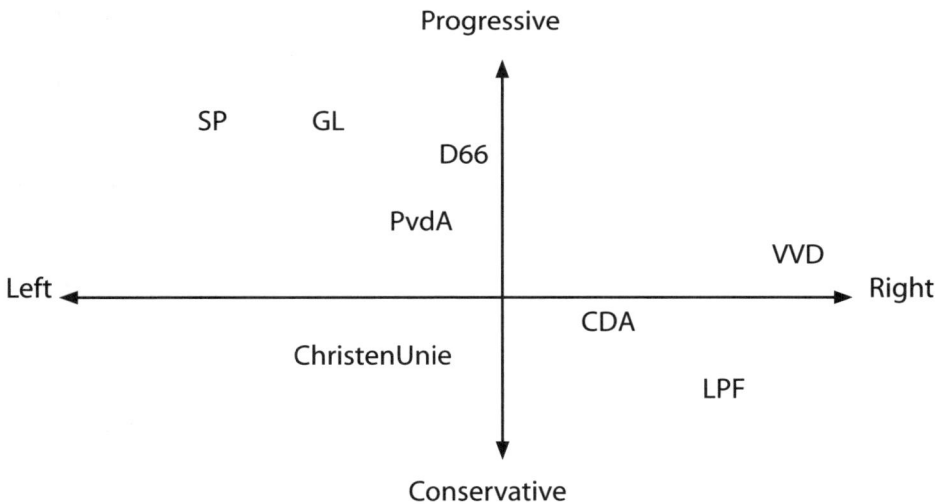

Progressive

SP   GL

D66

PvdA

VVD

Left ← → Right

CDA

ChristenUnie

LPF

Conservative

*Left versus Right and Progressive versus Conservative refer to respectively the socio-economic and the socio-cultural dimension.
Source: P. Pennings and H. Keman, "The Dutch Parliamentary Elections in 2002 and 2003. The Rise and Decline of the Fortuyn Movement", in: *Acta Politica*, 1 (2003) 59.

56   H. Pellikaan, T. van der Meer and S. de Lange, "The Road from a Depoliticised to a Centrifugal Democracy", in: *Acta Politica*, 1 (2003) 23-50; P. Pennings and H. Keman, "The Dutch Parliamentary Elections in 2002 and 2003. The Rise and Decline of the Fortuyn Movement", in: *Acta Politica*, 1 (2003) 51-68.
57   H. Masselink, "Wat paars niet zag", in: *Trouw*, 25 May 2002.

This position brings risks as well as opportunities in electoral competition. In the 2002 and 2003 elections, it may have contributed to the resurgence of the CDA as the largest party. Yet regardless of electoral outcomes, it also implies another step towards secularisation. A culturally homogeneous society, if it is to be a realistic goal at all, has to be secular - at least today, when most people treat religion as a private affair.

Conclusion

Hence, at the beginning of the 21st century Dutch Christian Democracy faces a difficult choice between three strategic options.
The first is to adapt itself to the secularisation of Dutch society and turn into a social conservative party at the risk of losing its more orthodox and/or progressive Christian supporters to the ChristenUnie, the PvdA or the GL. The second option is to emphasise its Christian identity but to lose its non-Christian conservative voters to the VVD or the LPF (assuming the latter will survive and establish its own niche in the Dutch party system). In the end the CDA might dwindle to the size of the ChristenUnie (and possibly merge with the latter). There may be a third option for the CDA, favoured at present by its political leader, Balkenende, other policy consultants of the party and members of the youth organisation: to defend communitarian and post-materialist values against the materialist individualism of the 'purple parties', the D66, PvdA and VVD, without relinquishing its Christian inspiration.[58] However, this may alienate important segments of traditional voters. So far, most CDA voters have scored rather low on post-materialism as measured by Inglehart, while most post-materialist voters tend to prefer parties like D66 and GL.[59] In the end, the third option might coincide with the first one: communitarianism in a conservative context, a goal Balkenende seems to be pursuing. Whatever option the party chooses, it will have to pay a price. Yet, rumours about its approaching decline and death - as voiced by observers like Van Kersbergen and Krouwel - have proven to be greatly exaggerated (to paraphrase Twain's famous response to newspaper reports of his death) given its spectacular resurrection at the beginning of the 21st century.

58   C.J. Klop, "Waarden en normen. Nieuwe scheidslijn?" in: M. Bovens, H. Pellikaan and M. Trappenburg (eds.), *Nieuwe tegenstellingen in de Nederlandse politiek?*, Amsterdam, 1998, 122-145; J.W.P. Wits, "Een strategische verkenning", in: *Christen Democratische Verkenningen*, 7/8 (1998) 378-380.

59   J. van Deth, "De stabiliteit van oude en nieuwe politieke oriëntaties", in: J.J.M. van Holsteyn and B. Niemöller (eds.), *De Nederlandse kiezer 1994*, Leiden, 1995, 126-141.

At the Centre of the State
Christian Democracy in Luxembourg

Philippe Poirier

The *Chrëschtlech-Sozial Vollekspartei* (CSV) is a key party within the political system of Luxembourg. Despite a loss of votes since its creation immediately after the Second World War (when it had almost an absolute majority), it still remains *Staatstragend* (state party). This refers to those political parties that are always (or most of the time) part of the government because of the influence and importance of their associative network (particularly trade unions and cultural organisations), their electoral roots and their ability to integrate and to recruit the ruling class.[1] Notwithstanding its dominance, the CSV always shared power in coalition governments with two other parties: the Liberal *Demokratesch Partei* (DP) or the *Lëtzebuerger Sozialistesch Arbechterpartei* (LSAP). However, it is worth noting that in 1974 after an unsatisfactory electoral result and though still the top party in the country, the CSV decided to go into opposition. A coalition government between the DP and the LSAP led by the Liberal Gaston Thorn (later to become President of the European Commission) was created, which lasted until 1979. Since 1984 there have been two governmental coalitions led by two different CSV prime ministers. Until he became President of the European Commission in 1995, Jacques Santer led a coalition of the CSV and LSAP. He was succeeded by Jean-Claude Juncker who continued as Prime Minster after the CSV exchanged the LSAP for the DP as its coalition partner in 1999.

Since the 1980s, the Luxembourg political scene, which had been traditionally dominated by the three aforementioned parties, has seen the rise of two new parties: the Green *Déi Gréng* (DG) and the sovereignist *Aktiounskomitee fir*

---

1   Its continuous, five-year participation in government from 1945 gave the CSV the opportunity to develop a state network, stronger than that of the other Luxembourg political parties. It is also another way of gaining legitimacy following the loss of importance of the Christian culture. The CRISP (Centre de recherche et d'information socio-politiques) uses the definition of 'dominating party': CRISP, *Grand-Duché de Luxembourg, systèmes et comportements électoraux. Analyse et synthèse des scrutins de 1974, 1979 et 1984,* Luxembourg, 1987.

Demokratie a Rentegerechtegkeet (ADR). Both parties have been challenging the position of the CSV as the DG wants to win over the new electorate in the suburbs of Luxembourg City which could be considered as 'post materialist' and as the ADR has the potential to attract a large part of the CSV's traditional, rural and rightist electorate. Insofar as its electorate is no longer representative of the whole country, the CSV has lost its position as 'the centre of the state'.

National election results, 1979-1999 (per cent)

	CSV	LSAP	DP	Extreme Left	DG	ADR
1979	36.4	28.9*	21.9	4.9		
1984	36.6	31.8	20.4	4.4	4.2	
1989	32.4	26.2	17.2	4.4	8.5	7.9
1994	30.3	25.4	19.7	1.7	9.9	9
1999	30.1	22.3	22.4	3.3	9.1	11.3

* Including the results of a dissident party
Source: F. Fehlen, I. Piroth and P. Poirier, *Les élections au Grand-duché du Luxembourg. Rapport sur les élections législatives du 13 juin 1999*, Luxembourg, 2000.

From a rural and Catholic party to a state party

The origins of the CSV go back to 19th century political Catholicism. A political party composed of different Catholic associations was founded only in 1903 with the establishment of the *Luxemburger Katholischer Volksverein* (Catholic People's Society of Luxembourg). In 1914 the party renamed itself the *Partei der Rechten* (Party of the Right) which mainly attracted the rural (and Catholic) electorate in the North and the East of the country. Consequently, the Catholic governments followed a rather agrarian and traditionalist approach. By the end of the 1930s however, a more social (leftist) approach started to dominate the party and the government. This was due to the rising influence of the Catholic trade unionists and the succesful joint campaign of the Socialists, Liberals and the Catholic trade unionists against the government proposal to ban the Communist party. This period of social reformism led to the establishment of a system of negotiation between employers and employees that secured social stability in the country's economy.[2]

2   A. Bové, *Le catholicisme politique au Luxembourg entre 1914 et 1940. Le parti de la droite*, Nancy, 1984.

Like everywhere else in Europe, the end of the Second World War worked as a catalyst on the social and ideological evolution of the right and left (non-communist) parties. The Catholic party dropped its conservative project for a clerical rural society from its political program. This project had become out of date in the face of the efforts required to rebuild the country and the decreasing number of farmers. Social Catholicism and support for European integration (this new direction was strongly influenced by the Luxembourg-born Robert Schuman) were perceived as the only option in this pervading climate of liberation. In a certain sense, the symbol of this shift, in 1944, was the new name chosen by the leadership of the party, *Chrëschtlech-Sozial Vollekspartei*.

The CSV became omnipresent within the state, managing to synthesise different interests, thanks to the control that the party exercised over public institutions but also to the charisma of some of its leaders.[3] In a certain way, the CSV gradually became a 'state party'.[4] At the same time, with the enlargement of the welfare state, the organisations affiliated to the Christian social sector gained a more central position. This resulted in an institutionalisation of the trade unions as a favourite partner in the social negotiations with the state as well as the growing importance within the CSV of the Catholic trade union and of civil servants. Catholic youth associations for their part provided the party with the means to attract the masses as well as to recruit a new political class.

Between 1968 and 1979, however, an electoral weakening in the CSV took place. There are different explanations for this development. First, despite the particular role of the Catholic Church in the Luxembourg institutional system, a *de facto* division between Church and State emerged, even though *de jure* the two entities were still unified.[5] Second, following the Second Vatican Council, the Church was internally divided and therefore could not rely on its internal strength to fight against this weakening of the CSV. Third, the pacification of the Catholic and lay forces in the political arena underlined how the cleavage between Christians and non-Christians had lost relevance. The CSV

---

3   This is especially true for Pierre Dupong, Prime Minister from 1937 to 1953, and Pierre Werner, Prime Minister from 1959 to 1974 and from 1979 to 1984.

4   J.-P. Chasseriaud, *Le parti de la démocratie chrétienne en Italie*, Paris, 1965.

5   A. Heiderscheid, "L'Eglise dans la société moderne sécularisée", in: *Nos cahiers. Lëtzebuerger Zäitschrëft fir Kultur*, 1 (1991) 188: "La société sécularisée prend le contre-pied de la société théocratique, et si elle ne se réalise pas ou pas tout de suite, 'de jure' la séparation de l'Eglise et de l'Etat, elle opère pour le moins une séparation 'de fait' entre la société civile et le religieux."

could no longer provide a coherent political discourse on libertarian ideas that would appeal to Luxembourg society.[6]

Between 1974 and 1979, for the first time since the First World War, the CSV was excluded from power. The CSV carried out an aggressive and intensive campaign against the LSAP-DP government, targeting particularly the law legalising abortion. Much more difficult to criticise was the creation of a new process of institutionalised consultation between government, employers and trade unions called the Tripartite Co-ordination Committee which had been founded to deal with the economic crisis. This new experience of being in opposition helped the CSV to rebuild its political identity and rethink its political principles. During these years of opposition a new political class arose within the CSV and a new institutional network was established. Internally, a renewed cohesion was reached with the signing of a temporary truce by the two opposite wings within the party, the liberal-conservatives and the Christian socials.

After the successful elections of 1979, the CSV entered a coalition with the DP. The main target was to fight the economic crisis, especially in the steel industry. The neoliberal-inspired fundamental reform of the industry gave the CSV new legitimacy even though its old image as a state party was preserved. The CSV was seen as both the party of a modernised country (its commitment to European integration and its support for the creation of Luxembourg as a financial centre) and the party for the defence of the social rights of the Luxembourg people.[7]

The grand coalition between the CSV and the LSAP (1984-1999) was characterised by a climate of ethical appeasement and a lack of social and economic competence. This paved the way for the populist ADR which gained votes among the most right-wing section of the CSV electorate. The success of the ADR proved the desire of some Luxembourgers for a restoration of the providential state but at the same time the need to find a solution to the inevitable reconstruction in the industrial sector. In this way, a new cleavage appeared between the section of society that depends on the public sector and that which is more vulnerable to internationalisation and competition.

---

6   V. Mouze, "Les relations Eglise-Etat au Luxembourg", in: *Forum für Politik, Gesellschaft und Kultur*, 1995, 8-12; ILRES, "Etude sur la relation Etat-Eglise", 1999.

7   M. Wurth, "Vers l'écu luxembourgeois", in: *D'Letzeburger Land*, 9 (1982) 5: "Face à la dévaluation du franc belge et l'impossible indépentatisme, il est nécessaire de créer une monnaie de référence européenne: l'ECU."

Electoral performances

The 60 members of the *Chambre des Députés* (legislative chamber) are directly elected by a proportional representation system from four constituencies for a term of five years. The electoral regions are the Center (Luxembourg City), the East (the wine region), the North (the agrarian region) and the South (the birthplace of the industrial revolution). These constituencies elect respectively 21, 7, 9 and 23 MPs. Parties present their candidates on lists. Voters can either vote for a list (each candidate on the list gets one vote) or for a candidate (in each region voters have as many votes as the number of MPs to be elected for that region) with a maximum of two votes per candidate. The voter can choose among the candidates on every list. Lists are not blocked. This very peculiar system is known as a 'panache' vote. It is undeniable that it favours well-known and popular candidates and institutional parties like the CSV. Following the adoption of a new electoral law in 2003, voting is now mandatory until 70 years of age.

As far as electoral geography is concerned, the electorate of the CSV has been traditionally concentrated in the agrarian constituencies (North and East). Since the 1974 elections, this situation gradually has changed with the take-off of Luxembourg as a financial centre. The elections of 1994 and 1999 show a (downward) homogenisation of the Christian Social vote at the regional level.

As far as the voters are concerned, one can distinguish two different types: traditional and new CSV voters. On the one hand, the CSV electorate is rather old, not very well educated, with a rural background or with strong links with the countryside (the North), concerned for the professional future of children and grandchildren, and relying on the protective arm of the Luxembourg state (the employer of around one third of this electorate). Because of the peculiar electoral system, these voters are also tempted to vote for the ADR or, if they live in the South, for the LSAP. On the other hand, the CSV also attracts an urban electorate, with a weak link to religion, working in the public or private sector but in secondary posts. Following European integration, these CSV voters are worried about limitations being imposed on the sovereign niche that Luxembourg has managed to create, namely its attractive fiscal system. Some of them have more liberal positions on ethical issues such as euthanasia and divorce. At the same time, they are all very attached to the use of the Luxembourg language. They believe that the introduction of dual nationality must lead to the assimilation of the newcomers, to a homogenous

Regional distribution of the CSV votes, 1974-1999 (per cent)

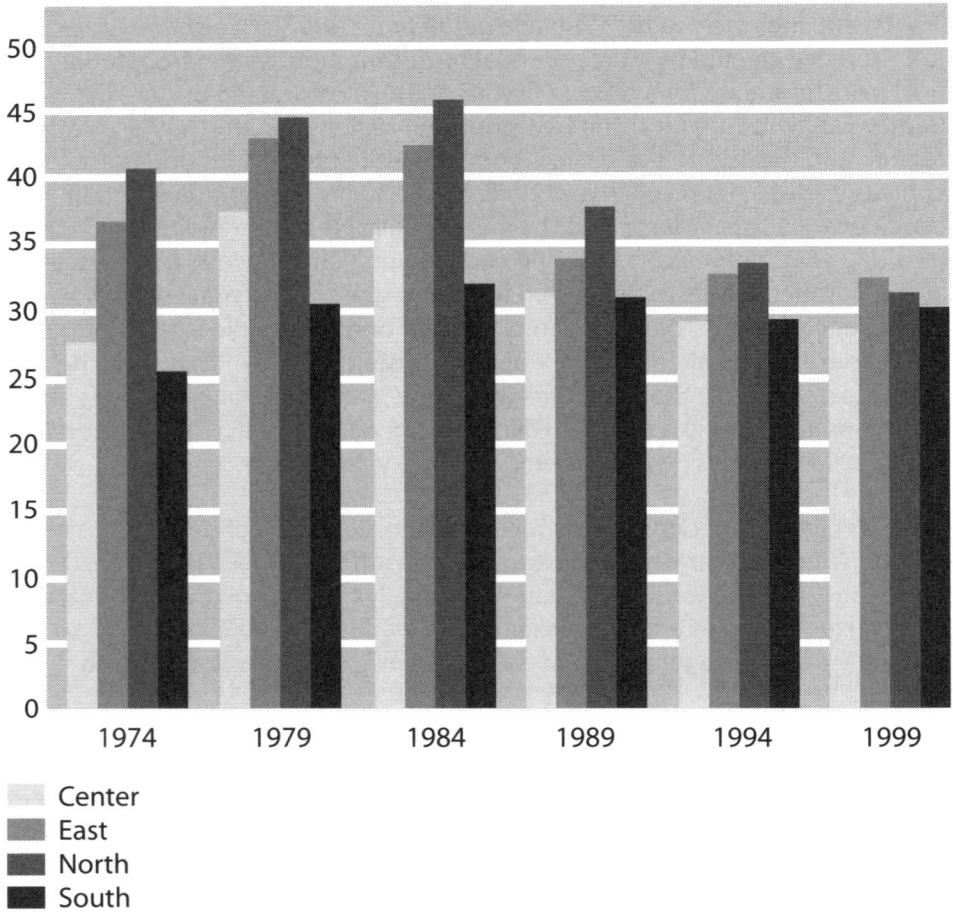

Center
East
North
South

Source: F. Fehlen, I. Piroth and P. Poirier, *Les élections au Grand-duché du Luxembourg. Rapport sur les élections législatives du 13 juin 1999*, Luxembourg, 2000.

culture characterised by the use of the Luxembourg language, despite the fact that Luxembourg society is trilingual (German, French and Luxembourg) and that French is the most spoken language in the country. This electorate is also close to the DP positions.

To further my analysis, I will use two snapshots of the Luxembourg electorate. The first was taken in 1999 after the legislative elections.[8] This research shows that the CSV voters, together with those of the LSAP and the DP, were the most convinced about voting for their respective parties before the election took place: 65% against with only 48% for the DG. This analysis also underlines that the LSAP and the CSV have a rather steady electorate, with 78 and 74% of their voters respectively choosing the same party in 1994 and 1999. This electoral continuity can be also found in the repartition of votes per age category. Among all parties, the CSV was the one with the most elderly electorate, 28% of the over-65 year olds had voted for the CSV as opposed to 7% of those aged between18 and 24 years old. It is worth noting that when the electoral reform was adopted, the CSV backed an increase of the mandatory voting age to 75 years. Among the voters who chose the 'panache' vote, the CSV obtained 34% of the vote. This percentage decreases to 28 among those who preferred to vote only for one list. In the North, East and Centre constituencies of the country, it appeared that the CSV candidates were often linked to DP candidates whereas in the South, the constituency of the incumbent Prime Minister Juncker, CSV voters chose LSAP candidates as well. Voters for the CSV, LSAP and ADR are people with a lower level of education. With more than 53%, women were fairly well represented in this category; only the DP and the DG had a higher percentage of the female vote, 55 and 57% respectively. Concerning the motivations that pushed people to vote for the CSV, a strong loyalty can be seen as one of the main driving forces. 74% declared they had confidence in the previous government (a coalition between the CSV and the LSAP) and 55% argued that the situa-tion had improved since the last legislative elections in 1994. 46% of CSV voters said they had made this decision on the basis of the accomplishments of the party during the previous 5 years, 31% on the basis of the candidate heading the list (against 17% as overall figure). Voters saw the CSV as more prepared to deal with various issues satisfactorily: 40% with family, social and health issues, 34% with educational issues, 29% with unemployment and 27% with security matters. In terms of the socio-economic left-right cleavage, the elec-

8   F. Fehlen, I. Piroth and P. Poirier, *Les Elections au Grand-duché du Luxembourg. Rapport sur les élections législatives du 13 juin 1999*, Luxembourg, 2000.

tors of the CSV and the DP are more rightist within the Luxembourg political system (58 and 63% respectively). In this way, there exists a contradiction
between the egalitarian approach of the CSV, which finds its inspiration in
social Catholicism, and the interviewees who voted for the CSV.

Another contradiction among CSV voters, even though it is one of the party's
strongest points, is their attitude towards European integration. Only 44%
them said they voted because of the pro-European approach of the party,
a smaller figure compared to that of the socialist electorate where 52% made
their choice on the basis of the European integration issue. On the contrary,
the wish to be conceived as a 'people's party' was well appreciated by all CSV
voters. More than 28% of them (for all interviewees the figure was between
10 and 22%) did not agree with the statement that class affects electoral
choice. The CSV electorate also was in agreement with the idea that personal
skills and education are fundamental in orienting personal life.

The second snapshot of the CSV electorate was made during research
conducted on Europeans and their values (European Values Studies).[9]
Concerning health, family and environmental issues, the CSV electorate does
not differentiate itself from the voters of other parties. More precisely, DP,
LSAP, DG and ADR voters all agree on the important role of the state in these
areas. The supporters of the CSV and the DG are more in favour of environmental improvement, of a fair distribution of income (72 and 83% respectively) and of tax increases (69 and 70% respectively). There is, however, a bigger
difference with regard to the role of religion and politics in society. CSV voters
are on average more 'politicised' than the voters of other parties, without this
necessarily implying a stronger engagement in the political life of the country. The differentiation between the CSV electorate and the others is always
based on religion. 62% of the CSV electorate deems religion as important as
politics whereas only one third of the other voters share this view. The CSV
electorate is also the only one that sees the influence of the Catholic Church
on national politics in a rather positive light (55% against a national average
of 33%). Besides, the CSV voters support the principle of the Church receiving
state subsidies (62, as against 42% on average). On the preference between
equality and liberty, the CSV electorate is less inclined to support liberty than
the LSAP electorate (49 and 51% respectively). Unlike the other centre-right
and right parties' (DP and ADR) electorates, CSV voters were more supportive

---

9   S. Besch, "Une citoyenneté en évolution", in: M. Legrand (ed.), *Les Valeurs au Luxembourg.*
     Portrait d'une société au tournant du 3ᵉ millénaire, Luxembourg, 2002.

of the idea that personal income was the responsibility of individuals and not of the state (59%), that this income should be a reward for personal efforts (65%), that competition is a healthy mechanism (55%) and that pensions should be based on capitalisation (55%). However, the state should have greater control over companies (55%). In this way, the CSV electorate can be seen as 'social liberal' to the extent that it supports personal freedom, even though it shows some distrust for private companies, mainly the big multinationals, while claiming a watch-dog role for the state in the area of social relations.

CSV voters have been the first to accept immigration for economic or political reasons. CSV supporters are, together with DG voters, less opposed to the building of mosques (66 and 74% respectively). Within the CSV electorate, this pro-foreigner stance goes together with a strong symbolic attachment to the country: 58% said they were proud of their citizenship (as against an average of 46%) and 53% said they were ready to fight for their country (against an average of 41%). On cultural pluralism *versus* foreigners' assimilation, CSV voters are, together with DP voters, split in two, 45 and 42% respectively. If foreigners were to have the right to vote, the CSV would by no means be penalised. For instance, within the Portuguese community, the largest group of foreigners, the CSV was the preferred party, although with a weak percentage (8.4%). Among all foreigners it was the second most favoured party (8.8%) after the DG (9.7%).[10] Within the political spectrum, CSV voters put themselves equally at the centre and on the right (in both cases 39%) and only 9% on the left. They are more to the right compared to DP voters (58% at the centre against 14% on the right) but also compared to the ADR (where 28% declared themselves to belong to the left).

Party organisation

With more than 9,500 members, the CSV is by far the largest party in the country. 4.2% of its voters are party members. By comparison, the LSAP and the DP have between 6,500 and 7,000 members. On the ground, the CSV is organised in different *Sektiounen* (sections) whose main task is to gather information on the local situation and prepare the

---

10   However, it is worth noting that 46.7% of the Portuguese and 42.2% of all foreigners could not answer this question: *Ibid.*, 449.

local elections.[11] At the top, the CSV consists of various specialised organisations. The youth organisation *Chrëschtlech Sozial Jugend* mainly focuses on ethical issues such as euthanasia, homosexual marriage and ecology, and traditionally asks for more young candidates in the elections. Besides its youth organisation, the party has a number of other organisations: one for women, *Chrëschtlech Sozial Fraen*, the only organisation that has a real independent status within the party, one for its local officials, *Chrëschtlech Sozial Gemengeréit*, which is mainly a training ground for members of local institutions and party candidates, and one for its aged, *CSV-Senioren*. The latter was founded only in 1998 with the aim of mobilising retired people in the private and public sector against the appeals of the ADR.

The CSV has a rather constraining democratic internal structure that every year finds its main expression in the *Nationalkongress* (National Congress) This congress represents the different sections, the regional committees and the various organisations. Its main task is to appoint the members of the two executive institutions, the *Nationalcomité* (National Committee) and the *Nationalrot* (National Council). Its agenda is, however, drafted and determined by these two bodies. More precisely, the National Committee is the party's central body that is responsible for its internal affairs.[12] It controls the general secretariat and is responsible for the production of the different documents for internal (only for the members of the party, the so-called *Am Bléckpunkt*) and external use (for example press statements and electoral campaigns). The high executives of the party, close to the CSV ministers, monopolise the committee. The National Council is the committee at large, with the addition of experts who give advice on specific topics and make the final arbitration.[13] The principal players in the CSV are the members of the government, and above all the prime minister. The recruitment of new politicians is mainly done within the most important ministries held by the CSV. From 1995 to 2003, the leadership of the party was assumed for the first time in its history by a woman, Erna Hennicot-Schoepges, Minister of Culture and Higher Educa-

11   The militants of the party can be involved via the *Bezierker* (regional sections) corresponding to the four electoral constituencies. Traditionally, the four presidents of the regional sections are always MPs and popular members of the party. Within companies it is also possible to take part in party life thanks to the *Bildungsarbeit*, even though they are not very active organisations. For this reason, the militants prefer to participate in the activities of the Christian trade union.

12   Its members are the party president, the secretary general, the two deputy presidents, one of whom has to be a woman, the president of the parliamentary group, the secretary of the parliamentary group, the presidents of the regional committees and of the specialised organisations of the party and other members appointed by the high executives of the party.

13   CSV, *Statuten*, beschlossen des außerordentlichen Nationalkongresses vom 17. March 2001.

tion in the current government. During this period, the party adopted a new charter of values and a public commitment to promote the role of women. Similar to the DG and the extreme left, the CSV introduced a policy of full equality between men and women inside the party.[14]

Ideological tendencies

One can distinguish two different ideological approaches inside the CSV. On the one hand, the social and technocratic wing believes that politics is not only the arena of ideological and partisan clashes, but that it must be open to all segments of the society, without making any moral judgment concerning the quantity or quality of the participation. The state is the only actor that can treat citizens neutrally. This approach favours a wide democratic consensus on issues such as the welfare state, European integration, the integration of foreigners in the party and Luxembourg society, etc., which is aimed at preventing ideological clashes.[15]

The most important supporters of this orientation can be found in the social associations close to the Church, such as the Catholic trade union, *Letzebuerger Chreschtleche Gewekschaftsbond*, and, in a more limited way, in Caritas and in the state apparatus. They have been able to appeal to the agricultural and food sector, the traditional electorate of the party, as well as to the supporters of sustainable development. This wing is looking with great interest at the choices made by some of the heirs of the Italian *Democrazia Cristiana* (DC), mainly those Christian Democrats who preferred to join the center-left coalition instead of making an alliance with Silvio Berlusconi's *Casa della Libertà* (Freedom House).[16] This social and technocratic wing has been controlling

14 *Ibid.*, Artikel 82:"Die Partei, ihre Gremien und Organe sowie ihre Unterorganisationen sind verpflichtet, die Gleichstellung von Frau und Mann in der Partei durchzusetzen. Die CSV setzt sich zum Ziel, alle Ämter innerhalb der Partei paritätisch zu besetzen. Gleiches gilt bei der Aufstellung der Kandidatenliste."

15 C. Delsol, *Le souci contemporain*. Brussels, 1996, 127. The assimilation stance, the argument in favour of a strong link between national community and citizenship, is promoted by Prime Minister Juncker who represents the leftist group within the party. Personally, however, he has argued for dual nationality: Speech given at the University Centre of Luxembourg in March 2002 and reproduced by ASTI (Association de Soutien aux Travailleurs Immigrés) in *Migrations. Les enjeux! Revue Ensemble*, 71-72 (2003) 11. See also: P. Poirier,"*La democratizzazione della società europea passa attraverso una riaffermazione del legame tra nazionalità e cittadinanza?*" Convegno nazionale della Società Italiana di Scienza Politica, 'La scienza politica e le sfide della democrazia post-nazionale', Università di Trento, 14-16 September 2003.

16 See the chapter "From Dominance to Doom? Christian Democracy in Italy" in this volume.

the party since the retirement of Pierre Werner as Prime Minister in 1984. The current Prime Minister, Juncker, and the party president elected in February 2003, also Minister of Labour, François Biltgen, are the main representatives.

The liberal-conservative wing, on the other hand, has occupied a secondary position only. However, it was revamped in 1999 with the creation of the independent think thank *Le Cercle Joseph Bech*. Its main supporters are very often thirty-year olds who are moving into key posts within the party, for instance Frank Engel, secretary of the parliamentary group. It's worth noting that Santer, Juncker and Biltgen held this post in the past. Jean-Loup Schiltz, a lawyer, who has been appointed secretary general of the party, represents the clerical stance of the liberal conservatives. Luc Frieden, Minister of Justice and Finance, also belongs to this wing and many political analysts see him as a future prime minister. The liberal-conservative wing accuses the social and technocratic wing of forgetting that every social and economic claim always belongs to the political sphere and that it is not possible therefore to make neutral decisions. Concerning the role of the state, they are critical of an omnipresent state intervening in all fields of human activity. They also oppose libertarian claims, such as euthanasia and civil marriage between two people of the same sex, emphasise the importance of individual responsibility and initiative and support a system of values based on family, nation and European integration.[17]

The doctrinal disagreements between the different wings within the party only rarely result in an open clash, at least publicly. This can be explained, on one hand, by the fact that the party has always presented itself as the 'party of harmony between the social classes', and, on the other hand, by the small political market. It would be very hard for candidates to go forward for election independently of the party, relying for their success on personal charisma and ideas only. In the same way, the actual leadership argues that the party cannot be labeled as purely 'rightist'.[18]

17   F. Engel, "Cercle Joseph Bech. Vérités et insinuations", in: *D'Letzeburger Land*, 18 (2001) 18: "Il appartient l'Etat de faire la part des choses vis-à-vis des revendications et positions de groupements d'intérêt en s'inspirant du seul bien commun. Celui-ci n'est par définition pas la source d'inspiration des groupements d'intérêt (…). Le Cercle Joseph Bech souligne aussi la nécessité de normes de référence pour la vie en société. De la famille, la société nationale et européenne."

18   See for instance: F. Biltgen, "Le parti chrétien social", in: M. Gerges (ed.), *Mémorial 1989. La société luxembourgeoise de 1839 à 1984*, Luxembourg, 1989, 80: "Le parti de la droite se voulait un parti populaire englobant, au contraire de ses adversaires directs, toutes les couches de la population, en vue de chercher un *'ausgleich'* dans l'intérêt du *'allgemeines volkswohl'.*"

In October 2002, for the first time since 1974, the CSV adopted a new fundamental programme. It is a mixture of the two tendencies, taking into consideration the recent structural evolution of its electorate. At the European level, the party considers the introduction of the euro to be neither the final objective nor a mere technical improvement but the start of a new era, one that will bring Europe closer to its citizens. European tax levels are too high to be globally competitive. The CSV is pushing for a quick enlargement of the European Union (EU), even though they seek radical institutional reforms to ensure a transparent and democratic union that works properly. In this respect, the members of the European Commission should have clear individual responsibilities. The subsidiarity principle must be interpreted in an 'integrationist' way: everything that can be done at the European level better than at the local, regional or national level should be dealt with in Brussels.[19] However, at the same time the party retains a certain sovereignist approach on fiscal competition inside the EU and on the right of small states to defend their interests in the future constitution of Europe.[20] For example, the CSV has gradually agreed with the abolition of the unanimity vote but, at the same time, it prefers to build a 'Europe of (member) states'. The CSV does not oppose globalisation but argues that attention has to be paid to the increase in social exclusion as significant minorities are pushed to the margins of the society, with a consequent development of organised crime. In what can be called a 'personalist' approach, the CSV believes also in an open society that respects the individual as a member of a family and of a wider community. Having fought against socialism and collectivism, the party has now begun to worry more about individualism and to oppose economic liberalism.[21]

At the social level, the CSV believes that parents should never be forced into making a choice between their children and their careers and that women should be given every encouragement to play a full part in public and profes-

19   CSV, *Programme électoral sur la politique européenne du Parti Chrétien Social. Luxembourg. Documents de campagne. Elections européennes*, Luxembourg, 1999, 3: "L'efficacité économique doit s'allier au contrepoids social (…). Dans ce sens, le CSV s'engage e.a. pour un revenu minimum européen et sollicite des prescriptions minimales pour le droit du travail, en vue d'éviter le dumping social."

20   *Ibid.*, 4: "Ils veilleront également à la consolidation de la place financière luxembourgeoise. Le CSV approuve une concurrence loyale en matière de systèmes fiscaux, refuse cependant une harmonisation, qui se limite uniquement aux impôts sur les revenus des capitaux (…). Pour qu'à l'avenir les questions fiscales puissent trouver une solution en accord avec le Luxembourg, le CSV maintient, dans ce domaine, le principe de l'unanimité."

21   CSV, *Jidder Eenzelen zielt. CSV Grundsatzprogramms. Personalität. Die Menschenwürde jedes Einzelnen ist unantastba*. Vorlage die am Nationalkongress vom 18. November 2002 votiert wurde, 8.

sional life.[22] For the first time, the CSV is trying to reconcile the social market, the free economy and sustainable development. It insists also on the risks of dehumanisation and the consequences of scientific progress, particularly in the field of genetics.[23] The CSV wants to ensure full employment. It supports increased liberalisation to boost competition throughout Europe and argues that the EU and the Luxembourg state must "avoid generating forests of regulations that discourage personal initiative".[24] That is why it believes in self-reliance and opposes regulation and intervention "where it is not clearly necessary. Quite often the state reinforces social illnesses rather than resolving them".[25] Having criticised the Tripartite Co-ordination Committee, the party now supports this institution for dialogue and negotiation between the social partners, even at the European level. The CSV is committed to greater social integration and to a kind of society that encourages equal opportunities and fights poverty and social exclusion.

Governmental policy

The CSV-LSAP coalition stayed in power for almost 15 years. With regard to the economic policies of this government, in 1984 they reintroduced an automatic inflation-linked increase in pensions and salaries, which had been abolished in 1979. However, the government can still suspend this measure in the event of a worsening of the economic and social situation or of a strong divergence between the internal inflation rate and the average inflation rate of the main trade partners, or loss of competitiveness of Luxembourg companies in the international arena. An agreement was also reached between the two coalition partners on the adoption of policies aimed at economic diversification, on a bill on mutual funds that consecrated Luxembourg as one of the main financial centres in Europe, on the privatisation of the telecommunications sector, on energy policy and on sustainable development by imposing very strict rules on environment protection.

22   *Ibid.*, 13: "Wir wollen die gesetzlich verankerte Gleichberechtigung von Frauen und Männern aktiv in allen Bereichen umsetzen. Frauen und Männern haben gleiche Rechte und gleiche Pflichten."
23   *Ibid.*, 22: "Wir treten ein für eine Marktwirtschaft, die sowohl sozial als auch ökologisch ist (…) für eine verantwortete Nutzung der Gentechnologie."
24   *Ibid.*, 14: "Die CSV hat sich in diesem Sinne traditionnel der Verbindung von Kapital und Arbeit verschrieben."
25   *Ibid.*, 14: "(…) eine erneuerte soziale Marktwirtschaft (…)."

In the area of social reform, the government introduced a minimum living allowance for 8% of families living in a very precarious financial state and for 18% of families right above the poverty line. Initiatives were also taken with regard to equality between men and women in the social security system, pre-retirement, harmonising the pension scheme between the private and the public sectors (especially with regard to civil servants), providing an independent living allowance for elderly people, introducing an insurance for unexpected expenses and making the health care system available to all (including non-Luxembourg resident workers).[26] Family policy (for instance, providing an allowance for school expenditures), was also one of the main areas of interest for the government during this period.[27]

The CSV-LSAP government strongly supported the development of scientific research and national cultural life. The purpose of these policies was the maintenance of the social and national cohesion of the Grand Duchy.
It was also an obvious strategy to assure the diversification of the Luxembourg economy in the field of new technologies. Public research centres were created, national cultural and heritage institutions were reorganised, a national research fund was created, advanced education was encouraged and a new broadcasting law establishing a *pax media* between the traditional leaders of the Luxembourg broadcasting market was adopted.

It is important to emphasise that these fifteen years of CSV-LSAP government were characterised by a favourable economic situation and the development of infrastructures: the improvement of the motorway network and of the railways, the development of the Kirchberg area (the area for European institutions and banks), the building of a European museum of contemporary art, the creation of a 'judiciary centre' and the modernisation of the energy supply. Yes, despite these favourable circumstances the two-party government failed to reach agreement on the creation of a ministry for women, environmental taxes, the opening of a site for industrial waste in Western Luxembourg, an integrated network of buses, trams and railways in Luxembourg City (because of the opposition of the DP-CSV coalition in the city council), the signing of conventions between the different churches and the state and the abolition of a third course on religion (besides confessional and moral) in primary schools.

26 At the request of the CSV ministers, higher levels were kept for the public sector for a period of 35 years. The socialists' criticism of this measure was one of the reasons for the loss in the 1999 national elections. The prominent trade union of civil servants was able to mobilise up to 35% of the Luxembourg electorate.

27 CSV, *E Programm fir lech. Weider an eisem fräien onofhängege Lëtzebuerg mat enger starker an dynamescher*, Luxembourg, 1989.

After the elections of 1999, a CSV-DP government was installed. The new coalition partner, the DP, managed to impose three types of reforms.[28] First, without strong opposition from the CSV, a bill for a new statute for civil servants (modelled on private sector rules) was voted in.[29] In compensation, the CSV demanded a cycle of negotiations, the so-called *Rentendësch* (Social Talks), with all social partners (trade unions, industrial associations and political parties), based on the model of the *tripartite*, with the aim of implementing a general reform of the pension situation. Both the CSV and the DP, however, did not agree with the proposition of the industrial association to introduce a universal private pension scheme. Second, the DP persuaded the CSV to prepare a bill for non-married (homosexual) couples, close to the French civil contract called *pacs*. In compensation, the CSV proposed unpaid leave for people with a family member suffering from an incurable disease. The two parties also agreed to ensure the development of palliative medicine instead of authorising active euthanasia (as in Belgium and the Netherlands). However, the liberal-conservative wing of the CSV blocked the aforementioned bill. In reaction, the caucus of the DP threatened to vote in the bill with the support of the LSAP and the DG.[30] Third, the coalition agreed to promote a competitive economy by implementing bold fiscal reforms: a balanced state budget, keeping the growth in ordinary expenditure less than the increase in the total budget, introducing tax cuts for employees and entrepreneurs with a commercial, agricultural or forest-linked activity, reducing fiscal pressure on companies, etc. These were compensated by a rise in the minimum wage (which is the highest in the EU) and a lowering of taxes in the highest tax bracket. With regard to the new European directive on fiscal harmonisation, the government pleaded for the preservation of banking secrecy laws in Luxembourg and for the adoption by its international competitors (within and outside the EU) of similar measures so as to prevent Luxembourg losing any of its competitiveness as a financial centre. In 2003, it was decided that that for an interim period Luxembourg (together with Austria and Belgium) would not be required to provide any information to the tax authorities of other EU countries on condition that they directly taxed investors themselves. The CSV presented this agreement as a succesful protection of Luxembourg's national interests in the EU.

---

28   Ministère d'Etat du Grand-Duché du Luxembourg, *Accord de coalition d'août 1999*, Luxembourg, 1999.

29   Foreigners are still forbidden access to the public sector. This was a specific demand by the trade union close to DP. In the mid-1990s, for strict electoral purposes, the DP adopted a large part of the demands of the Liberal trade union: P. Poirier, "Quelle(s) identité(s) politiques pour le Parti démocratique luxembourgeois?", in: P. Delwit (ed.), *Les libéralismes en Europe. Partis et cultures politiques*, Brussels, 2002, 247-262.

30   The mediation of Prime Minister Juncker is still going on with regard to these matters.

Conclusion

Historically, the CSV shifted from a rural and Catholic party to a so-called state party. In this way, it has always been 'at the centre' of Luxembourg politics. Gradually, it has developed a double identity: it has been the party of the 'sweet transition' that brought Luxembourg from a steel industrial-based economy to being an international financial centre but managed at the same time to preserve its image as a 'people's party' (attracting voters from all classes of society). The CSV has been challenged, on the one hand, by the collapse of religious practice, which forced the party to substitute the welfare state for the role of the Catholic Church in its programme, and on the other hand, by the combined effects of becoming one of the main financial centres worldwide and of European integration. Notwithstanding this, the CSV has been able to remain the largest party and lead the national government.

The enlargement of its electorate has been a key factor in its continuing success. The CSV has been able to attract voters beyond its rural reservoir in the North and the East of the country. Since the 1970s, the party has been drawing urban voters (especially the employees of the banking sector) who are less concerned by the personalist tradition and the traditional values of the CSV. However, parts of its core electorate have been disappointed by recent developments within Luxembourg society or have been excluded from the economic prosperity and have voted for the populist ADR.
At the same time, the CSV has never shifted completely towards neo-liberalism. Instead, it has kept its social profile by keeping the party as a point of reference for all those people, especially civil servants, who look to the state for protection. This social profile, however, has created an ideological gap between the electorate, which is more rightist, and the leadership of the party, which is more leftist. These two directions are also reflected in the party's liberal-conservative wing on the one hand and the social and technocratic wing on the other. At the same time, issues such as immigration, the role of foreigners and European integration, which question the political sovereignty (independence) of a small grand-duchy at the beginning of the 21st century, force the CSV to constantly rethink its position, programme and political strategy.

The Impossible Resurrection
Christian Democracy
in France

Alexis Massart

arc Sangnier, Georges Bidault, Robert Schuman for the politicians; the *Sillon* (Furrow), the *Ligue de la Jeune République* (League of the Young Republic), the *Républicains Démocrates* (Democratic Republicans), the *Parti Démocrate Populaire* (Democratic People's Party) for the political movements: these names, which have served as beacons for the French political scene, seem to demonstrate the continuing importance of Christian Democracy in France. Yet, the paradox is that although it has influenced political thought and inspired a great number of politicians, Christian Democracy has never been able to establish itself as a dominant partisan power in France. With the disappearance in November 1995 of the *Centre des Démocrates Sociaux* (CDS), the French political arena henceforth lack a clearly Christian Democratic party. Therefore in examining Christian Democracy in France in the 1990s, I will focus on the CDS' main successor, the *Union pour la Démocratie Française* (UDF).[1]

Post-war greatness and decline

ollowing a relatively chaotic beginning during the Third Republic, the Christian Democrats succeeded in structuring themselves into an efficient political formation, partly thanks to the activities of certain members during the Second World War. Moreover, the parliamentary nature of the system, which was particularly in tune with the political traditions of Christian Democracy, favoured such a development. However, the change of government in 1958 and the political environment of the time were to have the opposite effect. The presidentialisation of the Fifth Republic, the Christian Democrats' inability to adapt, and the Gaullist hegemony over the political scene are all factors that gradually brought about the relative decline of the political representation of French Christian Democracy.

1   A. Massart, *L'Union pour la Démocratie Française*, Paris, 1999.

Success during the Fourth Republic

The French Christian Democrats had the opportunity of participating actively in government during the Fourth Republic (1946-1958), through the *Mouvement Républicain Populaire* (MRP).[2] The end of the Second World War was particularly beneficial for them. Indeed, following the tragic death of Jean Moulin, it was Bidault, the figurehead of Christian Democracy, who took over the helm of the *Conseil National de la Résistance* (National Council of Resistance). As the first Christian Democrat in a top political position, he confirmed the strong commitment of the Christian Democrats to the Resistance.[3]
With the return to democracy, the MRP became the biggest party in France by winning 28.2% of the votes cast during the general elections in June 1946. This result was confirmed in November 1946. Nevertheless, this impact was short-lived and in fact, even at the time of Liberation, there was still no specific Gaullist political party. Subsequently, the commitment to the Resistance embodied by Bidault allowed the Christian Democrats to benefit from a major part of the support for General Charles de Gaulle.

The creation of the *Rassemblement du Peuple Français* (Rally of the French People) in April 1947 heralded the dramatic rise of Christian Democracy. Starting in 1947, the MRP consistently got between 12 and 15% of the votes cast during the various succeeding elections. They subsequently lost their central position on the national political scene, while maintaining a level of support that allowed them to participate in a number of governments and even occupy the post of *Président du Conseil* (prime minister) on several occasions. Through its governmental participation, Christian Democracy was to leave its mark on some of the nation's political tendencies and, particularly in the case of Schuman, on the question of the construction of Europe. However, as early as 1947, the Christian Democrats' key problem came to light - their differences with the Gaullists. This problem would only intensify from 1958 on with the creation of the Gaullist Republic.

2   P. Letamendia, *Le Mouvement Républicain Populaire*, Paris, 1995.
3   F.-G. Dreyfus, *Histoire de la démocratie chrétienne en France*, Paris, 1988.

The advent of the Fifth Republic and the decline of Christian Democracy

The Christian Democrats went into an irremediable decline with the advent of the Fifth Republic in 1958. In seeking a central position between a super-powerful Gaullist majority and a left-wing opposition structured around a strong Communist party that gradually allied with the Socialist movement, the Christian Democrats suffered from the polarisation of the French political system, owing to their inability to adapt to the regime's new rules of operation.

Following the disappearance of the MRP, Jean Lecanuet's attempt to revive Christian Democracy by standing for the presidential election in 1965 on the one hand and by creating the *Centre Démocrate* (Democratic Centre) on the other had no real effect.[4] The centrist branch was very quickly divided between the supporters of an autonomous centrist position - a system traditionally known as the 'centrist opposition' or even the 'third way' - and those within the *Centre Démocratie et Progrès* (Centre Democracy Prosperity), who preferred a collaboration with the Gaullist government.[5]

Certain centrists supported the candidacy of the Gaullist Georges Pompidou during the 1969 presidential election. The other section of the centrist contingency, grouped together within the *Centre Démocrate*, later joined the right-wing majority by calling on people to vote for Valéry Giscard d'Estaing during the first round of the 1974 presidential elections. In little more than five years, the Christian Democrat-inspired centrism that claimed to be in the opposition had taken hold in the right/left dichotomy, which it nevertheless attempted to refute. Paradoxically, it was during the important introduction of institutions whose functioning and presidential implications they contested, that the centrists finally pronounced themselves in favour of one camp to the detriment of the other. The option of the 'third way' - grouping together the right- and left-wing moderates - that the centrists defended did not survive the voting system or the structuring effect of the presidential election. The political autonomy of the centre, which the overall majority of Christian Democrats had claimed for a long time, seemed, in fact, to have been aban-

---

4   D. Dray, "Centre Démocrate", in: J.-F. Sirinelli (ed.), *Dictionnaire historique de la vie politique française au XXème siècle*, Paris, 1995, 146-148.

5   The *Centre Démocratie et Progrès* was created in July 1969 by Jacques Duhamel and Joseph Fontanet in order to anchor a section of the Christian Democrats within Georges Pompidou's presidential majority.

doned. A new phase of French Christian Democracy began, which would inexorably lead it towards an alliance with the entire right wing of French politics.

From 1974 onwards, the centrists became incontestably loyal partners in Giscard's government and continued to support the government completely. In the meantime, the centrist family was reconciled in May 1976 during the congress that led to the constitution of the CDS in Rennes. The CDS brought together the *Centre Démocrate* and the *Centre Démocratie et Progrès* in an attempt to recreate the former (relatively successful) MRP. Under a new name, symbolising the desire not to signal the simple absorption of one of these two movements by the other, the CDS grouped the centrists together. Responsibilities were distributed between the original members of both parties. Lecanuet, then Chairman of the *Centre Démocrate*, became the chairman of the new group, while Jacques Barrot, from the *Centre Démocratie et Progrès*, was appointed Secretary General. The purpose of this reunification was once again to give a new boost to structures whose impact on the population and representation within the government fell below the hopes of their respective leaders.

This endeavour did not, however, succeed as hoped. The first elections after the creation of the CDS - the municipal elections in 1977 - did not have any mobilising effect on the new structure. Furthermore, a gap developed very rapidly within the party between the leaders and the militants. When the president's reluctance became obvious, themes dear to the centrists were postponed, even before the rank and file had time to voice their opinions.[6] Lecanuet's declaration during his closing speech at the Rennes Congress, announcing that the centrists had to unite, "à ceux qui sont les plus proches de nous et qui, comme nous, veulent donner suite à la volonté de réforme du chef de l'Etat"[7] affected the deputies present like a "bombe à retardement"[8]. By encouraging a preferential agreement with the Liberals, reunited within the *Républicains Indépendants* (Independant Repbulicans) - the official representatives of Giscard's liberalism - the chairman of the new group dashed the hope that certain members of his party still had of being able to reconcile with the left, if it severed all its ties with the Communists. Integrating the

---

6   This would be the case, for instance, in discussions concerning a change in the voting system for the general elections, as a return to proportional representation had always been a major preoccupation of the centrists.
7   C. Ysmal, "Mort ou pérennité du centrisme", in: *Projet 112*, 1977, 141-151.
8   J.-N. Bergeroux, "CDS. La difficulté d'être", in: *Le Monde. Dossiers et documents. Les élections législatives de 1978*, 3 (1978).

Christian Democrats into the presidential majority would allow this majority to rely as much on the support of the CDS' militant network, comprised mainly of networks of Catholic associations, as on the electoral strongholds, essentially most of Western and Eastern France.[9]

The creation of the CDS in 1976 certainly helped to clarify the organisation of the centrist branch. The setting-up of a unique political party had an undeniably simplifying effect by putting an end to the competition between two parties claiming the same filiation, participating in the same government and developing almost identical political projects. Bringing together the leaders and elected members of the *Centre Démocrate* and the *Centre Démocratie et Progrès* within the same structure gave the Christian Democrats more weight on the political scene. However, the relative gap between a clear adherence to the presidential majority and the more separatist tradition cherished by part of the rank and file, and the difficulties associated with putting aside any presidential aspirations resulting from relations between centrist leaders and the head of state, led to a lack of clarity in the centrist strategy. This in all likelihood limited the impact of the new party on the people.

Just like the *Parti Républicain* (Repbulican Party) for the Liberals, the CDS did not become the major formation its initiators had hoped for. Some time after it was set up, it was not in a position either to promote the President of the Republic's message of reforms with the required impact or to oppose the Gaullists within the majority. Shortly before the general elections in 1978, no non-Gaullist group belonging to the majority was therefore in a position to match the *Rassemblement Pour la République* (RPR), the Gaullist formation created in 1976 by Jacques Chirac. Another formula had to be sought to maintain the representation of the non-Gaullists after March 1978. Part of the answer was to be found in the creation of a new federal political formation with the *Parti Républicain* and the *Parti Radical* (Radical Party). This was the UDF, which was founded on 1 February 1978.

However, within the militant world of what would become the UDF, the centrists in the CDS were identifiable by their clearly centre-left political positioning and by their genuine social awareness at the policy level. Compared with their Republican partners who were more inclined to favour a liberal

9   The Christian character of its voters is to be found in the electoral strongholds of French Christian Democracy. Both Western France (Brittany, Normandy) and Alsace are regions in which the general phenomenon of de-christianisation is less pronounced.

approach in economic matters and who leaned primarily towards the centre-right of the political spectrum, thus conveying a traditional image of the moderate right, the Christian Democrats represented a true Socialist centre-left within the majority itself. Without doubt, in 1978 the members of the CDS were still marked by the heritage of a culture of centrist opposition, whose links with the non-Communist left had undergone numerous developments from the beginning of the Fifth Republic. Nevertheless, if a certain distinction can be noted, it is above all due to the centrism they espoused and not a true adherence to the Christian Democrat movement.

The 1980s: dilution

Not long after it was set up, the UDF experienced a phenomenon that led to a significant reduction in internal ideological opposition. Indeed, the electoral body was moving in the same direction, since it appeared problematical that groups participating in the same confederation with a view to presenting common candidates during the various elections should develop different political programmes. At the same time, the rallying within the governmental majority as early as 1974 revealed an ideological proximity between these various parties.

Of course, it would have been unrealistic to expect that from the beginning of the common history of the UDF a Liberal and a Radical would agree on their vision of the state, and that a Christian Democrat and a Liberal would agree on the benefits of that agreement. Differences particular to each of the participants persisted and allowed the UDF's political system to be structured ideologically. Nevertheless, the initial differences between the participants evolved, resulting in a relative homogenisation. At a time then when divisions within the overall political arena were levelling out, the UDF was even more prone to this phenomenon as it was already engaged in a process of cooperation between the political formations that made their ideological proximity official.[10] But this streamlining within the UDF would not entirely answer to the developments within the confederation.

The UDF's commitment to working out a true political ideology had never been a priority. Though their importance cannot be ignored, from this time on ideological divisions between the constituent groups were not a major source of conflict. On the contrary, the reasoning that developed during the

  10   S. Guillaume, *Le consensus à la française*, Berlin, 2002.

preparations for the different media campaigns to present UDF doctrines was focused more on emphasising common points. This reasoning gradually became a priority because of the need for cohesion during the confederation's advertising campaign, which required a smoothing out of internal antagonisms. At no time was there any clear indication of the desire to construct a programme and an ideology especially for the confederation itself. A true UDF programme began to take shape as the confederation's activities progressed, starting with the ideological sources particular to each of the constituent groups . This smoothing over of ideological differences within the UDF happened gradually during the 1980s.

The possible preservation of certain divergences within the UDF had, above all, an internal interest. Indeed, in retaining the constituent groups on an organisational level within a confederation aiming to standardise itself, it was advisable for each constituent group to maintain a distinction capable of legitimising its existence and to resist the temptation to merge within a UDF that would become a more traditional type of political party. The programmatical divergences within the UDF were, from now on, as much an expression of specific traditional identities as the product of strategies aiming to demonstrate the existence of the various constituent groups. It is sometimes difficult even to determine which of these two factors was the most effective.

Nevertheless, the UDF in reality revealed a programmatical identity relatively common to all its constituent groups. The Republican and Christian Democratic tendencies drew closer, resulting in a formation marked by a socially-disposed liberalism, which the various actors in the confederation agreed upon in the 1980s. This compromise, which was sometimes subject to slightly different interpretations depending on the constituent groups or even on certain individual players, was reinforced by a strong European character.

This movement towards diluting the details particular to each constituent group was reinforced by the unitarian aspirations of the electorate and by pressure from the party leaders who were strongly in favour of local collaboration. The Christian Democratic electorate followed the same trend towards uniformity. From the end of the 1970s one can see a strong similarity with the electorate of the moderate right: an under-representation of workers and an over-representation of employers, executives, farmers and the liberal professions. The only remaining distinguishing mark was perhaps a slightly above-average interest in the construction of Europe.

The 1990s: an impossible autonomy

François Mitterrand's first term in office, which was particularly distinguished by the nomination of a coalition government of Socialists and Communists, led to a hardening of ideologies on the right and left. The general elections in March 1986 were seen as the revenge of the right for the 1981 presidential election, which was still considered a historical anomaly since the right had led the Fifth Republic from its beginnings. The start of Mitterrand's second term of office completely changed the situation and opened a period of great change in the political position of the French Christian Democrats. The first hope of change for the Christian Democrats would spring from the opportunity represented by a re-centring of French politics.

Political alliances were very much in fashion in 1988. Between the Mitterrand who stood for the left in 1981 and the Mitterrand who sought to renew his term in 1988 by presenting himself as the president of every French citizen and thus reaching a broader electorate, the nature of political confrontations evolved. This new acceptance of political alliances created the expectation that a place for the centrists would emerge. The beginning of the 1990s was then a time of real hope for this formation. However, political conservatism, largely reinforced by a voting system that left its mark on the political power struggles, and the significant presidentialisation of the system would not allow the Christian Democrats to take over what seemed to be their rightful place.[11] Paradoxically, other political players would gradually come to occupy the political space that the Christian Democrats were unable to hold, resulting in several party realignments within Christian Democracy.

The failure of parliamentary autonomy (1988-1993)

Raymond Barre's failure to be elected president in 1988, the departure of certain centrists for the Socialist government led by Michel Rocard, and the failed attempt involving certain Christian Democrats to renew the French right wing during the European elections in 1989, all left the centrist branch, still embodied by the CDS, in a position at the beginning of the 1990s where it was simply a back-up to the traditional right wing.

---

11   The two-round majority uninominal voting system generates strong political polarisation which leaves little room for a third-way centrist option.

However, one political event seemed to presage the return of the centrist branch. During the general elections in June 1988, the centrists decided to create an autonomous parliamentary group in the *Assemblée nationale* (French parliament), the *Union du Centre* (Union of the Centre). This decision arose from a desire to manage relations with the first majority, relating to the Fifth Republic led by Rocard, in a way that would be independent of the other right-wing political formations. Rejecting the process of systematic opposition, the centrists jumped at the opportunity of a political alliance, which was extremely popular at the time, to justify their distancing themselves from their traditional partners.

Furthermore, the creation of their own parliamentary group allowed the centrists to benefit from parliamentary procedures that would further enhance their strategy for autonomy. Whether it was a matter of speaking-time shared proportionately between the groups, of using parliamentary space or some other procedure based on French constitutional law and parliamentary regulations, there were plenty of opportunities to appear in a new light. Moreover, this independent position in the French parliament allowed a real distinction to be made between the centrists on the one hand, and the Gaullists and Liberals on the other.

However, this strategy did not pay off for the Christian Democrats. While seeking to free themselves from the constraints of the UDF through parliamentary autonomisation, the CDS nevertheless remained part of the UDF confederation. Consequently, the message intended by the creation of the *Union du Centre* was blurred because structural links with the other members of the UDF had been preserved. Moreover the UDF itself was engaged in a strong electoral alliance with the RPR.

Indeed, and this was a recurring problem for the Christian Democrats, the increasing number of elections resulting from the multi-level French politico-administrative organisation had engendered a strong habit of electoral coalitions which was difficult to abandon without the risk of losing a number of important elective positions. The views on autonomy held by the CDS leaders were not necessarily shared by the elected members at the various intermediate levels, whether mayors, departmental or regional councillors; they all were well aware that their election resulted from an alliance with the Liberals and the Gaullists. Questioning these relations risked an electoral defeat that these elected members naturally sought to avoid. Furthermore, the almost systematic repetition of this electoral strategy since the end of the 1970s had led to a high degree of dependency within the electorate, as is shown in the electoral studies and regular surveys on this issue. The voter - on whom the political system is based - who traditionally voted for a list of candidates, and the Christian Democratic candidate benefiting from a RPR-UDF nomination and to whom it had been explained over the past fifteen years that this was the only useful way of rising to power: both would have had some difficulty in understanding a strong party line. This issue was even more complex to manage in the case of opposition in the first round; it remained highly probable that the Christian Democrats would appeal to the nation to vote for their traditional partners in the second round. The quest for party independence was inevitably subject to electoral limits.

The withdrawal of Edouard Balladur (1993-1995)

In the euphoria following the overwhelming victory of the political right in March 1993, the Christian Democrats, like all the constituent groups of the RPR and UDF, followed the new prime minister, Edouard Balladur, into government. Simone Veil and François Bayrou, along with other centrists, occupied top governmental positions (social affairs and education respectively).
From this time on, the question of centrist autonomy gave way to the principle of governmental solidarity. The CDS obviously remained part of the UDF and tried, as best it could, to balance the majority in the face of the political machine represented by the Gaullist movement.

Interweaving of the Christian Democrats within the French right wing as a whole

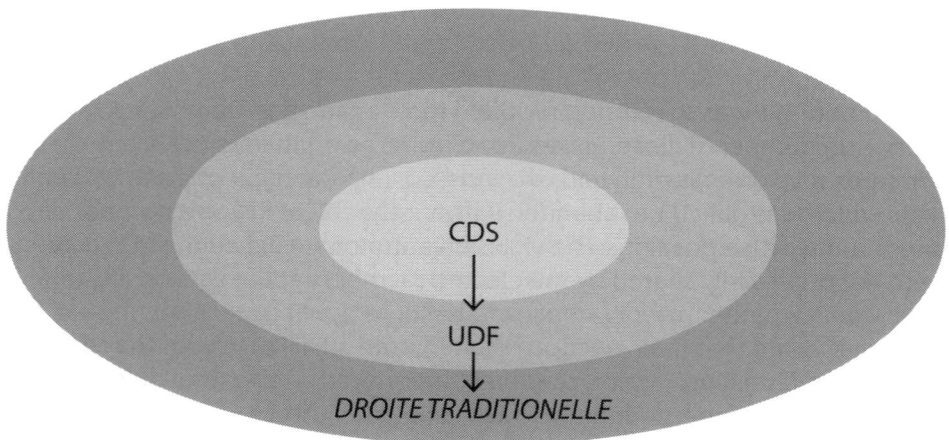

CDS
↓
UDF
↓
DROITE TRADITIONELLE

In the months following the setting up of the new government, the question of the preparations for the 1995 presidential election came up. Very rapidly, and despite a supposed sharing of the roles between Chirac, candidate for the presidential election, and Balladur, the great organiser of governmental action, the prospect of Balladur standing for president became apparent. His popularity, consensual style and his clear desire for reform quickly seduced many Christian Democrat politicians and voters.

Very rapidly, the CDS found itself in a situation where it could no longer put forward its own candidate during this crucial term of the Fifth Republic, a problem also encountered on a larger scale by the whole of the UDF. The Christian Democrats thus found themselves in a situation where they had to make a choice between various candidates from non-Christian Democrat political branches. After Rocard withdrew his candidacy - the consequence of his failure to be elected during the 1994 European elections - the Socialists hoped for a long time that Jacques Delors, the then president of the European Commission, would agree to take up the torch for the left in the 1995 elections. Given his basic centrist commitment to Europe and his strong and clear affiliation with the fundamental tenets of Christian Democratic thought, Delors was discreetly approached by the CDS leaders and in particular Bayrou. He was asked to consider a candidacy dedicated to political renewal which would be based around a wide-reaching centre, ranging from the fringes of the most moderate traditional right to the Social Liberal segment of the Socialist Party. Delors, however, did not accept this proposal which would have meant breaking with the traditional right/left divide of French politics, and so the centrists had to turn definitively to their traditional camp.

In the second half of 1994, the Christian Democrats were in a position to choose between two candidates from the same political branch, Gaullism, which though the usual ally was also still the eternal rival. Thanks to the above-mentioned qualities, Balladur rapidly received the overall support of the centrists. Moreover, they put their organisation and networks at Balladur's disposal, which he had been deprived of since the RPR had obviously decided upon Chirac as president. Since the Liberals also chose Balladur, the centrists and Liberals were brought together, leading to the gradual decline of the UDF.

By opting directly for a candidate from the Gaullist branch, the centrists abandoned the idea of presenting their own candidate. The functioning of the French political system is mostly based on the presidential election, which has a highly structuring effect. Any political formation that does not seek to play a major role by having a direct candidate is condemned to an inferior position in relation to the other political formations. By omitting to put forward a candidate in 1995, the centrists manoeuvred themselves out of choice positions in national politics.[12]

The deconstruction of the party (1995-)

The defeat of the outgoing prime minister precipitated a reorganisation of the UDF's internal forces. Because the UDF had supported a Gaullist candidate during the presidential election, it was all the more affected by the failure of its strategy. The second half of the 1990s was therefore to see a reorganisation of the French non-Gaullist right, which would seek to reposition itself on the political scene.

In November 1995, the CDS changed into the *Force Démocrate* (Deocratic Force) by uniting with a small element of the UDF, the *Parti Social Démocrate* (Social Democratic Party).[13] By accepting Social Democrat leaders and elected members within the *Force Démocrate*, this fusion put an end to the internal unity of the Christian Democrat formation. The Christian Democrats paid for seeking to revive their party structure by more or less losing their identity. The movement continued with the transformation of the *Parti Républicain* into the *Démocratie Libérale* (Liberal Democracy) in June 1997. The change of name and the accession of Alain Madelin to its leadership at the same time, marked the turning-point this formation intended to take.[14] Abandoning the option of 'advanced liberalism' previously developed by Giscard d'Estaing, i.e. a form of social conservatism balanced by a certain cultural liberalism, the French Liberals chose to follow from then on a system closer to traditional European liberalism, to the declarations of Madelin and to the ultraliberalism embodied by the British in the 1980s.

The constituent groups within the UDF therefore underwent a major reorganisation. At the end of 1997, only the *Parti Radical*, created in 1978, remained. This reorganisation led to a resurgence of internal rivalries between the two poles, the *Force Démocrate* and the *Démocratie Libérale*. The rejection of any internal compromise resulted in the *Démocratie Libérale* leaving the UDF in

---

12   P. Brechon, *La France aux urnes*, Paris, 1995.
13   M.-N. Denon-Birot, *De la Démocratie Chrétienne à Force Démocrate*, Paris, 2000.
14   A. Massart, "Y a-t-il un Parti Libéral en France?", in: P. Delwit (ed.), *Libéralisme et partis libéraux en Europe*, Brussels, 2002, 75-92.

May 1998. From then on, *le Nouveau UDF* (the new UDF) that Bayrou intended setting up would consist of former CDS members alongside several Liberals who refused to follow Madelin, the Radicals and the members of the former Giscard *Perspectives et Réalités* (Perspectives and Realities) clubs, renamed the *Parti Populaire pour la Démocratie Française* (People's Party for the French Democracy). This internal political reorganisation of the French right wing was completely contrary to the movement set in motion on a European scale within the European People's Party (EPP). While mergers are a fact within the European parliament, an arena considered as only moderately important by French political leaders in their party strategies, divisions can sometimes be intense within the French political scene, depending on the power struggles following major events such as the presidential and general elections.

This significant party evolution of the non-Gaullist right, partly a consequence of the presidential election results, weakened the different players in this process. By joining together within the UDF, the Liberals and Christian Democrats - both political forces of equal weight - became large enough to counterbalance the Gaullist branch in the right-wing sub-system. However, the split that occurred in 1998 now gave them the status of second-rate formations, far more vulnerable to leadership by the RPR.

A necessary step, a forced step, a strategic step: these different approaches remained conceivable as the events occurred. By separating themselves from the most Liberal wing of the UDF, the Christian Democrats appeared to be the majority in a new UDF led by one of their own members. The conditions would seem favourable for the reconstruction of a formation now clearly focused on the fundamentals of Christian Democracy. The narrowing of the ideological gap initially separating the different members of the UDF, and the disappearance of one of the two principal constituent groups, which resulted in less internal competition, meant the party could move towards a dynamic and rationalised party structure. This was the challenge issued by Bayrou at the end of 1998 when he envisaged a merger of the different formations in order to create a political party that was more in accordance with the normal French political system. However, this proposal was completely quashed by the reluctance of certain players within the UDF, such as the Radicals, who intended to keep their own identity particularly following the 2002 developments in the party.[15]

15   P. Perrineau and C. Ysmal, *Le vote de tous les refus*, Paris, 2003.

The image of the UDF at the end of the 1990s

The separation that occurred between the Liberals and the rest of the UDF, as we noted earlier, left the Christian Democrats largely in the majority within the UDF. Thus, it was at the end of the 1990s that this formation came closest to the Christian Democratic party model. However, as the historical connections with Christian Democracy were rarely mentioned, the UDF's image was more that of a centre-right political formation based on its position in the political scene, rather than of a party directly connected to a political ideology.

As the two following tables show, the UDF characteristically oscillates between the image of the *Démocratie Libérale* and the RPR, without having a clearly defined identity of its own. Besides getting slightly stronger support from professionals and a clear preference for the left expressed by those questioned - which fits with the more rightist positioning of the *Démocratie Libérale* and the RPR - the UDF does not, at any point, appear to outclass its partners/rivals in any specific domain. The general tendency is more to place it almost automatically in second position, while in some cases it is clearly rejected. This is especially the case for 18-24 year olds, shopkeepers, craftsmen and workers. Furthermore, taking stated party preferences into consideration, it would appear that the political future of the UDF lies more with the left-wing rather than with the right-wing supporters.

Question: *"Who would you feel closest to in the following general elections?"*

	Démocratie Libérale	UDF	RPR	None of these formations	Do not know
Total: %	15	17	24	35	9
GENDER					
Man	16	18	25	36	5
Woman	14	16	22	35	13

	Démocratie Libérale	UDF	RPR	None of these formations	Do not know
AGE					
18 to 24 years	17	15	25	33	10
25 to 34 years	20	20	19	33	8
35 to 49 years	13	17	20	40	10
50 to 64 years	12	16	25	39	8
65 years and over	14	16	30	29	11
PROFESSION OF THE HEAD OF HOUSEHOLD					
Shopkeeper, craftsman	22	16	27	29	6
Manager, white-collar worker	13	23	26	38	0
Intermediary profession and employee	17	18	18	40	7
Intermediary profession	15	18	17	45	5
Employee	20	18	18	34	10
Worker	17	14	17	39	13
Non-working, retired, etc.	12	16	30	31	11
PARTY PREFERENCE					
Left	13	20	10	51	6
Communist party	5	16	5	69	5
Socialist party	12	22	9	52	5
Green party	14	13	21	45	7
Right	21	19	41	14	5
UDF	11	55	15	11	8
Démocratie Libérale	66	13	10	8	3
RPR	12	7	65	14	2
Extreme-Right*	14	7	32	32	15
No party preference	2	3	12	46	37

*Due to the low level of numbers, the results should be interpreted with caution.
Source: Poll carried out for *Opinion Politique* on 31 March and 1 April 2000. Survey carried out according to the quota method on a national cross-section of 1,000 people representing the population aged 18 and over.

There is a recurring issue at the level of popular support when we look at themes that supposedly characterise the UDF. The UDF is primarily considered as the least modern and most old-fashioned of the right-wing political formations. Although the UDF has consistently wished to develop a more social centre-right image, it is the RPR which is usually associated with this image rather than the UDF. As for the future, 20% of those questioned would attribute this image to the UDF, a little more than for the *Démocratie Libérale* (18%) but a lot less than for the RPR (37%).

Question: "Here is a list of political parties: UDF, Démocratie Libérale and RPR. Amongst these three parties, tell me which one …?"

	UDF	Démocratie Libérale	RPR	Do not know
is the most modern	20	29	24	27
is the closest to people like you	22	16	30	32
is the most social	27	16	29	28
has the most ideas	23	19	26	32
has the best future	20	18	37	25
is the most youthful	19	36	19	26

The general image of the UDF at the end of the 1990s was therefore not very promising for the future. Shunned by the younger population, out of step with its social identity, incapable of mobilising a specific population group that would follow its development, there was particularly little prospect of the Christian Democrats in France reaching the political position attained by other Christian Democratic parties in Europe. This is one of the reasons for the gradual disintegration that would take place in the following period.

A similar destiny to the EPP's: exchanging ideology for political efficiency

When it was created in 1976, the EPP wanted to represent the Christian Democratic branch on a European scale, by bringing together the various political formations of the then European Community (EC) member countries that claimed to belong to this tradition. After the merger in 1996 with the

European Union of Christian Democrats (EUCD), the EPP found itself to be the sole representative of Christian Democratic thinking.[16]

Today, the EPP includes nearly forty parties from European Union (EU) member countries and therefore the strategic as well as ideological diversities within it may vary. For instance, in France the principal leaders of the new UDF are opposed to possible alliances with the extreme-right *Front National* (National Front), whereas in Austria the Christian Democrats concluded a governmental agreement with the extreme-right party. On a programmatical level, it is clear that the EPP is increasingly turning towards classical Liberalism at the expense of its initial purely Christian Democratic position. Recent party documents emphasise the need to resolve the economic crisis or the desire to accelerate renewed growth by reducing social costs, rather than emphasising the more traditional reflection on man's place in society and the actions necessary to correct the excesses of economic globalisation.

In short, this development is above all the fruit of expansionist politics developed by a parliamentary group essentially seeking to increase its influence in Strasbourg and Brussels, even if it means losing the principal ideological characteristics that have distinguished Christian Democracy. The loss of internal coherence within the EPP, which includes nearly all the Gaullist and non-Gaullist right-wing political groups, nevertheless allowed it to put an end to the traditional compromise of co-management with the Social Democrats in the European Parliament (EP). Choosing efficiency has paid off, even if it has meant leaving aside the initial divergences that existed between certain political formations which are today members of the EP.

Clearly, this kind of grouping also took place within the French right wing. From 1978 onwards with the creation of the UDF, and from 1981-82 with the regular RPR-UDF electoral alliances, a real ideological rapprochement was initiated between the different parties, between radicalism, Christian Democracy, liberalism and Gaullism. The succession of election platforms, or of other common government platforms, meant that supporters of these various parties became indifferent to their individual candidates. When the UDF and the RPR decided to present a different candidate or list of candidates in the first round, the transfer of votes was carried out under favourable conditions in the second round. From one election to the next, the political differences

16   For the EPP, see also the chapter "A Decade of Seized Opportunities. Christian Democracy in the European Union" in this volume.

between the various political parties dwindled as did the justification for their existence. This led Balladur in 1988 to suggest that one right-wing group be formed. During the 1980s and even more so in the 1990s therefore, the French Christian Democrats experienced a movement similar to the one that developed within the EPP. The only major difference was that the movement which in Europe benefited the Christian Democrat formation, in France led to its downfall.

Conclusion

At the end of the 1990s, the French Christian Democrats, viewed as a party, seemed to have had their day. Since the political calendar in France was mainly based on the presidential elections, it was even more the cycle beginning in 2002 that finally destructured the Christian Democrat formation, which was embodied partially by the UDF. Indeed, during the Spring 2002 elections, the right and the centre-right underwent a fairly intense reorganisation with the creation of the *Union pour un Mouvement Populaire* (UMP). The political upheaval that occurred during the second round of the presidential elections in France, marked by the opposition between the outgoing President Chirac and the extreme-right leader Jean-Marie Le Pen, resulted in a strong mobilisation around the President of the Republic. Immediately following the general elections, the presidential election allowed Chirac to completely change the traditional party rules by rallying the principal leaders of the French right wing around him in a show of unification. They rallied first in June 2002 in the form of an electoral coalition under the label *Union pour la Majorité Présidentielle* (Union for the Presidential Majority); this movement took final shape with the creation of the UMP, a designation that is close to that of the EPP.

This new political group, which claimed to be the President's party, is certainly based on the former RPR, but it has also integrated some of the UDF leaders and all of those belonging to the *Démocratie Libérale*. If the Liberals and the Radicals, who were members of the UDF, have mostly joined the UMP, this is also the case for the vast majority of the Christian Democrats. Whether they be Barrot, Pierre Méhaignerie or Philippe Douste-Blazy, the former leaders of the CDS have today become an integral part of the UMP and hold strategic posts (the three names cited are, respectively, parliamentary group Chairman of the Parliamentary Finance Committee, Chairman of the UMP and Secretary General of the UMP). At the intermediary levels (regions, departments and communes) the major Christian Democrat elected members have joined the new group as have the leaders of the departmental federations. Given this, the UDF can no longer legitimately claim to be the sole political representative of French Christian Democrats, just as the UMP cannot consider taking responsibility for the Christian Democratic heritage since it represents Gaullist, Liberal, Radical as much as Christian Democrat traditions.

The process started in June 2002 in the French political scene ultimately corresponds to that started a few years ago in the European political arena, that is, the organisation of a centre-right political formation combining various political traditions that have gradually merged in the EPP. The future of French Christian Democracy too would seem to be as part of a larger political party, which would allow the principal founders of this political ideology to survive.

Life at the Northern Margin
Christian Democracy
in Scandinavia

John T.S. Madeley

A s is the case with all parties or groups of parties, Scandinavian or, more properly, Nordic Christian Democracy is still marked by the circumstances of its birth and early development.[1] As compared to its counterparts further south in Europe, it is of relatively recent date. Although the parties' roots and origins at local level long predate their eventual emergence, they only appeared as significant players on the national political stage in Norway in 1945, in Finland and Denmark in the 1970s and in Sweden in the 1980s. By contrast with the more established traditions and parties of Continental Western Europe, the Scandinavian variant has understandably been relegated in the literature on Christian Democracy to the status of a virtual - and sometimes actual - footnote, along with the other 'lesser vehicle' Christian Democratic traditions of the United Kingdom or, until recently, of Central and Eastern Europe.[2]

Unlike all its counterparts elsewhere, Scandinavian Christian Democracy is the product of societies that remain overwhelmingly Protestant in their confessional identity and largely secular in terms of conventional religious belief and observance. Emerging against a background of the most highly developed forms of Social Democracy in the world, it appears to represent a very particular kind of protest, combining the defence of traditional Christian values with a centrist position on social and economic policy. In these respects it might be seen as replicating the classic features of Continental Christian Democracy of fifty years ago. It is perhaps all the more remarkable therefore that the 1990s should have seen a distinct rise in its political profile in Europe's far north at a time when this has sunk, and in places almost disappeared, further south. The Scandinavian Christian Democratic parties might thus

---

1   In its narrowest sense Scandinavia only includes Norway and Sweden while the less familiar term Nordic (from *Norden*) embraces in addition Denmark, Finland and Iceland, and their dependent territories.

2   See for example R.E.M. Irving, *The Christian Democratic Parties of Western Europe*, London, 1979, ix, 261-262; K. Van Kersbergen, *Social Capitalism. A Study of Christian Democracy and the Welfare State*, London, 1995, 255.

be seen as paradoxical cases which represent to their older Continental counter-parts both the past and the future: on the one hand, they cleave to their religious roots and to centrist social policies, while on the other their emergence, survival and occasional advances attest to the opportunities that continue to exist in the otherwise unpromising environment of highly secularised societies.

From its beginnings Scandinavian Christian Democracy has been distinctive. Unlike its Continental counterpart it did not emerge from the matrix of conflicts between Catholic religiosity and the secularising elites of the political Left that developed in the wake of the French Revolution. Nor can any of the parties in their origins, or even in their later development, be seen as church parties; in Scandinavia the existence of state or *folk* (people's) churches embracing (until recently at least) well over 90% of the population has traditionally militated against the idea that religious considerations should be brought into party political conflicts at all. In all four cases the parties grew instead out of traditions of religious dissent representing varying shades of dissatisfaction with the religious establishment among activist minorities. Typically, they were founded by the coming together of activists from surprisingly varied religious and political backgrounds.

The oldest of them, Norway's *Kristelig Folkeparti* (KrF), founded in 1933, reflected in the name it adopted then and still bears today, its roots among the country's *kristenfolk* (Christian people) whose principal identity was formed around voluntary lay mission organisations rather than the official church. As will be seen later, the other three, which followed the example of the Norwegian party some time after, also took their origin from movements of moral-religious protest, although they have all in recent years adopted the Continental Christian Democratic label: Finland's *Kristillisdemokraatit/ Kristdemokraterna* (Christian Democrats) founded in 1958, Sweden's *Kristdemokraterna* (Christian Democrats) founded in 1964 and Denmark's *Kristendemokraterne* (Christian Democrats) founded in 1970. Some authors even take the view that these parties are not really Christian Democratic at all and should instead be seen as minority Christian protest parties, whatever their recent name-changes may indicate. The alternative view is that they are certainly democratic as well as Christian and that they deserve to be seen as a distinctive local species of the genus Christian Democracy.[3]

3   This was the argument developed in: J.T.S. Madeley, "Scandinavian Christian Democracy. Throwback or Portent?", in: *European Journal of Political Research*, 3 (1977) 268.

In a number of respects Scandinavian Christian Democracy is markedly different from both the Continental and Anglo-Saxon forms identified by Fogarty.[4] As the product not of the Lutheran established churches but of independent revivalist traditions both outside and inside those churches, the parties have also tended for a long time to be religiously as well as politically more marginal than their Continental counterparts. Their rather modest size has denied them the central role often played by their sister parties, although this has been counterbalanced by the premium placed by bloc politics in the Nordic countries over recent decades on the role of small centrist parties.[5] All four of the parties have enjoyed periods of government office since 1990, with Norway's twice providing the political base of the prime minister.

It can also be argued that the Nordic parties tend to be more 'religious' than their Continental counterparts insofar as their membership tends to be restricted to religiously active minorities and their electoral appeal has tended to be more religiously accented. Each of them has certainly experienced serious tensions between those for whom politics is seen as an occasion to express their religious identity and purposes, and those for whom a common attachment to certain moral-religious values provides the opportunity to pursue a distinctive politics. These and other differences have furthermore made the parties cautious and, on occasion, positively suspicious in their attitudes to the other Christian Democratic traditions of Europe and further afield. The step-wise inclusion of Scandinavia in the processes of European integration has also posed particular problems. While there has been a distinct trend in favour of closer identification and cooperation with Continental Christian Democracy in the 1990s, none of the parties has been, or remains, untroubled by tensions arising in connection with European integration.

4   M.P. Fogarty, *Christian Democracy in Western Europe (1820-1953)*, London, 1957, 10.
5   J.T.S. Madeley, "Reading the Runes. The Religious Factor in Scandinavian Electoral Politics", in: D. Broughton and H-M. ten Napel (eds.), *Religion and Mass Electoral Behaviour in Europe*, London, 2000, 36-38.

The religious and party system background

The distinctiveness of Scandinavian Christian Democracy can only be understood against a background of five hundred years of religious and one hundred years of party system history. As far as religion is concerned, all the Nordic countries belong to (and, indeed, collectively constitute) Europe's sole mono-confessional Protestant region.[6] Unlike in other parts of Northern Europe where Protestant Reformation settlements were also successfully institutionalised, Roman Catholicism was almost completely eliminated among the native populations of the North. Indeed, until approximately the middle of the 19th century no religious competitors to established Evangelical Lutheranism were allowed to gain more than a toehold; something approaching full toleration for all faiths was not attained until well into the 20th century.[7]

The stability of the Reformation settlement, the lineaments of which are still to be seen in the Nordic countries, rested on the nature of the bargain that it represented: the Crown would support the Church in its spiritual mission while the Church, insofar as it continued to represent an entity separate from the state at all, would support the Crown in the exercise of its secular authority. An important legacy of the era of the confessional state in Scandinavia has been - alongside a continuing consensus on certain core notions of public, if not private, morality - the fact that an overwhelming proportion of the population continues to regard itself as Evangelical Lutheran.[8] If the predominant Lutheran identification has survived from the era of the confessional state however, religious uniformity and conformity has emphatically not.

Starting in the 18th century, as elsewhere among the Protestant populations of Europe and North America, religious uniformity began to be undermined as pietist. Other movements of religious revival emerged and grew on the one hand, while on the other religious indifferentism spread, particularly among the educated and urban dwellers. The revivalist movements, which

---

6   This makes the Nordic area, together with the Counter-Reformated South and the Orthodox East, one of the three historically mono-religious blocs occupying the corners of Europe: J.T.S. Madeley and Z. Enyedi (eds.), *Church and State in Contemporary Europe. The Chimera of Neutrality*, London, 2003, 27-34.

7   Thus in the case of Norway, while a Dissenters Act was passed in the mid-19th century, it was only in 1951 that the Constitution's ban on the entry of Jesuits into the country was finally abandoned, over the protests - it should be noted - of the KrF.

8   T. Petterson and O. Riis (eds.), *Scandinavian Values. Religion and Morality in the Nordic Countries*, Uppsala, 1994, 11.

typically arose in connection with unofficial and unlicensed lay preaching and attempts to suppress them by the use of the police powers of the confessional state, led to more or less intense - and even, on occasion, violent - local conflicts. As a result of the progressive relaxation of controls, successive waves of revivalism gave rise to more or less independent lay organisations, which undertook to launch and support mission work at home (e.g., through so-called inner-missions) and abroad.

By the time of the Second World War a significant religious pluralism both inside and outside the state churches was evident in all parts of Scandinavia and from the 1960s on, the presence of new groups of immigrants, especially those with a Muslim background and loyalty, extended the confessional range of this pluralism. Finally, the appearance in the 1980s of new, more or less exotic, religious movements, added a further element of diversity to broadening religious fringe, particularly evident in the metropolitan areas. The religious topography of the Nordic countries has thus become considerably more variegated than would appear from the bare statistics of church membership.

The political relevance of these changes in the religious sphere was not evident for a long time. While in Catholic Europe after the French Revolution a struggle developed between massive rival forces of secularism and religiosity, in Scandinavia as in the other Protestant regions of Europe more generally, the first religio-political tensions ranged religious nonconformists and revivalists against the upholders of church establishment.[9] The emergent systems of political competition and mass politics in Scandinavia first produced patterns where the political Left (in Norway and Denmark the Liberal parties took the name *Venstre*, literally 'the Left') often claimed to be just as religious as (if not actually more so than) the Right. Only later, with the gradual emergence at the end of the 19th century of Social Democratic parties with fraternal links to the Marxist parties of the Continent, in particular the German Social Democrats, did a markedly secularist strain begin to appear. With rapid economic development in the early 20th century, earlier culture-based patterns of opposition quickly gave way to the more materialist politics of class conflict. Finally, around the time of the first World War, when the final installments in suffrage extension coincided with the introduction of systems of proportional representation, patterns of political opposition resolved themselves more and more along lines of economic interest. While the emergent socio-economic

9   D. Martin, *A General Theory of Secularisation*, Oxford, 1978, 33-34. See for the British case
     S. Koss, *Nonconformity in Modern British Politics*, London, 1975.

left-right axis of party competition then became evermore dominant, the survival of an independent agricultural sector meant that the capital-labour opposition was supplemented with a third, centrist pole, representing the agrarian interest. As a representative of the rural economy and of the more peripheral areas this third pole continued to resonate some of the cultural and religious cleavages that had earlier been to the fore. In doing so it articulated a cross-cutting dimension, which counterposed inter alia moral-religious conservatives and secularists (or indifferents) of left and right. According, religious-political differences in Scandinavia crystallised more across than along left-right lines of opposition then, revivalists often deeming left and right to be equally astray on certain core issues of concern.

As to the emergent party systems of Scandinavia, the family resemblances have been strong ever since they finally took form around 1920.[10] From then, for some fifty years, three distinctive features remained prominent: a dominant left-right axis with the Social Democratic parties far outweighing that of any rivals to their right or left, and the existence, alongside Liberals and Conservatives, of Agrarian parties in the centre of the party spectrum. Adding the occasionally important Communist parties on the far left a typical five-party spectrum can be used to represent the Scandinavian party system between approximately 1920 and 1970.

The classic Scandinavian five party spectrum

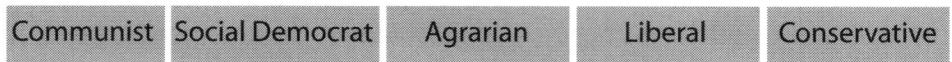

Communist	Social Democrat	Agrarian	Liberal	Conservative

Source: S. Berglund and U. Lindström, *The Scandinavian Party System(s)*, Lund, 1978, 16-18.

Although it was most closely exemplified in Sweden, this ideal-typical model was nowhere perfectly realised. In Norway from as early as 1933 the KrF had emerged in the centre of the spectrum, by 1945 establishing itself as a significant player, while in the 1950s (Finland), 1960s (Sweden) and 1970s (Denmark), the Christian Democratic parties were founded with the aim of emulating the Norwegian example. Thus in four of the five Nordic countries (Iceland only excepted) Christian - or Christian Democratic - parties had emerged onto the national political stage by the early 1970s, thus contrib-

10   S. Berglund and U. Lindström, *The Scandinavian Party System(s)*, Lund, 1978.

uting to, and benefiting from, a thaw in what had still seemed in the 1960s 'frozen' party systems.[11]

The emergence of the Christian (Democratic) parties

How and why the Christian parties came to take their place in the party systems of Scandinavia is not well understood, although there is now a sizable body of scholarship relating in particular to the longest-established party, Norway's KrF.[12] Rokkan's classic account of the development of the Norwegian electoral cleavage system traced the political engagement of different religio-political constituencies over fifty years before the KrF's actual emergence in 1933.[13] For most of this period revivalist circles in the South and West of the country aligned themselves with the Liberal Party, committed as it was in the 1920s to the defence of "the rural 'counterculture', an amalgam of prohibitionism, lay [religious] activism and support for the rural linguistic standard".[14] By the early 1930s, however, the prohibition of alcohol had been repealed after a national referendum and the Liberal Party leadership raised only a muted protest when a number of prominent leftist intellectuals openly lampooned Christian beliefs and morality.

Finally, when Nils Lavik, the general secretary of one of the main lay organisations in the West, was controversially passed over in the nominating convention of the Hordaland Liberal Party, he was quickly adopted as the leading candidate on an independent Christian list, that of the newly-formed KrF.[15] In addition to calling for resistance against what was seen as an organised assault on the country's treasured religious heritage, the new party

11   An unsuccessful attempt to launch an Icelandic party was made during the 1995 election campaign. The emergence of the Nordic Christian Democratic parties was not the only change that was eventually modified the uni-dimensional five party pattern described above. For an up-to-date review of the full spectrum of changes and their impact, see D. Arter, *Scandinavian Politics Today*, Manchester, 2002.

12   See for example the sources footnoted in L. Svåsand, "Die Konservative Partei und die Christliche Volkspartei Norwegens. Unbequeme Nachbarn im bürgerlichen Lager", in: H.-J. Veen (ed.), *Christlich-demokratische und konservative Parteien in Westeuropa. 4: Schweden, Norwegen, Finnland, Dänemark*, Paderborn, 1994, 133-227.

13   S. Rokkan, "Geography, Religion and Social Class. Crosscutting Cleavages in Norwegian Politics", in: S.M. Lipset and S. Rokkan, *Party Systems and Voter Alignments*, New York, 1967, 367-444. See for a critical appraisal of this account J.T.S. Madeley, "The Antinomies of Lutheran Politics. The Case of Norway's Christian People's Party", in: D. Hanley (ed.), *Christian Democracy in Europe. A Comparative Perspective*, London, 1994, 142-154.

14   S. Rokkan, "Geography, Religion and Social Class", 394.

15   A. Lomeland, *Kristelig Folkeparti Blir Til*, Oslo, 1979.

claimed that the politics of class division was undermining the prospects of surmounting the social and economic crisis of the time. It presented itself not so much as a new political party as a movement protesting against party politics as such. At the 1933 general election Lavik became the party's first representative in the *Storting* (Norwegian Parliament) and he was joined by a second from Hordaland at the next election in 1936.

It was only in 1945 however that KrF emerged as a national, rather than a regional, party. In the last months of the Nazi occupation, a number of prominent Christians, many unconnected with the lay revivalist organisations, started to make plans for the reassertion and strengthening of the country's religious heritage after the barbarism of war and occupation. These along with a number of other religious leaders, including representatives of non-Lutheran denominations as well as of the more churchly lay Lutheran organisations, rallied to KrF as it organised across the country for the first time - the official church leadership itself however remaining aloof. This, and the party's immediate success in taking 7.9% of the national vote, indicated that it had quickly become more than the voice of the 'radical' pietist tradition of Western Norway which it had principally been in the 1930s; "a completely new generation and a completely new type of Christianity began to make an impact - a new generation with a more *felleskirkelig* (cross-church) character".[16] This broader alignment made the party more representative of the nation as a whole. In addition to widening its geographical coverage it brought in urban middle-class Christians with a more urbane approach to secular culture and the arts, as well as supporters from free-church, dissenting traditions.

By 1953 KrF had established itself as a 10% party of the centre and in 1963, when Labour was briefly expelled from office for the first time since the Second World War, it joined the other three non-socialist parties in government. After the 1965 *Storting* election, when a non-socialist majority was finally elected, KrF took its place in the Borten government (1965-1971) with its leader as a controversial minister for Church and Education. In 1972 after Labour resigned following its failure to secure a referendum vote in favour of membership of the European Community (EC), a new KrF leader, Lars Korvald, became prime minister in a stop-gap minority coalition government, which was charged with re-negotiating the country's relations with the EC. One lesson of its eight years in government between 1963 and 1973 was that

16   O.S. Hove, "Kristen-Demokratene I Europa", in: *Idé. Tidsskrift for Kristen Demokratisk Samfunnsdebatt*, 4 (1972) 339-340.

it was possible for a Christian party to make an impact and to advance its agenda through bargaining and hard work. It was a lesson which Christians in the other Nordic countries duly noted as they sought to stem and, if possible, turn what they saw as a rapidly rising secularist tide.

Finland's *Suomen Kristillinen Liito* (literally, Finland's Christian League), as the Christian Democrats were called until the name-change in 2001, was launched in 1958 by a small group of activists who were concerned that the national drift towards the left was endangering the nation's religious heritage and that the Conservative party, *Kansallinen Kokoomus* (National Coalition), could not be relied upon to resist the trend.[17] 1958 was the year that the Communist-dominated Finnish People's Democratic Union became the largest parliamentary grouping, just ahead of the Social Democrats and the Agrarian Centre party. The Christian activists were mindful of the Norwegian example and the programme they adopted was "more or less a verbatim translation of the corresponding Norwegian document".[18] The party made little impact during its first twelve years however, receiving less than 1% of the national vote and so gaining no representation in the *Eduskunta* (Finnish Parliament).

While the Finnish party pioneers were associated particularly with the so-called new pietism of the post-war era, the party initially failed to attract the support of the more church-oriented Lutherans who tended to vote for the Conservatives, or of the Laestadian revivalists whose links with the Agrarian party remained solid particularly in North and East of the country, or of the Christian Swedish-speakers who tended to remain loyal to the *Svenska Folkpartiet* (Swedish People's Party). Only in 1970, after a decade in which, in Finland as elsewhere, 'permissive society' trends were seen to have made great inroads, did the party achieve its first breakthrough. Its 1.1% of the national vote in 1970 combined with a local electoral alliance with the Centre Party was sufficient for the election of its leader, Raino Westerholm. Despite these modest beginnings the party has ever since managed to return candidates at all subsequent elections, in 1979 achieving 4.8% of the national vote after Westerholm had raised the party's profile by standing in the 1978 presidential election.[19]

---

17   D. Arter, "Die bürgerlichen und konservativen Parteien Finnlands. Zentrumspartei, Nationale Sammlungspartei, Schwedische Volkspartei und Finnischer Christliche Bund", in: H.-J. Veen (ed.), *Christlich-demokratische und konservative Parteien in Westeuropa. 4: Schweden, Norwegen, Finnland, Dänemark*, 241-242.

18   L. Karvonen, "Christian Parties in Scandinavia. Victory over the Windmills?", in: D. Hanley (ed), *Christian Democracy in Europe. A Comparative Perspective*, 124.

19   In the presidential election Westerholm managed to attract 8.8% of the national vote.

Sweden's *Kristen Demokratisk Samling* (Christian Democratic Rally), as it was called at first, was launched in 1964 at a time when a number of moral-religious issues affecting government policy came to a head. Early that year a doctors' petition had expressed concern about rising rates of sexual promiscuity and the increased incidence of venereal disease. The action of the government's National Board of Social Affairs recommending municipalities to advise young people against attending the 'ecstatic meetings' of pentecostal movements was also considered ominous, while proposals to reduce the time devoted to religious instruction in secondary schools provoked an extraordinarily wide expression of concern as 2.1 million signatures (in a country with only five million adult citizens) were collected for a protest petition. Finally, there was also a sharp controversy over pornography and film censorship.

The time seemed auspicious for the launching of a party modelled on Norway's KrF to lead the fight in defence of conventional Christian values. The party began life under the wing of the Pentecostal leader Lewi Pethrus with his newspaper *Dagen* as a major source of publicity and support, even though the first party leader, Birger Ekstedt, was in fact an ordained minister in the state church.[20] Pethrus and the paper had been to the fore in promoting campaigns protesting against what was seen as the rapid and progressive 'de-christianisation' of Swedish society. At its first election the party achieved only 1.8% of the vote however and failed to gain representation in the *Riksdag* (Swedish Parliament). Six years later its prospects were further dimmed when a constitutional reform introduced a 4% threshold, excluding from representation all parties that received a lower quotient. Only twenty one years after its founding, in 1985, did the party finally succeed in winning its first seat. This was achieved, in the manner of its Finnish counterpart, on the basis of a local electoral alliance with the Centre Party. When the arrangement broke down three years later it was again excluded from parliament despite a modest advance in its electoral share.[21]

Denmark's Christian Democratic party was founded in 1970 under the name *Kristeligt Folkeparti* (Christian Peoples' Party), following the example - and copying the name - of its Norwegian counterpart. Its launch came towards

20   G.V. Johansson, *Kristen Demokrati på Svenska. Studier om KDS tillkomst och utveckling (1964-1982)*, Malmö, 1985.
21   B. Henningsen, "Die Konservativen parteien Schwedens. Die Gemässigte Sammlungspartei und die Christdemokratische Gesellschaftspartei", in: H.-J. Veen (ed.), *Christlich-demokratische und konservative Parteien in Westeuropa 4: Schweden, Norwegen, Finnland, Dänemark*, 105.

the end of three years of a non-socialist coalition government, which had dismayed moral-religious conservatives by its seeming contempt for conventional moral standards.[22] The 1960s had seen a progressive liberalisation of restrictions on abortion and pornography, which had already made Denmark an international byword for permissiveness. Less sensationally, plans to decrease the amount of time school pupils spent on religious instruction seemed, as in Sweden, to point in the same direction. Far from reversing these trends, however, the 1968-1971 non-socialist coalition had presided over an acceleration. Two pieces of legislation were taken to be symptomatic: one, introduced by a Conservative minister of justice in 1969, providing for the almost complete removal of controls on pornography; the other a year later introducing abortion on demand.[23]

At its first election in 1971 the party just failed to surmount the 2% threshold of the electoral system but at its next attempt two years later it took 4% of the vote and succeeded in getting seven candidates elected to the *Folketing* (Danish Parliament). This breakthrough occurred during Denmark's 'earthquake election' when the number of parties represented in parliament doubled and the four main established parties suffered very severe losses. Amongst those who switched their vote to the Christian Democratic Party were significant numbers of former Conservative and Liberal party voters. Even though it went on to take 5.3% of the votes in 1975, the Danish Christian Democrats remained decidedly a minor party, taking only approximately half that share at subsequent elections. Despite its small size, the party was nonetheless able to enjoy a share of government office between 1982 and 1988 in the Conservative-led 'Four-Leaf Clover' coalition.

As the difficulty with which they established themselves testifies, at their launch the Scandinavian Christian Democratic parties each entered crowded political marketplaces with little room for their stalls. Even the Norwegian party was only able to establish itself firmly on the national stage after twelve years (although five of those were accounted for by the country's occupation during the Second World War). Some of the parties' early difficulties have been connected with the fact that they sprang from dissident religious traditions, and secondly their particular concentration on issues of religion and

---

22   P.C. Andersen, *Kristen Politik. Kristeligt Folkeparti 13 April 1970-21 September 1971*, Odense, 1975.

23   M. Eysell, "Die Konservative Volkspartei, die Christliche Volkspartei und die Zentrum-Demokraten Dänemarks. Drei Wettbewerber in bürgerlichen Lager", in: H.-J. Veen (ed.), *Christlich-demokratische und konservative Parteien in Westeuropa. 4: Schweden, Norwegen, Finnland, Dänemark*, 351.

morality seemed to be at odds with orthodox Lutheranism's 'two regiments' doctrine, while at the same time seeming to imply that those who did not support them were not really or fully Christian at all. On left-right issues they tended to occupy the centre, close to the Centre and Liberal parties. The Conservative parties in each country, which had traditionally been supported by more conventional churchgoers, especially resented the implication that they were more con-cerned with the interests of business and the professions and the liberal culture of the middle classes than with defending and promoting Christian values. For them, with their more conventional concept of Christian values, there was no contradiction. Indeed, almost all the other parties argued that the Christian Democratic parties' seeming concentration on moral-religious issues was improper and misplaced, representing a distasteful sort of 'moral vigilantism'.[24]

The Christian Democratic parties were not alone however in disrupting the previously established five-party model, which had characterised Scandinavia from the 1920s. The emergence of left-socialist parties in Denmark and Norway in the late 1950s and of Green parties in Sweden and Finland from the 1980s onwards introduced other new sources and lines of cleavage, which gave expression to domestic and foreign policy divisions, general anti-establishment opinion and a new culture-radicalism. A third new group of parties, represented by the radical populist parties of the right, for instance in Denmark, which pioneered the trend in 1973, also had the effect of raising the political profile of ethical issues and cultural cleavages. As champions of general deregulation and opponents of 'nanny state' controls, for example on alcohol consumption, each of these so-called progress parties also defined themselves strongly in opposition to the Christian Democrats, an opposition which was only sharpened as the issues of immigration and third world aid became polarised. By 1990 the full series of party system changes had collectively contributed to and highlighted the distinctiveness of the Christian Democratic parties' stands across a range of policy areas. Having established themselves, albeit at widely differing levels of support, they had each tended to move beyond the narrowness and stridency that had characterised them in their earliest years.

---

24   D. Arter, "The Finnish Christian League. Party or Anti-Party?", in: *Scandinavian Political Studies*, 2 (1980) 143-162. While the charge seems merited particularly during the earliest developmental phase, for each party there were always other distinctive policy commitments, for example on social policy or international development.

Mixed fortunes since 1990

The period since 1990 has been one of mixed fortunes for Scandinavian Christian Democracy. In Denmark no advance has been made on the party's modest levels of performance in the 1980s (ranging between 2.0 and 2.7%). Indeed in 1994, after a short period of office in a Social Democrat-led coalition, the party suffered the indignity of losing all its seats, as it dropped below the 2% threshold for representation. The Finnish Christian Democrats have fared only slightly better. They have maintained a fairly steady level of modest representation albeit with a rising trend in their electoral support at the two most recent elections. The party's inclusion in the Centre Party-led Esko Aho coalition government from 1992 to 1994 did not lead to the same electoral reckoning as that suffered by the Danish. That period in government had ended unhappily when the party leader, Toimi Kankaanniemi, resigned from office over a fundamental disagreement about European policy. However, soon after, the party embarked on a programme of reform and reorientation under the new leadership of Bjarne Kallis. As will shortly be seen, this new departure has been associated with important changes of policy as well as of style. The fact that the party received no dividend for its increased share of votes by way of extra seats in 2003 was a result of the collapse of its former electoral agreement with the Centre Party.

While neither the Danish nor the Finnish party has quite escaped the electoral relegation zone since 1990, they have both been able to enjoy the fruits of office in government. As is evident from coalition theory, size is far from everything, especially for parties that occupy the centre of the party spectrum and are prepared to cooperate either to the left or right, provided they can advance their own policy agenda. In the Danish case, despite its low electoral support the party has been able to benefit from a fine parliamentary balance between left and right, which has gifted them the opportunity of exercising influence. On a number of occasions during the party's first twenty years they had learnt to engage with some success in the complicated parliamentary game of 'majority-mongering' as minority governments cast about for support, issue by issue. Having served in the 1980s in Conservative-led coalitions, from 1993 to 1994 they served in the Social Democrat-led coalition government of Poul Nyrup Rasmussen, thus neatly underlining their centrist credentials. These were the achievements of what, as of early 2004, still remain minor parties in Finland and Denmark, while the picture in Norway and Sweden has been one of increasingly substantial parties, well-placed in the new turbulence of the 1990s to make an impact.

National election results in Norway, Sweden, Denmark and Finland since 1989

NORWAY	1989	1993	1997	2001
Socialist Left	10.1	7.9	6	12.5
Labour	34.3	36.9	35	24.3
Centre	6.5	16.8	7.9	5.6
Christians	8.5	7.9	13.7	12.4
Liberal	3.2	3.6	4.5	3.9
Conservatives	22.2	17	14.3	21.2
Progress	13	6.3	15.3	14.7

SWEDEN	1991	1994	1998	2002
Left Party	4.5	6.2	11.9	8.3
Greens	3.4	5	4.5	4.6
Soc Dems	37.7	45.3	36.6	39.8
Centre	8.5	7.7	5.1	6.1
Christians	7.1	4.1	11.8	9.1
Liberals	9.1	7.2	4.7	13.3
Conservatives	21.9	22.4	22.7	15.2

DENMARK	1990	1994	1998	2001
Unity List	1.7	3.1	2.7	2.4
Soc Peoples	8.3	7.3	7.6	6.4
Soc Dems	37.4	34.6	35.9	29.1
Soc Libs	3.5	4.6	3.9	5.2
Christians	2.3	1.9	2.5	2.3
Liberals	15.8	23.3	24	31.3
Conservatives	16	15	8.9	9.1
D Peoples	6.4	6.4	7.4	12

FINLAND	1991	1995	1999	2003*
Left Alliance	10.1	11.2	10.9	9.9
Greens	6.8	6.5	7.5	8
Soc Dems	22.1	28.3	22.9	24.5
Centre	24.8	19.8	22.4	24.7
Christians	3.1	3	4.2	5.3
Sw Peoples	5.8	5.5	5.1	4.6
Nat Coaln	19.3	17.9	21	18.6
True Finns	4.8	1.3	1	1.6

*<www.stat.fi/tk/tp/tasku/taskue_vaalit.html> (12.03.2004)
Source: D. Arter, *Scandinavian Politics Today*, Manchester, 2002.

In the 1980s Norway's KrF had twice taken office in Conservative-led coalition governments, between 1983 and 1986 under Kåre Willoch and between 1989 and 1990 under Jan Per Syse. The 1980s had been the decade of the so-called *høyrebølgen* (Conservative wave) in Norwegian politics, when the Conservative party, despite being out-flanked to its right by the Progress Party, had enjoyed an Indian summer. Although as the largest of the country's three centrist parties, the Christian Democrats had played a significant part in the history of the Willoch government, they failed to prosper electorally, dropping back from over 12% in the 1970s to only 8.3% in 1985, approximately the level of support the party had been stuck at during the 1960s. The late 1990s however saw a definite resurgence in the party's fortunes as KrF attained a record level 13.7% in 1997. Its leader, Kjell Magne Bondevik, succeeded in becoming the first leader of a Christian Democratic party in the Nordic area to be elected prime minister in a general election.

The party had outshone its centrist allies (the Centre and Liberal parties), and successfully projected its leader as the people's choice for prime minister. Tensions between the Centre and Conservative parties over relations with Europe virtually ruled out the possibility of including the Conservatives in a broader non-socialist coalition however, and the Bondevik minority coalition consequently rested on a very narrow parliamentary base. The appointment of the government nonetheless symbolised the fact that the Christian Democrats had finally arrived at the very centre of Norwegian public life after a long pilgrimage from its origins on the geographical periphery. As the largest of the centrist parties it was able to benefit from the difficulties experienced by the larger parties to both left and right as they attempted to meet the challenges posed by more extreme rivals on their flanks. Despite the coalition's weak minority support-base, it proved to have a greater longevity than most commentators originally expected, lasting two-and-a-half years until it finally succumbed in 2000 on an energy and environment issue. Only eighteen months later however, after the 2001 election, Bondevik again became prime minister, this time of a more broadly-based centre-right government which now included the Conservative party.

In Sweden the 1980s had ended in disappointment. The party's single representative had failed to gain re-election in 1988 and the prospects again looked bleak. Beneath the surface, a number of changes were however occurring which in the 1990s were to foster a remarkable upturn in the party's fortunes. The party's leader since 1973 - and its solitary member of parliament between 1985 and 1988 - Alf Svensson, had been working for some time to transform the party "from a narrow evangelical band to an all-inclusive party based on non-dogmatic caring-Christian values".[25] From a Pentecostal background himself, Svensson presided over a distinct opening-up of the party. From initially representing a small minority of religiously active voters from low church and 'free church' denominational backgrounds the party started to project a wider, inter-faith image by having candidates from the Jewish and Islamic communities placed on its lists. In 2002 the country's leading imam called on Muslims to vote for the Christian Democrats on the grounds that their approach to social issues and family policy was closest to Islamic values.

The 1990s were an electoral roller-coaster for the Swedish party; unrepresented since 1988 (2.9%), in 1991 it enjoyed a surge of support to 7.1%, dipping to just over 4.0% in 1994, only to rise four years later to fully 11.8%. These vicissitudes were partly conjunctural as the decade first promised and then disappointed in terms of both a new world order and new patterns of domestic politics. In 1991 the party benefited along with the other non-socialist parties from the sense of a new era in international relations with the collapse of the Soviet Union, the start of negotiations for entry into the European Union (EU) and the perceived failure of the Social Democrats' economic management. Immediately following the 1991 election the party joined the centre-right coalition led by Carl Bildt, with Svensson as minister of foreign aid and development. As leader of the Conservative party, Bildt had campaigned for a new beginning in Sweden, promising to leave behind the corporatist over-regulation with which the Social Democrats were said to be identified and to press

25   D. Arter, "The Swedish General Election of 20th September 1998. A Victory for Values over Policies?", in: *Electoral Studies*, 2 (1999) 299.

on with negotiating entry into the EU. In both respects the leaderships of the other coalition partners, including the Christian Democrats, concurred, while putting a brake on some of the Conservatives' more neo-liberal policy commitments.

Three years later, after the country's worst economic crisis since the 1930s had undermined that coalition's claim to represent a successful new departure, the Christian Democrats suffered a major setback as they only just managed to retain their parliamentary representation, gaining a mere fraction above the 4% threshold. At the next general election in 1998, however, they bounced back by almost trebling that share of the vote and achieving a new highpoint with 11.8%. They appeared to benefit, as did the other big gainer in the election, the former communist Left Party, from emphasising values of solidarity and caring while the principal parties of left and right, the Social Democrats and the Conservatives, contested each others' policies and record in the area of overall economic management. This significant expansion of the party's electoral base clearly reflected a new ability to attract support beyond the narrow constituency of religious revivalism from which it had sprung. Electoral success thus underlined the party's change of profile from one of a narrowly Christian, almost single-issue protest movement to a more mature party concerned with a much broader range of issues, including questions of social justice and welfare at home and abroad.

All four of the parties have been committed - if with varying degrees of success - to broadening their appeal beyond the activist Christian minority to which they initially appealed and from whom they had taken their inspiration. This tended to occur in two stages, first by broadening the range of religious groups to which it could appeal and then calling for the support of any who endorsed the parties' aims and policies, regardless of their religious background. Despite some success in both these respects none of the parties can be said to have become catch-all parties however. In their early years, as already noted, they had each tended to concentrate on what were, for the campaigning groups that had pioneered them, 'core' moral-religious issues - the place of religion in the schools, the control of alcohol, drugs and pornography and issues such as abortion, homosexuality and so on - almost to the exclusion of others. The electoral core was not identified by particular social class characteristics however - like their Continental sister parties, the Christian Democratic parties share a cross-class electorate - but by its association with each country's activist religious subculture.[26] At a later stage, this has even enabled them to appeal for example to immigrant Muslim communities. In Sweden, as already noted, this appeal was endorsed at the highest level in the immigrant community, while in Norway and Denmark the parties were able to attract the support of a number of young Muslims, at least in the major urban areas. The parties' conservative views on issues such as homosexual rights and abortion and their vigorous condemnation of anti-immigrant sentiments on the part of radical populists of the right increased their attractiveness. In the Norwegian case, however, the rule that all party officials and candidates should be 'personal Christians' still presents a barrier to further widening in this direction at the urging of the party leadership. In Denmark in 2003, on the other hand when representatives of the party's old revivalist connections called for the formal adoption of a similar rule, the motion was withdrawn before it could be debated at the party conference.[27]

The Christian Democratic parties have however, over time, been required by their involvement in party-political competition to decide and adopt policy stands across all major areas of government policy and this has involved each of them in debating the social and political implications of religious faith and values. By the late 1960s and 1970s the Norwegian party, as the longest-established, the most developed, and the first to enjoy government office, had already developed a full range of policy positions in the context of a relatively vigorous debate on party principles and ideology. By the 1990s the other three parties had followed this lead, borrowing much from the Norwegian example while adding their own contributions.

The Swedish Christian Democrats in particular engaged in this broadening and deepening process and soon surpassed the Norwegians in their openness to new impulses. In some respects they had the furthest to travel. Although Pentecostalism like other charismatic movements tends to be remarkably tolerant of denominational differences, it is a distinctly minority religious tradition, all the more noticeable because of the contrast between its revivalist style and the rather staid atmosphere of the established church

---

26   O. Listhaug, *Citizens, Parties and Norwegian Electoral Politics (1957-1985). An Empirical Study*, Oslo, 1989, 161.

27   In 1994 a Muslim who had joined the party and who openly nursed the ambition to become a parliamentary candidate was prevented from succeeding when the party's executive ruled that it would "not approve a candidate publicly confessing any other religion than Christianity": private communication from the party's Secretary General, B.K. Johansen, 2 February 2004.

and the more conventional 'free churches'.[28] Party chairman Svensson realised early on that the party's only chance of breaking through the 4% barrier
for parliamentary representation was to broaden its appeal. Its initial name,
Kristen Demokratisk Samling (Christian Democratic Rally), reflected the intention of bringing all Christians who were both committed to democracy and
shared the party's concern for the nation's spiritual health together in a rally
(or union or coalition as the Swedish word *samling* can be variously trans-
lated). In 1991 the party changed its name to the *Kristdemokratiska Samhällspartiet* (Christian Democratic Society Party) in an attempt to advertise its
concerns with all aspects of Swedish society and politics. Its great surge in
support at the election, which followed later the same year, seemed to indicate the success of these efforts. Finally, in 1996 the party again changed its
name to simply *Kristdemokraterna* (Christian Democrats). Encouraged by the
Swedish example, party reformers in Finland and Denmark have argued for
a parallel shift in emphasis and successfully campaigned for a name change
to symbolise a growing identification with Continental Christian Democracy.
Thus in 2001 and 2003 respectively the Finnish and Danish parties also adopted the label 'Christian Democrats'.

Scandinavian Christian Democracy and the issue of European integration

The most dramatic impact in Scandinavia of the momentous changes in
the international system symbolised by the fall of the Berlin Wall was in
the field of relations with the EU. In Sweden and Finland the option of
EU membership opened up for the first time as the commitment to neutrality
between the superpowers, which had always been understood to preclude
membership, ceased to have the same purchase. Twenty years after turning
down membership in the 1972 referendum Norway was also faced with revis-
iting the question, while in Denmark - a member since 1973 - the ratification
of the Maastricht treaty raised cognate issues. It might have been supposed
that the new structure of opportunities that had opened up in Northern
Europe would have been particularly welcome to the Christian Democratic
parties - European integration can be seen after all as in large measure the

---

28   In 2000 the Swedish Evangelical Lutheran Church ceased officially to be the state church
although it retains a number of valuable links with the state: G. Gustafsson, "Church-State
Separation Swedish-Style", in: J.T.S. Madeley and Z. Enyedi (ed.), *Church and State in Contemporary Europe. The Chimera of Neutrality*, London, 2003, 51-72.

principal political project of Continental Christian Democracy. Far from providing the opportunity for a common endeavour and a rapprochement with their sister parties on the Continent however, the European issue has been a stumbling block and sign of contradiction. The different parties' divergent stands on European integration and the internal tensions each of them has experienced over the issue provide a graphic illustration of the continuing differences both within and between the individual parties, of Scandinavian Christian Democracy's remaining collective distinctiveness and, finally, of a discernible trend towards a growing identification with Continental Christian Democracy.

The Swedish Christian Democrats have been the most enthusiastic supporters of EU entry from the time around 1990 when it first opened up as a realistic prospect. On the basis of Ray's data measuring party orientations towards European integration it is evident that the party had by 1992 become overall a strong supporter.[29] At a special conference in the summer of 1994 a few months before the referendum the party confirmed its support and the leadership entered vigorously into the campaign in favour of a yes vote. Despite this official stance, party opinion was, however, by no means unanimous. As the Ray data indicates, there was significant internal dissent over the issue; at the 1994 conference concerns were expressed for example over the implications for both neutrality and the control of alcohol, and at the referendum a majority of party supporters actually voted against entry.

In neighbouring Finland meanwhile the Christian Democrats officially adopted the opposite stance on EU entry.[30] The Ray data places them as clearly the most vigorously Eurosceptic of Finnish parties throughout the period 1984 to 1996; it was also the party which was most united on the issue. In 1994 the party's leader left the Aho coalition in protest against the preparations for EU entry and as late as 1996 it was still calling for Finland to withdraw at the first opportunity while also fighting against adoption of the Euro. Nor can this stance be seen as a reflection of wider public opinion; although a significant minority of the electorate voted against entry, the Finnish majority in favour

29   L. Ray, "Measuring Party Orientations towards European Integration. Results from an Expert Survey", in: *European Journal of Political Research*, 2 (1999) 283-306. See the reanalysis of the data for the Nordic countries in J.T.S. Madeley and N. Sitter, *Differential Euroscepticism among the Nordic Christian Parties. Protestantism or Protest?*, paper presented at the Political Studies Association Conference, University of Leicester, April 2003.

30   K.M. Johansson and T. Raunio, "Partisan Responses to Europe. Comparing Finnish and Swedish Political Parties", in: *European Journal of Political Research*, 2 (2001) 239.

of European integration was considerable and the Christian Democratic party was one of only two small parties that were officially opposed to membership.[31]

For Norway and Denmark membership had been a live option since the 1960s. During Norway's 1972 referendum the Christian Democratic leadership had been evenly divided while the party members had voted overwhelmingly against entering the EC. Whereas the division of opinion was intense across the country and internally in most parties, KrF was able to survive intact, unlike the Liberal Party which split in two and almost disappeared althogether. For two decades the issue was firmly off the agenda as all leading parties feared a recurrence of the bitter conflict of 1972 but by 1990 it arose again unavoidable as the Finnish and Swedish applications were lodged. KrF adopted a negative stance on entry, regarding the European Economic Area Agreement as involving the maximum tolerable degree of integration, and a large majority of the party's supporters voted accordingly.

In Denmark the membership issue had been settled in 1972 and by the 1990s the Danish Christian Democrats were rated as largely, but not enthusiastically, in favour of European integration. Contemporaneously with the membership debates in Norway, Sweden and Finland however, the Danes had a referendum debate about the Maastricht Treaty and, when in June 1992 a majority narrowly voted against ratification, a great majority of Christian voters contributed to the no vote. Even though the country has experienced thirty years of EU membership, the Christian Democrats remain divided over the prospects for both deepening and widening. Latterly the party leadership has become much more open to these prospects and has introduced a rule that party members who stand in European elections must undertake to join the party group of the European People's Party (EPP) if elected.[32] The party remains committed to upholding Denmark's opt-out on Euro-membership.

Taken together the most surprising aspect of this record is the degree of Euroscepticism to be found in the Nordic Christian Democratic parties, at least in the early 1990s, given the almost unanimous support for European integration found among Christian Democrats further south. Even in Sweden

---

31   T. Raunio, "Facing the European Challenge. Finnish Parties Adjust to the Integration Process", in: *West European Politics*, 1 (1999) 145.

32   Previously, it had been possible for party members to stand as anti-EU candidates, for example on the so-called June Movement slate. See for the EPP(-ED) Group the chapter "A Decade of Seized Opportunities. Christian Democracy in the European Union" in this volume.

where the party leadership has been most supportive of European integration there has been a large section of party opinion that has been strongly opposed. The reason for this relative Euroscepticism cannot simply be ascribed to the overwhelmingly Lutheran Protestant heritage. The national Church leaderships, by contrast with the Christian Democratic parties, have tended to be clearly in favour of European integration.[33] Amongst parts of the evangelical religious minority, which form the core of the parties' historic support base, however the distinctive qualities of Scandinavia's Lutheran-Evangelical heritage, which they cherish and seek to uphold, have seemed to be threatened by accelerating European integration. For some in the parties the EU has always been seen to represent what in the Scandinavian languages are 'the three k's': Catholicism, Capitalism and Conservatism.[34] Moreover, for a relatively minor but nonetheless vocal fringe of fundamentalist believers, European integration is even of the devil.[35] With some extreme sectarian viewpoints and beliefs subsisting within the activist religious minorities it is not surprising that party leaderships should tread warily.

In none of the parties has the tension between often strongly opposed viewpoints disappeared, although it seems as if the balance between pro- and anti-integration supporters has tended to shift, often quite markedly, in favour of the former. This is partly a function of the fact that in Denmark, Finland and Sweden continued membership is no longer seen as a live issue. Whereas the pace and direction of both widening and deepening changes continue to be controversial both within the Christian Democratic parties and more widely, only a small minority espouses the option of withdrawal. Thus while recent referendum decisions have gone against adoption of the Euro in Denmark and Sweden - with and against, respectively, the stand of the respective Christian Democratic party leaderships - there has been a certain maturing of party opinion.

---

33   S. Sundback, "The Nordic Lutheran Churches and the EU Question in 1994", in: *Temenos. Studies in Comparative Religion*, 8 (2001) 191-208.

34   The Schuman plan was presented in Sweden in the 1950s as also representing another unwanted 'k' - Cartels: S. Gstoehl, *Reluctant Europeans. Norway, Sweden and Switzerland in the Process of Integration*, London, 2002, 53.

35   Thus Mathieu quotes one comment from the debate within the Danish party that 'portrays the Union as the forerunner of the anti-Christ' and other examples of this form of argumentation can be traced in the other countries: C .Mathieu, *The Moral Life of the Party. Moral Argumentation and the Creation of Meaning in the Europe Policy Debates of the Christian and Left-Socialist Parties in Denmark and Sweden (1990-1996)*, Lund, 1999, 163.

The most telling indicator of a trend within the parties in favour of a selfconscious alignment with Continental Christian Democracy is to be found in the shift of nomenclature. As already noted, the Swedish Christian Democrats have included an explicit reference to Christian Democracy in their namefrom the first. They finally moved to adopt the straightforward label *Kristdemokraterna* (Christian Democrats) in 1996 shortly after becoming the first full member of the EPP among the Nordic Christian Democratic parties.[36] In 2001 the Finnish Christian Democrats also decided under the reforming leadership of Bjarne Kallis to become known as *Kristillis-demokraatit/Kristdemokraterna* (Christian Democrats). And in 2003, finally, the Danish party also renamed itself the *Kristendemokraterne* (Christian Democrats). In each case those who pressed for the name change, often against strong opposition, saw it as symbolic of the parties realising their full political identity and connecting with their Continental counterparts.[37] As of early 2004 therefore three of the four parties now bear the Christian Democratic label, with only the Norwegian party holding fast to its original name as it does to its generally Eurosceptic stance. Other changes reflect a stepwise reorientation in favour of European integration; thus the Finnish and Danish Christian Democratic parties have followed their Swedish sister party into the EPP.[38] However, it remains the case that even the most Euroenthusiastic of the parties retain a certain caution about their countries' relations with the EU. Thus, the leadership of the Swedish party, which should according to one author be seen as a supporter of the federalist aims of the EPP programme, is required to stress that it opposes anything that would threaten to undermine Sweden's high standards of welfare provision, social insurance and environmental protection.[39]

36   The party was granted EPP associate member status in 1991 and full membership on Sweden's EU entry in 1995.

37   In Denmark the decision by over 70% of the delegates at the October 2003 party conference to change the name was strongly opposed by Finn Sjursen who had led the party for a decade up to 2002.

38   The Scandinavian Conservative parties - the Danish *Konservative Folkeparti* (Conservative People's Party), the Finnish *Kansallinen Kokomoos* (National Coalition), the Norwegian *Høyre* (Right) and the Swedish *Moderate Samlingspartiet* (Moderate Unity Party) all became permanent observers of EPP in 1993 and after the 1995 European election, with the exception of the Norwegian party, full members. In the case of Sweden the membership of the Christian Democrats in 1991 predated that of the Conservatives: T. Jansen, *The European People's Party. Origins and Development*, Basingstoke, 1998, 118.

39   K.M. Johansson, "EU och Partieväsendet", in: K.M. Johansson, *Sverige och EU*, Stockholm, 1999, 156.

Conclusion

Maier argued that Protestantism had made only a minimal contribution to the formation of Christian Democracy.[40] Kalyvas commented that "[w]ith the exception of the Dutch Calvinist parties, all other notable nineteenth-century confessional parties were Catholic, and 'Catholicness' was central to their identity".[41] Van Kersbergen has even claimed that the Scandinavian Christian Democratic parties should not be seen as 'Christian Democratic' at all but rather as Christian parties of moral protest.[42] As the account provided above shows however, even if they started out as moral protest parties - and even if they are still to an extent marked by these origins - Scandinavia's Christian Democratic parties have become much more self-consciously Christian Democratic, three of them having adopted the label itself and all of them developing growing links with their sister parties on the Continent.[43]

It could be argued that Scandinavian Christian Democracy provides an attractive alternative model to the more secular Continental model, one furthermore which is - paradoxically - more suited to the conditions of advanced secular societies. In this respect, Aardal points out that "[o]ne major difference between the Continental and the Nordic Christian parties is that economic issues tend to be predominant compared to particular religious issues in the former parties, while religious issues take precedence over economic issues in the latter parties".[44] As ethical issues ranging from abortion to world poverty, drug control to immigration policy, tend to increase in their political salience, it is perhaps in these areas, rather than in the fields of economic planning or welfare state development, that Christian Democrats have a distinctive contribution to make. Nor does this imply that Christian Democracy should become narrower or more 'sectarian', hiving itself off into a ghetto of moral protest. In Scandinavia where the legacy of half a millennium of Lutheran preaching has encouraged a general tendency to moralise social and political issues, the Christian Democratic parties have developed a propensity

40   H. Maier, *Revolution and Church. The Early History of Christian Democracy (1789-1901)*, Notre Dame, 1969, 5.
41   S.N. Kalyvas, *The Rise of Christian Democracy in Europe*, Ithaca, 1996, 1.
42   K. Van Kersbergen, *Social Capitalism*, 255.
43   Norway's KrF occasionally claims to be more truly Christian Democratic than the Continental Christian Democrats that are often seen as too much in thrall to market capitalism. See for instance K.M. Bondevik, *Det tredje alternativet. Kristendemokratisk 'på norsk'*, Oslo, 1994; E. Rimehaug, *Midtbanespilleren. Kjell Magne Bondevik og Kristelig Folkepart*, Oslo, 1997.
44   B. Aardal, *The Religious Factor in Political Life in the Nordic Countries*, paper presented at the 15th Nordic Conference in Sociology of Religion, Oslo, August 2000, 7.

for preaching 'values' - even the value of 'values' - across the whole range of policy areas, as though the religious-based values to which they conspicuously subscribe represented a sort of gold standard.[45]

The policy mix of the Scandinavian Christian Democratic parties distinguishes them from the Social Democrats and left socialists on their left as well as from their conservative and radical populist rivals on the right. While maintaining neighbourly relations with the Conservative parties with which they share membership in, or association with, the EPP at the European level, they self-consciously keep a policy distance. Aside from their particular commitments on protection-of-life issues, especially abortion, the combination of strong welfarism, antiracism, environmentalism and support for high levels of aid to the Third World has proved attractive to centrist voters beyond the rather narrow constituency of religious activists. In their advocacy of Third World development and in their commitment to generous support for the old, the sick and the handicapped, they typically refer to Christian moral obligations, rather than arguing in terms of a prudentially sound approach to social insurance. Equally, their generally strong endorsement of policies of environmental protection has been argued in terms of Christian notions of 'stewardship' of the world's resources. Could it be that while secularisation continues to advance in mainland Europe, an opposite, de-secularising trend is evident on the Continent's northern periphery? Or should the relatively new stirrings in the Nordic area merely be significant for negative reasons, as the previously hegemonic position of Scandinavian Social Democracy is degraded by economic globalisation and its consequences? Either way, it is curious and thought-provoking that in the 1990s, which saw a general recession in the fortunes of Christian Democracy across its heartland in Continental Europe, there has been a distinct resurgence of Christian Democracy, if perhaps only a modest one, in the previously unpromising territories of Europe's far north.

45   A graphic illustration of this was provided by the first Bondevik government (1997-2000) when it set up a Values Commission to undertake social scientific research on the value orientations of Norwegians with the hope of illuminating the nature and significance of the choices the country faced in moral as well as material terms.

Who Learns from Whom?
The Failure of Spanish Christian Democracy and the Success of the Partido Popular

Peter Matuschek

During the 1990s, no single centre-right or conservative party went through an evolution comparable to that of the Spanish *Partido Popular* (PP). The Spanish Conservatives delivered a remarkable success story, having transformed themselves from a post-Francoist minority party on the far right of the political spectrum into an apparently centrist party occupying a dominant position in the national party system.[1] The PP managed to develop successfully in the hostile climate that followed the long-lasting right-wing dictatorship, experienced a steady growth in votes and finally ousted the long ruling *Partido Socialista Obrero Español* (PSOE) from power in 1996. What is more, the PP was even able to increase its share of the vote in 2000 and to win an absolute majority of seats in the Spanish parliament, a development until then considered impossible by political scientists given the persistent centre-left orientation of the Spanish electorate.

The success of the PP stood in sharp contrast to the failure of many traditional centre-right parties in Western Europe during the 1990s, like the German Christian Democrats, the British Conservatives or the Italian Christian Democrats, and resulted in an exceptional position for the party. This position was exploited by the PP and its leader José María Aznar, who had assumed a leading role both within the European People's Party (EPP) and the Christian Democrat and People's Parties International, and is reflected in the increased presence of prominent PP members in leading positions in these transnational party organisations.[2]

---

1   The term 'success' is understood here as 'electoral success': a steady and persistent increase of the vote share on all levels during the 1990s.
2   See the chapter "A Decade of Seized Opportunities. Christian Democracy in the European Union" in ths volume.

Yes, despite this evolution, the PP has not inspired much research for a long time. The lack of research interest in Christian Democratic and centre-right parties in general is a commonplace that does not need to be repeated. It is particularly true of Southern European centre-right parties, especially in the countries of the so-called Third Wave, the latecomers to democratisation.[3] Both facts underline the necessity for further research and justify a closer inquiry into the reasons for the success of the PP and its implications.[4]

Why did Christian Democracy fail in Spain?

In the case of the Southern European latecomers to democracy (Spain, Portugal and Greece) which established a competitive party system only in the mid-1970s, the parties of the right, even of the democratic right, were forced to tackle particular problems of democratic legitimacy after decades (in the case of Spain and Portugal) of right-wing dictatorship. Apart from that, in the party system that emerged in Spain following the transition from Francoism to democracy, the right was fragmented into three main groups: a) the so-called bunker, represented by the extreme right-wing *Fuerza Nueva* (New Force), who opposed any development towards democracy and favoured maintaining the status quo of Francoism; b) the group around Manuel Fraga, a former minister in the Franco regime, which crystallized in the *Alianza Popular* (AP) and advocated political liberalisation, albeit limited and excluding the communists and some regionalists[5]; and c) the reformists grouped together by the Prime Minister Adolfo Suárez into the *Unión de Centro Democrático* (UCD),[6] the latter clearly promoting a democracy on the Western European model.[7] Another kind of division of the right and centre-right resulted from the vertical fragmentation into the nationwide parties mentioned and several parties on the regional level, especially in Catalonia and the Basque country.

3   S.P. Huntington, *The Third Wave. Democratisation in the Late Twentieth Century*, Norman, 1991.
4   Apart from the literature on the PP, this chapter is based on research of party documents, observation of party congresses and exclusive interviews with senior officials from the PP headquarters in Madrid.
5   Manuel Fraga Iribarne, born in the region of Galicia, was Minister of Information and Tourism under Franco from 1962 to 1969 and Spanish Ambassador to the UK between 1973 and 1975.
6   Adolfo Suárez González, born in the region of Old Castile, was Deputy Secretary General of the official party under Franco *Movimiento* (Movement) and Director of the Spanish Public Broadcasting Network in the early 1970s.
7   J. Hopkin, "Spain. Political Parties in a Young Democracy", in: D. Broughton and M. Donovan (eds.), *Changing Party Systems in Western Europe*, London/New York, 1999, 212-213.

Even more interesting is the fact that one particular kind of party did not emerge in post-dictatorship Spain. Like the question raised by Sombart as to why socialism did not emerge in the United States of America, one could ask why no Christian Democratic party was able to establish itself in Catholic Spain.[8] Indeed, the development of the Spanish party system after the transition to democracy has disproved all predictions about the nature of the centre-right spectrum that had been made during the 1960s and early 1970s. Both Linz and von Beyme had predicted the dominance of the centre-right in Spain by a large Christian Democratic party, deriving their assumptions from (the supposedly) existing similarities with Spain and Italy.[9] Several Christian Democratic groups, partly loyal to the Franco regime, had emerged during the 1950s and 1960s and since 1965 had even enjoyed international support from other Christian Democratic parties in Western Europe. During the 1977 election campaign especially (the first after Franco's death in 1975), the Spanish Christian Democrats had been backed - not least financially - by the German, Italian and Benelux Christian Democratic parties.[10] Opinion polls before the first elections had been quite favourable to these parties. However, against all expectations, no significant Christian Democratic party was able to establish itself, a fact that can be variously explained.

The first reason relates to the relevance of the religious cleavage in post-Franco Spain. It is noteworthy that the establishment of a Christian Democratic party was very much dependent on the intensity of the state-church cleavage in the competition between political parties. However, this cleavage was de-emphasised during the transition to democracy, and parties did not use religion in order to mobilise support. In contrast to the Second Republic during the 1930s, the Left in the new democracy was not openly anti-religious, nor militantly anti-clerical, and even the *Partido Comunista de España* (PCE), inspired by Eurocommunism, had developed moderate positions.[11]

---

8 W. Sombart, *Warum gibt es in den Vereinigten Staaten keinen Sozialismus?*, Tübingen, 1906.
9 J.J. Linz, "The Party System of Spain. Past and Future", in: S.M. Lipset and S. Rokkan (eds.), *Party Systems and Voter Alignments. Cross-National Perpectives*, New York/London, 1967, 267; K. von Beyme, *Vom Faschismus zur Entwicklungsdiktatur. Machtelite und Opposition in Spanien*, München, 1971, 120.
10 R. Gunther, G. Sani and G. Shabad, *Spain after Franco. The Making of a Comparative Party System*, Berkeley/Los Angeles/New York, 1988, 108.
11 C. Huneeus, La Unión de Centro Democrático y la Transición a la Democracia en España, Madrid, 1985, 181.

The second reason was the lack of an organisational infrastructure that only the Catholic Church would have been able to provide. The Church, however, rejected any intention of supporting the foundation of a Christian Democratic party, a condition that had already been mentioned by Linz as an indispensable pre-requisite for success.[12] The Spanish Church had increasingly distanced itself from the Franco regime since the 1960s in the aftermath of the Second Vatican Council and as a result of personnel renewal within its own hierarchy.[13] By the beginning of the 1970s, thanks to lessons learned from its close relationship with the Franco regime, it had adopted a position of abstention from direct political involvement.[14]

A third factor relates to the organisational weakness of the Christian Democratic proto-parties. The refusal of their leaders to merge their groupings into a single party before the first elections may be considered to have been crucial to their poor performance.[15] Instead, a considerable part of the Christian Democrat sector was absorbed elsewhere, as some groups finally joined Suárez' electoral alliance under the umbrella of the UCD, the coalition that became a partial 'substitute' for a Christian Democratic party.[16] It is significant that once the Christian Democratic sectors of the UCD left the party in 1982 and founded the *Partido Demócrata Popular* (PDP),[17] the only way to survive was in an electoral alliance with the rightist AP as a senior partner during the elections of 1982 and 1986, and that once it left the alliance after 1986 the PDP failed completely.[18] The PDP split and was renamed *Democracia Cristiana* (Christian Democracy). It was dissolved in 1989, with some prominent members joining the newly founded PP.

---

12   J.J. Linz, "The Party System of Spain", 267.

13   R. Gunther, G. Sani and G. Shabad, *Spain after Franco*, 110; C. Huneeus, *La Unión de Centro Democrático y la Transición a la Democracia en España*, 177-179.

14   In the long run, this neutrality turned out to be more beneficial for the Church than would have been the direct support of any political group. It allowed the Church to take more legitimate stances on issues such as abortion, divorce or educational reform: R. Cotarelo, "El sistema de partidos", in: J.F. Tezanos, R. Cotarelo and A. de Blas (eds.), *La transición democrática española*, Madrid, 1989, 367.

15   R. Gunther, G. Sani and G. Shabad, *Spain after Franco,* 108; C. Huneeus, *La Unión de Centro Democrático y la Transición a la Democracia en España*, 183-185.

16   J.J. Linz and J.R. Montero, "The Party Systems of Spain. Old Cleavages and New Challenges", in: L. Karvonen and S. Kuhnle (eds.), *Party Systems and Voter Alignments Revisited*, London/New York, 2001, 151.

17   This party was founded in 1982 and led by Óscar Alzaga who had defected from the UCD parliamentary group, together with a group of 20 other former UCD deputies.

18   Rather than revive the alliance with the AP, the PDP decided to run in a coalition with the two tiny parties in the 1987 regional, local and European elections. The outcome was disastrous.

The fact that an organised Christian Democratic party failed to emerge may finally be explained by the strategic errors of some Christian Democratic leaders (including the most prominent ones, Joaquín Ruiz Giménez and José María Gil Robles) during the 1977 election campaign. Their inability to unite was aggravated by the misguided campaign of Ruiz Giménez. His party, the *Izquierda Democrática* (United Democrats), ran a rather left-leaning campaign that never managed to connect with its potential electorate of rural and conservative voters.[19]

The failure of organised Christian Democracy in Spain is interesting from a theoretical point of view as it illustrates the dominance of political factors in the emergence of parties and party systems over purely sociological factors. A deterministic relationship does not exist between social structure or social change and the structure of party competition,[20] a misapprehension Panebianco has accurately called "the sociological prejudice".[21]

From the margin to the centre: the electoral evolution of the PP

As mentioned above, the Spanish Conservatives started as a small party on the right in 1977, with the AP gaining only 8% of the vote. In the general elections of 1982, the AP partly 'inherited' the electoral base of the UCD, which had been reduced to a minority party with 6% of the vote. On the one hand, the AP changed into the second largest party on the national level with 26% of the vote. This would be almost exactly the share of votes which the party would maintain in the three general elections during the 1980s, from an electorate that remained remarkably loyal in spite of internal party turmoil throughout that decade. On the other hand, the AP seemed unable to break through its electoral ceiling and seriously challenge the dominance of the governing Socialist Party despite its constant electoral losses. The parties who benefited from the PSOE's losses were the *Izquierda Unida* (IU), the nationwide *Centro Democrático y Social* (CDyS) and some regionalist parties.

19   C. Huneeus, *La Unión de Centro Democrático y la Transición a la Democracia en España*, 187; R. Gunther, G. Sani and G. Shabad, *Spain after Franco*, 111.
20   R. Gunther and J.R. Montero, "The Anchors of Partisanship. A Comparative Analysis of Voting Behavior in Four Southern European Democracies", in: P.N. Diamandouros and R. Gunther (eds.), *Parties, Politics and Democracy in the New Southern Europe*, Baltimore, 2001, 150-151.
21   A. Panebianco, *Political Parties. Organisation and Power*, Cambridge, 1988, 3.

It was only in the aftermath of the 'refounding' of the party in 1989, when it assumed the name *Partido Popular* and changed its programme, organisation and leadership - Aznar succeeded the party founder, Fraga, as president in 1990 - that the party began what can only be called an impressive success story on the electoral front.[22] The PP's electoral success during the 1990s is even more striking as the steady growth of the party involved all levels of the political system, from the local to the regional and national, up to the elections for the European Parliament.

Electoral results for the Spanish Congress, 1977-2000 (per cent)

	National parties					Regional parties		
	AP-PP	UCD/CDS	PSOE	PCE/IU	Others	UDC/CiU	PNV	Others
1977	8	34	28.9	9.2	7.8	2.8	1.7	3.2
1979	6.1	35.1	30.5	10.8	6.8	2.7	1.7	6.3
1982	26.5	6.5/ 2.9	48.4	4.0	2.5	3.7	1.9	3.6
1986	26.3	9.2	44.6	4.5	3.7	5.1	1.6	5.0
1989	25.9	7.9	39.9	9.1	5.5	5.1	1.2	5.4
1993	34.8	1.8	38.8	9.6	3.8	4.9	1.2	5.1
1996	38.8		37.5	10.6	1.8	4.6	1.3	5.4
2000	45.2		34.7	5.5	1.8	4.3	1.6	6.9

Source: P.N. Diamandouros and R. Gunther, *Parties, Politics and Democracy in the New Southern Europe*, Baltimore, 2001, 404-405.

The greatest progress was made between 1989 and 1993, when the PP increased its share of the vote by almost 10% and succeeded in absorbing the smaller centre-right parties on the national level. In 1996, the PP became the first party in the national party system, leaving the PSOE behind, although only by a narrow margin. In the 2000 general election, then, the party transformed itself into the dominant party of the system, extending its distance from the Socialist Party by over 10%. The party's number of seats almost doubled from 107 to 183 between 1989 and 2000, when it won an absolute majority in the *Congreso de los Diputados* (chamber of deputies).

22   José María Aznar López was born in Madrid and joined the AP in 1978. He was first elected to the Spanish Congress in 1982. In 1987 he became President of the Autonomous Community Castilla y León.

Electoral results AP-PP in local, regional and European elections, 1979-2003 (per cent)

	local elections	regional elections*	European elections
1979	3		
1983	25.9	34	
1987	20.7	27.8	24.7
1989			21.4
1991	25.3	33.3	
1994			40.1
1995	35.3	44.9	
1999	34.3	43.2	39.7
2003	34.3	42.5	

*All Autonomous Communities besides Catalonia, the Basque Country, Galicia and Andalusia
Source: J.I. Wert, "Poder, tiempo y espacio. Las elecciones municipales y autonómicas del 28-M", in: *Claves de Razón Práctica*, 54 (1995), 24-38; J.I. Wert, "Las urnas de San Antonio. Los votos y el poder tras el 13-J", in: *Claves de Razón Práctica*, 95 (1999), 14-23; G. Márquez Cruz, "Veinte años de democracia local en España. Elecciones, producción de gobierno, moción de censura, y élite política (1979-1999)", in: *Revista de Estudios Políticos (Nueva Época)*, 106 (1999), 289-334; D. Nohlen and A. Hildenbrand, *Spanien. Wirtschaft. Gesellschaft. Politik*, Opladen, 1992; own elaborations.

The same evolution can be traced on the local, regional and European levels. These elections have often served as a 'prelude' for developments to come in the 'first-order elections' on the national level. Beyond the statistics of the party's electoral development, some other trends can be discerned during the 1990s.

The social composition of the electorate

During the 1970s especially and the 1980s to a lesser degree, the AP-PP had fallen short of becoming a catch-all party as defined by Kirchheimer, especially as far as the social composition of its electorate was concerned.[23] The socio-structural characteristics of the AP-PP's support were broadly a higher educational level, rather advanced age, high educational status and higher income.

---

23 As one of the characteristics of this 'new' type of catch-all parties, Kirchheimer mentions the "deemphasis of the classe gardée, specific social-class or denominational clientele, in favour of recruiting voters among the population at large": O. Kirchheimer, "The Transformation of the Western European Party System", in: J. La Palombara and M. Weiner, *Political Parties and Political Development*, Princeton, 1966, 190.

This was especially true in the late 1970s, less so during the 1980s.[24] It was not until the 1990s that the catch-all approach of the PP became reflected in the composition of its voters. The increasing heterogeneity of the PP's electorate contrasted with the PSOE's return to a somewhat class-based support from the beginning of the 1990s. What took place was an inversion in the social composition of the electorates of the two dominant parties in the electoral competition.[25] This trend was already discernible in some results during the 1991 municipal and regional elections, but became much more evident in the 1994 European and the 1995 municipal and regional elections. While the PSOE increasingly won votes among the inactive strata of the population (pensioners, the unemployed, and out-of-work housewives), older people and less skilled employees, the PP managed to gain a clear catch-all profile with a notable increase among the employed, younger people, women and students.[26] Sections of the middle-class that had supported the PSOE during the 1980s were alienated from the Socialists and became more willing to cast their vote for the re-founded PP. The latter had become the real party of the middle-class.[27] However, interbloc volatility remained rather low in Spain on the national level even in 1996, with the PP winning the elections only by a slight margin. The landslide victory of the PP in the 'second-order elections' in 1994 (European) and 1995 (municipal and regional) and the repetition of those results in 1999 were clearly echoed in the watershed general election of 2000 when the PP succeeded in winning over significant groups of former PSOE voters, most strikingly the pensioners who had been the backbone of the Socialist party for more than a decade.[28]

---

24   M. Buse, *La nueva democracia española. Sistema de partidos y orientación del voto (1976-1983)*, Madrid, 1984, 297; J.R. Montero, "More than Conservative, Less than Neoconservative. Alianza Popular in Spain", in: B. Girvin (ed.), *The Transformation of Contemporary Conservatism*, London, 1988.

25   P. Chhibber and M. Torcal, "Elite Strategy, Social Cleavages and Party Systems in a New Democracy. Spain", in: *Comparative Political Studies*, 1 (1997) 27-54.

26   J.I. Wert, "Poder, tiempo y espacio. Las elecciones municipales y autonómicas del 28-M", in: *Claves de Razón Práctica*, 54 (1995) 32.

27   J. Hopkin, "Spain", 227. The alienation of the middle-classe can be partly explained by the leftist shift of the PSOE in terms of economic and fiscal policy in the late 1980s and the early 1990s. This shift was provoked by the success of the IU in the 1989 general elections and in the subsequent regional and local elections in 1991. The IU had capitalised on the trade unions' disenchantment with the economic policy of the PSOE government (labeled 'neoliberal' by its critics), which had led to a general strike in 1988.

28   R. Gunther and J.R. Montero, "The Anchors of Partisanship", 91; J.I. Wert, "¿Lluvia o diluvio? Una interpretación de las elecciones generales", in: *Claves de Razón Práctica*, 101 (2000) 20-30.

The ideological profile of the electorate

A notable transformation also took place during the 1990s in the ideological profile of the AP-PP's electorate. Where the party's electorate had been characterised by a clear rightist orientation during the 1970s and the 1980s, it acquired a much softer image during the 1990s. There were strong similarities between the attitudes of the AP's original electorate and those of voters for other right-wing parties on many issues: for example, they rejected the separation between church and state and increased rights for women, accepted the death penalty and more law and order, etc.[29] AP voters in the 1980s continued to reveal a highly religious profile and the majority clearly located itself on the right of the political spectrum.[30] This changed during the 1990s, although slowly. In the mid-1990s, with most Spanish voters locating themselves on the centre-left (4.7 out of 10), the PP succeeded in winning a notable portion of the centre segment of the Spanish electorate.[31]

The geographical distribution of the electorate

It is also interesting to follow the electoral evolution from a geographical perspective. The early AP had its strongholds in Old Castile, Galicia, Asturias and in the provinces of Toledo and those east of Madrid. Following the disintegration of the UCD, the AP inherited part of its electorate, and this was mirrored in the regional distribution of the AP vote after 1982 with strongholds in the North and Northwest of Spain, Old Castile and parts of New Castile.[32] The AP had been especially strong in rural areas and mid-size cities while the PSOE dominated the big cities and the provincial capitals. Here, too, the situation was inverted during the 1990s. The erosion of the Socialist vote in the urban centres and the improvement of the PP was already visible during the 1989 general election and continued in the 1991 municipal and regional elections with the victory of the PP in cities like Madrid and

29   M. Buse, La nueva democracia española, 302.
30   J.R. Montero, "More than Conservative", 155; J.R. Montero, "Los fracasos políticos y electorales de la derecha española: Alianza Popular (1976-1987)", in: J.F. Tezanos, R. Cotarelo and A. de Blas (eds.), La transición democrática española, Madrid, 1989, 529.
31   E.M. García-Guereta, Factores externos e internos en la transformación de los partidos políticos. El caso de AP-PP, Madrid, 1989, 557; J.J. Linz and J.R. Montero, "The Party Systems of Spain".
32   M. Buse, La nueva democracia española, 287-294.

Seville.[33] By the mid-1990s, a tremendous 'urbanisation' of the PP electorate had taken place.[34] At the end of the 1990s and in the 2000 election, the PP clearly had become the dominant party in all the urban centres besides those in Catalonia and the Basque country and governed in a vast majority of the 52 provincial capitals. As far as the Socialist strongholds during the 1980s are concerned, above all the South (Andalucía, Extremadura), the East (Valencia, Aragón) and the industrial North (Asturias), the PP managed to become the strongest party in all regions except Andalucía, Extremadura and Castilla-La Mancha in the 1995 regional elections, and won in all regions except Catalonia, the Basque country and Andalucía in the 2000 general elections.

Moreover, the PP has been able to advance in the most problematic regions, Catalonia and the Basque country, where it faced strong competition from regionalist centre-right parties. The clearest example is, once more, the 2000 general election, when the PP caught up with the Basque *Partido Nacionalista Vasco* (PNV) and became the third party in Catalonia. Whether this trend will also hold for the regional elections in the Autonomous Communities where voters usually tend to split their vote remains to be seen, especially in the case of Catalonia. Nevertheless, it seems that the PP has definitely overcome its long-lasting weakness in the so-called historical regions of Spain, which has for a long time hindered the PP from winning a clear majority.

The altered role of ideology in the PP's performance

The principal target of the PP during the 1990s was to shed the 'rightist' public image it had been projecting since its foundation. During the 1980s, the party had been associated with class favouritism, religiosity and traditionalism.[35] Following its 're-founding', the PP either tried to avoid controversial issues which had helped to identify the party with the traditional Spanish right or changed its position on religious issues (abortion, family values), its attitude to the welfare state and its conception of the *Estado de*

33   P. Heywood, "Spain" in: *Electoral Studies*, 3 (1989) 327; J.I. Wert, "Poder, tiempo y espacio", 37. The erosion of electoral support in the urban centers can be interpreted as a 'gauge' for developments throughout the rest of Spain. The urban electorate is more volatile in general and more sensitive to changes in the political environment. In this respect, the PP followed the path of the PSOE in the late 1970s, when the Socialists had started expanding their electorate in the urban centers before gaining in the country as a whole.
34   J.M. Vallès, "The Spanish General Election of 1993", in: *Electoral Studies*, 1 (1994) 90; J.I. Wert, "Poder, tiempo y espacio", 32.
35   J.R. Montero, "More than Conservative", 157.

las Autonomías (State of Autonomous Communities). One can distinguish a 'definite moderation' in the party on several crucial issues and a 'change in the overall image' of the party as perceived, however diffusely, by the Spanish electorate.

With regard to its public image, the PP under the leadership of Aznar and the new 'dominant coalition'[36] brought about a "drastic reduction in [the] party's ideological baggage", according to Kirchheimer an essential feature of a catch-all party.[37] On issues concerning the economy and the welfare state, the PP adopted the model of a social market economy at its 1989 party congress. This meant a moderation of its radical liberalism: state interventions in the economy ought to be limited, but the welfare state as constructed during the Socialist government should be maintained.[38] Although the PP had adopted some New Right positions during the early 1980s, such as the privatisation of public firms, the party had always acknowledged the value of the social contributions provided by the welfare state.[39] On the issue of the Spanish State of Autonomous Communities, the PP modified its position from one of rigid centralisation and Spanish nationalism towards one of acceptance and even made plans for further development. This was an important issue as it helped to reduce the gap between the traditionally centrist PP and potential allies such as the regionalist parties in Catalonia and the Basque country.[40] Moreover, the more pro-decentralisation stance of the PP was heavily influenced by its increasing importance on the regional level with the party assuming power in several Autonomous Communities. Perhaps the most important evolution was in questions relating to values. Where the party had formerly adopted a clearly conservative position on moral issues like divorce, family values and abortion, the change in leadership and the renewal in the

---

36 A. Panebianco, *Political Parties*. This new dominant coalition included both a younger generation of politicians from the former AP (such as Aznar himself) and recently recruited politicians who had seceded from the former UCD, the CDyS or the PDP.

37 O. Kirchheimer, "The Transformation of the Western European Party System"; G. Pasquino, "The New Campaign Politics in Southern Europe", in: P.N. Diamandouros and R. Gunther (eds.), *Parties, Politics and Democracy in the New Southern Europe*, 186-187. It should be added that a programmatic shift had already been initiated, albeit unsuccessfully, by Aznar's predecessor, Hernández Mancha in 1987 and 1988.

38 E.M. García-Guereta, *Factores externos e internos en la transformación de los partidos políticos*, 254.

39 A. Ruiz Jiménez, *Reshaping the Welfare State. New Right's Moral Arguments in Southern European Conservative Parties. The Spanish Partido Popular*, Madrid, 1997, 11.

40 E.M. García-Guereta, *La postura del PP ante los pactos autonómicos*, Madrid, 1993.

party brought a turnabout in its attitude on these issues.[41] For instance, legislation on abortion as approved under the PSOE government would not be abolished. Since 1989, and especially in the electoral programmes of 1993 and 1996, there has been a significant change in attitudes to gender-related issues as well.[42] The PP adopted a progressive stance on women's rights and their role in society, encouraging women to enter the labour market.[43]

With regard to its ideological profile, the PP has increasingly tried to define its ideology in a rather vague catch-all style, rejecting the terms 'right' or 'conservative'. Even the denomination of 'centre-right' was rejected and replaced by 'centre' or 'reformist centre'. Besides associating itself with the political 'centre', the PP started taking up key terms that had been used by the Socialist Party, such as 'modernity', 'progress', 'future', 'youth', 'new', 'innovation' and even 'Europe'. The new image created around the re-founded and renamed party has been at least as important for the PP's public appeal as have been the modifications in its programme.[44] The party has tried to project a rather technocratic image, downgrading ideology in general.[45] In promoting its new image, with a view to occupying the political 'centre', the party attacked its Socialist opponent by blaming it for being old-fashioned, corrupt and a symbol of the 'past'. The supposed 'inefficiency' and 'incompetence' of the PSOE government (and later the PSOE opposition) was compared with the 'efficiency' and 'skills' of the PP.[46] It is noteworthy that the Christian Democrats, who had become integrated in the party in 1989, have played a minor role in the PP's new programme. This is perfectly in line with the fact that the party has increasingly refrained from orienting its ideological image in any direction. The inclusion of some prominent Christian Democratic figures and some allusions to Christian Democracy in the party's public resolutions at

---

41 The AP parliamentary group had referred the bill liberalising legislation on abortion to the Constitutional Court in 1984: B. Barreiro, "Judicial Review and Political Empowerment. Abortion in Spain", in: P. Heywood (ed.), *Politics and Policy in Democratic Spain. No longer different?*, London, 1999, 153.

42 A. Ruiz Jiménez, "Cases that do not fit", ECPR Joint Sessions, Mannheim, 26-31 March 1999, 24.

43 A. Ruiz Jiménez, *Reshaping the Welfare State*, 9.

44 A fact frankly acknowledged retrospectively by Socialist Party leaders like the former Party President and Prime Minister Felipe González: F. González and J.L. Cebrián, *El futuro ya no es lo que era*, Madrid, 2002, 246-248.

45 An illustration is the statement of Ana Mato, member of the party executive, trying to define the political 'centre': "buena gestión sin descuidar lo social" ("good administration without forgetting the social side"): J. Tusell, "Introducción. Entre el centro y la derecha. El PP, desde la opsición al poder", in: J. Tusell (ed.), *El gobierno de Aznar. Balance de una gestión (1996-2000)*, Barcelona, 2000, 20.

46 See the slogans used by the PP in the different election campaigns using the terms 'solutions', 'promised', 'facts', etc.

the party congresses of 1989 and 1990 served the purpose of gaining public legitimacy both in the domestic political arena and abroad (especially among its European partners).[47]

However, it is important to consider the two components together: the adjustments and changes implemented by the party, necessary in order to reduce its 'ideological baggage', and the projection of a new image which goes along with these changes but refrains from defining the party's ideology exactly, beyond using terms like 'modern', 'centrist' or 'progressive'. This is both unavoidable and even useful for a party with a catch-all approach. As Pappas puts it, the dilemma of Conservative parties consists in "(...) either holding onto their traditional niches on the right of the political spectrum (while elaborating a new set of conservative principles) or moving toward the center, which held out the prospect of democratic legitimacy and a larger pool of votes, albeit at the expense of ideological clarity."[48] In this sense, the PP clearly preferred the latter approach, although they were somewhat late in doing so, compared with other Southern European Conservatives.

The PP in a system of increased competitiveness between parties

The Spanish party system represents a particular case among Western European party systems as we cannot speak of only one system but of several different party systems. We can differentiate between the 'statewide party system', some 'regional party systems' and a number of 'specific statewide party subsystems'.[49] Especially important in the case of the PP are the statewide party system and the regional party systems. One of the structural problems of the AP-PP in the electorate market is that it faces multilateral competition both on the national and the regional levels. On the national level, the AP-PP, following the implosion and disappearance of the UCD, had

---

47   As can be shown on several issues, the PP, on the contrary, distanced itself from the positions on family values or economic policy it had maintained until the mid-1980s, positions that might have been interpreted as closer to original Christian Democratic positions: P. Matuschek, "Aznars Ambitionen. Die spanische Volkspartei und ihr europäischer Führungsanspruch", in: *Blätter für deutsche und internationale Politik*, 1 (2002) 77-84.

48   T. Pappas, "In Search of the Center. Conservative Parties, Electoral Competition and Political Legitimacy in Southern Europe's New Democracies", in: P.N. Diamandouros and R. Gunther (eds.), *Parties, Politics and Democracy in the New Southern Europe*, 229.

49   J.J. Linz and J.R. Montero, "The Party Systems of Spain", 172.

to face competition from some smaller centre-right parties, especially the CDyS of former Prime Minister Suárez, and from its greatest opponent on the left, the PSOE.[50] On the regional level, the AP-PP was forced to compete with nationalist centre-right formations in Catalonia (*Convergència i Unió*, CiU) and in the Basque country, particularly the PNV, as well as in the Canary Islands. In other regions, such as in Navarra and Aragon during the 1990s, the PP reached agreements with regional centre-right parties, which form an electoral coalition with the PP and are part of the same parliamentary group in Congress. Hence, the PP is involved in party competition both on the left-right-axis and on the centre-periphery axis.

All these features notwithstanding, we can discern an increasingly stable party system in the 1990s. Even though the party system had been rather fragmented during the first years of democracy, leading to its categorisation as a "moderate multi-party system"[51] and even though in the 1990s it more or less conformed to a type of 'imperfect bipartism' with the dominant PSOE, a new version of 'moderate pluralism' has now emerged, together with a reduction in the number of statewide parties and an increase in the number of regionalist parties.[52] Nevertheless, on the national level, competition was centripetal from the very beginning and in the 1990s led to a concentration of the vote in the two major national parties. The existence of regional parties notwithstanding, bipolar competition on the national level has also been aided by institutional factors like the electoral law that establishes a system of proportional representation and tends to discriminate against minor national parties.[53] This institutional provision also makes the emergence of new parties highly unlikely.

---

50   The CDyS could best be described as a left-liberal centre party with a certain degree of populism. After an initial period characterised by a rather centre-left orientation, it collaborated increasingly with the AP in the late 1980s on the local level in order to bring down the PSOE-led town halls (the most prominent case being Madrid in 1989). Following heavy losses in several elections in 1989 and 1990, the party tried to recover its independence and turned towards the PSOE. The CDyS failed in the long run in its strategy of becoming a coalition partner for the PSOE on the national level, because of the persistent absolute majorities of the incumbent. It therefore lost much of its importance as a pivotal party.

51   A. Bar, "The Emerging Spanish Party System. Is There a Model?" in: *West European Politics*, 4 (1984) 139.

52   J.J. Linz and J.R. Montero, "The Party Systems of Spain", 171-172.

53   G. Pasquino, "The New Campaign Politics in Southern Europe", 220. The system comes close to 'winner takes all' electoral systems like those in the United States of America and the United Kingdom: R. Gunther, "Electoral Laws, Party Systems and Elites. The case of Spain", in: *American Political Science Review*, 3 (1989) 841.

One particular circumstance that the AP-PP had to face has turned out to be rather beneficial in the long run: the absence of a viable extremist, clearly anti-democratic party on its right.[54] On the one hand, this posed a serious problem of legitimacy as the AP-PP's competitors blamed it for being the only party representing the 'right' of the political spectrum. On the other hand, the AP-PP did not have to fear any direct competition from the right on the national level and could concentrate its resources on fighting its opponent on the left.

The PP as a textbook case of party change

In many respects, the PP can be considered a textbook case of party change. This is true not only of the changes in the party's programme, but also of the profound changes in its organisational structure, personnel (party staff and candidates for public office) and in the relation between the party in public office and the party's central office. The changed relationship of the party with civil society will be treated below.

Organisational structure

One crucial result of the process of 're-founding' was the change in the party's organisational structure. The symbolic name-change to *Partido Popular* was accompanied by a centralisation of the decision-making process, the specialisation and bureaucratisation of the party machine and a professionalisation of the party's strategy department.[55] The party's *Comité Ejecutivo Nacional* (executive committee) was granted more power, especially in the figure of the party's president.[56] In 1990, the seven vice-presidencies were abolished and the role of the secretary general was more clearly defined. Since 1993, the party's president combines the functions of chairman of the parliamen-

---

54 The Francoist *Unión Nacional* (National Union) disappeared as an alternative for the AP in 1982 when it lost its only seat in the *Congreso* which had been won in 1979.

55 F. Chadel, *Penser le changement dans les partis politiques. Le processus d'institutionnalisation au Partido Popular*, Barcelona, 2001, 13.

56 The president's power lies particularly in his powers of appointment. Most of the members of the party's executive committee are appointed or proposed by the party president, but he also controls the nomination process of candidates for public office through the Comité *Electoral Nacional* (National Electoral Committee). He also has at his disposal financial resources (appointing the treasurer and having the right to examine the party finances), ideological resources (as guardian of the coherence of all public declarations by the party's national organs) and disciplinary resources (appointing the president of the National Committee of Rights and Guarantees). *Ibid.*, 15.

tary group in the *Congreso de los Diputados*, the *Senado* (Senate) and of the PP's delegation in the European Parliament. The primary aim of this process of centralisation and concentration of power is to increase the internal cohesion of the party.

As far as the territorial structure of the PP is concerned, the party headquarters maintain vast powers over the organisation. For example, since 1993, all the regional and provincial congresses of the party are held in rapid succession, that is within a year of the last national congress, in order to guarantee a certain cohesion. Moreover, the central party maintains control over the territorial units by having professional employees in the provincial party offices directly answerable to the party headquarters. Any decision taken on a lower level can be undone by the party's central office in Madrid.[57] Although not publicly acknowledged, one consequence of the incompatibility rules introduced in 1993 was to prevent the concentration of a certain 'feudal' power in powerful local or regional 'barons'.[58] Since 1990, the statutes explicitly ban the creation of factions within the party. As far as professionalisation is concerned, since 1990 the strategic competencies in the party's central office have been organised into four main *áreas* (departments): organisation, elections, training and studies, and programme. Only slight modifications took place in 1999 and 2002. Another indication of the professionalisation of the party is the high number of its paid staff, now numbering more than 200, with 160 working in the headquarters in Madrid and 69 employed in the regions and provinces as secretaries.

Personnel

Besides the changes mentioned, since 1989 there has been a significant renewal in personnel. With the election of Aznar as party president, the party elite has experienced a sustained renewal, both in the party's central office and in the party in public office. Interestingly, the renovation in the party's executive committee was incremental in nature, as some older members were retained and new members were appointed by the president, with the overall number growing, especially in 1993. This model of 'renewal by aggre-

57   E.M. García-Guereta, *Factores externos e internos en la transformación de los partidos políticos*, 356-358.
58   These rules also prohibit combining executive positions at the provincial or regional level with a position at the national level: P. Gangas, *Desarrollo organizativo de los partidos políticos españoles de implantación nacional*, Madrid, 1995, 218-219; E.M. García-Guereta, *Factores externos e internos en la transformación de los partidos políticos*, 394.

gation' apparently was adopted at all levels down to the provincial. In qualitative terms, the renewal of the party elite meant the integration of members seceding from other parties, especially the former UCD, the small *Partido Liberal* (Liberal Party) or the Christian Democratic PDP,[59] as well as the inclusion of 'independents' or newcomers.[60] The same was true for candidates for public office. Although this process followed a somewhat different logic (as it was up to the electorate to decide), the new national executive committee accelerated changes here also by using its power to appoint and approve the closed and fixed lists of candidates.[61]

The election of Aznar as party president in 1990 meant a generation break in the party. One of the most striking features was the age - about 40 years on average - of the members of this new 'dominant coalition'. The positions in the new party executive were filled by young followers of the so-called Aznar generation, mainly co-workers who had formed part of the *Clan de Valladolid*, a group that had worked with Aznar when he was president of the Autonomous Community of Castilla y León from 1987 until 1989.

Besides this rejuvenation, there was also a change in leadership style. While his predecessor could be described as 'charismatic', Aznar falls into the category of 'non-charismatic' leaders. According to the definition of Ansell and Fish, 'non-charismatic' leaders are "often staid and untelegenic, they sometimes suffer as much derision outside the party for their unprepossessing personalities as they enjoy respect within the party for their organisational prowess".[62] Indeed, the 'non-charisma' of Aznar is closely linked to his effective control of the resources of power within the party (and the government) and contradicts the traditional view that strictly personal charisma is a crucial factor in the new Southern European democracies.[63] The new candidate for

59   It is worth noting that it was not the PDP as a whole (as the party had been dissolved before), but only individual members of the Democracia Cristiana (the predecessor of the PDP) who joined the PP in 1988 and 1989; this explains their limited influence, for instance on policy matters.

60   E.M. García-Guereta, *Factores externos e internos en la transformación de los partidos políticos*, 494.

61   Another factor that helped here was the good electoral performance of the PP which increased the number of candidates elected and 'poured' new politicians into parliament. It is clear that there was an interaction between the two phenomena.

62   C.K. Ansell and M.S. Fish, "The Art of Being Indispensable. Noncharismatic Personalism in Contemporary Political Parties", in: *Comparative Political Studies*, 3 (1999) 288.

63   In spite of the strong emphasis on the importance of personality and leadership in the literature on Southern European parties, there are examples, like the imploded UCD under Suárez, that provide evidence for the fact that personality (alone) without organisation leads to defeat.

the general elections in 2004, Mariano Rajoy, also seems to fit this pattern quite well. Rather like Aznar, Rajoy too falls into the category of an 'uncharismatic leader' and seems to have similar skills in intra-party organisation. In this respect, the leadership changeover shows more signs of continuity than of real change.

The relations between the different levels of the party

In the current literature on party change, a common hypothesis is that, among the different levels or 'faces' of the party (party on the ground, party central office and party in public office), the party in public office gains prominence over the party in central office or even tends to dominate it, because of the increasing number of party representatives in public office and the large financial and personal resources of the parliamentary groups in comparison with those of the party organisation.[64] The case of the PP is interesting in that it runs counter to the assumptions made by Katz and Mair, an aspect van Biezen has convincingly demonstrated for parties in Spain and Portugal.[65] In the case of the PP, the party in public office is clearly subordinated to the party in central office and does not enjoy any independence. A considerable personal overlap between the two spheres notwithstanding, the party executive dominates the parliamentary group due to several factors. First, the scarce financial resources provided to the parliamentary groups do not allow for any independence *vis-à-vis* the party in central office. Second, the *reglamento* of the parliamentary group explicitly guarantees the predominance of the party executive.[66] Third, the control maintained by the party executive and the president over the process of selecting candidates for public office leaves little room for manoeuvre to the party in public office and to the individual deputies who depend on the party (leadership) for re-election.[67] The strong position of the party's central office can be explained by the 'cohe-

---

64 R. Katz and P. Mair, "The Evolution of Party Organisations in Europe. The Three Faces of Party Organisation", in: *The American Review of Politics*, 4 (1993) 608-614; P. Mair, *Party System Change. Approaches and Interpretations*, Oxford, 1997, 144-145.

65 I. van Biezen, "On the Internal Balance of Party Power. Party Organisations in New Democracies", in: *Party Politics*, 4 (2000) 395-417.

66 P. Oñate, "Congreso, grupos parlamentarios y partidos", in: A. Martínez (ed.), *El Congreso de los Diputados en España. Funciones y rendimiento*, Madrid, 2000, 113. Note that this is a common feature of virtually all Spanish parties. However, in the case of the PP, this control of the parliamentary party by the party executive was further enhanced by the so-called *criterio de dependencia* in the party statutes: I. van Biezen, "On the Internal Balance of Party Power", 400.

67 P. Matuschek, "Spain. A Textbook Case of Partitocracy", in: J. Borchert and J. Zeiss (eds.), *The Political Class in Advanced Democracies*, Oxford, 2003, 336-351.

sion-seeking strategy'[68] of originally unstable and unconsolidated parties in the new democracies: the AP-PP had experienced constant turmoil within its parliamentary group throughout the 1980s and tensions between the party in public office and the party in central office had been frequent during the whole decade.[69] In short, where internal relations between the party in public office and the party's central office are concerned, here too, change has meant an increasing concentration of power in the new party executive.

In 1996, the PP became a party in public office at the national level. What have been the consequences of this new environment for the different levels or 'faces' within the party? The dominance of the party's central office (the party executive) has remained unchallenged. Within the strategic 'triangle' of government, parliamentary group and party in central office there is a high level of coordination in order to guarantee cohesive action. The cohesion is further enhanced by a personal overlap between the three spheres: Aznar combines the posts of party president and prime minister and from 1996 to 1999 Francisco Álvarez-Cascos combined the positions of head of the prime minister's office and secretary general of the party. Another means of improving coordination are the regular meetings that take place in the *Palacio de la Moncloa*, the prime minister's residence. These so-called *maitines* were institutionalised during the party congress of 1999 with the creation of the *Comité de Dirección* (Executive Board), which includes the president, the secretary general, the vice-secretary generals and the coordinators of the four departments in the party headquarters. More members can be invited, like the speakers of the parliamentary groups.

Undoubtedly, the conversion of the PP into a party in government has served as a catalyst for the processes initiated at the beginning of the 1990s. If the cohesion-seeking strategy of the party executive had been a necessary prerequisite for bringing the party to power, since 1996 it has became a *conditio sine qua non* for maintaining power. This explains why during the 1999 party congress, the party sought to continue with the specialisation and professionalisation of party activity.[70] The party elite has developed an obsession with preventing a gap between the party in government and the party's central office, a phenomenon that frequently occurs when a party holds power for more than one term.[71] The leadership also seeks to prevent

68   I. van Biezen, "On the Internal Balance of Party Power", 411.
69   F. Jáuregui, *La derecha después de Fraga*, Madrid, 1987.
70   F. Chadel, *Penser le changement dans les partis politiques*, 14.
71   M. Cotta, *On the Relationship between Party and Government*, Siena, 1999, 15.

the party from losing contact with civil society. However, this does not imply any kind of 'division of labour' between the two spheres: the role of the party clearly is to act as 'the government's voice' and it does not adopt an independent role but serves as a medium in order to 'explain' the government's performance to the wider electorate.

The PP and civil society: a successful penetration strategy

Parties acting as intermediaries between civil society and the state can adopt different strategies in order to establish linkages with the electorate. Poguntke distinguishes between organisational linkages and direct linkages. The latter are usually established via the mass media, while the former can be established via a) collateral organisations, b) membership organisations or c) new social movements.[72] It is clear that since the 1980s and especially the early 1990s, the AP-PP has followed an organisational strategy aimed at the penetration of civil society. The party has not followed the path of the traditional mass parties of the Christian Democratic type in Western Europe as it did not rely on close relations with (Christian) trade unions, religious or professional organisations (external collateral organisations). However, the PP has obviously employed all the other channels indicated by Poguntke.

Organisational linkages

The PP maintains two affiliated organisations (internal collateral organisations). The first is the youth organisation called *Nuevas Generaciones* (New Generations), which was founded in 1977 and has enjoyed an increase in membership similar to that of the party itself. It serves as an important 'transmission belt' for the party among the younger electorate as it offers a jumping-off point for potential party activists and candidates while at the same

---

72   T. Poguntke, *Parteiorganisation im Wandel. Gesellschaftliche Verankerung und Anpassung im europäischen Vergleich*, Opladen, 2000, 32. The collateral organisations can be subdivided into 'external' and 'internal' collateral organisations. The former embrace those organisations that came into being independently of a party's influence (for instance trade unions, religious organisations, interest groups, etc.). The latter were created by the party itself as part of a "focus group strategy" towards certain segments of society, for instance youth organisations, women's organisations, etc.: *Ibid.*, 40-41.

time projecting a youthful image towards the broader public.[73] The other affiliated organisation of the PP is the women's organisation *Mujeres para la Democracia* (Women for Democracy). Its membership is smaller than that of the youth organisation (about 15,000 members) but nevertheless it plays an important role in the party's strategy of attracting women's votes. The women's organisation was also founded rather early. Since the beginning of the 1980s, it has been providing several activities for women and is thought to serve as a 'gauge' of developments in society.[74]

The most important element in the party's penetration strategy has been the development and expansion of a large membership organisation. This certainly can be seen as offering the closest link between a party and civil society and the PP seems to have been quite aware of it. The party experienced a rapid growth in membership from the early 1980s, and particularly in the 1990s. The growth in membership was steady during the 1980s, but between 1990 and 1996 membership doubled from 280,000 to 540,000. Although numbers increased much more slowly with the PP in government, the party has not experienced any reduction due to possible disenchantment with its performance in government. If Spain, along with a few other countries, runs counter to the trend of declining levels of party membership, this is mainly due to the PP's membership growth during the 1990s.[75] In spite of repeated assertions about the declining importance of the 'party on the ground', party members continue to be an important asset which few political parties are willing to give up. As far as the PP is concerned, the most important benefits are legitimacy, outreach, labour and linkages.[76] In the context of linkages with civil society, members are supposed to act as 'opinion leaders' in their everyday lives, to spread the party's principal ideas and to mobilise support. Members can serve as a source of information for the party about public concerns. Apart from that, members constitute a potential pool of voluntary aid and unpaid labour, especially during election campaigns while their sheer number gives democratic legitimacy to the party.

---

73   In 2001, the PP's youth organisation had more than 60.000 members: Partido Popular, *Las propuestas del centro. Un nuevo impulso para España.* Memoria de gestión, Madrid, 2002, 47.

74   The links between the women's organisation and the party are fluid, although officially the women's organisation is registered as an NGO. However, it is located in the PP's headquarters in Madrid.

75   P. Mair and I. van Biezen, "Party Membership in Twenty European Democracies (1980-2000)", in: *Party Politics*, 1 (2001) 11.

76   S. Scarrow, *Parties and their Members. Organising for Victory in Britain and Germany*, Oxford, 1996, 42-47.

Number of AP-PP members, 1981-2002

1981	18,475	1994	429,293
1982	85,412	1995	490,223
1983	144,960	1996	540,218
1985	202,777	1997	570,879
1989	262,755	1998	584,341
1990	284,323	1999	600,374
1991	300,988	2000	619,658
1992	326,960	2001	632,566
1993	375,232	2002	644,311

Source: Numbers until 1998: E.M. García-Guereta Rodríguez, *Factores externos e internos en la transformación de los partidos políticos. El caso de AP-PP*, Madrid, 2001, 430; since 1999: Partido Popular, *Las propuestas del centro. Un nuevo impulso para España*. Memoria de gestión, Madrid, 2002.

As to the new social movements, the PP has established a department exclusively dedicated to contacts with societal actors, associations, NGOs, etc. This is the so-called *Área de participación y acción sectorial*. The party holds regular 'round tables' or 'fora' with representatives of all kinds of societal organisations in order to maintain contacts and acquire new input. However, with regard to the old social movements, since the 1990s the PP has cautiously avoided establishing privileged or exclusive relations with certain groups. Given the long-standing connection between the old AP and the Catholic Church as well as the steady influence on the party (not least on personnel) of the employers' organization *Confederación Española de Organizaciones Empresariales*, the PP clearly has tried to keep a distance from certain societal groups and to maintain its independence.

Direct linkages

At the same time, the PP has employed new means for communicating with the electorate as a whole. This process clearly is in line with the renovation and professionalisation of the party organisation during the 1990s. Apart from the most prominent channel, the mass media, in recent years the use of the internet has become more important for the party's communication with the wider electorate. The so-called *buzón popular* (mail-box) and the *Oficinas Parlamentarias* (parliamentary offices) provide the citizenry as a whole with new channels to participate in debates and make suggestions. This serves as an indicator to the party of developments in society, enlarges its possible target groups and emphasises its catch-all approach as a 'people's party'.[77]

The penetration strategy of the PP, especially the expansion of the membership organisation, can be seen as a result of its long period in opposition.
The party made a virtue of necessity as it lacked other means of establishing links with the electorate. Moreover, the PP seems to have learned from the strategic mistakes made both by the Socialists in power and by the defunct UCD in the early 1980s. In contrast to the PSOE, the PP seems to be able to keep its party organisation 'alive' while in government and attempts to maintain its linkages with civil society rather than relying exclusively on government policies.

The findings on the PP clearly reveal that one recurrent assertion in the literature on Southern European parties does not hold. Contrary to the thesis that parties in the new democracies have not made many efforts to establish closer linkages with civil society due to the special circumstances of late democratisation, the PP does seem to have succeeded to a considerable degree in its penetration strategy.[78] It is this aspect which, above all, gave the party a decisive competitive advantage over the PSOE during the 1990s.

Conclusion

Needless to say, measuring the influence of 'Europe' on the PP's politics and policies is a rather difficult endeavour. However, according to the five areas of Europeanisation highlighted by Ladrech, some final remarks can be made.[79] It would be an exaggeration to speak of profound changes in the PP's policy or programme as a direct result of Europeanisation. Nevertheless, it has had an indirect influence. Insofar as the issue of 'Europe' has been a source of modernisation for Spain in general and the self-presentation of the PSOE as the 'party of Europe' in particular, it pushed the PP to

77   F. Chadel, *Participation des adhérents au sein du Partido Popular. Analyse de l'implication des bases dans trois activités partisanes stratégiques*, Paris, 2002.

78   I. van Biezen, "Building Party Organisations and the Relevance of Past Models. The Communist and Socialist Parties in Spain and Portugal", in: *West European Politics*, 2 (1998) 43; L. Morlino, "Political Parties and Democratic Consolidation in Southern Europe", in: R. Gunther, P.N. Diamandouros and H.-J. Puhle (eds.), *The Politics of Democratic Consolidation. Southern Europe in Comparative Perspective*, Baltimore, 1995, 333.

79   R. Ladrech, "Europeanisation and Political Parties. Towards a Framework for Analysis", in: R. Ladrech (ed.), *The Europeanisation of Party Politics*. Special Issue of *Party Politics*, 4 (2002) 396-400.

adopt a more pronounced pro-European stance and downgrade its nationalist or patriotic rhetoric. It should be emphasised, however, that there has been
a general consensus between all the major Spanish parties as far as European
integration is concerned.[80] Given the highly positive connotation of 'Europe'
and the high approval rates for European integration among the Spanish
public, emphasising 'Europe' has been a necessity for a party with a catch-all
approach like the PP's. This stance is reflected in the party's modification of
its position on gender-related issues such as women's rights to both job and
family, a move that was induced by European integration.

Because 'Europe' was widely perceived by the Spanish as synonymous with
'modernity', it was crucial for the PP, and particular for Aznar as government
leader, that it be integrated with the EPP, a process that took place at the end
of the 1980s and the beginning of the 1990s. It was a means of gaining legitimacy on the national level, of shedding its image as an 'old' traditional Spanish rightist party tied to Francoism and of enhancing its international credibility. As mentioned above, Christian Democracy in Spain has not been able
to survive as a political party on its own and the re-founded PP has become
a refuge for former Christian Democratic politicians seceding either from the
tiny PDP or the dissolved UCD. The PP has skillfully used the influx of former
Christian Democrats in order to enhance its centrist character and thereby
increase its democratic legitimacy both in Spain and in Europe. Spanish Christian Democracy has paid the price of giving up its own identity but has also
gained access to political power.

If the acceptance, at least formally, of some Christian Democratic principles,
especially the vision on European integration, and the integration of Christian
Democratic politicians in the PP have been prerequisites for entering the EPP,
nowadays, however, it seems as if the roles have changed somewhat. The PP
has assumed a leading role within the EPP and influences the programme
of the transnational party by diluting authentically Christian Democratic
principles.[81] It is obvious that the success of the PP in the domestic arena
has helped to increase its weight on the European and international level in
recent years. After years of international isolation and longing for recognition from abroad, ironically, the PP nowadays might serve as a kind of model
for traditional Christian Democratic or centre-right parties in the established

---

80   B. Álvarez-Miranda, *El sur de Europa y la adhesión a la Comunidad. Los debates políticos*, Madrid, 1996.
81   P. Matuschek, "Aznars Ambitionen".

democracies, both on the programmatic and organisational levels. Thanks to its leap-frogging to modernity, the PP as a party embodying some features typical of parties in the new democracies, might anticipate some organisational developments yet to come for traditional mass parties in Western Europe. With its rather eclectic ideology, it might serve as a blueprint for the type of centre-right party that could become dominant in the new Europe in the future.

A Decade
of Seized Opportunities
Christian Democracy
in the European Union
Steven Van Hecke

The 1990s have in general been a challenging decade for the European People's Party (EPP) - the transnational party of Christian Democrats and Conservatives in the European Union (EU). Both the EU and the EPP have witnessed a fundamental change during this particular period. A far-reaching process of widening and deepening turned the Western European and mainly economic European Community (EC) into a Europe-wide political union. The EPP went through a parallel process of 'widening' and 'deepening'.[1] The party opened its doors to conservative parties on the one hand and enhanced its internal and external integration in developing into a transnational party organisation on the other. So far, this operation led to a clear victory in the 1999 European elections and has strengthened its position at various European forums. As far as policy outcome is concerned, the picture is more ambiguous. In this chapter I will analyse these widening and deepening processes as conditions for the EPP's recent record and evaluate the significance of the 1990s in this respect.[2]

First, a short history of the EPP will be presented in order to create a framework in which the events of the 1990s can be fully understood. Then, the widening and deepening of the EPP during the 1990s will be examined, with particular attention to some 'big' and 'controversial' enlargements and to the role of the EPP in the EU integration process. Additionally, the main organisational changes, the electoral performances, and the change in ideological

1   Although beyond the scope of this chapter, this thesis refers to the '(neo-)institutionalist' approach of European integration. For the theoretical assumptions of the parallelism, see S. Van Hecke, "Démocrates chrétiens et conservateurs au Parlement européen. Mariage d'amour ou de raison?", in: P. Delwit (ed.), *Démocraties chrétiennes et conservatismes en Europe. Une nouvelle convergence?*, Brussels, 2003, 334-337.

2   I would like to thank the members of the *Afdeling Politologie* (K.U.Leuven), Nelson Gonzalez (K.U.Leuven) and Michael Gehler (Universität Innsbruck) for their comments on this chapter.

profile will be assessed. To conclude, I will try to evaluate the significance and impact of the 1990s for European Christian Democracy and the EPP's near future.

Preliminary to our analysis is a definition of 'Christian Democracy in the European Union'. First of all, Christian Democrats in the EU have organised themselves into the EPP and their transnational party group in the European Parliament (EP). Although both cannot be totally separated, it remains important to underline the difference between the EPP as a transnational party and the EPP as a parliamentary group. Second, focusing on the EPP and its party group in the EP does not automatically exclude the national parties. They are present in an indirect way through their membership of the EPP and their delegation in the EPP Group. Therefore, when discussing the widening and deepening process of the EPP, reference has to be made to the parties at the national level. Third, a clear distinction between Christian Democrats and Conservatives often cannot be made. Therefore, we will consider all Christian Democrats and Conservatives of the EPP in our analysis, using a broad, pragmatic definition of 'Christian Democracy in the EU' but excluding Conservatives who are not linked to the EPP.

A short history of the EPP

Since the establishment of the European Coal and Steel Community in 1952, Christian Democratic deputies from the six founding countries formed one group in the Common Assembly, the forerunner of the EP. [3] As an offshoot, the 'Christian Democratic Group' was formally founded in 1953 and was composed of national parliamentarians from the Christian Democratic parties present in every member state: Belgium, France, the Federal Republic of Germany, Luxembourg, Italy and the Netherlands. The entry of the United Kingdom, Denmark and Ireland in 1973 brought new deputies to the Assembly (which has called itself the 'European Parliament' since 1962), but, because there were no Christian Democratic parties in the UK and Denmark, the Christian Democratic Group did not enlarge. Only the representatives of the Irish *Fine Gael* (Family of the Irish) joined the Christian Democratic Group. The British and Danish Conservatives created their own parliamentary group, the 'European Conservative Group', which was renamed the

3   For a long history of the EPP, see T. Jansen, *The European People's Party. Origins and Development, Basingstoke*, 1998; T. Jansen, "Die Europäische Volkspartei", in: H.-J. Veen (ed.), *Christlich-demokratische und konservative Parteinen in Westeuropa*, Vol. 5, Paderborn, 2000, 459-540.

'European Democratic Group' after the 1979 EP elections. While the entrance of delegates from the new Member States strengthened the Socialist group, the Christian Democrats were not able to gain from the new situation. Due to the electoral decline of the Christian Democratic parties and the 1973 enlargement, the Christian Democratic Group lost its absolute majority in the EP.

The prospect of the election of the EP by direct universal suffrage by the end of the 1970s and the entry of new member states, again without Christian Democratic parties, set the Christian Democrats of the original Six in motion.[4] Preparations were carried out within the Christian Democratic Group, and out of the twelve Christian Democratic parties the 'European People's Party' was formed on 29 April 1976.[5] The EPP consisted of the Belgian *Christelijke Volkspartij* (CVP) and *Parti Social Chrétien* (PSC), the French *Centre des Démocrates Sociaux* (CDS), the *Christlich Demokratische Union Deutschlands* (CDU) and the Bavarian *Christlich-Soziale Union* (CSU), the Italian *Democrazia Cristiana* (DC), the Irish *Fine Gael*, the Luxembourg *Chrëschtlech Sozial Vollekspartei* (CSV), and the three Dutch parties that merged into the *Christen Democratisch Appèl* (CDA) in 1980. The creation of a European Christian Democratic party was presented as another moment in a larger series of initiatives to build a federal Europe.[6] Only the Irish were not part of the EC original core and their party did not share the Christian Democratic tradition.

However, the foundation of the EPP masked a fundamental dispute between the CDU/CSU and the Italian and Benelux Christian Democrats. The Germans favoured the inclusion of the British and, to a lesser degree, of the Danish Conservatives as well as openness towards non-Christian Democratic parties from other European countries, which, in the long run, might become partners in the European integration process.[7] Nevertheless, the CDU/CSU strategy largely failed. A compromise between the two visions on the future

---

4   T. Jansen, "The Dilemma for Christian Democracy. Historical Identity and/or Political Expediency. Opening the Door to Conservatism", in: E. Lamberts (ed.), *Christian Democracy in the European Union (1945-1995)*, Leuven, 1997, 461-462.

5   Officially, the party was established as the 'European People's Party - Federation of Christian Democratic Parties of the European Community' in Luxembourg on 8 July 1976.

6   P. Chenaux, "Les démocrates-chrétiens au niveau de l'Union européenne", in: E. Lamberts (ed.), *Christian Democracy in the European Union (1945-1995)*, 449: "La création d'un Parti européen de la Démocratie chrétienne était replacée dans la continuité d'une action qui n'avait toujours eu qu'un seul objectif: la promotion d'une Europe fédérale (...)".

7   The impact of the fact that the CDU/CSU and the British Conservatives were both in opposition at that moment has to be considered. During the 1980s, when both parties were in power and developed opposite policies, particularly with regard to the European integration process, the relationship was less easy.

of European Christian Democracy was worked out whereby the EPP's ideology was based on the centrist model of the Italian and especially the Benelux Christian Democratic parties, membership of the EC was made a condition for EPP membership, and the (main) name of the party did not mention the term 'Christian Democratic'.

As for the CDU/CSU, the future positioning of the European Christian Democrats was not decided yet. Their point of reference was - and still is - a bipolar political party system in which the Christian Democrats are the dominant force on the right. The Germans kept seeking ways to stay in contact with the Conservative parties. However, the European Union of Christian Democrats (EUCD) did not include the British Conservatives and was nothing more than a rump organisation after the creation of the EPP.[8] The remaining members of the EUCD felt excluded from the EPP project. At the same time, the EPP decided not to create associate membership or observer status and the statutes of the EPP prohibited the membership of parties from countries outside the EC. In the end, the unwillingness of the EUCD and the EPP to establish a forum for a formal relationship between Christian Democrats and Conservatives led to the creation of a new organisation, the European Democratic Union (EDU).[9] It was founded in 1976, the same year that the EPP was established.[10] This German-modelled 'union', which was a cooperation not a federation, united "Christian Democratic, Conservative, and other non-collectivist parties" from eight countries. This initially successful revenge of the CDU/CSU and the *Österreichische Volkspartei* (ÖVP) strained relations within the EPP.[11] Various Christian Democrats accused their German colleagues of playing a double game. This situation severely damaged the EPP in its early years and paradoxi-

---

8 The EUCD was established in 1965 as the successor of the *Nouvelles Équipes Internationales*, a loose organisation of post-Second World War Christian Democrats (and their parties).

9 S. Hix, "The Transnational Party Federations", in: J. Gaffney (ed.), *Political Parties and the European Union*, London/New York, 1996, 315: "(…) the decision to form a broad right-wing alliance arose from a number of imperatives: the enlargement of the EC in 1973 (…); the particular desire of the CDU and the British Conservatives to overcome Conservative Party isolation in the EC; the formation of the CSP [Confederation of Socialist Parties], with members in every state; and the threat of a left-wing majority in the first elections."

10 The EDU was officially founded with the signing of the Klessheim Declaration in Salzburg on 24 April 1978.

11 The ÖVP had been one of the instigators of the EDU. As traditional Christian Democrats they felt excluded from the EPP project: M. Gehler, *Der lange Weg nach Europa. Österreich vom Ende der Monarchie bis zur EU*, Innsbruck, 2003, 447-448.

cally reaffirmed its anti-Conservative stance.[12] As a result, much of the EPP's initial potential remained unused.

The members of the Christian Democratic Group, renamed the Christian Democratic Group (Group of the European People's Party) in 1978 and later again the European People's Party Group (Christian Democratic Group) in 1979, were in the first election of the EP by direct universal suffrage relatively successful, taking into account that they were not represented in the UK and in Denmark. They won 107 seats out of 419. Nevertheless, the EPP deputies came second behind the Socialist Group who had 112 seats.

The 1979 election marked the end of a period in which most of the attention went into the creation of a single European Christian Democratic party federation. By contrast, the 1980s turned out to be a decade of consolidation. The EPP lost seats in successive EP elections but not in a way that its structure, membership or mission came under fire. In 1984, the EPP Group won 109 seats out of 434 and in 1989, 106 seats out of 518. As the EC enlarged steadily, new parties entered the EPP. After Greece's accession in 1981, the *Nea Dimokratia* (ND) joined the EPP Group in 1982 and became a full member of the EPP in 1983. Although a party without a Christian Democratic history but yet conservative and small, its accession took place without much ado. The same was true for the Portuguese *Partido do Centro Democratico Social* (CDSp) and the Spanish *Partido Democrata Popular* (PDP) - later renamed the *Democracia Cristiana* -, the Basque *Partido Nacionalista Vasco* (PNV), and the Catalonian *Unió Democràtica de Catalunya* (UDC). They entered the EPP Group after Spain and Portugal entered the EC in 1986.

The EU and the widening of the EPP

The European Christian Democrats faced a turning point at the end of the 1980s. With only 23.5% of the seats in the EP in 1989, the EPP had reached rock bottom.[13] Enlargement had not brought a profound reinforcement of the EPP Group, although the number of EPP members had increased. With the fall of the Berlin Wall and the rebirth of the EC, new countries would probably join the Community in the foreseeable future - again,

---

12   T. Jansen, "The Dilemma for Christian Democracy", 464: "Once the EDU had been set up, it became pointless for the EPP member parties to make any further attempt to agree a joint strategy for organised dialogue with the Conservatives."

13   The Socialists gained 34.7% of the seats, i.e. 11.2% more than the EPP.

without Christian Democratic parties - and the importance of the institutions, especially the EP, would increase. The Christian Democrats faced a fundamental dilemna: either stay independent of other political families at the risk of being marginalised, or build an alliance with other parties at the risk of losing its own identity and still being minimised. Both choices meant a loss for the European Christian Democrats. Under the leadership of the CDU/CSU, the EPP chose unequivocally for the latter, becoming a small group within a powerful alliance instead of performing as a single actor in a less influential constellation.[14]

Enlargement strategy

The (new) strategy was mainly conducted by Helmut Kohl, German Chancellor and President of the CDU, together with Wilfried Martens, former Prime Minister of Belgium and EPP President since 1990. The strategy aimed at (re)gaining a majority at the expense of the Socialists. In this respect the statement attributed to Kohl that "Europe has not been built by Christian Democrats to surrender it to the Socialists" is often quoted. Basically, this 'majority strategy' - to regain a majority in the EC, particularly in the EP - was an answer to the twofold challenge posed by the absolute and relative electoral decline of Christian Democracy in Europe. The absolute decline was mainly due to the shrinking electoral appeal of Christian Democratic parties in the Benelux and to the implosion of the DC in Italy. The relative decline was the result of the weak position or non-existence of Christian Democratic parties in most of the 'new' member states of the EU. This twofold challenge must be seen against the background of the growing politicisation ('deepening') on the one hand and the enlargement ('widening') of the EU on the other. This means that there would have simply been no need for a 'majority strategy' if the EC had stayed a non-political organisation, if the powers of the EP had not been increased, if there had been Christian Democratic parties in the 'new' member states, and/or if there had not been any enlargement at all. This not being the case, the 'majority strategy' was put into operation by enlarging the EPP to include parties of both the existing and future member states. The EPP was destined to have a significant member party in every country (representation requirement), resulting in a delegation relative to the size of each member state (proportionality requirement). The fulfilment of these two criteria - 'proportional representation' - was essential for realising the EPP's ambition to boost its credibility and to increase its numerical strength in the EU.

---

14   D. Hanley, "Christian Democracy and the Paradoxes of Europeanisation. Flexibility, Competition and Collusion", in: R. Ladrech (ed.), *The Europeanisation of Party Politics.* Special Issue of *Party of Politics*, 4 (2002) 473.

National electoral results of Christian Democratic parties in EP elections, 1979-1999 (per cent)*

	1979	1984	1989	1994	1999
CVP	29.5	19.8	21.1	17.0	13.5
PSC	8.2	7.6	8.1	7.0	4.9
CDU	39.1	37.5	29.5	32.0	39.3
CSU	10.1	8.5	8.2	6.8	9.4
CSV	36.1	35.6	34.9	31.5	31.9
CDA	35.6	30.0	34.6	30.8	26.9
DC	36.4	33.0	32.8		
ÖVP				29.6**	30.6

* Although the results of the EP elections are not always reflecting the outcome on the national level, the Christian Democratic performances at the European level have been chosen because of their relative high degree of comparability.
** The first Austrian election for the EP dates from 1996.
Sources: H.-J. Veen (ed.), *Christlich-demokratische und konservative Parteien in Westeuropa*, 5 Vol., Paderborn, 1983-2000; <www3.europarl.eu.int/election/default.htm> (13/01/2004).

Candidates for enlargement

Given the fact that its representation had to be strengthened in the 'old' and the 'new' member states, the EPP had no other choice in realising its majority strategy but to enlarge towards the other political parties in both groups of countries. Therefore, the classic *familles politiques* of the Socialists, Liberals, and Conservatives came into the picture.

As for the CDU/CSU - the promoter of the majority strategy -, the Socialists were the political opponents. It was their 'proportional representation' that the Christian Democrats were eager to match and, if possible, to surpass. This stance against the Socialists is a clear example of the Europeanisation of the bipolar party political system as it exists in Germany, as well as other countries, and contrasts with the situation for instance in the Benelux, where Christian Democrats participated in coalition governments with the Socialists, sometimes as their preferred partner. Because of the anti-Socialism of the CDU/CSU, the EPP was on the look out for conservatives as well as liberals. The latter were relatively well-organised in the European Liberal, Democrat and Reform Party (ELDR) and were often on the same side as the Christian Democrats in bipolar political systems. However, in 1991, an attempt by Valéry

Giscard d'Estaing, then President of the Liberals, to absorb them in the EPP Group failed. It is alleged that the confessional character of the EPP was the biggest obstacle in this operation.[15] By contrast, the Conservatives were, generally speaking, more a-confessional than anti-confessional and, further-more, were not very well-organised, partly due to their outspoken national orientation. Consequently, they did not invest in transnational networks and did not tend towards increasing cooperation and integration. The latter proved to be a clear advantage for the EPP's 'majority strategy'.

Pattern of enlargement

The EPP strategy was distinguished not only by its goal and target public; but equally important by its *modus operandi*. First of all, a 'big bang' opera-tion was never an option for two reasons: the Conservatives were not united in one organisation and the balance of power within the EPP would have been too severely disrupted. Therefore, a twofold incremental approach was worked out. On the one hand, enlargement towards new party members is done on a one-by-one basis. Each party joins the EPP individually. This clearly strengthens the negotiation position of the EPP and enables it to spread out (i.e. to weaken) potential criticism from within. On the other hand, each future member party has to complete several stages: Members of European Parlia-ment (MEPs) from the applicant party join the EPP Group on an individual basis, MEPs join the EPP Group as a group, the party becomes an EPP observer, and finally, the party is granted full membership. This step-by-step process makes is it easier for the new member party to be informed, to adapt to and accept the party culture and structure of the EPP. As for the EPP, the time interval both within and between the accessions of future member parties facilitates the practical organisation and makes it possible to antici-pate positive and negative political consequences. Finally, the enlargement process is not a bottom-up operation; at every stage, in each case and on both sides, the party leadership takes the lead and overcomes the internal opposition. This does not hinder the free character of the enlargement and no party has ever been forced into EPP membership. The EPP only offers a very lucrative win-win situation: more political power (information, staff, posi-tions, etc.) based on a mutual increase in numerical strength.

15   S. Hix and C. Lord, *Political Parties in the European Union*, Basingstoke, 1997, 103.

Enlargement cases

Naturally, each enlargement process has its own features. Despite the incremental approach, some of the member parties have challenged (and still do) the EPP due to their numerical size, their policy impact, and/or the internal protest it has generated.

The first and, for many participants the most crucial, enlargement was an immediate consequence of Spain's membership in 1986 in general and the relatively small number of Spanish MEPs who joined the EPP Group in particular. Only the Catalonian UDC had managed to win a seat in the EP. The MEPs from the Conservative *Allianza Popular* (AP) became members of the European Democratic Group. Because of the close links the AP maintained with the CSU and the fact that it did not feel comfortable in a parliamentary group dominated by the British Conservatives, it soon established contacts with the EPP. The poor results of the AP in the 1989 European election convinced President Manuel Fraga to reform the party into a centre-right political movement, the *Partido Popular* (PP), which a number of Christian Democrats joined, as well as Conservatives and Liberals. This development paved the way for the PP's integration into the EPP.[16] Some Christian Democrats had already joined the EPP Group after the 1989 election, such as José Maria Gil Robles, later to become President of the EP. When Fraga was succeeded by José Maria Aznar as president of the PP in the spring of 1990, the pro-European and moderate profile was finally established, a development warmly supported by the EPP. Soon after his election, Aznar made official contact with the EPP to discuss the steps that had to be taken in order to become a full member. On both sides, strong protest could be heard. Aznar had to overcome opposition from the Conservative right-wing of the PP. Within the EPP, Catalans and Basques were opposed for internal Spanish reasons while Italians, Belgians and Dutch were not convinced of the transformation of the Francoist AP into a modern people's party. Nevertheless, in the autumn of 1990, the PP was granted observer status. One year later, it became a full EPP member. Since then, the PP has gradually increased its political influence within the EPP and has used EPP membership as a tool to increase the party's internal and external power relations.[17]

16   T. Jansen, "The Dilemma for Christian Democracy", 468-469.
17   For instance, at the instigation of the PP, the PNV was expelled from EPP membership in 1999 due to its close relationship with the Basque separatists. For a full record of the relationship between the PP and the EPP and the benefits of the PP's membership, see S. Van Hecke and P. Matuschek, *Europeanisation and Political Parties. The Case of the Spanish People's Party and the European People's Party*, unpublished paper, 2004.

The relation with the British and Danish Conservatives was more controversial. In the 1970s, the exclusion of the Conservatives from the UK and Denmark did not cost a lot. However, with the widening and deepening of the EU, both sides wanted to profit from enhanced cooperation. As for the EPP, the relationship with the British Conservative and Unionist Party and *Det Konservative Folkeparti* (the Danish Conservative People's Party) had to be settled before the forthcoming enlargement of the mid-1990s. British and Danish Conservative MEPs applied for membership of the EPP Group after the 1989 EP elections.[18] Because of its controversial nature, their application was sent to the EPP itself who responded that the time had not yet come. This decision was mainly based on the hostile attitude of Margaret Thatcher, Prime Minister and leader of the British Conservatives, towards further European integration. Ongoing bilateral talks were given a decisive boost after Thatcher's resignation and her replacement by the less eurospectic John Major at the end of 1990. At the same time, Kohl and Martens pushed strongly for an agreement with the British Conservatives. Finally, the British and Danish Conservative MEPs joined the EPP Group in May 1992 as allied members.[19] An attempt to grant full membership has never been made because of protests inside the EPP and the reluctance of the Conservatives themselves to join a 'Christian Democratic party'. For the same reasons, in 1999 the group name of the was extended with 'European Democrats' int EPP-ED. Because the cost of integration would outnumber the benefits, cooperation was not maximised. Unlike their British allies, the Danish Conservatives applied for observer status in 1993 and two years later became a full EPP member. This successfully completed enlargement is however highly symbolic because of the party's relatively small size, with currently only one MEP delegated to the EPP Group. Similarly, another silent entry also took place thanks to a party's smallness. Instead of the Portuguese CDSp, which was excluded from EPP membership in 1993 due to its anti-European position (a decision difficult to justify given the rapprochement with the British and Danish Conservatives), the *Partido Social Democrata* (PSD) - Social Democratic only in name - became a full member in 1996, with the result that Portugal was again represented in the EPP.

The EPP enlargement that accompanied the entry of Austria, Finland, and Sweden into the EU in 1995 was of a totally different nature. Applicant parties were relatively small, their record was generally pro-European (e.g. supporting EU membership), and some had a historical relationship with European Christian Democracy. Unlike the previous Spanish, British and Danish enlarge-

18   T. Jansen, "The Dilemma for Christian Democracy", 469.
19   This led automatically to the dissolution of the European Democratic Group.

ment of the EPP, the countries of the parties concerned were not members of
the EU yet. The status of associate member was first granted to the Austrian
ÖVP and the Swedish *Kristdemokratiska Samhällspartiet* (Christian Democratic
Society Party) in 1991. These Christian Democratic parties were followed by
the Conservative parties - the Finnish *Kansallinen Kokoomus* (National Coalition), the Swedish *Moderata Samling* (Moderate Unity Party) and the Norwegian *Høyre* (Right) - which became 'permanent observers' in 1993. As for the
EPP, the point was to incorporate both Swedish and therefore rival parties.[20]
In 1995, all parties concerned were admitted as full members.[21] Consequently,
their MEPs could join the EPP Group immediately after their election.

Due to the implosion of the Italian DC - one of the original and strongest
pillars of the EPP - in 1994, the EPP lost its embedment in one of the larger
member states of the EU. Italian Christian Democrats (re)appeared in different kinds of parties, and as political opponents on the national level they
hampered each other's application for EPP membership. Apart from individual MEPs who allied themselves with the EPP Group before and after the 1994
EP election, and the *Partito Populare Italiano* (PPI) which continued the EPP
membership of the DC, the *Centro Cristiano Democratico* (CCD) and the
Cristiani Democratici Uniti (CDUi) became full EPP members in 1995.[22]
The *Unione Democratica per l'Europa* (UDEUR), founded only in 1999, became
a full member in 2001. Not surprisingly, the number of parties was inversely
proportional to their electoral appeal.[23] Therefore, the EPP still lacked a solid
and major Italian partner. Clearly, only *Forza Italia* (FI), the party of the media
tycoon and captain of industry Silvio Berlusconi, could fill this gap. This view
only emerged in the second half of the 1990s. As for the FI, the opinion grew
that membership of the EPP could be used to increase the respectability of
the party and its leader, especially after the fall of the first Berlusconi government in 1994 and in the run-up to the 2001 national election.[24] Moreover,
the EPP could serve as a tool to enhance Berlusconi's European network.

---

20   For this particular history, see T. Jansen, "The Dilemma for Christian Democracy", 471.
21   Because in the end Norway did not become a EU member, *Høyre* was granted the status of
      associate member.
22   The more rightist CCD and CDUi later on merged into the *Unione dei Democratici Cristiani e di
      Centro* (UDCi). See the chapter "From Dominance to Doom? Christian Democracy in Italy" in
      this volume.
23   Together the four parties mentioned gained only 9 of the 87 Italian EP seats in the 1999
      election.
24   This was clearly shown in February 2001 at the XIVth EPP Congress in Berlin where Berlusconi
      was presented and treated as one of the major leaders of the EPP to the detriment of the
      other but 'Christian Democratic' Italian party presidents.

Many Christian Democrats, particularly those from the Benelux, France and Italy, opposed any affiliation with the accursed Berlusconi; his coalition with the extreme-right especially was a bone of contention. Following a fierce debate and several possible scenarios, twenty deputies of the FI, mainly former DC members, joined the Group on an individual basis. Pressure to allow all the FI MEPs to enter came with the FI's threat to establish a European 'centre' party.[25] This would thoroughly upset the calculations of the EPP and jeopardise its majority strategy; everything had to be done to prevent the establishment of a rival party (group). To ease the pressure, the Christian Democratic leaders of the EPP in 1998 forced through the entry of individual FI MEPs, although this decision flew in the face of the wishes of many Christian Democratic deputies. In order to solidly anchor the MEPs of the FI after its victory in the 1999 European elections, party membership was granted at the end of 1999.[26]

Often neglected but equally important is the position of the French in the EPP. Similar to the Spanish and the Italian cases, the representation from France was for a long time disproportional to the country's size (and political power) in the EU. This was largely due to the unstable party system, the political fragmentation on the right of the political spectrum and the electoral decline of the Christian Democrats. In 1978 the CDS formed together with other parties the *Union pour la Démocratie Française* (UDF).[27] As a party federation, delegates were free to join a parliamentary group. MEPs from the UDF chose between the Liberal and the EPP Group. Following the failed attempt to absorb the Liberals into the EPP, several individual UDF delegates left for the EPP. This process continued after the 1994 and 1999 EP elections.[28] At the same time, deputies from *Démocratie Libérale* (Liberal Democracy) and the *Rassemblement pour la République* (RPR) joined the EPP Group. Having overcome protests from the UDF and widespread scepticism towards a Christian Democratic party within the RPR, the latter became a full EPP member in 2001. The RPR wanted to benefit from the informational and networking advantages of being part of a large transnational party (group), while the EPP for its part gained a stable and large basis for French representation.

---

25   FI's delegation in the EP, Forza Europa, would be the pivot of a future Conservative party (group), including the French Gaullists and the British Conservatives, potentially having more MEPs than the Liberal Group.

26   Apart from the *Südtiroler Volkspartei* (SVP), five Italian parties are now represented in the EPP.

27   The CDS itself was the successor of the once very successful *Mouvement Populaire Républicain* (Republican People's Movement).

28   Currently, only one French MEP is a member of the Liberal Group (as of 13 January 2004).

No surprise then that the EPP welcomed the recent establishment of the *Union pour un Mouvement Populaire* (UMP), which brought together the RPR, a part of the UDF, and *Démocratie Libérale* into one single people's party.

The EPP and deepening the EU

S imilar to the parallelism between the enlargement of the EU and the widening of the EPP, a process of deepening characterised the 1990s. European integration took some big leaps during this decade; in this section we will highlight the impact of this evolution on the EPP and, *vice versa*, the EPP's role in deepening the EU. On the other hand, the EPP went through a process of internal deepening (integration) - a topic to be discussed in the next section of this paper where we will examine successively the relation between the EPP and the EP, the European Council and the Commission.[29] Although the EU officially only recognises the role of political parties inside the EP, the single focus on party groups has moved away to the additional 'party politics' in the European Council and the Commission, due to the growing 'politicisation' of the EU in general.

The Parliament

During the 1990s, the EP underwent a true metamorphosis. Direct election by universal suffrage increased its legitimacy but, more important, with every new treaty more competences have been awarded. As a result of this 'emancipation', the EP changed from an advisory body into a player in the co-decision making process. The turning point came with the Single European Act (1987).[30] With the Treaty on the European Union (TEU) - the so-called Maastricht Treaty (1993) -, the role of the EP received a decisive boost, which was confirmed by the Treaty of Amsterdam (1999). The Nice Treaty (2003), however, did not decisively enlarge the competences of the Parliament. Overall, the 1990s changed the EP into a fairly 'political' institution. Due to the new legislative procedures the EP now matters both 'institutionally', due to the new competences, and 'politically'. Both developments have brought party politics into the heart of the EP.

---

29   Although there is an institutional difference between the Council (of Ministers) and the European Council, I will leave this aside because it has no direct relevance for this paper. Likewise, I will not discuss the relation between the EPP (Group) and the Committee of the Regions as it was established in 1994.

30   The dates of the treaties refer to the dates when they came into force.

The changing nature of the EPP Group serves as the example *par excellence* of this development. As mentioned already, the Christian Democrats originally formed one group, leaving the Conservatives out. The lack of cooperation between the Christian Democrats and the Conservatives did not cost either side much. However, with the prospect of several rounds of enlargement and new powers for the EP, the benefits of cooperation with like-minded parties in other member states outnumbered the advantages of a 'splendid isolation'. Therefore, the EPP chose for a majority strategy. Without the growing politicisation of the EP (and the political opportunities it generates), it is very unlikely that a rapprochement between the Christian Democrats and the Conservatives would have taken place.

The formation of a large parliamentary group is determined by the EP itself. Its Rules of Procedure facilitate a reduction in the number of EP party groups and a consolidation of the EPP. The size of the party group determines how much secretarial and research staff, financial resources and intra-parliament positions can be obtained.[31] Vice-presidents, committee positions, and *rapporteurs* are allocated proportionately to each party group's position (using the D'Hondt counting system, which favours the larger groups).[32] This allocation is then followed by a similar intra-group negotiation on how the party group's 'prizes' are to be distributed between the national delegations. Furthermore, the size of the party group is crucial to building majorities in the EP. As laid down in the treaties, EP majorities are necessary to pass legislation, but they are also needed to organise the Parliament itself, for instance in the election of the president (by absolute majority of the votes cast). For instance, in 1999 the EPP used its fresh (relative) majority to elect the EP president. The EPP rejected the 'grand coalition' with the Socialists, which had traditionally been the firm basis for the election of the president (pooling their votes in order to get their own candidates into the president's seat, each for half the term). With the support of the Liberal Group, Nicole Fontaine (UDF) was elected president. In 2002, the EPP-ED Group supported Pat Cox, the candidate of the Liberal Group. The election was a clear sign that the EPP-ED Group wanted to use its size to make and break majorities. Paradoxically, this was in opposition to Fontaine's personal opinion. Together with Martens, President of the EPP, she has always favoured the traditional cooperation with the Socialists to prevent the Parliament from being weakened in the broader

---

31   S. Hix, *The Political System of the European Union*, Basingstoke, 1999, 76.
32   *Ibid.*, 79. For instance, during the 1989-1994 parliamentary term, the EPP obtained 5 out of 18 committee chairs (27.8%). In 1999, 8 out of 17 committee chairmen were members of the EPP-ED Group (47.1%).

constellation of the EU by intra-parliament fights. Whether this alliance with the Liberal Group will last, especially in other, more policy oriented issues, and whether this development signals the end of the dominant 'grand coalition' still has to be researched.

The European Council

Although the majority strategy is first of all aimed at strengthening the EPP's position in the EP, it has its consequences for the European Council as well. On one hand, there is no institutional link between the political weight in the EP and the Council. The first depends on the result of the EP elections; the latter reflects the composition of the national governments based on national elections. On the other hand, the relative and absolute decline of Christian Democracy may decrease the number of government leaders and affect the composition of the Council. Therefore, the realisation of the majority strategy is crucial for the Council too. That party politics matter in the Council is clearly shown by the Commissioners' appointment and the treaty revision during the Intergovernmental Conferences (IGCs).[33]

The Commission

Finally, party politics have affected the Commission as well. Formally, Commission members are expected to act independently of their national and political affiliations. Nonetheless, the political background of the individual Commissioners (nominated by their respective national governments) and the political balance of the Commission as a whole are increasingly profiled. There is a growing tendency to respect, if not reflect, the outcome of EP elections in the representation of the different political parties in the Commission, especially since the appointment of the Santer Commission in 1995. This results in a very delicate exercise in finding a balance between the desires of the government leaders and the newly elected EP. In both cases, party political motivations and calculations are growing. For instance, in contrast with the CDU/CSU victory in the 1999 EP election, the German Red-Green government decided to put an end to the tradition whereby the majority appointed one commissioner and the opposition another. In the case of the appointment of the Prodi Commission, the EPP-ED Group disapproved

---

33   The European Council has the final say in the IGCs. Therefore, its political composition decides the outcome. See my chapter "Christian Democratic Parties and Europeanisation" in this volume.

EPP Commissioners since 1989

Commission	EPP Commissioners
Delors II (1989-1993)	Peter Schmidhuber (CSU) Sir Leon Brittan (British Conservatives) Filippo Maria Pandolfi (DC) Abel Matutes Juan (PP) Frans Andriessen (CDA) Christiane Scrivener (UDF) Jean Dondelinger (CSV)
Total of 17 Commissioners	7 EPP Commissioners (41.2%)
Delors III (1993-1995)	Raniero Vanni d'Archirafi (DC) Abel Matutes Juan (PP) Sir Leon Brittan (British Conservatives) Christiane Scrivener (UDF) João de Deus Rogado Pinheiro (PSD) Ioannis Paleokrassas (ND) Hans van den Broek (CDA) Peter Schmidhuber (CSU)
Total of 17 Commissioners	8 EPP Commissioners (47.1%)
Santer (1995-1999)	Jacques Santer (CSV) Sir Leon Brittan (British Conservatives) Hans van den Broek (CDA) João de Deus Rogado Pinheiro (PSD) Marcelino Oreja Aguirre (PP) Mario Monti* Franz Fischler (ÖVP)
Total of 20 Commissioners	7 EPP Commissioners (35%)

Commission	EPP Commissioners
Prodi** (1999-)	Loyola de Palacio del Valle-Lersundi (PP) Mario Monti* Franz Fischler (ÖVP) Chris Patten (British Conservatives) Michel Barnier (UMP) Viviane Reding (CSV)
Total of 20 Commissioners	6 EPP Commissioners (30%)

* Monti has no party membership but has been linked to the EPP ever since he became (Italian) Commissioner.
** Prodi attented several EPP meetings as Prime Minister of Italy. Since FI became linked to the EPP, he has presented himself as independent or linked to the Liberal ELDR.
Sources: <//europa.eu.int/comm>; <//epp-ed.europarl.eu.int>; <www.eppe.org> (13/01/2004).

of the under-representation of Christian Democrats and Conservatives.[34] Despite this reservation, six out of twenty Commissioners are recognised as linked with the EPP.[35] In the previous Santer Commission, seven Commissioners - including the president - were affiliated with the EPP. As for the EPP, 'EPP Commissioners' are full participants in the Congress, the Political Bureau, the Summits, and *ex officio* in the Presidency. In return, however, there are hardly any provisions for influencing the actions of the Commissioners.[36]

[34] Naturally, both cases are linked. Because there was no CDU/CDU Commissioner, the German Christian Democrats opposed the installation of the Prodi Commission. See for instance Hans-Gert Pöttering, Chairman of the EPP-ED Group, replying to President Designate Romano Prodi, European Parliament, 21 July 1999: "Mr Prodi, you repeated the view that the Commission is well balanced. I don't know what yardstick you are using to measure balance but I can tell you clearly and unequivocally that we in the EPP Group do not believe that this Commission is politically balanced. Therefore we should not allow the legend to emerge that the Commission is politically balanced. If you repeat the myth, you are not making it easier for us to approve the team you have put together, qualified as it may be. So Mr Prodi, I would be grateful if you would explain the criteria that you use to measure balance. You said that you did everything you could to put this new team together. You defended the choices made but in the case of Germany it was the Federal Chancellor who dictated the choices. This is contrary to the Treaty provisions because you as President Designate had no part in the German appointments. (...) It was a demonstration of arrogance by the Chancellor of the Federal Republic." See also his speech on the occasion of the vote on the Prodi Commission, European Parliament, 14 September 1999.
[35] See <http://www.eppe.org/network/cssrs.asp.> (13/01/2004).
[36] S. Hix and C. Lord, *Political Parties in the European Union*, 180.

Organisational changes

In 1990, on the occasion of the VIIIth EPP Congress in Dublin, the statutes were revised to adapt the party organisation towards widening (the enlargement of the EPP) and deepening (the growing political role of transnational parties).[37] Furthermore, the EPP started an integration (absorption) process with respect to the EDU and the EUCD. Despite these organisational changes, the continuity with respect to personnel has been remarkable.

One of the major changes in the first modification of the original EPP statutes of 1976 has been the introduction of the 'Conference of Party Leaders and Heads of Governments'. Article 11 regulates the composition only and does not address the tasks, voting procedure, convening details etc.[38] Nonetheless, the 'political' importance of these EPP Summits cannot be underestimated. First, they offer an opportunity for the EPP to present its political strength to the media and the public. While other EPP gatherings take place behind closed doors, they embody the EPP, especially on the eve of the European Council. In this case, full media coverage is guaranteed.[39] Second, they serve as a forum to outline the long-term policy of the EPP, internally and externally. Third, short-term difficulties can be resolved, for instance concerning enlargement and integration with the EDU and the EUCD. Fourth, they offer opportunities for bilateral networking, coalition building, exchange of information, etc. to the government and opposition leaders of the EPP. In this way, the EPP presents itself as an attractive forum to outsiders. As the political weight of the EPP grows, so does the importance of its summits (and the cost of non-attendance). For instance, following a long absence by France's leadership, the attendance of Jean-Pierre Raffarin, Prime Minister of France, was one of the

37 On the evolution towards transnational parties, see S. Van Hecke, "Het Europa van de opportunities. Analyse van de overlevingsstrategie van de christen-democraten in de Europese Unie", in: *Res Publica*, 4 (2003) 652-655.

38 The Conference of Party Leaders and Heads of Government is composed of those members of the EPP Presidency elected by Congress; the President of the EPP Group in the EP; the members of the European Council (Heads of Government); presidents of parties in coalition governments in EU member states in cases where the Head of Government is not a member of an EPP member party; the President of the largest opposition party in each member state of the European Union in the event that no EPP member party is part of the government (in cases where there is more than one EPP member party though not competing in the same region, the President of each party is invited); the President of the European Parliament if (s)he is member of EPP Member Party; the President of the European Commission or a Vice-President to represent members of the European Commission who are members of EPP member parties; and other personalities invited by the President.

39 Although the meetings also take place behind closed doors, they provide photo opportunities and arrange press conferences which attract a lot of interest.

highlights of the EPP Summit in Madrid on 20 June 2002.[40] Similarly, informal meetings of the European Christian Democratic leaders prepare solutions for the vexed questions of the EPP's internal organisation and external policy. Of importance in this respect are the so-called bungalow talks that took place in Kohl's country house outside Bonn where EPP leaders met regularly to discuss the evolution of the EPP.[41] Recently, such informal meetings have become semi-public.[42]

According as the majority strategy of the EPP began to bear fruit, the EPP network strengthened. The EPP became less dependent on its member parties, thanks to the increased financial resources and personnel of the EP. The EPP is, however, financially dependent from its group in the EP.[43] Besides, the EPP became more central to its side-organisations as well. Since enlargement had brought many parties from the EDU inside the EPP and the EUCD had acted as the EPP's 'waiting room', formal integration was on the agenda from the early 1990s.[44] The 1999 victory provided the opportunity to strike and a long period of preparation and negotiation ended in success. In February 1999, the EUCD was integrated into the EPP and since April 2000, the EDU has joined the EPP headquarters in Brussels, resulting almost in a fusion between the EPP and the EDU. Finally, the EPP can present itself as the single, dominant organisation of the European centre-right.

Notwithstanding the organisational changes in the EPP during the 1990s, there has been a striking continuity among the top personnel, probably a necessary condition for the success of the transition. The duration of the EPP presidency of Martens, which he combined in 1994-1999 with the presidency

---

40 See <www.eppe.org/news/n06h_raffarin_062.asp> (13/01/2004).

41 With regard to the integration of the EPP and the EUCD, see for instance K. Welle, "The European People's Party. A Political Family Reinvents Itself", in: EPP-ED Group, *Our Vision of Europe. Proximity, Competitiveness and Visibility*, Leuven/Apeldoorn, 2001, 251. Clearly, in this respect, the impact of personal affiliation (or 'political friendship') should not be underestimated, although this is not an exclusive intra-party phenomenon. See for instance the Kohl-Mitterrand tandem in drawing up the Treaty of Maastricht.

42 For instance the meeting in Sardinia on 9 September 2002. Silvio Berlusconi invited to his country house his colleagues from Spain, France, Portugal, the Netherlands and Luxembourg together with the EPP leadership, to discuss a draft of 'A Constitution for a Strong Europe' in the run-up to the EPP Congress in Estoril in October 2002.

43 The EPP is the only transnational party whose headquarters are separate from the buildings of the EP. On the direct financing of European political parties, see my chapter "Christian Democratic Parties and Europeanisation" in this volume.

44 K. Welle, "The European People's Party", 250: "(…) the EPP did not have to commit itself immediately to parties many of which were still short-lived, threatened with collapse and whose political content was difficult to evaluate precisely."

of the EPP Group in the EP, is certainly remarkable in this respect. Next, the party membership of the top personnel has almost been limited to the CVP (i.e. Martens), the CDU and the PP.[45] As for the CDU, Thomas Jansen and Klaus Welle have occupied crucial positions. The appointment of Alejandro Agag and Antonio Lopez, both former personal advisers to Aznar, reflects the ambition of the PP to become one of the leading parties of the EPP.[46]

EPP leadership posts since 1990

EPP President	Wilfried Martens (CVP)	1990-
EPP Secretary General	Thomas Jansen (CDU)	1983-1994
	Klaus Welle (CDU)	1994-1999
	Alejandro Agag (PP)	1999-2002
	Antonio Lopez (PP)	2002-
President EPP(-ED) Group	Egon Klepsch (CDU)	1984-1992
	Leo Tindemans (CVP)	1992-1994
	Wilfried Martens (CVP)	1994-1999
	Hans-Gert Pöttering (CDU)	1999-
Secretary General EPP(-ED) Group	Sergio Guccione (DC)	1986-1990
	Gerhard Guckenberger (CSU)	1991-1997
	Mario David (PSD)	1997-1999
	Klaus Welle (CDU)	1999-2003
	Niels Pedersen (Danish Conservatives)	2004-

Source: <www.eppe.org> (13/01/2004).

45 The appointment of Mario David as Secretary General of the EPP Group in 1997 was seen as a reward for his efforts in 1996 to detach the PSD MEPs from the Liberals and ally them with the EPP.

46 This stance was predominant when, after the 1998 electoral defeat of the CDU/CSU, the PP was the only major EPP party in government. See P. Matuschek, "Aznars Ambitionen. Die spanische Volkspartei und ihr europäischer Führungsanspruch", in: *Blätter für deutsche und internationale Politik*, 1 (2002) 77-84 and S. Van Hecke and P. Matuschek, *Europeanisation and Political Parties*.

Electoral performances

The electoral performances in the successive EP elections have been decisive for the development of the EPP. However, because of the specific nature of the European elections and the composition of transnational parties, national parties and their electoral performances are important as well.[47]

Before the election of the EP by universal suffrage, the Christian Democrats held the relative majority. After 1979, the Socialists took the first place and were able to increase their lead with every European election. In 1989 - the worst result for the EPP so far - the Party of European Socialists (PES) outnumbered the Christian Democrats by no less than 11.2%. Since the majority strategy started to pay off, the gap has constantly been narrowed, resulting in the 1999 victory (an increase of more than 40% since 1989). Currently, the difference between the EPP and the Socialists has been nearly inverted to 9.2%.[48] However, these figures disguise the growth in the number of EPP seats during the EP legislatures.[49] Taking these changes into account, the EPP won fewer than thirty seats in 1999. Generally, these figures show that the steady increase in the number of EPP seats is predominantly based on both enlargement and the specific nature of the 1999 election.

Since 1999, the EPP-ED Group has drawn MEPs from 31 parties, representing all 15 member states of the EU. The achievement of a relative majority is the direct result of the good performance of the big members.[50] The CDU/CSU won 6 seats and rose from 47 to 53, gaining more than half of the German MEPs. The PP, the only big EPP member which was nationally in office at the time of the elections, lost 2 seats but still delegated 28 MEPs to the EPP Group.

---

47   European elections are perceived as 'second-order national elections' which means that, inter alia, opposition parties will profit from high numbers of protest votes when European elections fall in the middle of a national parliamentary term. This particular mechanism can help to explain the EPP's victory in the 1999 EP elections while being a minority in the European Council. See S. Hix and C. Lord, *Political Parties in the European Union*, 88-89 and S. Van Hecke, "Het Europa van de opportunities", 666.

48   Figures from 13 January 2004: 232 EPP-ED seats (37.1%) and 175 Socialist seats (27.9%).

49   For figures at the beginning and at the end of each legislature, see L. Bardi, "Transnational Trends. The Evolution of the European Party System", in: B. Steunenberg and J. Thomassen (eds.), *The European Parliament. Moving Toward Democracy in the EU*, Lanham, 2002, 70. While the June 1999 figure of 224 reflects the number of seats chosen on EPP lists, Bardi counts 233 seats at the moment of the establishment of the EPP-ED Group in July 1999.

50   Although I discuss the results of the 9-13 June 1999 EP election, I refer to the figures of 13 January 2004. The differences between the numbers of seats are too slight to affect my analysis.

EP election results of the EPP and the PES, 1979-1999

	1979	1984	1989	1994	1999
Total EP seats	410	434	518	567	626
EPP(-ED) seats	107	110	122	157	224
PES seats	112	130	180	198	180
% EPP(-ED) seats	26.1	25.3	23.5	27.7	35.8
% PES seats	27.3	29.9	34.7	34.9	28.7
% EPP(-ED) seats - % PES seats	-1.2	-4.6	-11.2	-7.2	7.1

Source: <www3.europarl.eu.int/election/default.htm> (13/01/2004).

The biggest electoral success was for the British Conservatives. They more than doubled their size from 16 to 37 deputies. With an overall anti-European campaign, favoured by the proportional electoral system and thanks to a low national turnout, they became the largest national group but one in the EPP. Consequently, the British Conservatives demanded the EPP Group be renamed the EPP-ED, feeling more at ease in an alliance in which they constituted an almost separate entity. The renaming was crucial to selling their affiliation with the European Christian Democrats to the homeland party and the grassroots of the Conservative Party. In Italy, the FI performed very well with 22 MEPs, including the election of Silvio Berlusconi himself. With regard to France, 6 deputies from the *Démocratie Libérale* and 6 deputies from the RPR, together with the UDF MEPs brought the number of French seats to 21. Together, Germany, Spain, France, Italy, and the United Kingdom account for 173 seats, nearly three quarters of the total number of 232.[51] Within the Parliament as a whole, the delegations from the big five have a 67.7% share of the seats. This means that the small member states are slightly under-represented in the EPP-ED Group. Overall, the aim to have one solid partner in every member state, especially the big ones, and to include all the major Christian Democratic and Conservative parties, has been realised.

---

51   This figure of the big five includes the seats of some small parties: the Italian UDCi, PPI, SVP, UDEUR, *Partito Pensionati* (Pensioners' Party) *Rinnivamento Italiano-Dini* (Italian Renovation, Dini referring to Lamberto Dini, former Minister for External Affairs and Prime Minister) the Spanish UDC, and the Ulster Unionist Party.

Composition of the EPP-ED Group in the 5th parliamentary term,1999-2004

Member State	Party	Seats	% 1*	% 2**
Belgium	CVP	2	20	2.15
	PSC	1		
	CSP	1		
	MCC	1		
Denmark	Det Konservative Folkeparti	1	6.25	0.43
Germany	CDU	43	53.54	22.85
	CSU	10		
Greece	ND	9	36	3.88
Spain	PP	27	43.75	12.07
	UDC	1		
France	UDF	6	24.14	9.05
	Démocratie Libérale	1		
	UMP	14		
Ireland	Fine Gael	5	33.33	2.15
Italy	FI	22	39.08	14.66
	PPI	4		
	UDCi	4		
	Rinnovamento Italiana-Dini	1		
	UDE	1		
	Partito Pensionati	1		
	SVP	1		
Luxembourg	CSV	2	33.33	0.86
The Netherlands	CDA	9	29.03	3.88
Austria	ÖVP	7	33.33	3.02
Portugal	PSD	9	36	3.88
Finland	Kansallinen Kokoomus	4	31.25	2.15
	Suomen Kristillinen Liitto	1		
Sweden	Moderaterna	5	31.82	3.02
	Kristdemokraterna	2		
United Kingdom	Conservative Party	36	42.53	15.95
	Ulster Unionist Party	1		
Total		232		100

* Percentage number of national EPP-ED seats/number of Member State seats
** Percentage number of national EPP-ED seats/total number of EPP-ED seats
Source: <www.europarl.eu.int/home/default_nl.htm> (13/01/2004).

Ideological profile(s)

The EPP's establishment has taught us that the division between Christian Democratic 'purists' (from the Benelux and Italy) and 'realists' (mainly from Germany) is as old as the EPP itself.[52] The rapprochement with the Conservatives has not simplified this dichotomy. On the contrary, internal criticisms can easily be analysed along the lines of these two ideological visions about the essence of the EPP. For example, protest against the entry of the FI led to the foundation of the 'Athena Group', a faction of Flemish, Dutch and Irish MEPs (under the presidency of the former Irish prime minister John Bruton), which was set up to defend the Christian Democratic identity and named after the EPP Congress of 1992 in Athens in which the Basic Programme of the EPP was accepted. Even though the Athena Group could not prevent the FI from becoming a full EPP member, similar protest following the coalition of the Austrian ÖVP with the extreme-right in 2000 resulted in the establishment of the Schuman Group, named after the French Christian Democrat and founding father of the EU, Robert Schuman. Because of internal reasons, the French RPR and the Spanish PP joined the protests of the Belgian and Italian Christian Democrats.[53] Gaining from the weak position of the CDU due to a party financing scandal, they asked for the exclusion of the ÖVP; a compromise was reached whereby its membership was suspended. This measure was rectified after a positive report by the EPP wise men, a procedure to be copied by the European Council. As for the Schuman Group (presided over by UDF President François Bayrou), its members prefered a renewal of the Christian Democratic identity and wanted to free the EPP of its Conservative absolute majority.[54]

Despite these protests, the official party discourse still emphasises its centrist programme, position and character in referring to the Christian inspired personalist concept of man, the principle of subsidiarity, a federal Europe and the *Soziale Marktwirtschaft* (social market economy).[55] To a certain degree, 'purist' Christian Democrats traditionally had a major say in the establishment of the EPP's doctrine because the 'realists' could care less. Therefore, as in the

---

52   On this terminology, see D. Hanley, "Christian Democracy and the Paradoxes of Europeanisation", 463.

53   M. Gehler, "Präventivschlag als Fehlschlag: Motive, Intentionen und Konsequenzen der EU 14-Sanktionsmassnahmen gegen Österreich im Jahre 2000", in: W. Loth (ed.), *Das europäische Projekt zu Beginn des 21. Jahrhundert*, Opladen, 2001, 342-344.

54   S. Van Hecke, "Démocrates chrétiens et conservateurs au Parlement européen. Mariage d'amour ou de raison?", 340.

55   EPP, *Basic Programme adopted by the IXth EPP Congress*, Athens, 14 November 1992.

Statutes, only the name 'Christian Democrats' is mentioned. In more 'political' documents however, the realists' anti-socialism reflects the reality of the EPP composition of Christian Democrats and Conservatives.[56] The renewed mission statement adjusting the EPP programme to the enlargement with the Conservatives, accepted at the Berlin Congress in February 2001, shows a more balanced approach.[57]

As far as voting behaviour in the EP is concerned, the outcome is equally ambiguous. Overall, research has shown that the political landscape is predominantly two-dimensional, dominated by the left-right divide (social affairs, environment, and redistributive policy) and the pro- versus anti-European (federalism) divide.[58] For both dimensions, the EPP(-ED) Group shows a high degree of cohesion. This cohesion level was higher before the rapprochement with the Conservatives but is, similar to the Socialist and the Liberal Group, rising. The British Conservatives are the only large party located some distance from the majority group positions: they are more right-wing and more sceptical of further EU integration. With regard to ethical questions, the EPP(-ED) differs from the Socialist and the Liberal Group. According to the research on the post-1999 Parliament, the left-right dimension has become more dominant and therefore the cleavage between the EPP-ED and the Socialists is widening. The British Conservatives are the single largest group whose position is distinct from the majority group position, both within the EPP-ED Group and the Parliament as a whole. As the only group without full membership of the EPP, the Conservatives are the outsiders, *de jure* and *de facto*, within the EPP-ED Group.[59]

---

56 See for instance EPP, *Action Programme 1999-2004*. On the Way to the 21st Century adopted by the XIII Congress, 6 February 1999, Brussels, 2, 4: "Europe must not be one-sidedly dominated by a Socialist majority. (…) That is why the EPP is going into the 1999 European Elections determined to become the strongest force in the European Parliament and once again to ensure the political balance in the European institutions. (…) The EPP is determined to vehemently fight attempts to introduce a Socialist agenda in Europe. (…) We call for a strong stand against Socialism."

57 EPP, *A Union of Values. Final text agreed at the XIV Congress*, Berlin, 13 January 2000. Note that *A Union of Values* is simply a 'text' and therefore not replacing the (Christian Democratic) Basic Programme.

58 On this 'cleavage' approach and the research on roll call votes in the EP, see S. Van Hecke, "Démocrates chrétiens et conservateurs au Parlement européen", 331-334.

59 This de facto outside position is another argument for some British Conservatives to leave the EPP-ED Group. See for instance J. Collett and M. Ball, *Conservative MEPs and the European People's Party. Time for Divorce*, The Bruges Group, London, 1999.

Conclusion

This chapter shows that the 1990s changed the nature of the EPP and that this development ran parallel with the widening and deepening of the EU.[60] Moreover, the EPP's history has taught us that the 1990s marked a qualitative and quantitative leap in a process that had already been initiated in the previous decades but that reached fruition in the 1990s. The same is true of the dispute between 'purists' and 'realists'.

With the majority strategy, the German bipolar model was introduced to the EPP. As for the CDU/CSU, its decision to overcome the relative decline of Christian Democracy was crucial to its moving forward in a wider and deeper EU. t was presented as the only way to survive politically at the European level. Due to the absolute decline of some Christian Democratic parties, an alternative (e.g. a split) has never been seriously considered.[61] As far as these parties are concerned, the majority strategy does not provide a solution for their absolute decline and is therefore not a 'survival' strategy. Another relative failing in enlargement is the position of the British Conservatives. Although the EPP-ED Group sometimes gives way, the position of the British Conservatives is the true Achilles heel.[62]

The widening and deepening of the EPP proved successful at the 1999 European elections (vote-seeking) and through the EPP's presence in the Parliament, the Council and the Commission (office-seeking). Ideologically, there is a tendency away from traditional Christian Democratic priorities (policy-seeking). In this matter, the party has shown considerable pragmatism and flexibility, except for the issue of European integration. Although traditional Christian Democrats seem to dominate the discussion about the EPP's doctrine, how long this situation will last (e.g. in terms of personnel) and what the real impact is of these basic Christian Democratic principles are questions that remain unanswered.[63]

60   Insofar as the developments within the EPP are subsidiary to those of the EPP, the traditional claim of an essential relationship between Christian Democracy and European integration has been thoroughly questioned. See F. Horner, "Parteienkooperation der europäischen Christdemokraten. Möglichkeiten und Grenzen. Ein Kommentar", in: M. Gehler, W. Kaiser and H. Wohnout (eds.), *Christdemokratie in Europa im 20. Jahrhundert*, Vienna, 2001, 738-739, 742-743.

61   A break between the 'realists' and the 'purists' happened among the respective youth organisations. See A. De Brouwer, "Le parti populaire européen. Son identité et son nécessaire élargissement", in: M. Caciagli (ed.), *Christian Democracy in Europe*, Barcelona, 1992, 119.

62   See for instance the establishment of the European Ideas Network, a conservative think-tank sponsored by the EPP-ED Group: <www.europeanideasnetwork.org.> (13/01/2004).

All in all, the EPP has seized the political opportunities of the 1990s.[64] Obviously, this has brought costs (policy) and benefits (power). In the long run, however, the outcome is uncertain because another major challenge is on its way: Eastern enlargement. As for the EPP, the particular period of the 1990s will 'politically' finish with this new window of opportunity in 2004.

---

63 D. Hanley, "The European People's Party. Towards a New Party Form?", in: D. Hanley (ed.), *Christian Democracy in Europe. A Comparative Perspective*, London, 1994, 191.

64 On this phrase, see EPP, *A Europe of Opportunities. Election Manifesto 1999*, s.l.

European Christian Democracy in the 1990s
Towards a Comparative Approach

Emmanuel Gerard and Steven Van Hecke

"(...) Christian Democrats['] (...) hopes, defeats, and victories can still inform our understanding of how people in any time are shaped by and reshape their world."[1]

Political parties cannot be isolated from the environment in which they operate. Consequently, research on political parties must take into account the circumstances that do not merely refer to parties' developments, directly or explicitly, for these circumstances contribute to explain party change. This volume's aim has been to analyse the evolution of Christian Democratic parties in the European Union (EU). Each chapter has examined one or more parties by, *inter alia*, highlighting the intra-party or inter-party changes. In the concluding chapter of this volume, we try to synthesise these findings and to explain the changes of European Christian Democracy in the 1990s within its context.[2]

The end of Christian Democracy in Western Europe?

During the 1990s, quite a lot of political observers have predicted the end of Christian Democracy in Western Europe. A number of successive electoral failures was said to be this thesis' cause and illustration at the same time. In 1994, the Dutch *Christen Democratisch Appèl* (CDA) suffered its worst defeat ever and was deprived off government participation for the first time in its, albeit short, history; the once dominant *Democrazia*

---

1   C. Strikwerda, "Parties, Populists and Pressure Groups. European Christian Democracy in Comparative Perspective", in: T. Kselman and J.A. Buttigieg (eds.), *European Christian Democracy. Historical Legacies and Comparative Perspectives*, Notre Dame, 2003, 287.

2   By succeeding in explaining the changes of European Christian Democracy in the 1990s, we prove that our first and third assumption - that European Christian Democracy is a distinctive political phenomenon and that the 1990s constitute a politically distinct period - are justified.

Cristiana (DC) collapsed and disappeared from the Italian political scene; and the *Österreichische Volkspartei* (ÖVP) was not able to structurally stop its electoral losses. This tendency seemed more than local and accidental when, in 1998, the *Christlich Demokratische Union* (CDU) and *Christlich-Soziale Union* (CSU) lost the federal elections and the chancellorship in Germany; the electorate of the CDA shrank once more. In 1999, the Belgian *Christelijke Volkspartij* (CVP) and *Parti Social Chrétien* (PSC) also lost power and left the government while the ÖVP reached rock bottom. With the exception of the Luxembourg *Chrëschtlech-Sozial Volekspartei* (CSV), all Christian Democratic strongholds were in deep crisis.

The idea of a structural crisis was reinforced by the fact that for most of the parties the electoral defeats also signaled the end of long periods of government participation, if not domination, and/or the end of being the largest party: the CDA and its predecessors had continuously shared power in the Netherlands since 1917 and had been the biggest party since its foundation in 1980; the Belgian Christian Democrats were sent to opposition for the first time in 40 years while being outnumbered for the first time by both the Socialists and the Liberals; the CDU/CSU, personified in Chancellor Helmut Kohl, had lead the federal government of Germany for an exceptionally long period of 16 years; the DC had taken part of every government since its foundation in 1945 and had been the largest party in Italy between 1948 and 1992. In this way, the 1990s seemed to sound the death-knell of European Christian Democracy.

Contrary to 'the end of Christian Democracy' thesis, the sudden and clear resurrection of some Christian Democratic parties at the beginning of the new decade has been remarkable. In 2002, the CDU/CSU won the federal elections after a long series of *Land* victories but was unable to break the ruling coalition of Socialists and Greens[3]; the ÖVP became the largest party in Austria for the first time since 1966 and continued to lead the federal government with the defeated extreme-right, for which the ÖVP had been maligned by many Christian Democratic and non-Christian Democratic parties and politicians; the CDA became again the largest party, returned to power, even providing the prime minister, and confirmed its position in 2003. As the CSV still led the Luxembourg government, only the Belgian Christian Democrats were not able to make a strong stand during its 2003 election campaign. The

---

3   After the 2002 federal elections, the series of *Länder* victories continued of which the 68.9% result of the CSU in the Bavarian elections of 2003 was the most spectacular.

Christian Democratic successes were preceded by the victory of the European People's Party (EPP) in the 1999 European elections, gaining the relative majority in the European Parliament (EP) for the first time since 1979 when direct elections were introduced.

If one takes a closer look at the overall evolution since the end of the Cold War, including the Christian Democratic performances in Scandinavia, a number of assessments can be made.[4] Firstly, there is no single linear trend towards failure or success. One must therefore differentiate with regard to parties and periods. For those parties that gain more than 15%, there is an almost steady decline until 1998-1999, with the exception of the sharp fall in the case of Italy due to the sudden implosion of the DC in 1994. However, it is worth noting that since then the Christian Democratic votes still count for 20% of the Italian electorate. Secondly, at the beginning of the new decade, the share of Austrian, German and Dutch Christian Democrats started to rise again (Belgium being the exception). The results of the Scandinavian Christian Democratic parties (with the exception of the Finnish) show an inverse tendency: an increase until 1997-1998 and a loss of votes at the beginning of the new decade (but no return to the previous low results for the Norwegians and the Swedish). Taken together, one can distinguish the period since the end of the Cold War in two phases.

4   We leave aside the performances of the French and Spanish Christian Democrats, as they have hardly respectively not stand for election as a separate party. As the picture would become too complicated, we also leave aside the EPP's results in the European elections because it only reflects the addition sum of its member parties, neutralising the failure of the one by the success of the other and *vice versa*.

National election results of Christian Democratic parties, 1989-2003 (per cent)

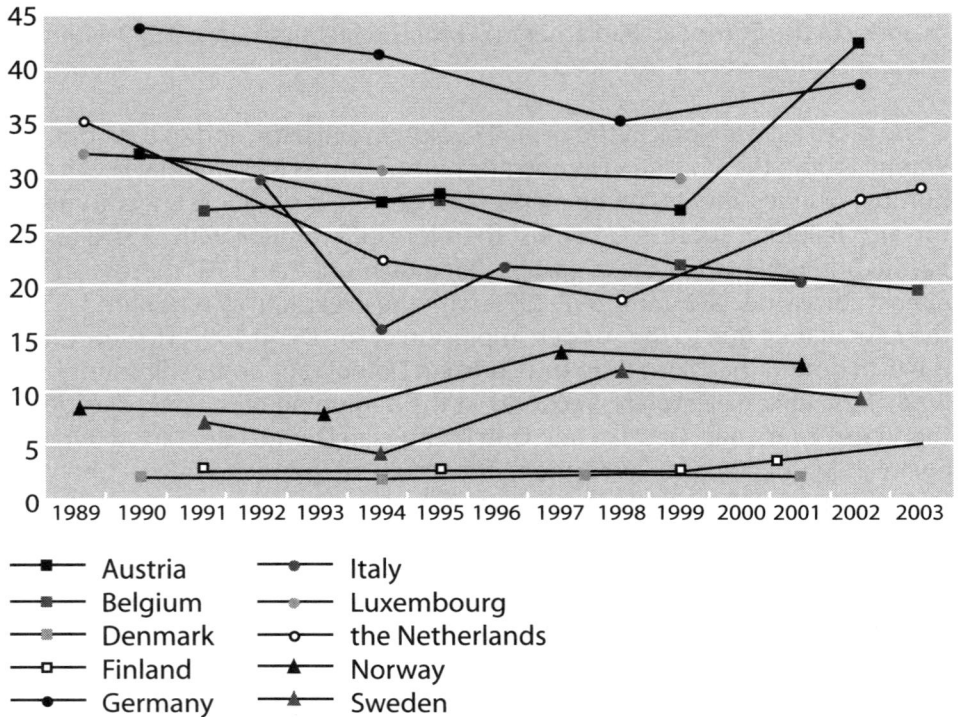

━■━	Austria	━◆━ Italy
━■━	Belgium	━●━ Luxembourg
━▨━	Denmark	━○━ the Netherlands
━□━	Finland	━▲━ Norway
━●━	Germany	━▲━ Sweden

Thirdly, the recent success of some Christian Democratic parties covers both centre (CDA) and centre-right (ÖVP) parties. In this way, the so-called shift to the right from the beginning of the new decade should be questioned.[5] Fourthly, not all parties, especially the Christian Democratic ones, have regained their previous results from the beginning of the 1990s (in terms of relative share of the overall electorate). Finally, with regard to government participation, only two out of four core parties of European Christian Democracy that were sent to opposition have returned to power.[6]

5   The thesis of parties winning elections (not about parties themselves moving to the right) and therefore shifting the political pendulum refers to the series of victories of right parties in Western Europe: the *Partido Popular* (PP) in 2000 gaining absolute majority (outnumbering its previous success in 1996), *Forza Italia* (FI) in 2001, and the Portuguese and French right in 2002.

6   We consider the Belgian Christian Democrats as a single part of the Christian Democratic core. We also leave the CSV aside as it did not lose power in Luxembourg in the 1990s.

Christian Democrats in National Government, 1989-2003

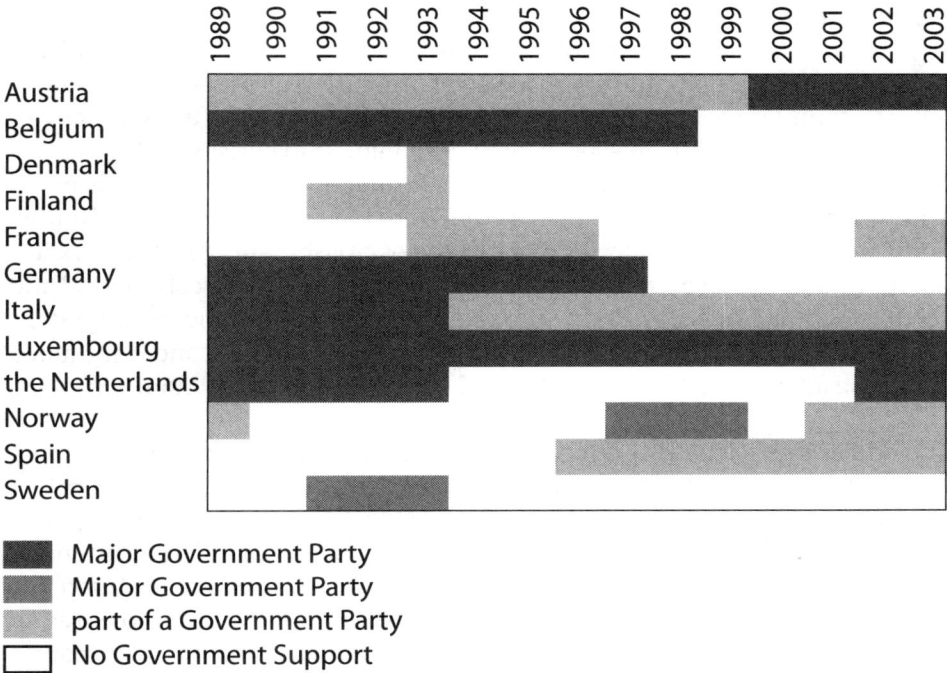

	1989	1990	1991	1992	1993	1994	1995	1996	1997	1998	1999	2000	2001	2002	2003
Austria															
Belgium															
Denmark															
Finland															
France															
Germany															
Italy															
Luxembourg															
the Netherlands															
Norway															
Spain															
Sweden															

- ■ Major Government Party
- ■ Minor Government Party
- ▨ part of a Government Party
- ☐ No Government Support

We will try to explain this particular evolution of the Christian Democratic parties by focussing on (1) the acceleration of the European integration process, (2) the emergence of new parties and issues, (3) a changing pattern of political ideologies and (4) party change(s). It is, however, impossible to totally isolate these various events and evolutions, let alone distinguish dependent from independent factors, because in one way or the other, they are closely linked with the end of the Cold War. Therefore, we will first of all present - in four 'clusters' - those events and evolutions that have been characteristic for European society and politics since the end of the Cold War: the implosion of communist regimes in Central and Eastern Europe, Economic and Monetary Union (EMU), the deepening of the EU and the issue of migration.

The end of the Cold War

The sudden collapse of Communist regimes in Central and Eastern European countries has been of paramount importance for the overall history of Europe. Communism as a way of organising all aspects of society fell into complete discredit. It also affected Socialism as the leftist alternative of Western capitalism. However, instead of running into crisis, Socialism gradually incorporated the principles of its former enemy: (neo)liberalism. This new synthesis became known as the 'Third Way'. The transition of Central and Eastern European countries towards the establishment of social market economy and liberal democracy also challenged the economical, political and security architecture of Western Europe, particularly the European integration process and the transatlantic defence partnership NATO. Rules and institutions had to be adapted to ensure a stable and prosperous reunited Europe.

The end of the Cold War also meant the end of the artificial split between the two Germanys. In exchange for European (particularly French) support for the (re)unification of Germany, the Treaty of Maastricht started, *inter alia*, the process towards EMU that finally led to the introduction of a single currency, called 'euro' (which replaced the *de facto* dominance of the German *Mark*). The so-called Maastricht criteria the EU countries had to meet in order to enter EMU severely limited the latitude for national budgetary and socio-economic policies. This no-nonsense convergence process was imposed on every government (coalition), irrespective of its composition, because in most of the EU countries it was widely accepted that there was no alternative to EMU (and that EMU offered the opportunity to finally reorganise public finances in a structural way). Consequently, differences between political parties' programmes and policies became blurred or non-existent (something out of which the extreme left and extreme right made profit).

Apart form EMU, the Treaty of Maastricht also created new institutions and competences at the European level. On the one hand, this further weakened the decision-making capacity at the national level, a process that is not exclusively caused by but received its major qualitative and quantitative boost from the ongoing European integration process. On the other hand, the position of the EP was strengthened *vis-à-vis* the other EU institutions and *vis-à-vis* the national parties and politicians operating at the European level. Consequently, the importance of transnational parties and party groups as fora of policy-making (lobbying, coordination, decision-making, etc.) increased. As the EP tends to be organised as a bipolar political system, transnational parties' compositions and alliances question the various organisations of party politics at the national level (and *vice versa*).

Migration became a more prominent issue in Western European politics from the late 1980s onwards. The end of the Cold War - particularly the 'implosion' of Cold War regimes in Central and Eastern Europe and Black Africa and wars in Yugoslavia and the Middle East - led to an 'explosion' of asylum seekers and economic immigrants in Western Europe, whether legally or not. This wave of migration was clearly part of a broader process of globalisation (that had also economical and cultural effects). At the same time, tensions with 'old' mainly Muslim immigrants from Northern Africa were rising in many Western European societies (especially in deprived urban areas). Confrontations, although non-violent in most of the cases, between 'old' and 'new' citizens (relatively speaking), generated a debate about the identity of (Western) European society, its values, its so-called *Leitkultur* (dominant culture), etc. It also caused and resulted in a bipolarisation of the political debate (with regard to this issue) in general and the emergence of extreme-right parties in particular

Acceleration in the European integration process

The progress in the European integration process during the 1990s was not without impact on Christian Democratic party politics.[7] Firstly, as abovementioned, EMU did not leave much latitude to pursue a 'Christian Democratic' policy.[8] Programmatic differences with Socialists, Liberals and Conservatives, whether in government or in opposition, became subsidiary to government policies that were mainly directed towards fulfilling the Maastricht criteria.[9] Therefore, protest voters had no choice but to support Green or extreme-right parties.[10] In the Netherlands, the CDA was not able to present itself as an alternative for the 'neoliberal consensus' of the ruling

---

7   We leave the issue of Europeanisation aside as it has already been extensively discussed in the chapter "Christian Democratic Parties and Europeanisation" in this volume.

8   In the Italian case, it is said that EMU took away the money that had facilitated the consociational policies of the DC for so long. See the chapter "From Dominance to Doom? Christian Democracy in Italy" in this volume.

9   See for instance: A. Volkens and H.-D. Klingemann, "Parties, Ideologies and Issues. Stability and Change in Fifteen European Party Systems (1945-1998)", in: K.R. Luther and F. Müller-Rommel (eds.), *Political Parties in the New Europe. Political and Analytical Challenges*, Oxford, 2002, 143-167.

10   In Germany, the Netherlands and Wallonia, the Greens profited from this situation. Austria, France and Flanders saw the rise of extreme-right parties.

Socialists and Liberals as many voters believed that the CDA would pursue the same kind of policies.[11] Moreover, as Christian Democrats took the lead in implementing neoliberal reform, they were blamed for neglecting the social dimension of Christian Democracy. Social and Church organisations criticised the CDU and the ÖVP of *Soziale Kälte* (social coldness). Generally, traditionally close linkages with socio-economic organisations, especially Christian trade unions, came under pressure. In Belgium, the Christian Labour Movement was caught in a dilemma as it could not agree with the social cuttings of the Christian Democratic government but realised that a government without the Christian Democrats would probably take even fewer notice of its demands. By contrast, Scandinavian Christian Democrats tried to broaden their appeal by emphasising their strong welfarism (against government's social cuttings).

Secondly, it has already been mentioned, the growing importance of the EP strengthens the trend towards a bipolar political landscape as a dominant feature of Continental European party politics. For some Christian Democratic parties, particularly the CDU/CSU and the ÖVP, the situation in the EP simply resembles the actual (or desired) political landscape at the national level. Moreover, the CDU/CSU actively support the Europeanisation of the German 'model', i.e. the rapprochement of the EPP towards Liberals and Conservatives from new and old EU member states. For others, particularly the Christian Democrats in the Benelux, France and Italy, this bipolarisation undermines their traditional centrist position.[12] Either they do not feel comfortable anymore in the EPP; either they join Liberals and/or Conservative forces at the national level: the result is no matter which choice they make a loss of power and influence at the national or the European level.

Thirdly, the 1990s saw a qualitative and quantitative increase in European competences. This directly led to the weakening of the decision-making capacity at the national level. In many countries, the erosion of the national level has been reinforced by the growing importance of the regional level.

11   It should be noted that ruling Christian Democratic parties - the CDU, the CSV and the CVP/
      PSC - also profited from this situation, as Socialist or Liberal opposition parties could not
      present any reliable alternative to the government policies. However, once EMU had been
      met, the situation changed dramatically. The job had been done so it was time to change
      government, as occurred in Germany, Belgium and the Netherlands.
12   The so-called "two versions of the Christian Democratic world view, the principled and the
      minimalist" largely coincide with Christian Democratic parties in, respectively, a multipolar
      and a bipolar political system. See: D. Hanley, "Conclusion. The Future of Christian Democ-
      racy in Europe", in: D. Hanley (ed.), *Christian Democracy in Europe. A Comparative Perspective*,
      London, 1994, 213.

Irrespective of the existence of a strong regional level, the evolution contributes to the growing irrelevance of national party political differences. By contrast, European party politics have become more important. Therefore, coordination, common strategies and tactics are needed to push Christian Democratic core issues on the agenda of the EU and to make Christian Democrats' political actions efficient and effective through a well-equipped and well-developed Christian Democratic organisation at the European level. It is mainly in this respect that the change of the EPP during the 1990s has to be understood. However, the EU itself also offers a forum for national government leaders to show their (European) leadership: the European council. In this way, the loss of power of political parties at the national level is compensated by its political leaders' performances. In their respective countries, Kohl, Jean-Luc Dehaene, Ruud Lubbers, Jacques Santer and Jean-Claude Juncker successfully 'nationalised' their European leadership.

Emergence of new parties and issues

The 1990s saw, the emergence of new parties and issues. As migration gradually became a hot issue in Western European society and politics, it placed many Christian Democrats, especially in Austria, Germany and the Netherlands, in a dilemma. Churches and other Christian organisations expected a so-called humane policy towards asylum seekers and immigrants that takes special care of those people living at the margin of society. With regard to the 'old' immigrants, the integration of Muslims in Christian Democratic parties was all but self-evident. It referred to the very identity of Christian Democratic parties: are they open for everyone with a religious inspiration or are they the fierce defenders of Christian values and therefore excluding other religions by definition? The CDA explicitly opened its doors for non-Christian religious politicians but maintained its traditionally strong emphasis on the party's religious origins. The Flemish Christian Democrats took a more moderate stance with regard to Muslims and Christian values. Their francophone colleagues dropped references to Catholicism and made many efforts to establish close relations with the Muslim community. By contrast, the CDU and the ÖVP have been reluctant to attract Muslims in their party organisations.

Rightist and extreme-rightist parties whipped up the Christian Democrats to take a strong stand against immigration and pursue a so-called tough policy. Especially Austria, Flanders, France and Italy saw the breakthrough of extreme-right parties in the course of the 1990s. Although different in terms of origins and organisation, they successfully claimed the monopoly on the immigration issue (and so-called related problems such as the fight against crime). In attacking the political institutions and its establishment (accused of bureaucracy, corruption, elitism, etc.), they became the opponents of the Christian Democrats as one of the traditional *familles politiques* that rule the country. Depending on the particular political situation, Christian Democratic parties have defined their positions towards extreme-right parties in divergent, sometimes conflicting ways.

In Germany, unification prevented a nation-wide breakthrough of the extreme-right. The CDU and the CSU have been in the forefront in demanding legal actions against extreme-right parties and excluding coalition agreements (similar to the ban on the extreme-left former Communists) but taking rightist positions with regard to migration issues. Although in a different political environment (not the fear of but the existence of relatively large extreme-right parties), French and Flemish Christian Democrats also proclaimed a self-ban on sharing power with the extreme-right. By contrast, the ÖVP, being confronted with the existence of a large extreme-right party, has chosen the opposite strategy: tame the extreme-right through government participation and introducing severe migration limitations. Rightist Christian Democrats in Italy also joined governments with a separatist and a (former) extreme-right party. Their Leftist colleagues however took together with Dutch, French, Spanish and Belgian francophone Christian Democrats the lead in condemning the strategy of the ÖVP. This led to fierce discussions inside (and outside) the EPP. The latter finally adopted a double position (that resembled the German concerns to a large degree): explicit political opposition against the extreme-right but understanding (support) for the position (decision) of the ÖVP.

Ethics and bioethics have equally been central issues on the political agenda of the 1990s. Moreover, they go to the heart of Christian Democratic politics. Many issues such as abortion, euthanasia, gay marriage, cloning, stem cell research, etc. confront Christian Democrats with a question that is related to the essence of their political ideology: are Christian Democratic programmes and policies based on a Christian view of mankind? If so, what does that mean? On the one hand, Christian Democrats should display some pragmatism as they do not represent an absolute majority of the people, they take part of coalition governments (with Liberals and Socialists) and many of its voters have become secularised. On the other hand, if they do not defend Christian principles in (bio)ethics, who will? Extreme-right parties? And what about the critics of the Churches and its affiliated organisations (that, to some degree, compose the Christian Democratic core electorate)?

Unification led to a more liberal image of the CDU with regard to moral issues (e.g. abortion). This tendency was reinforced due to the leadership change in 1998-1999. Since 11 September 2001 however, the German Christian Democrats took the lead in the *Leitkultur* debate that stressed the superiority of Western democracy and Christian values in society, a debate that equally referred to the migration issue. In this way, the CDU/CSU criticised the permissive society and the role of the red-green coalition therein in particular. The position the CDA developed is close to that of the Germans: opposition against the libertarianism of the Socialist-Liberal government, e.g. legalisation of euthanasia, and instigation of an overall *normen en waarden* (norms and values) debate. In the same way, the CDA has become very critical towards the concept of the 'multicultural society'. The Belgian, particularly the Flemish Christian Democrats have taken a more moderate position: opposition to legalisation of abortion, drugs, euthanasia and gay marriage (but hesitantly supported in the end) but less emphasis on values, norms and the integration issue.

Clearly, Continental and Scandinavian Christian Democracy differ from each other in this respect. Whereas Continental parties have more or less incorporated the developments towards secularisation in a permissive society, Scandinavian parties are rooted this tendency but as a counter-reaction.[13] Support for Christian values and opposition against ethical libertarianism has been the main *raison d'être* of Scandinavian Christian Democracy. However, as the 1990s saw a kind of backlash (not with regard to secularisation but with regard to the degree of permissiveness in society, privately as well as publicly), Continental and Scandinavian Christian Democracy came closer to each other: the first increasingly criticised the so-called excesses of the permissive society; the latter de-emphasised its originally rigid positions, both to broaden their electoral appeal. Therefore, one can say that while Continental Christian Democracy (re)discovered one of its unique selling propositions, Scandinavian Christian Democracy realised the necessity of attracting voters beyond its core electorate.

13   See for the complex problem of secularisation and its impact on party politics, D. Broughton and H.-M. ten Napel (eds.), *Religion and Mass Electoral Behaviour in Europe*, London/New York, 2000.

Changing pattern of political ideologies

Since the end of the Cold War, Liberal, Socialist and Conservative ideas have successively dominated the public debate and have therefore shaped the intellectual framework in which European Christian Democracy has been discussed. This has evidently had an impact on the ideological positioning of Christian Democratic parties.

Neoliberalism

As Marxism (or 'real socialism' as it was called) was no longer an alternative to the Western way of organising the society economically and politically, liberalism became the dominant paradigm for both the old and the new Europe. Moreover, Fukuyama announced the end of history worldwide.[14] Although Conservative, his ideas support Western democracy and the market economy in a way that suits (the ideology of) Liberalism best.[15] Fukuyama's thesis illustrated the crisis of the left at the turn of the decade, but challenged the Christian Democratic concept of the welfare state as well. For neoliberalism preaches privatisation of public firms and services, small or minimal state (intervention only), austere budget politics, etc. that are diametrically opposed to traditional welfare state recipes such as universal social assurance, state intervention during economic crisis, labour market rules, etc. Together with the EMU burden, this critique of the welfare state has boosted neoliberal ideas, tendencies and wings inside Christian Democratic parties and brought the latter closer to the Conservatives (who are traditionally more liberal than Christian Democrats as far as economic affairs are concerned).

Indeed, CDU/CSU policies became gradually more neoliberal during the 1990s, despite the presence of the more leftist Christian Democrats from the Eastern *Länder* after unification and protests from Churches and social organisations during the Kohl Chancellorship. Some party branches, such as the one of Baden-Württemberg, have traditionally been liberal in economic affairs: its successful (neoliberal) economic policy became a model for the whole CDU. Unlike Austria, Belgium and Luxembourg, there has never been strong or institutionalised links with Christian Democratic labour movements and trade

---

14   F. Fukuyama, "The End of History?", in: *The National Interest*, 16 (1989), 3-18; F. Fukuyama, *The End of History and the Last Man*, New York, 1992.
15   See for instance, A. Vincent, *Modern Political Ideologies*, Oxford, 1992, p. 13: "The 'end of ideology' was an ideological position committed to a form of pragmatic liberalism. There was a clear failure, which permeated the 'end of ideology' perspective, to analyse liberalism as ideology."

unions. It is only after the 1998 defeat that the CDU tempered its neoliberal positions and stressed its social profile in order to regain the centrist voters from the Social Democrats. The position of the ÖVP has been remarkably similar to that of the CDU: its policies became more neoliberal; at the same time the concept of 'eco-social market economy' was introduced in response to growing environmental concerns (but market mechanisms continued to prevail); reproaches of *Soziale Kälte*; and a weak or non-existent liberal party. Since its rapprochement with Conservatives and Liberals, the EPP(-ED) Group became more neoliberal in economic affairs as well.

In the Benelux, France and Scandinavia however, there exist relatively strong Liberal parties. To emphasise the difference with the rightist Liberal party, the CDA has been critical towards neoliberal recipes for economic crises despite its own government policy in the second half on the 1980s. Unlike Belgium, Austria and Luxembourg, the party has no *standen* or a faction that is in favour of neoliberal economic policies. In Belgium and Luxembourg, Liberal parties won the elections in the 1990s. However, policies have only slightly shifted in neoliberal direction, particularly because of the Single Market and EMU. Strong links with Catholic trade unions and social organisations came under pressure but the latter have kept their informal dominance inside the party (for instance with Prime Ministers such as Dehaene in Belgium and Juncker - leading a coalition with the Liberal party - in Luxembourg). The French Christian Democrats have traditionally been more liberal in economic terms (since its left wing merged with the Socialists) but were weakened by attractiveness of Liberal parties and tendencies. By contrast, Scandinavian Christian Democrats strongly opposed neoliberal ideas. With regard to the welfare state, there position was close(r) to that of the Social Democrats.

The Third Way

The triumph of neoliberalism forced Socialism (as a heir of Marxism) onto the defensive in a way that some predicted the end of Social Democracy. However, in the middle of the 1990s a 'radical' alternative was presented: the reconciliation between neoliberalism and Socialism in the so-called Third Way developed by Giddens.[16] Although Giddens was to a certain degree an answer to Fukuyama, both theories were endemic to the *Zeitgeist* of the so-

---

16   A. Giddens, *Beyond Left and Right. The Future of Radical Politics*, Cambridge, 1994; A. Giddens, *The Third Way. The Renewal of Social Democracy*, Cambridge, 1998.

called 'endism'.[17] The 'Third Way' was presented as the final synthesis of left (Socialism) and right (neoliberalism). Similar to neoliberalism, there was no alternative for the Third Way.[18] Its exclusiveness made the Christian Democratic concept of society redundant. Moreover, the writings and ideas of Giddens took over the originally Christian Democratic terms and concepts of 'the middle', 'the centre', 'the third way', etc. As Socialism shifted towards the centre and Socialist parties focused on centrist voters, Christian Democracy was threatened in its original positioning and directed towards rightist Liberalism and Conservatism.[19] In turn, this changing pattern of ideologies strengthened the tendency towards bipolar political systems. This is particularly challenging for those countries in which parties exist right of the Christian Democratic centre.

'The Third Way' has not played a major role in every country and during the same period.[20] As it increasingly became an electoral strategy to attract centrist voters, the idea of a new political ideology was not on the agenda of Socialists parties that led national governments (as was the case in Austria, France and the Netherlands). In Germany, *die Neue Mitte* (the new centre) lost momentum after the Social Democrats came to power in a way that the CDU/CSU was able to present itself as 'people's party' with a truly social alternative (close to the party profile in, for instance, Northrhine-Westfalia and Saarland). The ÖVP also combined the people's party's self definition and strong antisocialism, the latter becoming even stronger as the ÖVP excluded a coalition with the Social Democrats in the 1999 election campaign. In Belgium and the Netherlands, the coalition governments of Socialists and Liberals stood for much of the Third Way idea. However, as centrist parties, the Christian Democrats had difficulties to oppose these governments with regard to economic policy. In Luxembourg, the threat of becoming redundant was already over-

---

17   Derrida uses the concept of 'endism' to refer to and criticise the theses of the end of history, ideology, modernity, subject, politics, etc.: S. Sim, *Derrida and the End of History*, Cambridge/New York, 1999.

18   See for instance: C. Hamilton, "The Third Way and the End of Politics", in: *The Drawing Board. An Australian Review of Public Affairs*, 2 (2001), 89-102.

19   Even in Britain, a country without a Christian Democratic party, this change has been discussed: N. Huntington and T. Bale, "New Labour. New Christian Democracy", in: *Political Quarterly*, 1 (2002), 44-50. Moreover, Prime Minister Tony Blair has been characterised as a (Continental) Christian Democrat. See: P. Stephens, *Tony Blair. The Making of a World Leader*, New York, 2004.

20   See for a critique of the exclusivity of the Third Way as it was 'realised' in British and German politics: S. Bastow, J. Martin and D. Pels, "Introduction. Third Ways in Political Ideology", in: *Journal of Political Ideologies*, 3 (2002), 269-280.

come in the late 1970s. Since then, the CSV has managed to keep its pivotal (third way) position between Socialists and Liberals.

Neoconservatism

Although the 'end of ideology' turned out to be an ideology itself, the idea that ideological distinctions had lost much of their significance continued to prevail long after the end of the Cold War. It is in this way that the revival of Conservatism (neoconservatism) in Western Europe at the turn of the century has to be understood.[21] Conservatism offers an alternative to Socialism and neoliberalism without claiming to be 'ideological' and without undermining (or attacking) the fundamentals of the social market economy. Common sense, law and order, traditional values, civil society, etc. are presented as the answers for the growing problem of insecurity (nationally and internationally) and as an alternative to the permissive society of the previous decades in which only economics mattered.[22] Although these ideas are not overall accepted, they challenge the distinctiveness of Christian Democracy in a particular way. Insofar Conservatism rejects libertarian solutions for ethical-cultural problems and insofar Conservativism rejects leftist (etatist) solutions for current socio-economic problems (retirement, unemployment, state services, etc.), Conservatives pursue the same policy based on the same concept of society as Christian Democrats. With regard to party politics, this conclusion has far-reaching implications for Christian Democratic parties in those countries where there exist direct competition with Conservatives.[23]

Unlike the Benelux and French Christian Democrats, the CDU/CSU and the ÖVP have never had a major problem to call themselves 'Conservative'. In Hessian and Schleswig-Holstein, for instance, the CDU has traditionally

---

21   Insofar neoconservatism stands for a neoliberal organisation of the economy, it comes close to the so-called New Right (that already exists since the 1970s). However, as this volume focuses on European politics, we leave the developments in the United States of America aside. The 'bible' of the recent conservative revival in Europe is R. Scruton, *The Meaning of Conservatism*, Basingstoke, 2001. Whereas its first edition of 1980 strongly attacks Marxism, the 2001 edition criticises the dominant position of neoliberalism in political ideology. See also J. Gray, *Enlightment's Wake. Politics and Culture at the Close of the Modern Age*, London, 1995, 87.

22   It is in this respect that the recent interest of Christian Democrats for 'communitarianism' and 'social capital(ism)' (which are based on traditional principles of Christian Democracy) has to be understood.

23   Some authors consider Christian Democratic parties to be moderate Conservative parties or the left-wing branch of traditionalism: E. Lamberts, "General Conclusions", in: E. Lamberts (ed.), *Christian Democracy in the European Union (1945-1995)*, Leuven, 1997, 473-474.

been Conservative, not to speak of the Bavarian CSU. The CDU campaigned against former Communists as a means of attracting Conservative voters. As to the CDU/CSU, it has been their strategy to be and to stay the single party of the right. As to the ÖVP, being the single party on the right of the political spectrum has become a major goal. This had not prevented the Austrian and German parties to strongly oppose the extreme-right (be it for the ÖVP through government participation). Austrian Chancellor Wolfgang Schüssel himself has a liberal-conservative profile, keeps close links to the Business League and presents his party as non-extremist that stands 'beyond left and right' (to paraphrase the title of one of Giddens' books). Positively, the ÖVP has borrowed ideas form communitarianism and launched the concept of *Bürgergesellschaft* (civil society, but in its meaning diametrically opposed to the Flemish Liberal translation of *Burgermaatschappij*).

In Italy Christian Democrats split along the left-right axis with the Conservative Christian Democrats being the minor heir of the DC (that was predominantly centre-left). The CDA flirted with Conservatism in its debate on ideology as well as strategy. Given the absence of a strong rightist party, social (not neoliberal) Conservatism strengthened the ideology of the party although the term has not been officially used. In Flanders, the same debate occurs outside the party: many political observers (and opponents) wanted the CVP to become a Conservative party to establish an effective alternative for the extreme-right. Communitarianism also found its way in Dutch and Flemish Christian Democracy. Overall, Christian Democratic parties (as 'people's parties') stood for 'social integration' and increasingly criticised societal individualism (liberalism) and welfare etatism (socialism). Luxembourg Christian Democrats for their part found opposition from a new Conservative party despite the existence of a Liberal-Conservative, business-minded wing within the party (of which Santer was one of the protagonists). Scandinavian Christian Democrats equally opposed their much bigger Conservative opponents. French Christian Democrats had to compete with both the traditional right and the extreme-right (and, to a certain degree, the left). Spanish Christian Democrats failed to establish a single party and became part of the Conservative *Partido Popular* (PP). Paradoxically, the PP has been presented to Christian Democrats as a successful example. At the European level, the EPP changed from nature (and size) by successive enlargement operations with Conservative (and Liberal) parties from old and new member states of the EU.

Party change(s)

Apart from the emergence of new parties and issues, the 1990s have also been characterised by an acceleration of the speed and direction of party change.[24] Political parties have gradually and fundamentally changed with respect to organisation, communication, ideology, and their relationship *vis-à-vis* the state, the mass media, civil society, the electorate, etc. In many European countries, this process has been concomitant with - winning back the public/electorate in light of - the assumed crisis in party politics or the growing gap between politics and the public. Party change has in its various aspects been both cause and effect of this 'crisis'.[25] Naturally, Christian Democratic parties have been subject of this change respectively crisis, whether actively or passively.

The electoral decline in the 1990s have particularly been characterised by the structural decrease of the Christian Democrat core electorate (churchgoing, rural, old-aged). This decrease has been so dramatic (especially with regard to secularisation but also due to the changing nature of the society itself) that it has led to the abovementioned thesis of the end of Christian Democracy. However, without denying this irreversible trend, some parties have managed to recruit voters far beyond the core electorate. In everything but comparable circumstances, in the case of the CDU, the ÖVP, the CDA and the CSV, young secularised urban professionals, quite the opposite of the core electorate, have been voting Christian Democratic, next to other kinds of voters.[26] This may in part be due to a generational effect. Voters that went the fist time to the polls in the 1970s and 1980s seem to have been 'lost' whereas Christian Democratic parties (at least some of them) have been able to breach the electoral 'limits' in the late 1990s by attracting youngsters (that are not aware of

24   Luther and Müller-Rommel identify five main dimensions of recent change within and between Western European polities that have affected political parties: socio-economic change (towards a post-industrial and post-modernised society), alterations to the political values and behaviour of individual citizens and in due course also to national political cultures, a radical transformation in the structure of political communication, a significant change in respect of the political issues and policy agendas shaping political discourse, reform of fundamental aspects of constitutional systems and European integration: K.R. Luther & F. Müller-Rommel, "Political Parties in a Changing Europe", in: K.R. Luther and F. Müller-Rommel (eds.), *Political Parties in the New Europe*, 2002, 7-10.

25   Although related, this 'crisis' is less far-reaching than the 'decline of parties' thesis and the 'party failure' cases. See: K. Lawson and P.H. Merkl (eds.), *When Parties Fail. Emerging Alternative Organisations*, Princeton, 1988, R.S. Katz and P. Mair (eds.), *How Parties Organise. Change and Adaptation in Party Organisations in Western Democracies*, London, 1994, 375.

26   In its attempt to become a real 'people's party', the PP managed to enlarge its electorate in a similar way.

the 'past' and/or the confessional roots of these parties) for which the Christian Democrats are nothing more but nothing less than a reliable alternative with which they can politically identify themselves.

Leadership has been one of the means to attract 'old' and 'new' voters. Whether perceived or not, it is said to play a major role in the election campaigns, irrespective of the fact that the leaders are Christian Democratic, Socialist, Liberal, etc. Leadership as an issue to convince voters has often been combined with the party's record with regard to government stability, credibility, seriousness, effective and efficient public policy, etc.[27] This was clearly the favourite campaign strategy of the CDU and CSU, especially in the series of *Länder* election after its 1998 defeat. It was also used by the ÖVP, this time against the failing coalition partner. The CDA also successfully used its public policy record and its new leadership amidst the chaos after a political murder whereas the Belgian Christian Democrats could not valorise its public policy record during their 2003 election campaign.

As mentioned above, many Christian Democratic parties made profit of the Europeanisation of their party leaders, provided that they were leading the national government. In the same way, the mass media, especially television, contribute to the so-called presidentialism of party and government politics by increasingly focussing on party and government leaders' private and public life. In turn, the parties' electoral campaigns are organised in line with the mass media formats. In Belgium, the CVP (with prime ministers Leo Tindemans, Wilfried Martens and Dehaene) has been a forerunner in this respect. The CDU witnessed the advantages as well as the disadvantages (in terms of party organisation) of the Kohl Chancellorship. The CDA and ÖVP initially lacked the so-called prime minister bonus but once they were leading the government they did not leave much to make a profit. Furthermore, mass media offer an alternative for direct communication with the electorate as the impact of traditional communication channels (for Christian Democrats as well as for other traditional parties) have dramatically decreased.

At the same time, but also as an answer to the crisis of traditional channels (of communication, recruitment, voting behaviour, etc.), Christian Democratic parties have developed new initiatives and strategies to bridge the credibility gap in general and to (directly) involve its members in the party's organisa-

---

27   Obviously, policy performance is neither an exclusively Christian Democratic means of attracting voters. See: K.R. Luther & F. Müller-Rommel, "Parties and Party Research in the New Europe", in: K.R. Luther and F. Müller-Rommel (eds.), *Political Parties in the New Europe*, 337-338.

tion in particular. In the case of the ÖVP, this led to increased intra-party fight. As a result, experiments were not prolonged. The Benelux Christian Democrats introduced, among other things, the direct election of the party president. Paradoxically, this undermined the internal cohesion of the party in case the president could not count on the overall support of the senior officials. The problem of leading but not controlling the party caused serious damage in the case of the francophone PSC. By contrast, the CDU and the CSU did not take new initiatives. They rebuilt respectively relied on their decentralised (*Länder*) party organisation to overcome its 1998 electoral defeat and, for the CDU, financial scandal of 1999-2000.

Finally, we pay special attention to the role of political affiliations, civil society and churches because they constitute one of the particularities of Christian Democratic parties. As abovementioned, the crisis of these traditional channels of communication, recruitment and voting behaviour has had an impact on the Christian Democratic parties' performances.

Christian Democratic parties traditionally have different affiliations or side-organisations for youth (students), women, pensioners, employees, employers, farmers and/or local deputies.[28] In Austria, Belgium, Italy and Luxembourg the employees', employers' and farmers' organisations (or leagues) are called '*standen*' because they have great influence on the party's programme, policies and personnel.[29] However, during the 1990s their power basis has weakened because of neoliberal critique on corporatism (particularly trade unionism), the growing independence of (professional) party organisations (cartelisation) and the establishment of direct linkages between the party members and the party's central office. Sometimes, these affiliated organisations distanced themselves from the Christian Democratic parties once they were in opposition. This was clearly the case in the Netherlands and, to a lesser degree, in Belgium as political parties became increasingly isolated from society.

---

28   The CDU and the CSU have also organisations for Germans that live abroad (refugees), the CDU hosts an organisation for pupils, and the CDA is the only party with a permanent multi-cultural platform.

29   In Germany, there exist no real *standen* but relations with socio-economic organisations can differ between political parties and between *Länder*. For instance, the CSU is said to be more corporatist than the CDU.

The influence of youth, women and pensioners organisations and their interest aggregation has not increased either but they have provided the party a basis for recruitment, established contacts with civil society and contributed to the party's profile (image) in terms of youthfulness and gender equality. The multifunctionality of these organisations whose existence is said to be crucial for 'people's parties' has led to their further development in the PP and the EPP.[30] In this way, one can argue that the PP has become more 'Christian Democratic'. However, this evolution should not be overestimated given the increasing importance of networking between political parties and non-political (social, economical, environmental, religious, etc.) actors.

During the 1990s, the distance between Christian Democracy and the Churches increased (a process that begun with the establishment of Christian Democratic non-confessional parties after the Second World War).[31] It has already been mentioned, Churches (or affiliated organisations) strongly criticised neoliberal economic and social policies of CDU and ÖVP (and with regard to the latter also its migration policy and its concept of *Burgergesell-schaft*). The 1994 basic programme of the CDU still referred to God and Christianity but publicly the party avoided to be associated with Christianity, particularly since the party stood for election in the highly secularised Eastern *Länder*.[32] The Austrian Catholic church distanced itself from the ÖVP by organising a dialogue with all political parties. The ÖVP from its part accused the extreme-right of Christian fundamentalism, emphasising its attachment to the Liberal constitutional state and its openness towards non-Catholic voters.

In Bavaria and Italy Catholicism is still dominant and uncontested which makes explicit religiousness in politics less problematic. In the Italian case, the Vatican supported the idea of a single Christian Democratic party after the collapse of the DC. With the diaspora of Christian Democrats in various parties and alliances, the Vatican lost much of its influence in Italian politics and policies. As for the successors of the DC, the establishment of privileged relations with the Catholic Church and its affiliated organisation is an intra-competition

30   The development of the EPP associations is obviously a result of the growing importance of political parties at the European level. See the chapter "A Decade of Seized Opportunities. Christian Democracy in the European Union" in this volume; T. Jansen, *The European People's Party. Origins and Development*, Basingstoke, 1998, 138-146.

31   In Bavaria, Belgium, France, Italy, Luxembourg and Spain, Christian Democracy is solely Catholic, in Scandinavia it is solely Protestant, whereas the CDU and the CDA gather both Catholics and Protestants.

32   Unlike any other Christian Democratic party, CDU/CSU have a permanent forum for dialogue with the Evangelical Church, called *Evangelische Arbeitskreis*.

criterion to prove their respective 'Christian Democratic' identity. In Belgium, the distance with the hierarchy of the Catholic Church gradually grew (almost leading to mutual indifference). There are no longer advantages of an exclusive relationship since the once dominant positions of the Catholic Church and the Christian Democrats in Flemish society and politics have disappeared. In Wallonia, the Catholic Church and Christian Democracy historically hold a minority position. It is therefore no surprise that the francophone Christian Democrats dropped references to Catholicism in order to attract (more) non-Catholic voters.

To a certain degree, religiousness did not disappear from politics but changed from institutionalised and exclusive relations with Christian Democratic parties into individual engagements in all parties (e.g. priests and imams being elected in parliament). However, this does not prevent the Flemish and francophone Christian Democrats to strongly defend Christian values and institutions (schools, hospitals, etc.). The CDA also combined openness towards other religions and defence of Christian values in society but maintained its traditional strong emphasis on the party's religious origins, as it has to compete with two small Protestant parties. While Belgian and Dutch Christian Democratic parties opened their doors for non-Christian religious politicians, the churches did not develop into 'NGOs' that regularly criticise government policies (as it has been the case in Austria and Germany).

Whither European Christian Democracy?

The analysis of the impact of the end of the Cold War on Christian Democratic parties in Europe has produced a complex pattern of particularities and universalities. Various developments point to different directions, not to speak of the many dilemmas and contradictions (for instance, the end of Communism that led to electoral success for the CDU and the implosion of the DC, to name just one example). To conclude, we select three findings that at the same time constitute fundamental challenges for future Christian Democracy in what is said to be a post-industrial, post-ideological and post-Christian Europe.

The parties of the core countries of European Christian Democracy have faced electoral decline in a period that was characterised by the re-establisment of Social Democracy, the realisation of EMU and a growing tendency towards private and public libertarianism. 'The end of the end of the Cold

War' seems to have turned the tide. In the aftermath of 11 September 2001 Christian Democratic parties have benefitted from a kind of renaissance of old ideological antagonisms and party rivalries between left and right, widespread criticism towards the permissive society and their government record of reorganising the public sector (this time to be applied to the problem of ageing population).

Secularisation and in some cases depillarisation have continuously undermined the core electorate of Christian Democratic parties. With the dissolution of the confessional issue that dominated politics from the fall of the Bastille until the fall of the Berlin Wall, Christian Democracy has lost one of its unique selling propositions. Moreover, other, predominantly non-Christian confessions force Christian Democratic parties to rethink the role of its origins in contemporary programmes and policies. As Christian values have become less 'confessional' and more 'societal' and as Muslims share common ground with Christians in many respects, some parties have proved that it is not impossible to broaden the electoral basis without losing its distinct religous position and profile.

Christian Democratic parties have not only 'suffered' the particular circumstances that have constituted the period since the end of the Cold War. Many of them have to a large extent contributed to the government policies at the national and the European level. In turn, this governmental record, especially in socio-economic affairs, has been used (by the parties as well by the voters) to distinguish themselves from other political parties. Although fairly pragmatically and contrary to other (sometimes one-issue) parties, it seems to support the continued existence of European Christian Democracy as a political distinct phenomenon. In other words, bearing government responsibilities (office) has not only been a disadvantage in electoral terms (votes). As the introductory citation of Strikwerda suggests, Christian Democrats have not only been shaped by but also have shaped the Europe of the 1990s.

Bibliography

Adler, E. "Seizing the Middle Ground. Constructivism in World Politics". *European Journal of International Relations*, 3 (1997) 319-363.

Alberti, P. *Il coraggio della moderazione. Dalla Dc al Ppi di Mino Martinazzoli*. Brescia: La Quadra, 2000.

Andersen, P.C. *Kristen Politik. Kristeligt Folkeparti 13 April 1970-21 September 1971*. Odense: Odense Universitetsforlag, 1975.

Andeweg, R. "Afscheid van de verzuiling" in J.J.M. van Holsteyn and B. Niemöller, eds. *De Nederlandse kiezer 1994*. Leiden: DSWO Press, 1995, 111-125.

Anker, H, "Kiezers, politici en partijkeuze" in: J.J.M. van Holsteyn and B. Niemöller, eds. *De Nederlandse kiezer 1994*. Leiden: DSWO Press, 1995, 205-222.

Ansell, C.K. and Fish, S.M. "The Art of Being Indispensable. Noncharismatic Personalism in Contemporary Political Parties". *Comparative Political Studies*, 3 (1999) 283-312.

Arter, D. "The Finnish Christian League. Party or Anti-Party?". *Scandinavian Political Studies*, 2 (1980) 143-162.

Arter, D. "Die bürgerlichen und konservativen Parteien Finnlands. Zentrumspartei, Nationale Sammlungspartei, Schwedische Volkspartei und Finnischer Christliche Bund" in H.-J. Veen, ed. *Christlich-demokratische und konservative Parteien in Westeuropa. 4: Schweden, Norwegen, Finnland, Dänemark*. Paderborn: Schöningh, 1994, 229-326.

Arter, D. *Scandinavian Politics Today*. Manchester: Manchester University Press, 2002.

Bar, A. "The Emerging Spanish Party System. Is There a Model? "*West European Politics*, 4 (1984) 128-155.

Bardi, L. "Parties and Party Systems in the European Union. National and Supranational Dimensions" in: K.R. Luther and F. Müller-Rommel, eds. *Political Parties in the New Europe. Political and Analytical Challenges*. Oxford: Oxford University Press, 2002, 293-321.

Bardi, L. and L. Morlino, "Italy. Tracing the Roots of the Great Transformation" in R.S. Katz and P. Mair, eds. *How Parties Organize. Change and Adaptation in Party Organisations in Western Democracies*. London: Sage Publications, 1994, 242-277.

Barreiro, B. "Judicial Review and Political Empowerment: Abortion in Spain" in: P. Heywood, ed. *Politics and Policy in Democratic Spain: No Longer Different?* London: Cass, 1999, 147-162.

Becker, W. "The Emergence and Development of Christian Democratic Parties in Western Europe" in E. Lamberts, ed. *Christian Democracy in the European Union (1945-1995)*. KADOC-Studies 21. Leuven: University Press Leuven, 1997, 109-120.

Boogards, M. "The Favourable Factors for Consociational Democracy. A Review". *European Journal of Political Research*, 4 (1998) 475-496.

Boogards, M. "The Uneasy Relationship between Empirical and Normative Types in Consociational Theory". *Journal of Theoretical Politics*, 4 (2000) 395-423.

Bornewasser, J.A. *Katholieke Volkspartij 1945-1980. II Heroriëntatie en integratie (1963-1980)*. Nijmegen: Valkhof, 2000.

Bösch, F. *Die Adenauer-CDU. Gründung, Aufbau und Krise einer Erfolgspartei (1945-1969)*. Stuttgart/München: Deutsche Verlags-Anstalt, 2001.

Bösch, F. *Das konservative Milieu. Vereinskultur und lokale Sammlungspolitik (1900-1960)*. Göttingen: Wallstein Verlag, 2002.

Bösch, F. *Macht und Machtverlust. Die Geschichte der CDU*, Stuttgart/München: Deutsche Verlags-Anstalt, 2002.

Bové, A. *Le catholicisme politique au Luxembourg entre 1914 et 1940. Le parti de la droite*. Nancy: Université de Nancy II, 1984.

Brezzi, C. *I partiti democratici cristiani d'Europa*. Milano: Teti, 1979.

Broughton, D. "The CDU-CSU in Germany. Is There Any Alternative?" in: D. Hanley, ed. *Christian Democracy in Europe. A Comparative Perspective*. London: Pinter, 1994, 101-118.

Broughton, D. and ten Napel, H.-M., eds. *Religion and Mass Electoral Behaviour in Europe*. London/New York: Routlegde, 2000.

Buchanan, T. and Conway, M., eds. *Political Catholicism in Europe (1918-1965)*. Oxford: Clarendon Press, 1996.

Bufacchi, V. and Burgess, S. *Italy Since 1989. Events and Interpretations*. Basingstoke: Palgrave, 2001.

Buse, M. *La nueva democracia española. Sistema de partidos y orientación del voto (1976-1983)*. Madrid: Union Editorial, 1984.

Caillaud, B. and Tirole, J. "Parties as Political Intermediaries". *The Quarterly Journal of Economics*, 4 (2002) 1453-1491.

Cary, N.D. *The Path to Christian Democracy. German Catholics and the Party System from Windthorst to Adenauer*. Cambridge: Harvard University Press, 1996.

Chadel, F. *Penser le changement dans les partis politiques. Le processus d'institutionnalisation au Partido Popular*. Barcelona: Institut de Ciències Polítiques i Socials, 2001.

Checkel, J.T. "Social Construction and Integration". *ARENA Working Paper*, University of Oslo, 14 (1998).

Chhibber, P. and Torcal, M. "Elite Strategy, Social Cleavages and Party Systems in a New Democracy. Spain". *Comparative Political Studies*, 1 (1997) 27-54.

Chryssochoou, D.N. *Theorising European Integration*. London: Sage, 2001.

Clemens, C. and Patterson, W.E., eds. *The Kohl Chancellorship*. Special Issue of *German Politics*, 1 (1998).

Conway, M. "Introduction" in: T. Buchanan and M. Conway, eds. *Political Catholicism in Europe (1918-1965)*. Oxford: Clarendon Press, 1996, 1-33.

Conway, M. "The Age of Christian Democracy. The Frontiers of Success and Failure" in: T. Kselman and J.A. Buttigieg, eds. *European Christian Democracy. Historical Legacies and Comparative Perspectives*. Notre Dame: University of Notre Dame Press, 2003, 43-67.

Cotarelo, R. "El sistema de partidos" in: J.F. Tezanos, R. Cotarelo and A. de Blas, eds. *La transición democrática española*. Madrid: Editorial Sistema, 1989, 347-388.

Cotta, M. *On the Relationship between Party and Government*. Siena: Centro di Ricerca sul cambiamento politico, 1999.

Bibliography

CRISP, *Grand-duché de Luxembourg. Systèmes et comportements électoraux. Analyse et synthèse des scrutins de 1974, 1979 et 1984.* 2 Vol. Brussels: CRISP éditions, 1995.

De Rosa, G. *La transizione infinita. Diario politico 1990-1996.* Bari: Laterza, 1997.

De Vries, J. and Wiggers, J.W. "Je kunt een plantje niet aan zijn blaadjes de grond uittrekken. Een blik op de CDA-campagne" in: P. Kramer, T. van der Maas and L. Ornstein, eds. *Stemmen in stromenland. De verkiezingen van 1998 nader bekeken* Den Haag: Sdu, 1998, 29-37.

Decker, F. *Parteien unter Druck. Der neue Rechtspopulismus in den westlichen Demokratien.* Opladen: Leske und Bundrig Verlag, 2000.

Delsol, C. *Le souci contemporain.* Brussels: Editions Complexe, 1996.

Denon-Birot, M.-N. *De la Démocratie Chrétienne à Force Démocrate.* Paris: L'Harmattan, 2000.

Deschouwer, K. "De smeltende ijsschots. Religie, kerkpraktijk en stemgedrag", in: M. Swyngedouw and J. Billiet, *De kiezer heeft zijn redenen. 13 juni 1999 en de politieke opvattingen van Vlamingen,* Leuven: Acco, 2002, 27-38.

Dewachter, W., Gerard, E., Lamberts, E. et al. *Tussen staat en maatschappij (1945-1995). Christen-Democratie in België,* Tielt: Lannoo, 1995.

Dewachter, W., Gerard, E., Lamberts, E. et al. *Un parti dans l'histoire (1945-1995). 50 ans d'action au Parti Social Chrétien,* Louvain-la-Neuve: Duculot, 1996.

Dierickx, G. "Christian Democracy and Its Ideological Rivals" in: D. Hanley, ed. *Christian Democracy in Europe. A Comparative Perspective.* London: Pinter, 1994, 15-30.

Donovan, M. "Democrazia Cristiana. Party of Government" in D. Hanley, ed. *Christian Democracy in Europe. A Comparative Perspective.* London: Pinter, 1994, 71-86.

Donovan, M. "Italy. A Dramatic Case of Secularisation?" in D. Broughton and H.-M. ten Napel, eds. *Religion and Mass Electoral Behaviour in Europe.* London: Routledge, 2000, 140-156.

Dreyfus, F.-G. *Histoire de la démocratie chrétienne en France.* Paris: Albin Michel, 1988.

Durand, J.D. *L'Europe de la Démocratie Chrétienne?* Brussels: Editions Complexe, 1995.

Durand, J.-D. "La Mémoire de la Démocratie chrétienne en 1945. Antécédents, expérience et combats" in E. Lamberts, ed. *Christian Democracy in the European Union (1945-1995).* KADOC-Studies 21. Leuven: University Press Leuven, 1997, 13-26.

Einaudi, M. and Goguel, F. *Christian Democracy in Italy and France.* Notre Dame: University of Notre Dame Press, 1952.

Elchardus, M., Chaumont, J.M. and Lauwers, S. "Morele onzekerheid en nieuwe degelijkheid" in: K. Dobbelaere, M. Elchardus, J. Kerkhofs, L. Voyé and B. Bawin-Legros, eds. *Verloren zekerheid. De Belgen en hun waarden, overtuigingen en houdingen.* Tielt: Lannoo, 2000, 153-192.

Eysell, M. "Die Konservative Volkspartei, die Christliche Volkspartei und die Zentrum-Demokraten Dänemarks. Drei Wettbewerber in bürgerlichen Lager" in: H.-J. Veen, ed. *Christlich-demokratische und konservative Parteien in Westeuropa. 4: Schweden, Norwegen, Finnland, Dänemark.* Paderborn: Schöningh, 1994, 327-528.

Fallend, F. "Austria". *European Journal of Political Research* (Political Data Yearbook 1997), 3-4 (1997) 311-323.

Fallend, F. "Austria". *European Journal of Political Research* (Political Data Yearbook 1998), 3-4 (1998) 347-356.

Fallend, F. "Austria". *European Journal of Political Research* (Political Data Yearbook 1999), 3-4 (1999) 327-337.

Fallend, F. "Austria". *European Journal of Political Research* (Political Data Yearbook 2000), 3-4 (2000) 323-337.

Fallend, F. "Austria". *European Journal of Political Research* (Political Data Yearbook 2001), 3-4 (2001) 238-253.

Fedele, M. *Democrazia referendaria.* Roma: Donzelli, 1994.

Fehlen, F., Piroth, I. and Poirier, P. *Les Elections au Grand-duché du Luxembourg. Rapport sur les élections législatives du 13 juin 1999.* Luxembourg: Centre universitaire de Luxembourg, 2000.

Fogarty, M.P. *Christian Democracy in Western Europe (1820-1953).* London: Routledge/Paul Kegan, 1957.

Follini, M. *C'era una volta la DC.* Bologna: Il Mulino, 1994.

Freeden, M. *Ideologies and Political Theory.* Oxford: Clarendon Press, 1998.

Fukuyama, F. *The End of History and the Last Man.* New York: Free Press, 1992.

Gaffney, J., ed. *Political Parties and the European Union.* London: Routledge, 1996.

Gangas Peiró, P. *Desarrollo organizativo de los partidos políticos españoles de implantación nacional.* Madrid: Centro de Estudios Avanzados en Ciencias Sociales, 1994.

García-Guereta, E.M. *La centralización de Alianza Popular.* Madrid: Centro de Estudios Avanzados en Ciencias Sociales, 1993.

García-Guereta, E.M. *La postura del PP ante los pactos autonómicos.* Madrid: Centro de Estudios Avanzados en Ciencias Sociales, Madrid, 1993.

García-Guereta, E.M. *Factores externos e internos en la transformación de los partidos políticos: el caso de AP-PP.* Madrid: Centro de Estudios Avanzados en Ciencias Sociales, 2001.

Gehler, M., Kaiser W. and Wohnout, H., eds. *Christdemokratie in Europa im 20. Jahrhundert/ Christian Democracy in 20th Century Europe/La démocratie chrétienne en Europe au XXe siècle,* Vienna: Bohlau, 2001.

Gerard, E. "Christen-democratie in België tussen 1891 en 1945. De 'archeologie' van de Christelijke Volkspartij". *Trajecta,* 2 (1993) 154-175.

Gerard, E. "El catolicismo social en Bélgica" in: A.M. Pazos, ed. *Un siglo de catolicismo social en Europa (1891-1991).* Pamplona: Universidad de Navarra, 1993, 155-194.

Giddens, A. *Beyond Left and Right. The Future of Radical Politics.* Cambridge: Polity Press, 1994.

Giddens, A. *The Third Way. The Renewal of Social Democracy.* Cambridge: Polity Press, 1998.

Giovagnoli, A. *La cultura democristiana tra Chiesa cattolica e identità italiana (1918-1948).* Roma: Laterza, 1991.

Giovagnoli, A. *Il Partito Italiano. La Democrazia Cristiana dal 1942 al 1994.* Bari: Laterza, 1996.

Bibliography

Goldstein, J. and Keohane, R.O. "Ideas and Foreign Policy. An Analytical Framework" in: J. Goldstein and R.O. Keohane, eds. *Ideas and Foreign Policy. Beliefs, Institutions and Political Change*. New York: Cornell University Press, 1993, 3-30.

Grabow, K. *Abschied von der Massenpartei. Die Entwicklung der Organisationsstruktur von SPD und CDU seit der deutschen Wiedervereinigung*. Wiesbaden: Deutscher Universitäts-Verlag, 2000.

Gray, J. *Enlightment's Wake. Politics and Culture at the Close of the Modern Age*. London: Routledge, 1995.

Gstoehl, S. *Reluctant Europeans. Norway, Sweden and Switzerland in the Process of Integration*. London: Boulder, 2002.

Gunther, R. "Electoral Laws, Party Systems and Elites. The case of Spain". *American Political Science Review*, 3 (1989) 835-858.

Gunther, R., Diamandouros P.N. and Puhle, H.J., eds. *The Politics of Democratic Consolidation. Southern Europe in Comparative Perspective*. Baltimore: Johns Hopkins University Press, 1995.

Gunther, R. and Montero, J.R. "The Anchors of Partisanship. A Comparative Analysis of Voting Behavior in Four Southern European Democracies" in: P.N. Diamandouros and R. Gunther, eds. *Parties, Politics and Democracy in the New Southern Europe*. Baltimore: Johns Hopkins University Press, 2001, 83-152.

Gunther, R., Sani, G. and Shabad, G. *Spain after Franco. The Making of a Competitive Party System*. Berkeley: University of California Press, 1988.

Gustafsson, G. "Religious Change in the Five Scandinavian Countries (1930-1980)" in: T. Petterson and O. Riis ,eds. *Scandinavian Values. Religion and Morality in the Nordic Countries*. Uppsala: Acta Universitatis, 1994, 11-57.

Gustafsson, G. "Church-State Separation Swedish-Style" in: J.T.S. Madeley and Z. Enyedi, eds. *Church and State in Contemporary Europe. The Chimera of Neutrality*. London: Cass, 2003, 51-72.

Guzzini, S. "A Reconstruction of Constructivism in International Relations". *European Journal of International Relations*, 2 (2000), 147-182.

Hanley, D., ed. *Christian Democracy in Europe. A Comparative Perspective*. London: Pinter, 1994.

Hanley, D. "Introduction. Christian Democracy as a Political Phenomenon" in: D. Hanley, ed. *Christian Democracy in Europe. A Comparative Perspective*. London: Pinter, 1994, 1-11.

Hanley, D. "The European People's Party. Towards a New Party Form?" in: D. Hanley, ed. *Christian Democracy in Europe. A Comparative Perspective*. London: Pinter, 1994, 185-201.

Hanley, D. "Conclusion. The Future of Christian Democracy in Europe" in: D. Hanley, ed. *Christian Democracy in Europe. A Comparative Perspective*. London: Pinter, 1994, 212-214.

Hanley, D. "Christian Democracy and the Paradoxes of Europeanisation. Flexibility, Competition and Collusion" in: R. Ladrech, ed. *The Europeanisation of Party Politics*. Special Issue of *Party Politics*, 4 (2002) 463-481.

Heiderscheid, A. "L'Eglise dans la société moderne sécularisée". *Nos cahiers. Lëtzebuerger Zäitschrëft fir Kultur*, 1 (1991) 187-211.

Heinisch, R. "Success in Opposition - Failure in Government. Explaining the Performance of Right-Wing Populist Parties in Public Office". *West European Politics*, 3 (2003) 91-130.

Henningsen, B. "Die Konservativen parteien Schwedens. Die Gemässigte Sammlungspartei und die Christdemokratische Gesellschaftspartei" in: H.-J. Veen, ed. *Christlichdemokratische und konservative Parteien in Westeuropa. 4: Schweden, Norwegen, Finnland, Dänemark.* Paderborn: Schöningh, 1994, 23-130.

Heywood, P. "Spain". *Electoral Studies*, 3 (1998) 322-330.

Hillebrand, R. *De antichambre van het parlement. Kandidaatstelling in Nederlandse politieke partijen.* Leiden, DSWO Press, 1992.

Hix, S. and Lord, C. *Political Parties in the European Union.* Basingstoke: Macmillan, 1997.

Hix, S. and Goetz, K.H. "Introduction. European Integration and National Political Systems" in: S. Hix and K.H. Goetz, eds. *Europeanised Politics? European Integration and National Political Systems?* Special Issue of *West European Politics*, 4 (2000) 1-26.

Hobsbawm, E. *Age of Extremes. The Short Twentieth Century (1914-1991).* London: Vintage, 1994.

Höcker, B., ed. *Handbuch politischer Partizipation von Frauen in Europa.* Opladen: Leske und Budrich, 1998.

Hopkin, J. "Spain. Political Parties in a Young Democracy" in: D. Broughton and M. Donovan, eds., *Changing Party Systems in Western Europe.* London: Pinter, 1999, 207-231.

Horn, G.-R. and Gerard, E., eds. *Left Catholicism. Catholics and Society in Western Europe at the Point of Liberation (1943-1955).* KADOC-Studies 25. Leuven: Leuven University Press, 2001.

Horner, F. and Zulehner, P.M. „Kirchen und Politik" in: H. Dachs et al., eds. *Handbuch des politischen Systems Österreichs. Die Zweite Republik,* Vienna: Manz Verlag, 491-505.

Huneeus, C. *La Unión de Centro Democrático y la Transición a la Democracia en España.* Madrid: Centro de Investigaciones Sociológicas, 1985.

Huntington, N. and Bale, T. "New Labour. New Christian Democracy". *Political Quarterly,* 1 (2002) 44-50.

Huntington, S.P. *The Third Wave. Democratisation in the Late Twentieth Century.* Norman: University of Oklahoma Press, 1991.

Irving, R.E.M. *The Christian Democratic Parties of Western Europe.* London: Allen & Unwin, 1979.

Irwin, G. "Tussen de verkiezingen" in: J.J.M. van Holsteyn and B. Niemöller, eds. *De Nederlandse kiezer 1994.* Leiden: DSWO Press, 1995, 9-26.

Jansen, T. *The European People's Party. Origins and Development.* Basingstoke: Macmillan Press, 1998.

Jansen, T. "The Integration of the Conservatives into the European People's Party" in: D.S. Bell and C. Lord, eds. *Transnational Parties in the European Union.* Aldershot: Ashgate, 1998, 102-116.

Johansson, G.V. *Kristen Demokrati på Svenska. Studier om KDS tillkomst och utveckling (1964-1982).* Malmö: Gleerup, 1985.

Johansson, K.M. "EU och Partieväsendet" in: K.M. Johansson. *Sverige och EU.* Stockholm: SNS, 1999.

Johansson, K.M. "Vers une théorie des fédérations européennes de partis" in: P. Delwit, E. Külachi and C. Van de Walle, eds. *Les fédérations européennes de partis. Organisation et influence.* Brussels: Editions de l'Université de Bruxelles, 2001, 21-38.

Bibliography

Johansson, K.M. "Party Elites in Multilevel Europe. The Christian Democrats and the Single European Act" in: R. Ladrech, ed. *The Europeanisation of Party Politics.* Special Issue of *Party Politics*, 4 (2002) 423-439.

Johansson, K.M. and Raunio, T. "Partisan Responses to Europe. Comparing Finnish and Swedish Political Parties". *European Journal of Political Research*, 2 (2001) 225-249.

Jörs, I. "East Germany. Another Party Landscape". *German Politics*, 1 (2003) 135-158.

Kalyvas, S.N. *The Rise of Christian Democracy in Europe.* Ithaca: Cornell University Press, 1996.

Kalyvas, S.N. "Unsecular Politics and Religious Mobilisation. Beyond Christian Democracy" in T. Kselman and J.A. Buttigieg, eds. *European Christian Democracy. Historical Legacies and Comparative Perspectives.* Notre Dame: University of Notre Dame Press, 2003, 293-320.

Karvonen, L. "Christian Parties in Scandinavia. Victory over the Windmills?" in: D. Hanley, ed. *Christian Democracy in Europe. A Comparative Perspective.* London: Pinter, 1994, 121-141.

Katz, R. and Mair, P. "The Evolution of Party Organisations in Europe. The Three Faces of Party Organiation". *The American Review of Politics*, 4 (1993) 593-617.

Katz, R.S. and Mair, P. eds. *How Parties Organise. Change and Adaptation in Party Organisations in Western Democracies.* London: Sage, 1994.

Katz, R. and Mair, P. "Changing Models of Party Organisation and Party Democracy. The Emergence of the Cartel Party". *Party Politics*, 1 (1995) 5-28.

Kitschelt, H. "Formation of Party Cleavages in Post-Communist Democracies. Theoretical Prepositions". *Party Politics*, 4 (1995) 447-472.

Kitschelt, H. and McGann, A. *The Radical Right in Western Europe. A Comparative Analysis.* Ann Arbor: University of Michigan Press, 1995.

Klingemann, H.-D. and Kaase, M., eds. *Wahlen und Wähler. Analysen aus Anlaß der Bundestagswahl 1998.* Wiesbaden: Westdeutscher Verlag, 2001.

Klop, K. "Waarden en normen. Nieuwe scheidslijn?" in: M. Bovens, H. Pellikaan and M. Trappenburg, eds. *Nieuwe tegenstellingen in de Nederlandse politiek?* Amsterdam: Boom, 1998, 122-145.

Koff, S. and Koff, S. *Italy. From the First to the Second Republic.* London: Routledge, 2000.

Koole, R.A. "Ledenpartijen of staatspartijen? Financiën van Nederlandse politieke partijen in vergelijkend en historisch perspectief" in: *Jaarboek 1996 DNPP.* Groningen: Documentatiecentrum Nederlandse Politieke Partijen, 1997, 156-182.

Koole, R.A., "The Societal Position of Christian Democracy in the Netherlands" in E. Lamberts, ed. *Christian Democracy in the European Union (1945-1995).* KADOC-Studies 21. Leuven: University Press Leuven, 1997, 137-153.

Korte, K.-R. *Deutschlandpolitik in Helmut Kohls Kanzlerschaft. Regierungsstil und Entscheidungen (1982-1989).* Stuttgart: Deutscher Universitäts-Verlag, 1998.

Kriechbaumer, R. *Parteiprogramme im Widerstreit der Interessen. Die Programmdiskussionen und die Programme von ÖVP und SPÖ 1945-1986.* Vienna: Verlag für Geschichte und Politik/Oldenbourg Verlag, 1990.

Kselman, T. and Buttigieg, J.A., eds. *European Christian Democracy. Historical Legacies and Comparative Perspectives.* Notre Dame: Notre Dame University Press, 2003.

Küberl, F. "Dialogbedarf und gemeinsame Aufgaben von Kirche und ÖVP" in: M. Wilhelm and P. Wuthe, eds. *Parteien und Katholische Kirche im Gespräch. Fünf Studientage der Österreichischen Bischofskonferenz mit FPÖ, Liberales Forum, SPÖ, ÖVP, Die Grünen.* Graz/Vienna: Verlag Zeitpunkt, 1999, 141-154.

Ladrech, R. "Europeanisation and Political Parties. Towards a Framework for Analysis" in: R. Ladrech, ed. *The Europeanisation of Party Politics.* Special Issue of *Party Politics,* 4 (2002) 389-403.

Lamberts, E., ed. *Christian Democracy in the European Union (1945-1995).* KADOC-Studies 21. Leuven, Leuven University Press, 1997.

Lamberts, E. "General Conclusions" in: E. Lamberts, ed. *Christian Democracy in the European Union (1945-1995).* KADOC-Studies 21. Leuven: Leuven University Press, 1997, 473-481.

Legard, M., ed. *Les valeurs au Luxembourg. Portrait d'une société au tournant du 3e millénaire.* Luxembourg: Editions Saint-Paul, 2002.

Leonardi, R. "Political Party Linkages in Italy. The Nature of the Christian Democratic Party Organisation" in: K. Lawson, ed. *Political Parties and Linkage. A Comparative Perspective.* New Haven: Yale University Press, 1980, 243-265.

Leonardi, R. and Wertman, D.A. *Italian Christian Democracy. The Politics of Dominance.* Houndmills: Macmillian, 1989.

Letamendia, P. *Le Mouvement Républicain Populaire.* Paris: Beauchesne, 1995.

Lijphart, A. "Consociational Democracy". *World Politics,* 2 (1969) 207-225.

Lijphart, A. *Democracy in Plural Societies. A Comparative Exploration.* New Haven: Yale University Press, 1977.

Lijphart, A. *Patterns of Democracy.* New Haven: Yale University Press, 1999.

Linz, J.J. "The Party System of Spain. Past and Future" in: S.M. Lipset and S. Rokkan, eds. *Party Systems and Voter Alignments. Cross-National Perspectives.* New York: Free Press, 1967, 197-282.

Linz, J.J. and Montero, J.R. "The Party Systems of Spain. Old Cleavages and New Challenges" in: L. Karvonen and S. Kuhnle, eds. *Party Systems and Voter Alignments Revisited.* London: Routledge, 2001, 150-196.

Lipset, S.M. and Rokkan, S. "Cleavage Structures, Party Systems and Voter Alignments. An Introduction" in: S.M. Lipset and S. Rokkan. *Party Systems and Voter Alignments. Cross-National Perspectives.* New York: Free Press, 1967, 23-56.

Listhaug, O. *Citizens, Parties and Norwegian Electoral Politics (1957-1985). An Empirical Study.* Oslo: Tapir, 1989.

Lösche, P. and Walter, F. *Die SPD. Klassenpartei, Volkspartei, Quotenpartei. Zur Entwicklung der Sozialdemokratie von Weimar bis zur deutschen Vereinigung.* Darmstadt: Wissenschaftliche Buchgesellschaft, 1992.

Lucardie, P. "De ideologie van het CDA. Een conservatief democratisch appèl?" in: K. van Kersbergen, P. Lucardie and H.-M. ten Napel, eds. *Geloven in macht: de christendemocratie in Nederland.* Amsterdam: Spinhuis, 1993.

Lucardie, P. and H.-M. ten Napel. "Between Confessionalism and Liberal Conservatism. The Christian Democratic Parties of Belgium and the Netherlands" in: D. Hanley, ed. *Christian Democracy in Europe. A Comparative Perspective.* London: Pinter, 1994, 51-70.

Lucardie, P. "From Family Father to DJ: Christian Democratic Parties and Civil Society in Western Europe" in: E. Lamberts, ed. *Christian Democracy in the European Union (1945-1995)*. KADOC-Studies 21. Leuven: Leuven University Press, 1997, 210-221.

Lucardie, P. "Greening and Ungreening the Netherlands" in: M. Jacobs, ed. *Greening the Millennium? The New Politics of the Environment*. Oxford: Blackwell, 1997, 183-191.

Lucardie, P. "Vox populi of vox diaboli? Het debat over het referendum in de Nederlandse politieke partijen" in: *Jaarboek 1996 DNPP*. Groningen: Documentatiecentrum Nederlandse Politieke Partijen, 1997, 109-128.

Lucardie, P. and Voerman, G. "Party Foundations in The Netherlands" in: K.-H. Nassmacher, ed. *Foundations for Democracy. Approaches to Comparative Political Finance*. Baden-Baden: Nomos, 2000, 321-339.

Luther, K.R. "The Self-Destruction of a Right-Wing Populist Party? The Austrian Parliamentary Election of 2002". *West European Politics*, 2 (2003) 136-152.

Luther, K.R. and Müller-Rommel, F. "Political Parties in a Changing Europe" in: K.R. Luther and F. Müller-Rommel, eds. *Political Parties in the New Europe. Political and Analytical Challenges*. Oxford: Oxford University Press, 2002, 3-16.

Luther, K.R. and Müller-Rommel, F. "Parties and Party Research in the New Europe" in: K.R. Luther and F. Müller-Rommel, eds. *Political Parties in the New Europe. Political and Analytical Challenges*. Oxford: Oxford University Press, 2002, 325-346.

Madeley, J.T.S. "Scandinavian Christian Democracy. Throwback or Portent?" *European Journal of Political Research*, 3 (1977) 267-286.

Madeley, J.T.S. "The Antinomies of Lutheran Politics. The Case of Norway's Christian People's Party" in: D. Hanley , ed. *Christian Democracy in Europe. A Comparative Perspective*. London: Pinter, 1994, 142-154.

Madeley, J.T.S. "Reading the Runes. The Religious Factor in Scandinavian Electoral Politics" in: D. Broughton and H-M. ten Napel, eds. *Religion and Mass Electoral Behaviour in Europe*. London: Routledge, 2000, 28-43.

Madeley, J.T.S. "A Framework for the Comparative Analysis of Church-State Relations in Europe" in: J.T.S. Madeley and Z. Enyedi, eds. *Church and State in Contemporary Europe. The Chimera of Neutrality*. London: Cass, 2003, 23-50.

Maier, H. *Revolution and Church. The Early History of Christian Democracy (1789-1901)*. Notre Dame: University of Notre Dame Press, 1969.

Mair, P. *Party System Change. Approaches and Interpretations*. Oxford: Oxford University Press, 1997.

Mair, P. "The Limited Impact of Europe on National Party Systems". *West European Politics*, 4 (2000) 27-51.

Mair, P. and van Biezen, I. "Party Membership in Twenty European Democracies (1980-2000)". *Party Politics*, 1 (2001) 5-21.

Márquez Cruz, G. "Veinte años de democracia local en España. Elecciones, producción de gobierno, moción de censura, y élite política (1979-1999)". *Revista de Estudios Políticos (Nueva Época)*, 106 (1999) 289-334.

Martin, D. *A General Theory of Secularisation*. Oxford: Blackwell, 1978.

Massart, A. *L'Union pour la Démocratie Française*. Paris: L'Harmattan, 1999.

Massart, A. "Y a-t-il un Parti Libéral en France?" in: P. Delwit, ed. *Libéralismes et partis libéraux en Europe*, Brussels: Editions de l'Université de Bruxelles, 2002, 75-92.

Matuschek, P. "Aznars Ambitionen. Die spanische Volkspartei und ihr europäischer Führungsanspruch". *Blätter für deutsche und internationale Politik*, 1 (2001), 77-84.

Matuschek, P. "Spain. A Textbook Case of Partitocracy" in: J. Borchert and J. Zeiss, eds. *The Political Class in Advanced Democracies*. Oxford: Oxford University Press, 2003, 336-351.

Mayeur, J.-M. *Des partis catholiques à la démocratie chrétienne (XIXe-XXe siècles)*. Paris: Colin, 1980.

McCarthy, P. *The Crisis of the Italian State. From the Origins of the Cold War to the Fall of Berlusconi.* Palgrave: Macmillan, 1995.

Montero, J.R. "More than Conservative, Less than Neoconservative. Alianza Popular in Spain" in: B. Girvin, ed. *The Transformation of Contemporary Conservatism*. London: Pinter, 1988, 145-163.

Montero, J.R. "Los fracasos políticos y electorales de la derecha española. Alianza Popular (1976-1987)" in: J.F. Tezanos, R. Cotarelo and A. de Blas, eds. *La transición democrática española*. Madrid: Editorial Sistema, 1989, 495-542.

Morlino, L. "Political Parties and Democratic Consolidation in Southern Europe" in: R. Gunther, P.N. Diamandouros and H.-J. Puhle, eds. *The Politics of Democratic Consolidation. Southern Europe in Comparative Perspective*. Baltimore: Johns Hopkins University, 1995, 315-388.

Morlino, L. *Democracy between Consolidation and Crisis. Parties, Groups and Citizens in Southern Europe*. Oxford: Oxford University Press, 1998.

Mouze, V. "Les relations Eglise-Etat au Luxembourg". *Forum für Politik, Gesellschaft und Kultur*, 1995, 8-12.

Müller, W.C. "Die Österreichische Volkspartei" in: H. Dachs et al., ed. *Handbuch des politischen Systems Österreichs. Die Zweite Republik*. Vienna: Manz Verlag, 1997, 265-285.

Müller, W.C. "Das Parteiensystem", in H. Dachs et al., eds. *Handbuch des politischen Systems Österreichs. Die Zweite Republik*. Vienna: Manz Verlag, 1997, 215-234.

Müller, W.C. "Austria. Tight Coalitions and Stable Government" in: W.C. Müller and K. Strøm, eds. *Coalition Governments in Western Europe*. Oxford: Oxford University Press, 2000, 86-125.

Müller, W.C., "Evil or the 'Engine of Democracy'? Populism and Party Competition in Austria" in: Y. Mény and Y. Surel, eds. *Democracies and the Populist Challenge*. Basingstoke: Palgrave, 2002, pp. 155-175.

Müller, W.C. and Jenny, M. "Abgeordnete, Parteien und Koalitionspolitik. Individuelle Präferenzen und politisches Handeln im Nationalrat". *Österreichische Zeitschrift für Politikwissenschaft*, 2000, 137-156.

Müller, W.C., F. Plasser and Ulram, P.A. "Schwäche als Vorteil, Stärke als Nachteil. Die Reaktion der Parteien auf den Rückgang der Wählerbindungen in Österreich" in: P. Mair, W.C. Müller and F. Plasser, eds. *Parteien auf komplexen Wählermärkten. Reaktionsstrategien politischer Parteien in Westeuropa*. Vienna: Signum Verlag, 1999, 201-245.

Müller, W.C. and Steininger, B. "Christian Democracy in Austria. The Austrian People's Party" in: D. Hanley, ed. *Christian Democracy in Europe. A Comparative Perspective*. London: Pinter Publishers, 1994, 87-100.

Bibliography

Müller, W.C. and Ulram, C. "The Social and Demographic Structure of Austrian Parties (1945-93)". *Party Politics*, 1 (1995) 145-160.

Neuhaus, F. *DGB und CDU. Analysen zum bilateralen Verhältnis von 1982 bis 1990*. Cologne: Bund-Verlag, 1996.

Newell, J.L. *Parties and Democracy in Italy*. Brookfield: Ashgate, 2000.

Nohlen, D. and. Hildenbrand, A. *Spanien. Wirtschaft. Gesellschaft. Politik*. Opladen: Leske und Budrich, 1992.

Oñate, P. "Congreso, grupos parlamentarios y partidos" in: A. Martínez, ed. *El Congreso de los Diputados en España: funciones y rendimiento*. Madrid: Tecnos, 2000, 95-139.

Panebianco, A. *Political Parties. Organisation and Power*. Cambridge: Cambridge University Press, 1988.

Papini, R. *The Christian Democratic International*. London: Rowman & Litlefiedl, 1997.

Pappas, T.S. "In Search of the Center. Conservative Parties, Electoral Competition and Political Legitimacy in Southern Europe's New Democracies" in: P.N. Diamandouros and R. Gunther, eds. *Parties, Politics and Democracy in the New Southern Europe*. Baltimore: Johns Hopkins University Press, 2001, 224-267.

Parisella, A. "La base sociale della Democrazia cristiana. Elettorato, iscritti e organizzazione" in E. Lamberts, ed. *Christian Democracy in the European Union (1945-1995)*. Leuven, KADOC-Studies 21. Leuven, University Press Leuven, 1997, 189-209.

Pasquino, G. "The New Campaign Politics in Southern Europe" in: P.N. Diamandouros and R. Gunther, eds. *Parties, Politics and Democracy in the New Southern Europe*. Baltimore: Johns Hopkins University Press, 2001, 183-223.

Pelinka, A., Plasser, F. and W. Meixner, W. "Von der Konsens- zur Konfliktdemokratie? Östereich nach dem Regierungs- und Koalitionswechsel" in: A. Pelinka, F. Plasser and W. Meixner, eds. *Die Zukunft der österreichischen Demokratie. Trends, Prognosen und Szenarien*. Vienna: Signum Verlag, 2000, 439-464.

Pellikaan, H., van der Meer, T. and de Lange, S. "The Road from a Depoliticised to a Centrifugal Democracy". *Acta Politica*, 1 (2003) 23-50.

Pennings, P. and Keman, H. "The Dutch Parliamentary Elections in 2002 and 2003. The Rise and Decline of the Fortuyn Movement". *Acta Politica*, 1 (2003) 51-68.

Peters, B.G. *Institutional Theory in Political Science. The 'New Institutionalism'*. New York: Pinter, 1999.

Petterson, T. and Riis, O., eds., *Scandinavian Values. Religion and Morality in the Nordic Countries*. Uppsala: Acta Universitatis, 1994.

Pijnenburg, B. "De 'C' van CDA. Een analyse van het christen-democratisch electoraat" in: K. van Kersbergen, P. Lucardie and H.-M. ten Napel, eds. *Geloven in macht. De christen-democratie in Nederland*. Amsterdam: Spinhuis, 1993, 117-140

Plasser, F. and Ulram, P.A. "Konstellationen und Szenarien des Parteienwettbewerbs in Österreich" in: W.C. Müller, F. Plasser and P.A. Ulram, eds. *Wählerverhalten und Parteienwettbewerb. Analysen zur Nationalratswahl 1994*. Vienna: Signum Verlag, 1995, 505-524.

Plasser, F. and Ulram, P.A. *Das österreichische Politikverständnis. Von der Konsens- zur Konfliktkultur?* Vienna: WUV-Universitätsverlag, 2002.

Plasser, F. and Ulram, P.A., eds. *Wahlverhalten in Bewegung. Analysen zur Nationalratswahl 2002*. Vienna: WUV-Universitätsverlag, 2003.

Poguntke, T. *Parteiorganisation im Wandel. Gesellschaftliche Verankerung und organisatorische Anpassung im europäischen Vergleich.* Opladen: Westdeutscher Verlag, 2000.

Poirier, P. "Quelle(s) identité(s) politiques pour le Parti démocratique luxembourgeois?" in: P. Delwit, ed. *Les libéralismes en Europe. Partis et cultures politiques.* Brussels: Editions de l'Université de Bruxelles, 2002, 247-262.

Pridham, G. "Christian Democrats, Conservatives and Transnational Party Cooperation in the European Community. Centre-Forward or Centre-Right?" in Z. Layton-Henry, ed. *Conservative Politics in Western Europe.* London: MacMillan Press, 1982, 318-346.

Puhle, H.-J. "Mobilisers and Late Modernisers. Socialist Parties in the New Southern Europe" in: P.N. Diamandouros and R. Gunther, eds. *Parties, Politics and Democracy in the New Southern Europe.* Baltimore: Johns Hopkins University Press, 2001, 268-328.

Pühringer, J. "Als Christ Politik machen. Der Beitrag der Kirche zu einer menschlichen Gesellschaft" in: M. Wilhelm and P. Wuthe, eds. *Parteien und Katholische Kirche im Gespräch. Fünf Studientage der Österreichischen Bischofskonferenz mit FPÖ, Liberales Forum, SPÖ, ÖVP, Die Grünen.* Graz/Vienna: Verlag Zeitpunkt, 1999, 155-168.

Putnam, R., Leonardi, R. and Raffaella, R. *Making Democracy Work. Civic Traditions in Modern Italy.* Princeton: Princeton University Press, 1993.

Putnam, R. *Bowling Alone. The Collapse and Revival of American Community.* New York: Simon and Schuster, 2000.

Raunio, T. "Facing the European Challenge. Finnish Parties Adjust to the Integration Process". *West European Politics*, 1 (1999) 138-159.

Ray, L. "Measuring Party Orientations towards European Integration. Results from an Expert Survey". *European Journal of Political Research*, 2 (1999) 283-306.

Reichardt-Dreyer, I. *Macht und Demokratie in der CDU. Dargestellt am Prozess und Ergebnis der Meinungsbildung zum Grundsatzprogramm 1994.* Wiesbaden: Westdeutscher Verlag, 2000.

Rokkan, S. "Geography, Religion and Social Class. Crosscutting Cleavages in Norwegian Politics" in: S.M. Lipset and S. Rokkan. *Party Systems and Voter Alignments.* New York: Free Press, 1967, 367-444.

Ruggie, J.G. "What Makes the World Hang Together? Neo-Utilitarianism and the Social Constructivist Challenge". *International Organisation*, 4 (1998) 855-885.

Ruiz Jiménez, A.M. *Los Nuevos Temas en los Partidos de Derecha. El Feminismo del Partido Popular.* Madrid: Centro de Estudios Avanzados en Ciencias Sociales, 1996.

Ruiz Jiménez, A.M. *Reshaping the Welfare State. New Right's Moral Arguments in Southern European Conservative Parties. The Spanish Partido Popular.* Madrid: Centro de Estudios Avanzados en Ciencias Sociales, 1997.

Ruiz Jiménez, A.M. *Mecanismos del cambio ideológico e introducción de políticas de género en partidos conservadores. El caso de AP-PP en España en perspectiva comparada.* Madrid: Centro de Estudios Avanzados en Ciencias Sociales, 2002.

Sartori, G. *Parties and Party Systems. A Framework for Analysis.* Cambridge: Cambridge University Press, 1976.

Scarrow, S. *Parties and their Members. Organising for Victory in Britain and Germany.* Oxford: Oxford University Press, 1996.

Bibliography

Scarrow, S. "Parties without Members? Party Organisation in a Changing Electoral Environment" in: R.J. Dalton and M.P. Wattenberg, eds. *Parties without Partisans. Political Change in Advanced Democracies.* Oxford: Oxford University Press, 2000, 79-101.

Schedler, A. "Zur (nichtlinearen) Entwicklung des Parteienwettbewerbs (1945 bis 1994)". *Österreichische Zeitschrift für Politikwissenschaft*, 1 (1995) 17-34.

Schmid, J. *Die CDU. Organisationsstrukturen, Politiken und Funktionsweisen einer Partei im Föderalismus.* Opladen: Leske und Budrich, 1990.

Schneider, H. *Ministerpräsidenten. Profil eines politischen Amtes im deutschen Föderalismus.* Opladen: Leske und Budrich, 2001.

Schröder, W. "Das katholische Milieu auf dem Rückzug. Der Arbeitnehmerflügel der CDU nach der Ära Kohl" in: T. Dürr and R. Soldt, eds. *Die CDU nach Kohl.* Frankfurt am Main: Fischer, 1998, 175-191.

Scoppola, P. *La Repubblica dei Partiti. Evoluzione e crisi di un sistema politico (1945-1996).* Bologna: Il Mulino, 1997.

Sorge, B. *I Cattolici e l'Italia che verrà.* Casale Monferrato: Piemme, 1994.

Scruton, R. *The Meaning of Conservatism.* Basingstoke: Palgrave, 2001.

Smits, J. "De organisatie en werking van de CVP-PSC", in: W. Dewachter, ed. *Tussen staat en maatschappij. De christen-democratie in België tussen 1945 en 1995.* Tielt: Lannoo, 1995, 142-169.

Strikwerda, C. "Parties, Populists and Pressure Groups. European Christian Democracy in Comparative Perspective" in: T. Kselman and J.A. Buttigieg, eds. *European Christian Democracy. Historical Legacies and Comparative Perspectives.* Notre Dame: Notre Dame University Press, 2003, 267-292.

Sundback, S. "The Nordic Lutheran Churches and the EU Question in 1994". *Temenos. Studies in Comparative Religion*, 8 (2001) 191-208.

Svåsand, L. "Die Konservative Partei und die Christliche Volkspartei Norwegens. Unbequeme Nachbarn im bürgerlichen Lager", in: H.-J. Veen, ed. *Christlich-demokratische und konservative Parteien in Westeuropa. 4: Schweden, Norwegen, Finnland, Dänemark.* Paderborn: Schöningh, 1994, 133-227.

Ten Napel, H.-M. *"Een eigen weg". De totstandkoming van het CDA (1952-1980).* Kampen: Kok, 1992.

Thelen, K. and Steinmo, S. "Historical Institutionalism in Comparative Politics" in S. Steinmo, K. Thelen and F. Longstreth, eds. *Structuring Politics. Historical Institutionalism in Comparative Analysis.* Cambridge: Cambridge University Press, 1992, 1-32.

Tsoukas, H. "False Dilemmas in Organisation Theory. Realism or Social Constructivism?". *Organisation*, 3 (2000) 531-535.

Tusell, J. "Introducción. Entre el centro y la derecha. El PP, desde la oposición al poder" in: J. Tusell, ed. *El gobierno de Aznar. Balance de una gestión (1996-2000).* Barcelona: Crítica, 2000, 9-40.

Vallès, J.M. "The Spanish General Election of 1993". *Electoral Studies*, 1 (1994) 87-91.

Van Beveren, C. and Moerman, I. "Organisatorische vernieuwingen in het Christen-Democratisch Appèl" in: I. Hartman, ed. *Sporen van vernieuwing: een inventarisatie van recente organisatorische veranderingen in acht politieke partijen.* Amsterdam: Instituut voor Publiek en Politiek, 1996, 6-20.

van Biezen, I. "Building Party Organisations and the Relevance of Past Models. The Communist and Socialist Parties in Spain and Portugal". *West European Politics*, 2 (1998) 32-62.

van Biezen, I. "On the Internal Balance of Party Power. Party Organisations in New Democracies". *Party Politics*, 4 (2000) 395-417.

Van der Kolk, H. "Het afnemende belang van godsdienst en sociale klasse" in: J. Thomassen, K. Aarts and H. van der Kolk, eds. *Politieke veranderingen in Nederland 1971-1991*. The Hague: Sdu, 2000, 121-138.

Van Deth, J. "De stabiliteit van oude en nieuwe politieke oriëntaties" in: J.J.M. van Holsteyn and B. Niemöller, eds. *De Nederlandse kiezer 1994*. Leiden: DSWO Press, 1995, 126-141.

Van Hecke, S. "Démocrates chrétiens et conservateurs au Parlement européen. Mariage d'amour ou de raison?" in: P. Delwit, ed. *Démocraties chrétiennes et conservatismes en Europe. Une nouvelle convergence?* Brussels: Editions de l'Université de Bruxelles, 2003, 323-343.

Van Holsteyn, J.J.M. and Irwin, G.A. "Never a Dull Moment. Pim Fortuyn and the Dutch Parliamentary Election of 2002". *West European Politics*, 2 (2003) 41-66.

Van Kersbergen, K. "The Distinctiveness of Christian Democracy" in D. Hanley, ed. *Christian Democracy in Europe. A Comparative Perspective*. London: Pinter, 1994, 31-47.

Van Kersbergen, K. *Social Capitalism. A Study of Christian Democracy and the Welfare State*. London/New York: Routledge, 1995.

Van Kersbergen, K. "Hopen op macht. De neergang van de Nederlandse christendemocratie in vergelijkend perspectief" in: *Jaarboek 1995 DNPP*. Groningen: Documentatiecentrum Nederlandse Politieke Partijen, 1996, 92-112.

Van Kersbergen, K. "Contemporary Christian Democracy and the Demise of the Politics of Mediation" in: H. Kitschelt et al., eds. *Continuity and Change in Contemporary Capitalism*. Cambridge: Cambridge University Press, 1999, 346-370.

Van Kersbergen, K. and Krouwel, A. "De strategische opties van de christen-democratie". *Socialisme & Democratie*, 4 (2002) 14-22.
Van Praag, P. "The Winners and Losers in a Turbulent Political Year". *Acta Politica*, 1 (2003) 5-22.

Veen, H.-J., ed. *Christlich-demokratische und konservative Parteien*, 5 Vol., Paderborn: Schöningh, 1983-2000.

Veen, H.-J., ed. *Christlich-demokratische und konservative Parteien in Westeuropa. 4: Schweden, Norwegen, Finnland, Dänemark*. Paderborn: Schöningh, 1994.

Volkens, A. and Klingemann, H.-D. "Parties, Ideologies and Issues. Stability and Change in Fifteen European Party Systems (1945-1998)" in: K.R. Luther and F. Müller-Rommel, eds. *Political Parties in the New Europe. Political and Analytical Challenges*. Oxford: Oxford University Press, 2002, 143-167.

von Beyme, K. *Vom Faschismus zur Entwicklungsdiktatur. Machtelite und Opposition in Spanien*. München: Piper, 1971.

Wendt, A. "Collective Identity Formation and The International State". *The American Political Science Review*, 2 (1994), 384-396.

Wert, J.I. "Poder, tiempo y espacio. Las elecciones municipales y autonómicas del 28-M". *Claves de Razón Práctica*, 54 (1995) 24-38.

Wert, J.I. "Las urnas de San Antonio. Los votos y el poder tras el 13-J". *Claves de Razón Práctica*, 95 (1999) 14-23.

Bibliography

Wert, J.I. "12-M. ¿Lluvia o diluvio? Una inter-pretación de las elecciones generales". *Claves de Razón Práctica*, 101 (2001) 20-30.

Wewer, G., ed. *Bilanz der Ära Kohl. Christlich-liberale Politik (1982-1998)*. Opladen: Leske und Budrich, 1998.

White, J.H. *Catholics in Western Democracies. A Study in Political Behaviour*. Dublin: Gill/Macmillan, 1981.

Woldendorp, J. "Christen-democratie en neo-corporatisme. Het CDA en het maatschap-pelijk middenveld" in: K. van Kersbergen, P. Lucardie and H.-M. ten Napel, eds. *Geloven in macht: de christen-democratie in Nederland*. Amsterdam: Spinhuis, 1993, 141-161.

Zielonka-Goei, M.L. and Hillebrand, R. "De achterban van parlementariërs: kiezers en partijleden" in: *Jaarboek 1987 DNPP*. Groningen: Documentatiecentrum Neder-landse Politieke Partijen, 1988, 116-137.

Zohlnhöfer, R. *Die Wirtschaftspolitik der Ära Kohl. Eine Analyse der Schlüsselentscheidungen in den Politikfelder Finanzen, Arbeit und Entstaatlichung (1982-1998)*. Opladen: Leske und Budrich, 2001.

Zulehner, P.M., Hager, I. and Polak, R. *Kehrt die Religion wieder? Religion im Leben der Menschen (1970-2000)*. Ostfildern: Schwaben-verlag, 2001.

Zwart, R.S. *"Gods wil in Nederland". Christelijke ideologieën en de vorming van het CDA (1880-1980)*. Kampen: Kok, 1996.

List of Abbreviations

ADR	*Aktiounskomitee fir Demokratie a Rentegerechtegkeet*	Action Committee for Democracy and Social Justice (Luxembourg)
AGALEV	*Anders Gaan Leven*	Living Differently (Belgium: Flanders and Brussels)
AN	*Alleanza Nazionale*	National Alliance (Italy)
AP	*Allianza Popular*	People's Alliance (Spain)
CCD	*Centro Cristiano Democratico*	Christian Democratic Centre (Italy)
CDA	*Christen Democratisch Appèl*	Christian Democratic Appeal (the Netherlands)
CDH	*Centre Démocrate Humaniste*	Democratic Humanist Centre (Belgium: Wallonia and Brussels)
CDS	*Centre des Démocrates Sociaux*	Centre of Social Democrats (France)
CDSp	*Partido do Centro Democratico Social*	Party of the Democratic and Social Centre (Portugal)
CDyS	*Centro Democrático y Social*	Democratic and Social Centre (Spain)
CDU	*Christlich Demokratische Union Deutschlands*	Christian Democratic Union of Germany (Germany)
CDUi	*Cristiani Democratici Uniti*	United Christian Democrats (Italy)
CD&V	*Christen-Democratisch en Vlaams*	Christian Democratic and Flemish (Belgium: Flanders and Brussels)
CiU	*Convergència i Unió*	Convergence and Union (Spain: Catalonia)
CSP	*Christlich-Soziale Partei*	Christian Social Party (Belgium: German-speaking Community)
CSU	*Christlich-Soziale Union*	Christian Social Union (Germany: Bavaria)
CSV	*Chrëschtlech-Sozial Vollekspartei*	Christian Social People's Party (Luxembourg)
CVP	*Christelijke Volkspartij*	Christian People's Party (Belgium: Flanders and Brussels)
DC	*(Partido della) Democrazia Cristiana*	Christian Democratic Party (Italy)
DE	*Democrazia Europeo*	European Democracy (Italy)
DG	*Déi Gréng*	The Greens (Luxembourg)
DP	*Demokratesch Partei*	Democratic Party (Luxembourg)
DS	*Democratici di Sinistra*	Democrats of the Left (Italy)
ECOLO	*Ecologistes Confédérés pour l'Organisation des Luttes originales*	Confederal Ecologists for the Organisation of Original Struggles (Belgium: Wallonia and Brussels)
FDF	*Front Démocratique des Francophones*	Democratic Front of French-speakers (Belgium: Wallonia and Brussels)
FDP	*Freie Demokratische Partei*	Free Democratic Party (Germany)

FI	*Forza Italia*	Go Italy (Italy)
FPÖ	*Freiheitliche Partei Österreichs*	Freedom Party of Austria (Austria)
GL	*Groen Links*	Green Left (the Netherlands)
IU	*Izquierda Unida*	United Left (Spain)
KrF	*Kristelig Folkeparti*	Christian People's Party (Norway)
LN	*Leefbaar Nederland*	Liveable Netherlands (the Netherlands)
LPF	*Lijst Pim Fortuyn*	List Pim Fortuyn (the Netherlands)
LSAP	*Lëtzebuerger Sozialistesch Arbechter-partei*	Socialist Labour Party of Luxembourg (Luxembourg)
MCC	*Mouvement des Citoyens pour le Changement*	Citizen's Movement for Change (Belgium: Wallonia and Brussels)
MSI	*Movimento Sociale Italiano*	Italian Social Movement (Italy)
MRP	*Mouvement Républicain Populaire*	Republican Popular Movement (France)
ND	*Nea Demokratia*	New Democracy (Greece)
NVA	*Nieuw-Vlaamse Alliantie*	New Flemish Alliance (Belgium: Flanders and Brussels)
ÖVP	*Österreichische Volkspartei*	Austrian People's Party (Austria)
PCE	*Partido Comunista de España*	Communist Party of Spain (Spain)
PCI	*Partito Comunista Italiana*	Italian Communist Party (Italy)
PDP	*Partido Democrata Popular*	Democratic People's Party (Spain)
PDS	*Partei des Demokratischen Sozialismus*	Party of Democratic Socialism (Germany)
PDSi	*Partito Democratico della Sinistra*	Democratic Party of the Left (Italy)
PNV	*Partido Nacionalista Vasco*	Basque Nationalistic Party (Spain: the Basque country)
PP	*Partido Popular*	People's Party (Spain)
PPI	*Partito Populare Italiano*	Italian People's Party (Italy)
PRL	*Parti Libéral Réformateur*	Liberal Reformist Party (Belgium: Wallonia and Brussels)
PS	*Parti Socialiste*	Socialist Party Belgium: Wallonia and Brussels)
PSC	*Parti Social Chrétien*	Christian Social Party (Belgium: Wallonia and Brussels)
PSD	*Partido Social Democrata*	Social Democratic Party (Portugal)
PSI	*Partito Socialista Italiana*	Italian Socialist Party (Italy)
PSOE	*Partido Socialista Obrero Español*	Spanish Socialist Party (Spain)
RI	*Rinnovamento Italiano*	Italian Renovation (Italy)
RPR	*Rassemblement Pour la République*	Rally for the Republic (France)
SP	*Socialistische Partij*	Socialist Party (the Netherlands)
SPA	*Socialistische Partij Anders*	Socialist Party Differently (Belgium: Flanders and Brussels)
SPD	*Sozialdemokratische Partei Deutschlands*	Social Democratic Party of Germany (Germany)
SPÖ	*Sozialdemokratische Partei Österreichs*	Social Democratic Party of Austria (Austria)
SVP	*Südtiroler Volkspartei*	People's Party of South Tirol (Italy: South Tirol)
UCD	*Unión de Centro Democrático*	Union of the Democratic Centre (Spain)

UDC	*Unió Democràtica de Catalunya*	Democratic Union of Catalonia (Spain: Catalonia)
UDCi	*Unione dei Democratici Cristiani e di Centro*	Union of the Centrist and Christian Democrats (Italy)
UDE(UR)	*Unione dei Democratici per l'Europe*	Union of Democrats for Europe (Italy)
UDF	*Union pour la Démocratie Française*	Union for the French Democracy (France)
UDR	*Unione dei Democratici per la Repubblica*	Union of Democrats for the Republic (Italy)
UMP	*Union pour un Mouvement Populaire*	Union for a Popular Mouvement (France)
VLD	*Vlaamse Liberalen en Democraten*	Flemish Liberals and Democrats (Belgium: Flanders and Brussels)
VU	*Volksunie*	People's Union (Belgium: Flanders and Brussels)

EC	*European Community*
EDU	*European Democratic Union*
ELDR	*European Liberal, Democrat and Reform Party*
EMU	*Economic and Monetary Union*
EP	*European Parliament*
EPP	*European People's Party*
EPP-ED	*European People's Party - European Democrats*
EU	*European Union*
EUCD	*European Union of Christian Democrats*
IGC	*Intergovernmental Conference*
MEP	*Member of European Parliament*
PES	*Party of European Socialists*
TEU	*Treaty on the European Union (a.k.a. Maastricht Treaty)*

List of Tables and Figures

Index

Notes on Contributors

Paolo ALBERTI (°1972) is writing a Ph.D. dissertation from the European Institute of the London School of Economics and Political Science (UK) with a dissertation entitled 'Christian Democracy: Towards a Framework for Analysis'. He studied Political Science at the Università degli Studi di Milano (Italy) and the Economics of Cooperation at the Università di Bologna (Italy). His research interests include comparative politics, politics in Italy and the European Union, party politics, centre parties, Christian Democracy, consociational theory, and political moderation. He is the author of *Il Coraggio della Moderazione. Dalla DC al PPI di Mino Martinazzoli* (La Quadra, 2000).

Wouter BEKE (°1974) has a doctorate in Social Science. He obtained a Ph.D. at the K.U.Leuven (Belgium) with a dissertation entitled *De Christelijke Volks-partij tussen 1945 en 1968. Breuklijnen en pacificatiemechanismen in een catch-allpartij*. He studied Political Science at K.U.Leuven (Belgium) and Social Law at Vrije Universiteit Brussel (Belgium). His research and publications focus on the political history of Belgium, Christian Democracy, and political parties.

Frank BÖSCH (°1969) is a Junior Professor in the History Department of the Ruhr-Universität Bochum (Germany). He obtained a Ph.D. in History at the Georg-August Universität Göttingen (Germany). His main research areas are the history of political parties, media and mass culture. He is the author of *Die Adenauer-CDU. Gründung, Aufbau und Krise einer Erfolgspartei 1945-1969* (DVA, 2001), *Das konservative Milieu. Vereinskultur und lokale Sammlungspolitik 1900-1960* (Wallstein-Verlag, 2002) and *Macht und Machtverlust. Die Geschichte der CDU* (Deutsche Verlag-Anstalt, 2002).

Franz FALLEND (°1965) is a Lecturer in the History and Political Science Department of the Universität Salzburg (Austria). He obtained a Ph.D. in Political Science at the Universität Salzburg (Austria) with a dissertation on regional cabinet systems and decision-making processes. His research focuses on federalism, parliamentarianism, the executive and political parties. He is co-author of *Länderpolitik. Politische Strukturen und Entscheidungsprozesse in den österreichischen Bundesländern* (Signum-Verlag, 1997) and covers Austria in the annual *Political Data Yearbook* of the *European Journal of Political Research*.

Emmanuel GERARD (°1952) is Dean of the Faculty of the Social Sciences and Vice-President of KADOC at the K.U.Leuven (Belgium). He obtained a Ph.D. in History at the K.U.Leuven (Belgium) with a dissertation on the Catholic party in Belgium during the interbellum. His research interests include Christian Democracy, Catholic parties, Christian labour movements, the Belgian Parliament and the decolonisation of the Congo. He is co-editor of *Histoire du mouvement ouvrier chrétien en Belgique* (University Press Leuven, 1994), *Left Catholicism. Catholics and Society in Western Europe at the Point of Liberation 1943-1955* (University Press Leuven, 2001), and *Histoire de la Chambre des Représentants de Belgique 1830-2002* (2003).

Robert LEONARDI (°1945) is Jean Monnet Senior Lecturer in European Union Politics at the European Institute of the London School of Economics and Political Science (UK), where he is also Director of the Socio-Economic Cohesion Laboratory. He obtained a Ph.D. in Political

Science at the University of Illinois at Champaign-Urbana (USA) with a dissertation entitled *The Politics of Choice. An Inquiry into the Causes of Factionalism in the Italian Christian Democratic Party*. His current research is on regions, economic development and institutional capacity in the management of development policies in European Objective 1 Regions. He is co-author of *Italian Christian Democracy. The Politics of Dominance* (St. Martin's Press, 1989) and editor of *Italy. Politics and Policy* (Ashgate Press, 1996; 2003).

Paul LUCARDIE (°1946) is a Research Associate at the Documentation Centre on Dutch Political Parties of the Rijksuniversiteit Groningen (the Netherlands). He obtained a Ph.D. in Political Science at Queen's University (Canada). His research interests focus on political ideologies and political parties in the Netherlands, Canada and Germany. He is co-editor of *Geloven in macht. De christen-democratie in Nederland* (Het Spinhuis, 1993) and *The Politics of Nature. Explorations in Green Political Theory* (Routledge, 1995).

John T.S. MADELEY (°1944) is a Lecturer in Government at the Government Department of the London School of Economics and Political Science (UK) and was until recently Dean of the Graduate School. His research interests include the government and politics of the Nordic countries, European politics more widely and, in particular, religion and politics in Europe. He is editor of *Religion and Politics* (Aldershot, 2003) and co-editor of *Church and State in Contemporary Europe. The Chimera of Neutrality* (Frank Cass, 2003).

Alexis MASSART (°1969) is Dean of the Law Faculty at the Université Catholique de Lille (France). He is currently a member of the advisory committee on education in France. He obtained a Ph.D. in Political Science at the Université de Lille 2 (France). His main research areas are political parties and elections in France and Europe. He is the author of *L'Union pour la Démocratie Française* (L'Harmattan, 1999).

Peter MATUSCHEK (°1973) is a research assistant in the Centre for European and North American Studies at the Georg-August Universität Göttingen (Germany) where he is writing a Ph.D. dissertation on the Spanish People's Party. He studied Political Science at the Georg-August Universität Göttingen (Germany), the Universidad Complutense de Madrid (Spain) and Uppsala Universitet (Sweden). His research and publications focus on political parties, the democratisation processes and the European Union.

Philippe POIRIER (°1971) is a Lecturer and researcher in Political Science at the Université du Luxembourg (Luxembourg) and an associate researcher at the Centre d'études et de recherches autour de la démocratie-Centre national de la recherche scientifique at the University of Rennes I (France). He obtained a Ph.D. in Political Science from the Université de Rennes I (France) with a dissertation entitled *Les droites 'extrêmes' en Europe. Histoire et identité(s)*. The main research areas on which he has published are citizenship and multiculturalism, economic and regional governance, right wing parties and regionalist parties.

Steven VAN HECKE (°1974) is a Research Assistant of the Fund for Scientific Research Flanders (Belgium) in the Political Science Department of the K.U.Leuven (Belgium). He is writing a Ph.D. dissertation on Christian Democracy and Conservatism in Western Europe since the mid-1970s. He studied Philosophy and Political Science at the K.U.Leuven (Belgium) and the University of Hull (UK). His research focuses on Christian Democracy, political parties, European integration, political ideology and the principle of subsidiarity.

Colophon

Final Editing
Luc Vints
Lieve Claes

Translations
Maria Kelly
Benedict Perquy

Lay-out
Alexis Vermeylen
Johan Mahieu (cover)

Printing Office
Peeters, Herent

KADOC
Documentation- and Research Centre
for Religion, Culture and Society
Vlamingenstraat 39
B - 3000 Leuven
tel. +32 16 32 35 00
fax +32 16 32 35 01
e-mail: postmaster@kadoc.kuleuven.ac.be
www.kadoc.kuleuven.ac.be